Merrimack College Library

North Andover, Massachusetts

LUTHER'S WORKS

American Edition

VOLUME 54

*Published by Concordia Publishing House
and Fortress Press in 55 volumes.
General Editors are Jaroslav Pelikan (for vols. 1-30)
and Helmut T. Lehmann (for vols. 31-55)*

LUTHER'S WORKS

VOLUME 54

Table Talk

EDITED AND TRANSLATED BY
THEODORE G. TAPPERT

GENERAL EDITOR
HELMUT T. LEHMANN

FORTRESS PRESS / PHILADELPHIA

© 1967 by Fortress Press

Library of Congress Catalogue Number 55-9893

Printed in the United States of America 1-354

GENERAL EDITORS' PREFACE

The first editions of Luther's collected works appeared in the sixteenth century, and so did the first efforts to make him "speak English." In America serious attempts in these directions were made for the first time in the nineteenth century. The Saint Louis edition of Luther was the first endeavor on American soil to publish a collected edition of his works, and the Henkel Press in Newmarket, Virginia, was the first to publish some of Luther's writings in an English translation. During the first decade of the twentieth century, J. N. Lenker produced translations of Luther's sermons and commentaries in thirteen volumes. A few years later the first of the six volumes in the Philadelphia (or Holman) edition of the *Works of Martin Luther* appeared. But a growing recognition of the need for more of Luther's works in English has resulted in this American edition of Luther's works.

The edition is intended primarily for the reader whose knowledge of late medieval Latin and sixteenth-century German is too small to permit him to work with Luther in the original languages. Those who can will continue to read Luther in his original words as these have been assembled in the monumental Weimar edition (*D. Martin Luthers Werke.* Kritische Gesamtausgabe, Weimar, 1883-). Its texts and helps have formed a basis for this edition, though in certain places we have felt constrained to depart from its readings and findings. We have tried throughout to translate Luther as he thought translating should be done. That is, we have striven for faithfulness on the basis of the best lexicographical materials available. But where literal accuracy and clarity have conflicted, it is clarity that we have preferred, so that sometimes paraphrase seemed more faithful than literal fidelity. We have proceeded in a similiar way in the matter of Bible versions, translating Luther's translation. Where this could be done by the use of an existing English version—King James, Douay, or Revised Standard—we have done so. Where it could not, we have supplied our own. To indicate this in each specific instance would have been pedantic; to adopt a uniform procedure would have been artificial—especially in view of Luther's own inconsistency in this regard. In each volume the translator will be responsible primarily for matters of text and language, while the responsibility of the editor will extend principally to the historical and theological matters reflected in the introductions and notes.

Although the edition as planned will include fifty-five volumes, Luther's writings are not being translated in their entirety. Nor should they be. As he was the first to insist, much of what he wrote and said was not that important. Thus the edition is a selection of works that have proved their importance for the faith, life, and history of the Christian church. The first thirty volumes contain Luther's expositions of various biblical books, while the remaining volumes include what are usually called his "Reformation writings" and other occasional pieces. The final volume of the set will be an index volume; in addition to an index of quotations, proper names, and topics, and a list of corrections and changes, it will contain a glossary of many of the technical terms that recur in Luther's works and that cannot be defined each time they appear. Obviously Luther cannot be forced into any neat set of rubrics. He can provide his reader with bits of autobiography or with political observations as he expounds a psalm, and he can speak tenderly about the meaning of the faith in the midst of polemics against his opponents. It is the hope of publishers, editors, and translators that through this edition the message of Luther's faith will speak more clearly to the modern church.

J.P.
H.T.L.

CONTENTS

General Editors' Preface	v
Abbreviations	viii
Introduction to Volume 54	ix
Table Talk Recorded by Veit Dietrich, 1531-1533	3
Table Talk Recorded by George Rörer, 1531-1535	115
Table Talk Recorded by John Schlaginhaufen, 1531-1532	123
Table Talk Collected by Conrad Cordatus, 1532-1533	167
Table Talk Recorded by Anthony Lauterbach and Jerome Weller, 1536-1537	201
Table Talk Recorded by Anthony Lauterbach, 1538-1539	251
Table Talk Recorded by John Mathesius, 1540	365
Table Talk Recorded by Caspar Heydenreich, 1542-1543	411
Table Talk Recorded by Jerome Besold, 1544	465
Indexes	477

ABBREVIATIONS

CIC	— *Corpus Iuris Canonici,* edited by E. Friedberg (Graz, 1955).
C.R.	— *Corpus Reformatorum,* edited by C. G. Bretschneider and H. E. Bindseil (Halle/Salle, 1834-1860).
LW	— American Edition of *Luther's Works* Philadelphia and St. Louis, 1955-).
PE	— *Works of Martin Luther.* Philadelphia Edition Philadelphia, 1915-1943).
St. L.	— *D. Martin Luthers sämmtliche Schriften,* edited by Johann Georg Walch. Edited and published in modern German, 23 vols. in 25 (2nd ed., St. Louis, 1880-1910).
WA	— *D. Martin Luthers Werke.* Kritische Gesamtausgabe (Weimar, 1883-).
WA, Br	— *D. Martin Luthers Werke.* Briefwechsel (Weimar, 1930-).
WA, DB	— *D. Martin Luthers Werke.* Deutsche Bibel (Weimar, 1906-1961).
WA, TR	— *D. Martin Luthers Werke.* Tischreden (Weimar, 1912-1921).

INTRODUCTION TO VOLUME 54

As a result of the Reformation the Augustinian friars who had previously lived in the Black Cloister in Wittenberg abandoned their monastic life. However, Martin Luther continued to dwell there, and from the time of his marriage to Katherine von Bora in 1525 until his death in 1546 it was also the home of his family. The spacious building was almost constantly overrun by all sorts of people. "A miscellaneous and promiscuous crowd inhabits Dr. Luther's home," a friend reported in 1542, "and on this account there is great and constant disturbance."[1] In addition to Luther and his wife and the six children who were born to them, the Black Cloister was for years the home of a maiden aunt of Katherine and several orphaned nephews and nieces of the Reformer. Several poor students roomed and boarded there in return for clerical and other services, there was a constant flow of guests from near or far, and a few servants completed the number.

In Luther's household the day began at sunrise, and the principal meal of the day was eaten about ten o'clock in the morning. About five o'clock in the afternoon supper was served, and this meal was often shared by exiled clergymen, escaped nuns, government officials, visitors from abroad, and colleagues of Luther in the university who frequently stopped in, men like Philip Melanchthon, John Bugenhagen, and Justus Jonas. The relaxed atmosphere of the hospitable home was conducive to spirited conversation, and John Mathesius, who was often present in 1540, has left this description of what the scene was like:

> Although our doctor often took weighty and profound thoughts to table with him and sometimes maintained the silence of the monastery during the entire meal, so that not a word was spoken, yet at appropriate times he spoke in a very jovial way. We used to call his conversation the condiments of the meal because we preferred it to all spices and dainty food.
> When he wished to get us to talk he would throw out a question,

---

[1] Letter of George Held to Count George of Anhalt, February 23, 1542, in Theodor Kolde, *Analecta Lutherana* (Gotha: F. A. Perthes, 1883), p. 378.

"What's new?" The first time we let this remark pass, but if he repeated it—"You prelates, what's new in the land?"—the oldest ones at the table would start talking. Dr. Wolf Severus,[2] who had been the tutor of his royal majesty of the Roman Empire, sat near the head of the table and, unless there was a stranger present (like a traveling courtier), he got something started.

If the conversation was animated, it was nevertheless conducted with decent propriety and courtesy, and others would contribute their share until the doctor started to talk. Often good questions were put to him from the Bible, and he provided expert and concise answers. When at times somebody took exception to what had been said, the doctor was able to bear this patiently and refute him with a skilful answer. Reputable persons often came to the table from the university and from foreign places, and then very nice talks and stories were heard.[3]

Some of the men who listened to these conversations at table began to take notes.[4] There was nothing strange about this. After all, the same persons were taking notes of Luther's lectures and sermons, and they were interested in recording the opinions he expressed at table too. Not everything that was said was noted but only what interested one recorder or another. The notes were taken for private use—as personal remembrances of a revered teacher or as guides for the solution of problems—and were not intended for publication.

Conrad Cordatus claimed to have been the first man to record Luther's conversation at table and asserted that Luther "never indicated by as much as a word that what I did displeased him."[5] As a teacher Luther was accustomed to seeing open notebooks and poised pens before him. In fact, he sometimes challenged the notetakers to record especially outrageous statements by saying, "Make a note of this!" "Write it down!" "Mark this well!"[6] When his

---

[2] Wolfgang Schiefer (Severus) is often mentioned in John Mathesius' notes for the year 1540. He was the tutor of Archduke Maximilian, who later became Emperor Maximilian II.

[3] Georg Buchwald (ed.), *Mathesius' Predigten über Luthers Leben* (Stuttgart: Paul Rocholls Verlag, 1904), pp. 155-156.

[4] The only extensive study in English is Preserved Smith, *Luther's Table Talk: A Critical Study* (New York: Columbia University Press, 1907). Although this book was written before investigation of the Table Talk reached all of its present conclusions, it remains a useful introduction.

[5] See p. 169.

[6] See No. 246; cf. Nos. 463, 1525.

wife jestingly complained that those who were taking notes ought to pay for this additional instruction, Luther in effect defended those who were recording the conversation.[7] On another occasion, however, Philip Melanchthon was annoyed by something that Cordatus had recorded, and the latter wrote, "He asked me again and again for the notebook in which I was accustomed to write what I heard, and at length I gave it to him. After he had read a little he wrote this couplet:

'Everything don't try to tell,
Silence would at times be well.' "[8]

I

Early editions of the works of Martin Luther did not include the Table Talk. It was with some misgivings that Johann Georg Walch finally decided to incorporate the Table Talk in his edition, which was published in twenty-four volumes in Halle between 1739 and 1753. Walch was aware that many Protestants were embarrassed by some things in the Table Talk—for instance, the earthy language which Luther occasionally employed and the freedom with which he criticized the composition and contents of some books of the Bible. It was feared that Protestants in general and Lutherans in particular would be exposed to damaging attacks at the hands of Roman Catholic polemicists if the Table Talk were included in an edition of Luther's works. Attempts were even made to deny its genuineness, to claim that it was an unfriendly fabrication and forgery.[9]

It was not that the Table Talk had been unknown. The fact of the matter is that it was widely known in an edition published separately by John Aurifaber in 1566 and frequently reprinted thereafter. John Aurifaber (whose name was Latinized from Goldschmidt after the humanistic fashion of the day) had been born in Mansfeld, probably in 1519, and after studying in Wittenberg for three years had returned to his homeland to serve as a tutor to a young count of Mansfeld and thereupon to serve for a time as

---

[7] See No. 5187.
[8] *WA*, TR 2, No. 2068.
[9] *D. Martin Luthers Sämtliche Schriften*, herausgegeben von Johann Georg Walch (24 vols.; Halle: J. J. Gebauer, 1739-1753), XXII, 4, 15, 21, 23-24, 30-38.

military chaplain. In 1545 he was back in Wittenberg to continue his studies. This time he became more intimately acquainted with Luther, was made his famulus or secretary, and as such lived in Luther's home for less than a year until the Reformer died on February 18, 1546. While he lived with Luther and ate at his table Aurifaber made notes of the conversation he heard, and he also made a record of what Luther said and did on his last journey and on his deathbed. Afterward, when Aurifaber was court chaplain in Weimar and pastor in Erfurt, he was an indefatigable collector of the writings and sayings of Luther. He was one of the editors of the Jena edition of Luther's works (1553-1556), put out two volumes of Luther's letters (1556, 1565), and finally edited a collection of the Table Talk in German under the title *Tischreden oder Colloquia Doct. Mart. Luthers* (Eisleben: Urban Gaubisch, 1566).

At the close of the preface in the last-named work Aurifaber explained his own purpose and procedure:

> After having had several volumes of the previously unpublished books, sermons, writings, and letters of Dr. Martin Luther printed in Eisleben, I have now also prepared this volume of colloquies or table conversations and have had it published. It was originally compiled from the Rev. Master Anthony Lauterbach's collections of colloquies, which he himself set down from the hallowed lips of Luther and which were afterward arranged by me under certain commonplace topics. The collection was in several places enlarged and improved in the light of the notebooks of colloquies written by other godly and learned persons who had been table companions of Dr. Martin Luther many years ago. Such were Master Veit Dietrich, Master Jerome Besold, Master John Schlaginhaufen (pastor in Cöthen), and Master John Mathesius. There were also others who were constantly in Dr. M. Luther's company and associated with him daily, like the late Master George Rörer. Afterward I also took many good things from the manuscript collection of colloquies by the late Master John Stolz and Master James Weber (pastor in Ordorf) and incorporated them in this volume. Moreover, since I, John Aurifaber, was also in Dr. M. Luther's company a great deal in the years 1545 and 1546, before Dr. Martin Luther's death, and diligently recorded many splendid stories and anecdotes as well as other useful and necessary things that were spoken at table, I have included and inserted them here as well. . . .
>
> Inasmuch as I have for many years had a large heap of manuscripts of Luther's colloquies in my home, I could not with good conscience

allow this treasure of Luther's table conversations to continue to be hidden and allow such a talent to remain buried and forgotten or allow it to get lost or be destroyed in some way after my death. I have decided to share it through publication with the Christian church, which can be strengthened by such teaching, can use it with blessing as crumbs fallen from Luther's table, and with it can satisfy the spiritual hunger and thirst of men's souls. For under no circumstances should one allow such table conversations of Luther, which deal with lofty spiritual matters, to be lost. On the contrary, they must be esteemed and valued because one may receive all sorts of instruction and consolation from them.[10]

There are several things in this account that need to be underscored.

The first is that many of Luther's students and friends who had an opportunity to do so took notes of the Reformer's conversation at table. Aurifaber mentioned only a few of these. It is known that in addition to those he named, Nicholas Medler, Conrad Cordatus, Jerome Weller, Caspar Heydenreich, John Forster, John Kraft, George Plato, Caspar Cruciger, Justus Jonas, and Ferdinand von Maugis also took notes.[11] More than a score of men are known to have recorded the conversation at Luther's table. Not all of these took notes simultaneously, for most of them were not in Wittenberg at the same time, but at least one of them was there virtually every year between 1531 and Luther's death in 1546.

The second thing to notice is that in his compilation Aurifaber made use of "a large heap of manuscripts of Luther's colloquies." Inasmuch as by his own admission he had been in a position to record Luther's conversation only during the last year of the Reformer's life, he was dependent on the notes that others had taken in earlier years. He probably had made copies of these, as others before him had done. In fact, he mentioned as his chief source the large collection which Anthony Lauterbach had made from his own notes and the notes copied from several other men. This collection

---

[10] See the critical edition of the Aurifaber version in Karl Eduard Förstemann and Heinrich Ernst Bindseil (eds.), *D. Martin Luther's Tischreden oder Colloquia, . . . nach Aurifaber's erster Ausgabe . . . herausgegeben und erläutert* (4 vols.; Berlin: Gebauer'sche Buchhandlung, 1844-1848), IV, xxii, xxiii.

[11] See Ernst Kroker, in WA, TR 5, xxxiv.

was later published in a Latin version by Henry Peter Rebenstock,[12] and a comparison of this with Aurifaber's German collection reveals to what an extent both are dependent on the Lauterbach collection. It is obvious that the texts which Rebenstock reproduced in Latin often derive from the same source as Aurifaber's German version. The two are not identical throughout, however, because Aurifaber did not include some items that appear in the Lauterbach-Rebenstock version, because Aurifaber added some items from other manuscript sources, and because Aurifaber introduced changes which were unique with him.

A third thing that merits attention is that Aurifaber was interested in making public those conversations which might "satisfy the spiritual hunger and thirst" of readers and might furnish them with "instruction and consolation." Although he placed on his title page a quotation from John 6:12, "Gather up the fragments left over, that nothing may be lost," Aurifaber did not include all "the crumbs fallen from Luther's table" but only those that suited his purpose. In fact, he did not limit himself to what Luther had said at table but inserted portions of the letters, sermons, and published works of Luther. Professor A. F. Hoppe identified one hundred and forty instances of the introduction of such alien materials, which Aurifaber sometimes furnished with fabricated introductions to simulate table talks.[13] In keeping with his purpose of edifying the reader, Aurifaber followed the example of Lauterbach in arranging his collection topically. He did so under eighty heads—for example, the Christian life, worship, marriage, civil authority, sickness and death, resurrection and judgment, councils, ecclesiastical property, patristic and scholastic theologians, soldiers, lawyers, schools. The sayings of Luther were thus removed from their chronological and historical context to serve the topical or systematic interests of the editor, and presumably of the reader.

In this form the Table Talk became widely known. Edition after edition was printed in Germany, either complete or abridged,

---

[12] *Colloquia, meditationes, consolationes, consilia, judicia, sententiae, narrationes, responsa, facetiae D. Martini Lutheri, piae et sanctae memoriae, in mensa, prandii et coenae, et in peregrinationibus observata et fideliter transcripta* (2 vols.; Frankfurt-am-Main, 1571).

[13] *St. L.* 22, 20-24.

down to our own time.[14] In this form the Table Talk was reproduced in the editions of Luther's complete works during the eighteenth and nineteenth centuries.[15] Translations were made from the same text of Aurifaber into other tongues.[16] Captain Henry Bell published an abridged English translation with a somewhat curious introduction as early as 1652.[17] About two centuries later William Hazlitt made a new translation containing about a fourth of Aurifaber's text,[18] and an even briefer condensation of this abridgment has had some currency.[19]

II

During the last decades of the nineteenth and the early decades of the twentieth century it gradually became manifest that in spite of all his diligence and devotion and in spite of his occasionally faithful renderings into German, Aurifaber had actually obscured and distorted the Table Talk. One after another, manuscripts containing contemporary reports of Luther's conversations were discovered in remote archives or rediscovered in libraries where they had long been overlooked. Some were edited and published, and these contained the notes taken by Anthony Lauterbach,[20] Conrad Corda-

---

[14] Kurt Aland included a volume of selections from the Aurifaber version in Vol. IX of his series, *Luther Deutsch* (Berlin: Evangelische Verlagsanstalt, 1948). He gave as his reason that this is the form in which the Table Talk has come to be widely known.

[15] The Walch edition (1739-1753), the Erlangen edition (1826-1857), and the St. Louis edition (1880-1910). Professor A. F. Hoppe, who edited the volume of the Table Talk (Vol. XXII) in the St. Louis edition, made a not very successful attempt to incorporate some of the new finds in his edition.

[16] For example, in French, *Les Propos de Table de Martin Luther,* traduits par Gustave Brunet (Paris: Gernier Frères, 1844).

[17] *Dris. Martini Lutheri Colloquia Mensalia, or Dr. Martin Luther's Divine Discourses at his Table.* . . . Translated from the High German into the English Tongue by Captain Henry Bell (London: William Du-Gard, 1652). This was reprinted several times into the nineteenth century (1840). For a discussion of this and subsequent editions in English, see Gordon Rupp, *The Righteousness of God: Luther Studies* (New York: Philosophical Library, 1953), pp. 56-77.

[18] *The Table-Talk or Familiar Discourses of Martin Luther,* translated by William Hazlitt, Esq. (London, 1848). This was frequently reprinted, most recently by the United Lutheran Publication House in Philadelphia, without date.

[19] *The Table Talk of Martin Luther,* edited with an introduction by Thomas S. Kepler (Cleveland: World Publishing Co., 1952).

[20] *M. Anton Lauterbach's Tagebuch auf das Jahr 1538.* . . . Aus der Handschrift herausgegeben von Johann Karl Seidemann (Dresden: Justus Naumann, 1872).

tus,[21] John Schlaginhaufen,[22] and John Mathesius.[23] Still other manuscripts were found to contain notes by Veit Dietrich and collections of sayings recorded by various other writers. All together, more than thirty manuscripts were found. None of these represents the original form of the notes taken at table. This is so because the writers expanded their skeletal notes, smoothed out the style, and wrote fair copies when they returned to their rooms. At best we have texts which are a product of such reworking; at worst we have copies of such copies, and copies made in turn from these copies, with all the slips, misreadings, and attempted improvements that usually accompany such repeated copying. However, there can be no doubt that these manuscripts take us much closer to the actual conversations at Luther's table than the text offered by Aurifaber. It was the achievement especially of Ernst Kroker, whose painstaking editorial work made the six volumes of the Table Talk in the Weimar edition a model of literary and historical reconstruction, to demonstrate this.

A comparison of items in the manuscripts with Aurifaber's text is illuminating. Some of the changes made by Aurifaber are minor, as may be seen in the case of a translation of the opening sentence in *WA, TR* 4, No. 4397:

Lauterbach	*Aurifaber*
"Duke George would not permit an official of his to hold his command in contempt. . . ."	"Neither N. N. nor another prince and lord would permit an official of theirs to hold their command in contempt. . . ."

It might appear at first sight that Aurifaber was reluctant to mention Duke George of Albertine Saxony, a bitter foe of the Reformation, but elsewhere he named him without scruple. The change he made in the text must therefore be attributed either to caprice or

---

[21] *Tagebuch über Dr. Martin Luther geführt von Dr. Conrad Cordatus, 1537.* Zum ersten Male herausgegeben von H. Wrampelmeyer (Halle: Max Niemeyer, 1885).

[22] *Tischreden Luthers aus den Jahren 1531 und 1532 nach den Aufzeichnungen von Johann Schlaginhaufen.* Aus einer Münchner Handschrift herausgegeben von Wilhelm Preger (Leipzig: Dörffling & Franke, 1888).

[23] *Luthers Tischreden in der Mathesischen Sammlung.* Aus einer Handschrift herausgegeben von Ernst Kroker (Leipzig, 1903).

to an attempt to transform Luther's observations and opinions into timeless truths. More typical of Aurifaber's procedure is the expansion of his sources by inserting material of an edifying nature. An example of this, from WA, TR 4, No. 5223, follows:

Mathesius

"When he was asked whether the devil knew Christ in the flesh, the doctor said, 'Yes. He is well acquainted with the Scriptures and hears what we sing, but because Christ behaved humbly the devil did not pay attention to him. For the devil is farsighted; he watches out only for big people and attaches himself to them; he does not see what is low or beneath him.

"'But God does just the opposite; he sees only what is low down and lets go of what is high up.'"

Aurifaber

"When somebody asked whether the devil knew Christ according to the flesh, Dr. Martin answered, 'Yes. He knows the Scriptures well: "Behold, a young woman shall conceive and bear a son" [Isa. 7:14], and "To us a child is born" [Isa. 9:6], etc. The devil also hears us sing every day: "The Word was made flesh" and "He was incarnate by the Holy Spirit and was made man." But because Christ conducted himself so humbly and associated with sinful men and women, and as a consequence was not held in great esteem, the devil overlooked him and did not recognize him. For the devil is farsighted; he looks only for what is big and high and attaches himself to that; he does not look at what is low down and beneath himself.

"'The eternal and merciful God does just the opposite; he sees what is low down, as Psalm 113 [:5-6] declares, "The Lord our God, who is seated on high, looks far down," and Isaiah 66 [:2],"This is the man to whom I will look, he that is humble and contrite in spirit and trembles at my word." On the other hand, he lets go of what is high. Indeed, it is an abomination to him, as Christ says in Luke 16 [:15], "What is exalted among men is an abomination in the sight of God." ' "[24]

It will be observed how the sharp and pointed reply of Luther, as reported by Mathesius, is embroidered by Aurifaber. One must concede that Aurifaber showed some skill and imagination in expanding the notes of earlier reporters. In the case before us he did not alter or deflect the point of Luther's remarks so much as he tended to bury it under pious farcing, and he resorted to the use of biblical proof texts in a manner alien to the Reformer. Aurifaber was not above altering what Luther said, however, as the following excerpt from Luther's long admonition to a man afflicted with melancholy (WA, TR 1, No. 122) will illustrate:

Dietrich

" 'Having been taught by experience I can say how you ought to restore your spirit when you suffer from spiritual depression. When you are assailed by gloom, despair, or a troubled conscience you should eat, drink, and talk with others. If you can find help for yourself by thinking of a girl, do so.' "

Aurifaber

" 'I have learned from experience how one ought to conduct oneself in temptation. Anybody who is assailed by grief, despair, or a troubled heart and has a worm in his conscience should first of all cling to the comfort of the divine Word. Afterward he should eat and drink and seek the company and conversation of godly and Christian people. In this way he will get better.' "

---

[24] The reader may wish to compare the translation of this piece by William Hazlitt (No. dxcix): " "The devil well knew the Scripture, where it said: "Behold, a virgin shall conceive and bear a child." Also: "Unto us a child is born." But because Christ has carried himself humbly and lowly, went about with public sinners, and by reason thereof was held in no esteem, — therefore the devil looked another way over Christ, and knew him not; for the devil looks a-squint upwards, after that which is high and pompous, not downwards, nor on that which is humble and lowly. But the everlasting merciful God does quite the contrary; he beholds that which is lowly, as the 113th Psalm shows. ... Therefore he that intends to climb high, let him beware of the devil, lest he throw him down; for the nature and manner of the devil is, first to hoist up into heaven, and afterwards to cast down into hell.' "

Here Luther's counsel apparently did not please Aurifaber and so he changed it. Luther was talking to (not about) a man who appears to have found no comfort in the gospel, and therefore Luther did not belabor him with this. Instead, Luther suggested that the man first eat and drink (rather than fast) and cultivate fellowship with the people from whom he had withdrawn. Not only did Aurifaber insist inflexibly that the man "should first of all cling to the comfort of the divine Word," but he found the idea of "thinking of a girl" so distasteful in this context that he simply deleted it. For another example of the liberties which Aurifaber took with earlier texts of the Table Talk see No. 5207.[25]

III

One of the striking differences between the Aurifaber edition of Luther's Table Talk and the earlier manuscripts, whose texts have been reproduced in the Weimar edition, is that the former is in German and the latter is in a curious mixture of German and Latin. The following is an example of the original macaronic style, with the Latin words set in roman type and the German words in italics to make it easier to distinguish them (for an English translation see No. 315):

> In administratione oeconomiae et politiae *mus* lex *seyn, das man es nit haben will,* ut aliquid peccetur. Econtra *wenn es geschehen, sol* remissio peccatorum *dazu kommen, sonst so verderbt mans.* Maritum oportet multa dissimulare in uxore et liberis, et tamen non obmittere debet legem. *So ists in allen stenden.* . . .[26]

The manuscripts do not distinguish between Latin and German words, for all words were written in the same handwriting. Many abbreviations were used (especially for Latin words)—for example, *oes* for *omnes, pnt* for *possunt*—and symbols were also employed for commonly recurring words and phrases. The editor of the texts of the Table Talk in the Weimar edition expanded all abbreviations and provided the equivalent words for all symbols, as in the example given above.

---

[25] In passing it may be remarked that Aurifaber uniformly changed *scheissen* into *schmeissen,* a reflection of a change in taste within a generation after Luther.

[26] For William Hazlitt's translation of Aurifaber's expanded text see Hazlitt's No. ccli.

The macaronic style in the manuscripts can be accounted for by two observations.

The first is that long before the Reformation students had developed a primitive kind of shorthand for taking notes in the classroom, and this was also used by persons who performed secretarial tasks of one kind or another. Since Latin was the language of the schools, the abbreviations and symbols that were used applied to this language. When it became necessary to take notes of something said in German, it was often quicker for the experienced reporter to write a Latin translation of what was being said rather than to reproduce the German original in longhand, without benefit of abbreviations and symbols. However, words or phrases which could not be translated adequately on the spur of the moment, or which the recorder preferred to keep in the original because of their aptness or color, were put down in German. This explains why many of Luther's sermons, recorded by auditors, are in a similar mixture of Latin and German although it is of course absurd to suppose that he preached in a macaronic style to the townspeople in Wittenberg. In the case of the Table Talk, then, one should not assume that Luther actually spoke in each language exactly what was reported in that language.

Nevertheless, a second thing needs to be borne in mind. Luther himself and those who gathered about him at his table were bilingual. In the informal atmosphere of a hospitable home it was natural for them to slip from one language into another. Technical theological matters were more readily expressed in Latin, and domestic matters could be referred to more easily in German. The matter is not quite so simple, however, as an examination of even the one sample given above should make clear. Luther and most of his table companions were capable of putting the same thing in either Latin or German. When, in the summer of 1527, John Bugenhagen visited the sick Luther he found the Reformer in bed, "with clear words calling now on God the Father and then on Christ the Lord, first in Latin and then in German." Luther presumably prayed in both languages because he was bilingual and not because the contents of the several parts of his prayers required one language or the other. A recent linguistic study[27] of a portion of the

---

[27] Birgit Stolt, *Die Sprachmischung in Luthers Tischreden: Studien zum Problem der Zweisprachigkeit* (Stockholm: Almqvist & Wiksell, 1964). The quotation from Bugenhagen appears in this study, p. 14.

Table Talk contends that the macaronic sentences in the earliest manuscripts are on the whole identical with the mixture of Latin and German in Luther's own speech. Although this thesis is supported by industriously assembled evidence and ingeniously constructed arguments, it is not entirely convincing, and the author herself concedes, "We are here operating on a frontier; thorough investigation from the psychological side is also necessary fully to illuminate these processes." [28] Although one cannot say that even our earliest texts reflect precisely the use of Latin and German at Luther's table, it remains true that he and his companions employed both languages. Both this bilingualism and the "stenography" of the sixteenth century help to explain how the macaronic texts came into existence.

It has sometimes been conjectured that Luther said some things in Latin to spare his wife and other women who were at the table.[29] We now know that Luther's wife Katherine von Bora understood Latin quite well[30] and that what might appear to be offensive to our taste today did not always appear so to her and her contemporaries. In a time in which it was accepted practice to empty the contents of chamber pots in the street[31] one should not expect the same delicacy of speech that is characteristic of modern urban life. Even the Jesuit scholar Hartmann Grisar, who was anything but sympathetic with him, conceded that Luther was "improper rather than obscene, coarse rather than lascivious." With reference to the Table Talk in particular Grisar expressed the judgment: "We may peruse many pages of the notes without meeting anything in the least offensive but much that is both fine and attractive. . . . Much of what was said was true, witty, and not seldom quite edifying." [32] A comparison of Luther's robust language with that of his contemporaries has often been made.[33] The assertion of John Mathesius, one of the later reporters of the Table Talk, that he had never heard a shameful word from Luther's lips,[34] is to be understood in the

---

[28] *Ibid.*, p. 303.
[29] See Smith, *Luther's Table Talk*, p. 91.
[30] Cf. *WA*, TR 4, No. 4860.
[31] See Gerhard Belgum (ed.), *The Mature Luther* ("Martin Luther Lectures," Vol. III [Decorah, Iowa: Luther College Press, 1959]), pp. 11, 12.
[32] Grisar, *Luther* (6 vols.; London: Herder, 1913-1917), III, 229, 234.
[33] See Heinrich Boehmer, *Luther and the Reformation in the Light of Modern Research* (New York: Dial Press, 1930), pp. 176-187.
[34] Buchwald, *Mathesius' Predigten*, p. 162.

context of the proprieties of that time. Certainly one does not encounter in Luther the bawdiness that was characteristic of William Shakespeare,[35] not to speak of Giovanni Boccaccio or Margaret of Navarre, who were nearer to Luther in time.

It should not astonish the reader that the polemical spirit of the age of the Reformation should be reflected in Luther's informal conversations as well as in his correspondence, sermons, lectures, and published treatises. Popes and bishops, monks and priests, scholastic theologians and canon lawyers were the objects of sharp attack. Equally devastating were Luther's criticisms of humanists like Desiderius Erasmus and religious enthusiasts like Andrew Karlstadt and Thomas Münzer. The lines between right and wrong, truth and error were so firmly drawn that Luther's exceptional gentleness toward deviant views was noted with some amazement (e.g., No. 515). He was aware of his own vehemence (e.g., Nos. 197, 397). In a letter he once observed, "This I know for sure: if I fight with dirt I shall always get dirty, whether I win or lose." [36]

Questions have often been raised concerning the reliability of the reports of the Table Talk that have come down to us. Aurifaber's version, as we have already noted, is far less trustworthy than the manuscripts that were rediscovered at the end of the nineteenth and beginning of the twentieth century. There is no doubt that the manuscripts take us much closer to what was actually said than Aurifaber's text does. But it is too much to claim that even the manuscripts provide us with verbatim reports. In some cases we have parallel accounts of the same conversation by two reporters, and these are not identical, as the following brief example shows:

Dietrich	*Schlaginhaufen*
"'Laurentius Valla was the best Italian I've ever seen or heard of in all my life. He argued well about free will. He strove for honesty simultaneously in piety and in letters...'" (*WA*, TR 1, No. 259).	"'Laurentius Valla was a good man—upright, honest, skilful, straightforward. He bore more fruit than all the rest of the Italians ever did.... He argued well about free will. He conjoined piety with letters'" (*WA*, TR 2, No. 1470).

---

[35] Eric Partridge, *Shakespeare's Bawdy: A Literary and Psychological Essay and a Comprehensive Glossary* (New York: E. P. Dutton, 1960).
[36] Letter to Nicholas Amsdorf, March 11, 1534. *WA*, Br 7, 29.

As a rule Veit Dietrich was more accurate in his reporting than John Schlaginhaufen,[37] and this appears to be the case here, too, for the former seems to have caught Luther's manner of speaking while the latter has recast essentially the same thoughts in a more artificial style. The difference between the two reports must be ascribed to the relative skill of the two men in taking notes and the extent to which the original notes taken at table were later revised by the writers themselves and subsequently altered by copyists. Although it cannot be said that available texts of the Table Talk reproduce word for word what was actually said at Luther's table, it must nevertheless be added that the texts are reasonably trustworthy in reporting the subject matter and the directions which the conversation took. In other words, the Table Talk is less reliable than writings which we have from Luther's own hand but not on this account to be dismissed as fiction.

IV

What is presented in this volume is only a selection from the six volumes of Table Talk reproduced in the Weimar edition.[38] This selection represents about one-tenth of the total bulk of what is known as the Table Talk. It is therefore of some importance to explain on what basis the selection was made.

1. Excluded at the outset were all the less trustworthy texts of John Aurifaber, including those which are elaborations of his own notes made in the last year of Luther's life. Excluded, too, were notes whose authorship is unknown. The selection was accordingly made from the most reliable texts and those which can be read, to some extent at least, in a concrete historical context. For this reason the reports of conversations are here reproduced not in a topical arrangement but in the chronological order established by the editor of the Table Talk in the Weimar edition. For purposes of convenience they are also numbered as in the Weimar edition.

---

[37] Cf. Adalbert Wahl, "Beiträge zur Kritik der Überlieferung von Luthers Tischgesprächen der Frühzeit," in *Archiv für Reformationsgeschichte*, XVII (1920), 11-40.

[38] In addition to the six volumes of WA, TR, there are more texts of the Table Talk in WA 48, 365-719.

2. Parallel texts, where two writers reported the same conversation, were excluded and the better text was translated. Also excluded as a rule were parallels of another kind, where Luther discussed the same topic in essentially the same way on different occasions, usually years apart. Exceptions to this rule were made in cases in which variations in Luther's statements, or at least in the reports of Luther's statements, have been debated by historians. For example, several accounts have been included of Luther's so-called tower experience (Nos. 3232c, 4007, 5518) and his first mass (Nos. 623, 3556A, 4574).

3. As has just been intimated, there is a good deal of autobiographical material in the Table Talk. Luther often spoke about his early home and parents, his education, his decision to become a monk, his experience in the monastery, his rediscovery of the gospel, his attacks on scholasticism and the papacy, his journey to Worms, his marriage to Katherine von Bora, the Marburg Colloquy, and so on. As many pieces of this kind as possible were included. In addition, conversations that throw light on Luther's temperament and nature were selected—his humor and anger, his cheerfulness and melancholy, his candor and liberality, his critical acumen and credulity, his gentleness and blustering defiance. Recorders of the Table Talk occasionally indicated that Luther smiled or wept or spoke in irony, but as a rule the text itself suggests his changing moods.

4. A special effort has been made to include pieces that have played a role in later polemical literature, pieces that have often been cited with triumph by unsympathetic writers or that have often been hidden with embarrassment by friendly writers. There are examples which show to what an extent Luther shared superstitions of his time and was guilty of "coarseness" in speech. It must be admitted that instances of the last kind presented particular problems in translation, for it has not always been easy to find English equivalents that have precisely the same connotation to modern readers as the German or Latin expressions had to auditors or readers in the sixteenth century. The same is true with respect to the powerful invective which Luther directed against his opponents.

5. Unlike Aurifaber's version, the selection from the Table Talk here is not intended to serve the interests of edification. To be sure, many of the things that Luther said were and still are edifying.

Pieces have not been omitted on this account, but the basis for selection has been to offer a representative sampling of the variety that is characteristic of the whole. Included accordingly were not only expositions of biblical passages, treatments of doctrines, and examples of pastoral counsel but also discussions of current events, fashions and tailoring, proposals for calendar reform, the benefits of mothers' milk, the blessings and problems of marriage, physicians and medicine, the conferring of degrees in the university, printers and books, dancing and fishing, ghosts and witches, lawyers and lawsuits. That a subjective element was involved becomes apparent when the selection offered in this volume is compared with the quite different selections in other recent publications, but the principles of selection were also different.[39]

The reader will notice that while most of the conversations were held at Luther's table, some of them were not. As has been suggested above, many of the reporters who took notes lived in the home of the Reformer. Sometimes they walked with him in the garden and recorded what he said to them there. Sometimes they heard, or overheard, Luther's conversation with his wife and jotted this down. Sometimes they accompanied him on a journey and reported what was said on the way. The term "Table Talk" has been used more loosely than this, for an early manuscript even included in the Table Talk a recipe for making ink.[40]

It is necessary to call attention to several editorial procedures peculiar to this volume. 1) Even in the earliest of the extant manuscripts the Table Talk is divided into separate "talks" or "pieces," and this practice has been followed in the Weimar edition, where the pieces are numbered consecutively in approximate chronological order. The division is sometimes capricious, for now and then

---

[39] Unlike the present volume, moreover, the following do not reproduce the selected pieces in their entirety: Preserved Smith and Herbert P. Gallinger, *Conversations with Luther* (Boston: Pilgrim Press, 1915), introduce a new topical arrangement; Otto Clemen, *Tischreden*, Vol. 8 of *Luthers Werke in Auswahl* (Berlin: Walter de Gruyter, 1930), reproduces selections in the original mixture of Latin and German; Hermann Mulert, *Luther lebt!* (Berlin: Propyläen-Verlag, 1935), also employs a topical arrangement; Reinhard Buchwald, *Luther in Gespräch* (Stuttgart: Alfred Kröner, 1938), puts selected conversations in chronological order; Heinrich Fausel, *Tischreden*, third supplementary volume in the Munich edition of selected works of Luther (Munich: Christian Kaiser Verlag, 1963), returns to a topical order.
[40] WA, TR 1, No. 321, n. 8.

what obviously forms a unit is separated into two or more pieces (e.g., Nos. 3798, 3799). Because the pattern of reference to piece numbers is now generally followed it has been adhered to here. 2) In the earliest manuscripts there were no headings for the individual pieces. Captions were added later and varied from edition to edition. New headings have been introduced below and are intended to indicate the contents of each piece. 3) Only Anthony Lauterbach took pains to furnish the dates of the conversations he recorded. The dates of the talks recorded by others can in some cases be determined by references in them to known events or seasons (e.g., No. 1416). On the assumption that the order of pieces in the earliest manuscripts is the order in which the notes were taken, undated talks probably occurred before or after those whose dates have been determined. It must be recognized that there is some uncertainty therefore about some of the dates. 4) There are no quotation marks in the macaronic texts that were used. Such marks have been inserted in the translation to assist the reader. It needs to be pointed out, however, that Luther was fond of the device of putting words into other people's mouths. He often dramatized a situation by simulating a conversation with somebody else. The most obvious examples of this are his debates with the devil. Accordingly Luther did not in every instance mean to suggest that he was actually quoting; where he was, the quotations are identified in the footnotes in so far as possible. 5) Words enclosed in brackets are always additions inserted by the translator. In some cases these are readings from one or another of the more than thirty early manuscripts whose variants are noted in the critical apparatus of the Weimar edition, and in other cases these are interpolations borrowed from Aurifaber's version. The footnotes indicate which of these two sources applies in each instance. Most of the words enclosed in brackets (and for these no explanations are given in the footnotes) were added by the translator to suggest the probable meaning of otherwise obscure texts.

T.G.T.

LUTHER'S WORKS

VOLUME 54

TABLE TALK RECORDED BY VEIT DIETRICH

1531-1533

INTRODUCTION

The pieces numbered 1 to 656 in *WA, TR* 1 were recorded by Veit Dietrich in the years 1531-1533. About one-fourth of these have been selected for translation and inclusion in this edition.

Between 1531 and 1533 John Schlaginhaufen and Conrad Cordatus, among others, were also taking notes of the conversation at Luther's table. When more than one of these men recorded the same conversation, a comparison of their notes reveals that Dietrich had a gift for getting the substance of Luther's remarks on paper but was even less interested than Schlaginhaufen in reporting the particular circumstances in which Luther spoke or the particular situation to which the Reformer was addressing himself. Moreover, the notes of both Dietrich and Schlaginhaufen give an impression of greater authenticity than those of Cordatus, which were afterward revised.

Veit Dietrich[1] was born in Nürnberg in the year 1506. He went to Wittenberg as a student in 1522, when he was sixteen years old, and received his master's degree there in 1529. Before receiving his degree he had attracted the favorable attention of Martin Luther and Philip Melanchthon. He was invited to live in Luther's home and eat at his table, in return for which he served as Luther's amanuensis. In this capacity he helped Luther in the preparation of his *House Postil* and accompanied the Reformer to the Marburg Colloquy in 1529 and to Castle Coburg, where Luther stayed during the Diet of Augsburg in 1530. His contemporaries criticized Dietrich for his hot temper and his fondness for disputation, but none of this is reflected in his notes of the Table Talk.

---

[1] Biographical information concerning Dietrich and some of the other recorders of the Table Talk may be had in compendious form in the *Allgemeine deutsche Biographie* (56 vols.; Leipzig, 1875-1912); *Neue Deutsche Biographie* (Berlin, 1953-   ); *Die Religion in Geschichte und Gegenwart* (3rd ed., 7 vols.; Tübingen, 1957-1965); *The New Schaff-Herzog Encyclopedia of Religious Knowledge* (13 vols. and 2 supplementary vols.; Grand Rapids, 1908-1955).

In 1535 Dietrich returned to his native Nürnberg, where he remained as preacher in St. Sebald's Church until his death in 1549. There he attacked the practice of elevating the host in the celebration of the Lord's Supper, for which he was unjustly called a Zwinglian by some opponents, and opposed the laying on of hands at ordinations. As these controversies might suggest, Dietrich was concerned about a proper relation between the practice of the church and its theology. The same concern found expression in his preparation of a manual for pastoral acts, his preparation of devotional works, his writing of hymns, and his publication of some of his own sermons.

TABLE TALK RECORDED BY VEIT DIETRICH

How Luther Handled Troublesome Thoughts
Summer or Fall, 1531   *No. 19*

"When I'm troubled by thoughts which pertain to political questions or household affairs [said Martin Luther], I take up a psalm or a text of Paul and fall asleep over it. But the thoughts which come from Satan demand more of me. Then I have to resort to more difficult maneuvers before I extricate myself, although I easily get the upper hand in thoughts of an economic or domestic character. However, when I'm angry with God and ask him whether it's he or I who's wrong, then it's more than I can handle."

Value of Knowledge Gained by Experience
Summer or Fall, 1531   *No. 46*

"A doctor of the Scriptures ought to have a good knowledge of the Scriptures and ought to have grasped how the prophets run into one another. It isn't enough to know only one part—as a man might know Isaiah, for example—or to know only one topic of the law or of the gospel. Now, however, doctors are springing up who scarcely have a right comprehension of one topic.

"Teachers of law can humble their students when the students try to put on airs about their learning, because they have a court and get practical experience. On the other hand, we can't humble our students because we have no practical exercises. Yet experience alone makes the theologian."

Luther's Evaluation of His Wife
Summer or Fall, 1531   *No. 49*

"I wouldn't give up my Katy[1] for France or for Venice—first,

---

[1] Luther was married to Katherine von Bora (1499-1552), a former nun, on June 13, 1525. See Clara S. Schreiber, *Katherine, Wife of Luther* (Philadelphia: Muhlenberg Press, 1954).

because God gave her to me and gave me to her; second, because I have often observed that other women have more shortcomings than my Katy (although she, too, has some shortcomings, they are outweighed by many great virtues); and third, because she keeps faith in marriage, that is, fidelity and respect.

"A wife ought to think the same way about her husband."

Opinions About Some of the Church Fathers
Summer or Fall, 1531   *No. 51*

"Jerome[2] was neither a theologian nor an orator but was like the Swabian Altenstaig.[3] In his controversy with the Pelagians, Augustine[4] became a strong and faithful defender of grace. Gregory[5] was leprous when it came to ceremonies; he considered it a mortal sin to break wind. Ambrose[6] was a straightforward defender of faith against a reliance on works; if he had been involved in controversy he would perhaps have excelled all others."

The Difference Between Men and Women
Summer or Fall, 1531   *No. 55*

"Men have broad shoulders and narrow hips, and accordingly they possess intelligence. Women have narrow shoulders and broad hips. Women ought to stay at home;[7] the way they were created indicates this, for they have broad hips and a wide fundament to sit upon [keep house and bear and raise children]." [8]

---

[2] Jerome (d. 420), one of the most learned of the Western fathers of the church, was often criticized by Luther for his interpretation of the Bible.

[3] John Altenstaig (d. *ca.* 1525), humanist in Württemberg.

[4] Aurelius Augustine (354-430), most influential of the Western church fathers, wrote extensively against Pelagius, roughly a contemporary, and against his followers.

[5] Gregory the Great (*ca.* 540-604) was probably in Luther's mind here.

[6] Ambrose, bishop of Milan (*ca.* 340-379), was a writer of ascetic literature.

[7] Greek: *oikouros*.

[8] Text in brackets from later variant of John Aurifaber.

What It Takes to Understand the Scriptures
Fall, 1531 No. 81

"I wonder whether Peter, Paul, Moses, and all the saints fully and thoroughly understood a single word of God so that they had nothing more to learn from it, for the understanding of God is beyond measure.[9] To be sure, the saints understood the Word of God and could also speak about it, but their practice did not keep pace with it. Here one forever remains a learner. The scholastics illustrated this with a ball which only at one point touches the table on which it rests, although the whole weight of the ball is supported by the table.

"Though I am a great doctor, I haven't yet progressed beyond the instruction of children in the Ten Commandments, the Creed, and the Lord's Prayer. I still learn and pray these every day with my Hans and my little Lena.[10] Who understands in all of its ramifications even the opening words,[11] 'Our Father who art in heaven'? For if I understood these words in faith—that the God who holds heaven and earth in his hand is my Father—I would conclude that therefore I am lord of heaven and earth, therefore Christ is my brother, therefore all things are mine, Gabriel is my servant, Raphael is my coachman, and all the other angels are ministering spirits[12] sent forth by my Father in heaven to serve me in all my necessities, lest I strike my foot against a stone. In order that this faith should not remain untested, my Father comes along and allows me to be thrown into prison or to be drowned in water. Then it will finally become apparent how well we understand these words. Our faith wavers. Our weakness gives rise to the question, 'Who knows if it is true?' So this one word 'your' or 'our' is the most difficult of all in the whole Scripture. It's like the word 'your' in the first commandment, 'I am the Lord your God' [Exod. 20:2]."

---

[9] Cf. Ps. 147:5.
[10] Luther's son John was born in 1526 and his daughter Magdalene was born in 1529.
[11] Of the Lord's Prayer. Cf. Matt. 6:9.
[12] Cf. Heb. 1:14.

About Augustine and Justification
Early November, 1531   No. 85

"It was Augustine's[13] view that the law, fulfilled by the powers of reason, does not justify, even as works of the moral law do not justify the heathen, but that if the Holy Spirit assists, the works of the law do justify. The question is not whether the law or the works of reason justify, but whether the law, kept with the Spirit's help, justifies.

"I reply by saying No. Even if in the power of the Holy Spirit a man were to keep the law completely, he ought nevertheless to pray for divine mercy, for God has ordained that man should be saved not by the law but by Christ. Works never give us a peaceful heart. Christ would never have been sad in spirit unless he had been pressed hard by the law, to which he subjected himself for our sake."

Man's Arrogance and Self-Assurance
Early November, 1531   No. 87

"It's remarkable that men should be so arrogant and secure when there are so many, indeed countless, evidences around us to suggest that we ought to be humble. The hour of our death is uncertain. The grain on which we live is not in our hands. Neither the sun nor the air, on which our life depends, lies in our power, and we have no control over our sleeping and waking. I shall say nothing of spiritual things, such as the private and public sins which press upon us. Yet our hearts are hard as steel and pay no attention to such evidence."

The Order of the Ten Commandments
Early November, 1531   No. 88

"The first to the seventh commandments follow one another in good order. Murder is a graver sin than adultery, adultery is a

---

[13] Luther probably was thinking of Augustine's *Against Two Epistles of the Pelagians*, 3, 20.

graver sin than stealing, etc. The order of the other three commandments is not so apparent. Although I do not presume to make a judgment, it is my opinion that the last three commandments speak, as it were, of the ground or circumstances of the preceding commandments, for it is with the mouth and with coveting (these are the two things that are forbidden in the last three commandments) that one sins against all the other commandments. The order certainly appears to shift in the eighth commandment, for to bear false witness is not a graver sin than to covet your neighbor's wife, nor is it a graver sin to covet your neighbor's house than his wife."

God's Punishment of the Godless
Early November, 1531   *No. 94*

"While I was in Erfurt I once said to Dr. Staupitz,[14] 'Dear Doctor, our Lord God treats people too horribly. Who can serve him as long as he strikes people down right and left, as we see he does in many cases involving our adversaries?' Then Dr. Staupitz answered, 'Dear fellow, learn to think of God differently. If he did not treat them this way, how could God restrain those blockheads? God strikes us for our own good, in order that he might free us who would otherwise be crushed.'

"When I was in Coburg[15] these comments about adversaries taught me the meaning of the words in the Decalogue, 'I the Lord your God am a jealous God.'[16] It is not so much a cruel punishment of adversaries as it is a necessary defense of ourselves. They say that Zwingli recently died thus;[17] if his error had prevailed, we would have perished, and our church with us. It was a judgment of God. That was always a proud people. The others, the papists, will probably also be dealt with by our Lord God. They

---

[14] Luther was recalling this conversation which he had with John Staupitz (d. 1524), then vicar-general of the Augustinian Observantists in Germany, while Luther was still in the Augustinian monastery in Erfurt.
[15] During the Diet of Augsburg in 1530 Luther was in Castle Coburg. See *LW* 34, 5-8.
[16] Exod. 20:5. In Luther's *Small Catechism* these words appear at the conclusion of the Ten Commandments.
[17] Huldreich Zwingli, the Swiss Reformer, died in battle on October 11, 1531.

TABLE TALK

invoked the bread[18] as God, and now he will become as hard as iron toward them. Oecolampadius[19] called our Lord's Supper a Thyestian banquet[20] [and ridiculed participants in it as] flesh-eaters, blood-drinkers, etc. Now we say to them: Here you have what you asked for. God has spoken once for all: he will not hold him guiltless who takes his name in vain.[21] Surely they blasphemed when they invoked God in the bread or called us flesh-eaters, blood-drinkers, God-devourers. The same will happen to our papists who have burdened themselves with the blood of the godly. God grant that by Pentecost they may be destroyed root and branch! They themselves say that they want either to smother doctrine or leave nothing behind. Amen. Let it be as they wish! How can our Lord God repay them better than by giving them what they want?"

Rejection of Transubstantiation
November 9, 1531   *No. 96*

"In the sacrament of the altar Thomas[22] invented transubstantiation. I think that the bread and wine remain, just as the water remains in baptism and just as the human voice remains when I preach. Yet it is in truth the power of God, as Paul calls it." [23]

Luther's Own Call to the Ministry
Between November 9 and 30, 1531   *No. 113*

"Unless those who are in the office of preacher find joy in him who sent them, they will have much trouble. Our Lord God had to ask Moses as many as six times.[24] He also led me into the office in the same way. Had I known about it beforehand, he would have

---

[18] I.e., the transubstantiated bread of the Roman Mass.
[19] John Oecolampadius, co-laborer of Zwingli in Switzerland, died in Basel on November 24, 1531, shortly after this conversation in Wittenberg.
[20] Thyestes was a mythological figure who was served his own son to eat.
[21] Cf. Exod. 20:7.
[22] Thomas Aquinas (d. 1274), greatest of the medieval scholastic theologians. Cf. *LW* 36, 32-35, 271-273.
[23] Cf. Rom. 1:16.
[24] Cf. Exod. 3, 4.

had to take more pains to get me in. Be that as it may, now that I have begun, I intend to perform the duties of the office with his help. On account of the exceedingly great and heavy cares and worries connected with it, I would not take the whole world to enter upon this work now. On the other hand, when I regard him who called me, I would not take the whole world not to have begun it. Nor do I wish to have another God. Others before me, like Erasmus,[25] criticized the life that people lived under the papacy, but I never thought I would be able to attack the two pillars on which the papacy rests, the mass and the [monastic] vows, for to do so seemed to me like an attack on God and his creation."

Contempt for and Love of God's Word
Between November 9 and 30, 1531 No. 115

When there was talk about contempt for the Word of God among peasants, noblemen, and townspeople, he [Martin Luther] said, "Such contempt ought to be both a consolation and a warning to us, so that we give thanks to God for the blessing of being among those who love his Word, diligently hear and learn God's Word, and find delight in the Holy Scriptures. For it is a great punishment and a severe judgment of God if a man so hates God and his Word that he is unwilling to hear it and neither honors nor esteems the ministers of the Word."

Luther's Early Study of the Bible
Between November 9 and 30, 1531 No. 116

Once when he was a young man he [Martin Luther] happened upon a Bible. In it he read by chance the story about Samuel's mother in the Books of the Kings.[26] The book pleased him immensely, and he thought that he would be happy if he could ever possess such a book. Shortly thereafter he bought a postil; it also

---

[25] Desiderius Erasmus (1466-1536), Dutch humanist whose early support of Luther turned to opposition. See Preserved Smith, *Erasmus* (New York: Harpers, 1923).
[26] Cf. I Sam. 1:1-11. For a discussion of this episode, see W. J. Kooiman, *Luther and the Bible* (Philadelphia: Muhlenberg Press, 1961), pp. 1-9.

pleased him greatly, for it contained more Gospels[27] than it was customary to preach on in the course of a year.

When he became a monk he gave up all his books. Shortly before this he had bought a copy of the *Corpus iuris*[28] and I do not know what else. He returned these to the bookseller. Besides Plautus[29] and Vergil[30] he took nothing with him into the monastery. There the monks gave him a Bible bound in red leather. He made himself so familiar with it that he knew what was on every page, and when some passage was mentioned he knew at once just where it was to be found.

"If I had kept at it," he said, "I would have become exceedingly good at locating things in the Bible. At that time no other study pleased me so much as sacred literature. With great loathing I read physics, and my heart was aglow when the time came to return to the Bible. I made use of the *glossa ordinaria*.[31] I despised Lyra,[32] although I recognized later on that he had a contribution to make to history. I read the Bible diligently. Sometimes one important statement occupied all my thoughts for a whole day. Such statements appeared especially in the weightier prophets, and (although I could not grasp their meaning) they have stuck in my memory to this day. Such is the assertion in Ezekiel, 'I have no pleasure in the death of the wicked,' etc. [Ezek. 33:11]."

Recollection of Accident in Student Days Between November 9 and 30, 1531   No. 119

When he [Martin Luther] set out for home and was on the way, he accidentally struck his shin on his short sword and cut an artery in his leg. At the time he was alone in the open field except for one companion, and he was as far from Erfurt as Eutzsch is

---

[27] Appointed lections of the church year. A postil was a collection of sermons or commentaries on the appointed lessons of the church year.

[28] The collection of canon law which he had intended to use in his study of law.

[29] T. M. Plautus (d. 184 B.C.), a Roman writer of comedies.

[30] Vergilius Maro (70-19 B.C.), a Roman poet.

[31] Walafried Strabo's (*ca.* 808-849) exposition of the Scriptures.

[32] Nicholas Lyra's (*ca.* 1270-1340) fifty-volume exposition of the Scriptures was used by Luther to the end of his life.

distant from Wittenberg, that is, a half mile. The blood gushed from the wound and could not be stopped. When he pressed his finger on the wound, his leg became greatly swollen. Finally a surgeon was fetched from the town, and he bound up the wound. There he [Luther] was in danger of death and cried out, "Mary, help!" "I would have died," he now added, "with my trust in Mary." Afterward, during the night, while he was in bed, the wound broke open. He almost bled to death and again prayed to Mary. This happened on the Tuesday after Easter.[33]

The Friar Martin Luther and Sex
November 30, 1531   *No. 121*

"When I was a monk I did not feel much desire. I had nocturnal pollutions in response to bodily necessity. I didn't even look at the women when they made their confession, for I didn't wish to recognize the faces of those whose confessions I heard. In Erfurt I heard the confession of no woman, in Wittenberg of only three women."

Treatment of Melancholy, Despair, Etc.
November 30, 1531   *No. 122*

"When I was in spiritual distress[34] a gentle word would restore my spirit. Sometimes my confessor said to me when I repeatedly discussed silly sins with him, 'You are a fool. God is not incensed against you, but you are incensed against God. God is not angry with you, but you are angry with God.' This was magnificently said, although it was before the light of the gospel.[35]

"Right here at this table, when the rest of you were in Jena, Pomeranus[36] sometimes consoled me when I was sad by saying,

---

[33] Probably April 16, 1503.
[34] *In tentatione; in Anfechtung.*
[35] Luther refers to his experience as a monk before the beginning of the Reformation.
[36] John Bugenhagen (1485-1558), of Pomerania, prominent co-laborer of Luther. The reference is probably to August, 1527, when the university was temporarily moved from Wittenberg to Jena on account of the pestilence and Bugenhagen stayed behind with Luther.

'No doubt God is thinking: What more can I do with this man? I have given him so many excellent gifts, and yet he despairs of my grace!' These words were a great comfort to me. As a voice from heaven they struck me in my heart, although I think Pomeranus did not realize at the time what he had said and that it was so well said.

"Those who are troubled with melancholy," he [Martin Luther] said, "ought to be very careful not to be alone, for God created the fellowship of the church and commanded brotherliness, as the Scriptures testify, 'Woe to him who is alone when he falls,' etc. [Eccles. 4:10]. To be gloomy before God is not pleasing to him, although he would permit us to be depressed before the world. He does not wish me to have a long face in his presence, as he says, 'I have no pleasure in the death of the wicked' [Ezek. 33:11] and 'Rejoice in the Lord' [Phil. 4:4]. He desires not a servant who does not expect good things of him.

"Although I know this, I am of a different mind ten times in the course of a day. But I resist the devil, and often it is with a fart that I chase him away. When he tempts me with silly sins I say, 'Devil, yesterday I broke wind too. Have you written it down on your list?' When I say to him, 'You have been put to shame,' he believes it, for he does not want to be despised. Afterward, if I engage him in further conversation, I upbraid him with the pope and say, 'If you do the same as he does, who is your pope that I should celebrate him? Look what an abomination he has prepared, and it continues to this day!' Thus I remind myself of the forgiveness of sin and of Christ and I remind Satan of the abomination of the pope. This abomination is so great that I am of good cheer and rejoice, and I confess that the abomination of the papacy after the time of Christ is a great consolation to me. Consequently those who say that one should not rebuke the pope are dreadful scolds. Go right ahead and inveigh against the pope, especially if the devil disturbs you about justification. He often troubles me with trivialities. I don't notice this when I'm depressed, but when I feel better I recognize it easily.

"Well, then, our furious foe has done us much harm. I know that I shall see him and his flaming missiles in the last day. As long as we have pure teaching he will not harm us, but if the teaching is wrong we are done for. But praise be to God, who gave us the Word and also allowed his only Son to die for us! He did not do this in vain. Accordingly we should entertain the hope that we are saints, that we are saved, and that this will be manifest when it is revealed. Since Christ accepted the thief on the cross[37] just as he was and received Paul after all his blasphemies and persecutions,[38] we have no reason to despair. As a matter of fact, all of us must be saved just as the thief and Paul were. Good God, what do you think it means that he has given his only Son? It means that he also offers whatever else he possesses. We have no reason, therefore, to fear his wrath, although we must continue to fear on account of the old Adam, who is still unable to understand this as it ought to be understood. If we had only the first three words of the Creed,[39] 'I believe in God the Father,' they would still be far beyond our understanding and reason. In short, it does not occur to man that God is Father. If it did, man could not live for a single moment. Accordingly in this infirm flesh we must have faith, for if we were capable of fully believing, heaven would already be here. There is therefore no reason to fear, in so far as the object of fear is concerned, and yet we cannot understand and are compelled on account of the weakness of our flesh to suffer assaults of fear and desperation. Thus the catechism remains lord,[40] and there is nobody who understands it. I am accordingly compelled to pray it every day, even aloud, and whenever I happen to be prevented by the press of duties from observing my hour of prayer, the entire day is bad for me. Prayer helps us very much and gives us a cheerful heart, not on account of any merit in the work, but because we have spoken with God and found everything to be in order.

"Having been taught by experience I can say how you ought to restore your spirit when you suffer from spiritual depression. When you are assailed by gloom, despair, or a troubled conscience

---

[37] Cf. Luke 23:39-43.
[38] Cf. Gal. 1:13.
[39] The first three words of the Apostles' Creed in Latin: *Credo in Deum*.
[40] I.e., the catechism (e.g., Luther's *Small Catechism*), which contains the Creed and an explanation of it.

you should eat, drink, and talk with others. If you can find help for yourself by thinking of a girl, do so.

"There was a bishop who had a sister in a convent. She was disturbed by various dreams about her brother. She betook herself to her brother and complained to him that she was again and again agitated by bad dreams. He at once prepared a sumptuous dinner and urged his sister to eat and drink. The following day he asked her whether she had been annoyed by dreams during the night. 'No,' she responded. 'I slept well and had no dreams at all.' 'Go, then,' he said. 'Take care of your body in defiance of Satan, and the bad dreams will stop.'

"But this you ought to know, that other remedies are suitable for other persons. Copious drinking benefits me when I am in this condition. But I would not advise a young person to drink more because this might stimulate his sexual desire. In short, abstinence is beneficial for some and a drinking bout for others. Augustine says wisely in his rule, 'Not equally for all because you are not all equally strong.'[41] So he speaks about the body and so we can speak about illnesses of the spirit."

"Are You the Only One who Is Right?"
Between November 30 and December 14, 1531   No. 130

"Above all, we must be certain that this [our] teaching is the Word of God. When this is established, we shall be sure that the cause must and will remain and that no devil can suppress it. God be praised, I am certain that it is the Word of our Lord God, I have driven from my heart all other beliefs in the world, whatever they may be, and I have almost overcome that most difficult of all thoughts which arises in the heart, 'Do you claim to be the only one who has the true Word of God and no one else has it?' In this sense—that is, in the name of the church—they are now attacking us most severely. I find this argument [of our opponents] everywhere in all the prophets, to whom men said, 'We are the people of God; you are only a few.' Only in such a way should one rely

---

[41] *Rule of St. Augustine*, chap. II, "Prayer and Fasting." This rule of the Augustinian Order was not actually written by Augustine.

upon oneself and say, 'All the rest of you are wrong.' But a consolation is added when the Word declares, 'I shall give you children, people who will accept it.'"[42]

The Duplicity of Desiderius Erasmus
Between November 30 and December 14, 1531   No. 131

"Erasmus[43] is an eel. Nobody can grasp him except Christ alone. He is a double-dealing man. When Elector Frederick[44] asked him in Cologne why Luther was condemned, what wrong he had done, Erasmus replied, 'He has done much wrong who attacks the monks in their bellies and the pope in his crown.' Frederick said to Spalatin,[45] 'He is a strange fellow. One does not know what to make of him.' He at once recognized the man's cunning. It was the remarkable astuteness of Satan that captivated the world when he attacked the superstitions of the pope. Then he corrupted the youth with the wicked opinions he expressed in his colloquies.[46] God keep him in check! The stratagem of Satan is violent."

God's Grace Is Hard to Believe
Between November 30 and December 14, 1531   No. 137

"It's very difficult for a man to believe that God is gracious to him. The human heart can't grasp this. What happened in my case? I was once terrified by the sacrament which Dr. Staupitz carried in a procession in Eisleben on the feast of Corpus Christi.[47] I went along in the procession and wore the dress of a priest. Afterward I made confession to Dr. Staupitz, and he said to me, 'Your thought is not of Christ.' With this word he comforted me well.

---

[42] Cf. Isa. 54:13; Matt. 13:8.
[43] Desiderius Erasmus. Cf. No. 113, n. 25.
[44] Elector Frederick the Wise of Saxony (1463-1525).
[45] George Spalatin (1484-1545), secretary of Elector Frederick.
[46] *Colloquia familiaria*, first published in 1518. Craig R. Thompson (trans.), *The Colloquies of Erasmus* (Chicago: The University of Chicago Press, 1965).
[47] This incident probably occurred on June 7, 1515. First observed in 1264 as a day to commemorate the institution of the Lord's Supper, Corpus Christi was marked by a solemn procession in which the host (the body of Christ) was carried. *Corpus Christi* is the Latin for body of Christ. On Staupitz, cf. No. 94, n. 14.

This is the way we are. Christ offers himself to us together with the forgiveness of sins, and yet we flee from his face.

"This also happened to me as a boy in my homeland when we sang in order to gather sausages.[48] A townsman jokingly cried out, 'What are you boys up to? May this or that evil overtake you!' At the same time he ran toward us with two sausages. With my companion I took to my feet and ran away from the man who was offering his gift. This is precisely what happens to us in our relation to God. He gave us Christ with all his gifts, and yet we flee from him and regard him as our judge."

Original Sin Is Like a Wound
Between November 30 and December 14, 1531   No. 138

"After baptism original sin is like a wound which has begun to heal. It is really a wound, yet it is becoming better and is constantly in the process of healing, although it is still festering, is painful, etc. So original sin remains in the baptized until their death, although it is in the process of being rooted out. It is rendered harmless, and so it cannot accuse or damn us."

Luther Drinks to God's Honor
Between November 30 and December 14, 1531   No. 139

"If our Lord God can pardon me for having crucified and martyred him for about twenty years [by saying mass],[49] he can also approve of my occasionally taking a drink in his honor. God grant it, no matter how the world may wish to interpret it!"

The Epistle to the Galatians
Between December 14, 1531,
and January 22, 1532   No. 146

"The Epistle to the Galatians is my dear epistle. I have put my confidence in it. It is my Katy von Bora." [50]

---

[48] In Luther's youth, when mendicancy was a way of life, it was customary for students to support themselves by begging for food. Like other forms of begging, this practice was forbidden where the Reformation was introduced.
[49] Text in brackets from a later variant by John Aurifaber.
[50] I.e., I love it as I love my wife. Cf. No. 49, n. 1.

Cheerfulness and Reverence Before God
Between December 14, 1531, and January 22, 1532   *No. 148*

"If it is true that God speaks with us in the Holy Scriptures, either he must be a rascal who does not do what he says or he must be the highest majesty who, when he opens his mouth, does three times as much as he promises. With one word he created the whole world, Genesis 1. It is therefore established that God speaks, and so one will learn to esteem his word highly. David recognized and believed this, and so he wrote, 'God has spoken to me in his sanctuary' [Ps. 60:6]. He had to pay for this, too, and that is why God put him to such severe trials, involving murder, adultery, exile, etc. So David wrote in a psalm, 'Serve the Lord with fear, and exult with trembling' [Ps. 2:11]. Let somebody bring this into harmony for me: exult and fear! My son Hans[51] can do it in relation to me, but I can't do it in relation to God. When I'm writing or doing something else, my Hans sings a little tune for me. If he becomes too noisy and I rebuke him a little for it, he continues to sing but does it more privately and with a certain awe and uneasiness. This is what God wishes: that we be always cheerful, but with reverence."

Judges Decide on the Basis of Evidence
Between December 14, 1531, and January 22, 1532   *No. 149*

[Dr. Martin Luther was asked,][52] Did David do the right thing when he killed the man who said that he had slain Saul but (if I am not mistaken) had not really done so?[53]

"I reply that he did the right thing. So a judge also does right if he makes a wrong judgment in a case in which he relies on the testimony of witnesses. No one can be sure of witnesses. One must believe them and be content with this. Lawyers also carry on their task by faith. They can safely rely on testimonies, even if they discover afterward that they were false, for 'on the evidence of two

---
[51] See No. 81, n. 10.
[52] Text in brackets from a later variant by John Aurifaber.
[53] Cf. II Sam. 1:1-16.

witnesses, or of three witnesses, shall a charge be sustained' [Deut. 19:15]. Besides, they have a rule, 'A judge should pronounce sentence according to the charges and the proofs.'

"A jurist can be a scoundrel but a theologian ought to be a godly man. The reason is that a jurist has power over the bodily things with which he deals, but it requires a godly man to be a theologian because God himself, his heaven and all his gifts, righteousness, the forgiveness of sin, and everything else are entrusted to him. God himself relies upon him, for it is written, 'If you forgive the sins of any, they are forgiven' [John 20:23]."

Practical Versus Speculative Theology
Between December 14, 1531,
and January 22, 1532   No. 153

"True theology is practical, and its foundation is Christ, whose death is appropriated to us through faith. However, today all those who do not agree with us and do not share our teaching make theology speculative because they cannot free themselves from the notion that those who do good [will be rewarded].[54] This is not what is written, but rather, 'Whoso feareth the Lord, it shall go well with him at the last' [Ecclus. 1:13]. Accordingly speculative theology belongs to the devil in hell. So Zwingli[55] speculated, 'The body of Christ is in the bread, but only spiritually because I think it is in the bread.' Such is the theology of Origen[56] also. David did not do it thus but acknowledged his sin and said, 'Have mercy on me, O God' [Ps. 51:1]."

Luther Is Occupied with Many Duties
Between December 14, 1531,
and January 22, 1532   No. 154

"I am very busy. Four persons[57] are dependent on me, and

---

[54] Text in brackets from later variant by John Aurifaber.
[55] Cf. No. 94, n. 17.
[56] Origen (ca. 182-ca. 251) was a prolific writer of the ancient church whose biblical interpretations had continuing influence.
[57] In addition to Luther's wife and two children, the servant Wolfgang Seberger (Sieberger) may have been in the Reformer's mind here, although the

each of them demands my time for himself. Four times a week I preach in public, twice a week I lecture, and in addition I hear cases,[58] write letters, and am working on a book for publication. It is a good thing that God came to my aid and gave me a wife. She takes care of domestic matters, so that I do not have to be responsible for these too."

Luther Stricken with a Sudden Illness
January 22, 1532   *No. 157*

In January, 1532, he [Martin Luther] foretold that he would be sick, that in March he would be overtaken by a grave illness. The illness was not so far away, however, for on January 22 a violent illness assailed him, so that he had to lie down all day. About four o'clock in the morning he was troubled by a ringing in his ears, and this was followed by an extraordinary faintness in his heart. He commanded Master Philip Melanchthon, Master Eisleben (who was then present), and me[59] to be summoned at once in order that he might have somebody to speak to and might listen to our conversation. When he overheard us say that if he died it would give great satisfaction among the papists, he said confidently, "But I am not going to die now. I know this of a certainty. For God will not strengthen the papistic superstition through my death so shortly after the death of Zwingli and Oecolampadius.[60] God will not give them [the papists] such an occasion for rejoicing. To be sure, Satan would gladly kill me if he could. Every moment he is pressing me, is treading on my heels. Yet what he wishes will not be done, but what God wills."

---

house was constantly overrun with relatives, student boarders, and visitors as well.

[58] Matrimonial cases. While John Bugenhagen (see No. 122, n. 36) was in Lübeck from 1530 to 1532, Luther substituted for him in the pulpit in Wittenberg as well as in the hearings of matrimonial cases.

[59] Philip Melanchthon (1497-1560) was Luther's younger friend and colleague in the university in Wittenberg; see Clyde L. Manschreck, *Melanchthon, the Quiet Reformer* (Nashville: Abingdon Press, 1958). John Agricola (1494-1566), a native of Eisleben and often at odds with Luther, was visiting in Wittenberg at this time. The "me" refers to the recorder, Veit Dietrich.

[60] Cf. No. 94, nn. 17, 19.

Thereupon Philip said, "You have sure testimony of his interest. Christ said, 'Even the hairs of your head are all numbered' [Matt. 10:30]."

The physician was also present, and after inspecting the [patient's] urine he said that he [Luther] had been close to apoplexy but would recover from his illness. Although he did not hear the doctor, Luther said, "I cannot believe that my illness is natural. I suspect Satan, and therefore I am the more inclined to take it lightly."

Nature Is Not Abolished by Grace
Between January and March, 1532   No. 165

"Grace does not entirely change nature but uses nature as it finds it. So if somebody is kind when converted through faith, he becomes a gentle preacher like Master Hausmann.[61] If he is by nature irascible and severe, like Cordatus,[62] he preaches after this fashion. On the other hand, if he is fitted by nature with some slyness, intelligence, and power of reason, like Philip,[63] he uses these qualities for the benefit of mankind."

A Man Marries His Daughter and Sister
Between February and March, 1532   No. 183

"The penalty which the pope imposed on an adulterous party, namely, that a husband who commits adultery should not demand but only fulfil his marital duty, is bad, for it gives occasion to whoring. I should rather have imposed a penalty of fasting with bread and water, or something similar.

"The following happened in Erfurt: A certain man at one and the same time took his natural daughter and his sister as his wife; although he did not know it, he had had intercourse with his mother and afterward married the unrecognized daughter borne by his mother. The matter was kept from the papal confessors, for neither

---

[61] Nicholas Hausmann, a mild-mannered pastor and intimate friend of Luther. Cf. No. 4084, n. 274.
[62] Conrad Cordatus (1480-1546), evangelical pastor and a collector of Luther's table talks.
[63] Philip Melanchthon. Cf. No. 157, n. 59.

the man nor his wife knew about it, and only the mother had made confession of it. The couple lived honorable lives with each other, and it was a true marriage before God. Thus the mother kept the deed to herself, which she should not have done.

"I have made concessions in many cases, but I have considered the consciences and not the wickedness of people. On this account I shall not permit anyone to exploit the concessions."

Controversy About Christ's Presence
Between February and March, 1532   No. 184

"Bucer[64] argues that the ungodly do not receive the body of Christ [in the sacrament] because they do not believe. Then one should be permitted to argue that because the ungodly do not believe the Ten Commandments, therefore the commandments do not exist, or because the ungodly do not believe in laws, therefore laws do not exist. They ought to give half their lives if this conclusion were correct, for then nobody would be damned and everything could be excused and set free. I wish that this argument would be put into practice for them in this way: The ungodly person does not believe in God's creation, and therefore the ungodly has no money that might be taken from him. But it is the greatest folly to argue from the impiety of the godless to the truth of God. Is one to argue that if the ungodly cannot receive Christ spiritually, they therefore cannot receive him corporally? They are godless men, stricken with madness!"

Marriage Should Begin with Prayer
Between February and March, 1532   No. 185

"Marriage consists of these things: the natural desire of sex, the bringing to life of offspring, and life together with mutual fidelity. Yet the devil can so rupture marriage that hate is never more bitter than here. This comes from our beginning everything

---

[64] Martin Bucer, or Butzer (1491-1551), reformer of Strassburg and mediating theologian. See Hastings Eells, *Martin Bucer* (New Haven: Yale University Press, 1931).

without prayer and with presumption. A God-fearing young man who is about to be married should pray, 'Dear God, add thy blessing!' But this is not done. Everybody is like Dolzig,[65] and the most important things are begun presumptuously. What is our Lord God to do under the circumstances? It is implied that his name is false: Almighty, Creator, the Giver of all things. Accordingly, dear Master Veit,[66] do as I did. When I wished to take my Katy I prayed to God earnestly. You ought to do this too. You have never yet prayed to God earnestly for a wife."

Judgment Concerning Peter Lombard
Between February and March, 1532   No. 192

"These are said to be the sons of nuns: Peter Lombard,[67] the greatest theologian; Gratian,[68] the greatest canon lawyer; and Comestor,[69] the greatest historian of his times. Peter Lombard was adequate as a theologian; none has been his equal. He read Hilary,[70] Augustine,[71] Ambrose,[72] Gregory,[73] and also all the councils. He was a great man. If he had by chance come upon the Bible he would no doubt have been the greatest."

Luther's Analysis of Himself
End of March, 1532   No. 197

"I am free from avarice, my age and bodily weakness protect me from sensual desire, and I am not afflicted with hate or envy

---

[65] The Saxon marshal Hans von Dolzig, who, Luther said elsewhere (WA, TR 6, No. 6912), began his reckoning without God and without prayer.
[66] Veit Dietrich, the recorder of these early table talks, was contemplating marriage. Cf. pp. 5-6.
[67] Peter Lombard's (d. ca. 1160) *Four Books of Sentences* was the standard manual of dogmatics at the close of the Middle Ages.
[68] Gratian compiled the influential *Decreti Magistri Gratiani* between 1139 and 1142, but otherwise little is known about him.
[69] Peter Comestor (d. 1179 or 1198), professor in Paris and author of the *Historia scholastica*.
[70] Hilary (ca. 401-ca. 450), bishop of Arles.
[71] See No. 51, n. 4.
[72] See No. 51, n. 6.
[73] See No. 51, n. 5.

toward anybody. Up to now only anger remains in me, and for the most part this is necessary and just. But I have other sins that are greater."

Future Complaint About Weak Faith
End of March, 1532 No. 203

"When we are brought to life on the last day we shall spit on ourselves and say, 'Fie on you for not having been bolder in believing on Christ, since the glory is so great! If I were in the world I would have ten Turks trample me underfoot.'"

Luther's Father Dies Comforted
End of March, 1532 No. 204

When Luther's father, who was on his deathbed, was asked by his pastor[74] whether he believed the consolations which Luther had written to him, he replied, "Of course! If I didn't believe them I'd be a knave."

Threatened Invasion by the Turks
April, 1532 No. 206

"At this time some rumors are circulating about an advance of the Turks.[75] Accordingly our [papists] are saying that the Turks are coming on account of my teaching and that God will dash Germany to the ground because Luther has not been extirpated. Then Faber[76] and others started to hold processions. What should our Lord God do with the Turks? He must brand the blind and perverse people. I should be glad if the Turks were defeated, but I hardly know how to pray because our people look upon the

---

[74] Michael Coelius, pastor in Mansfeld. Luther's letter to his father, dated February 15, 1530, is translated in Theodore G. Tappert (ed.), *Luther: Letters of Spiritual Counsel* ("Library of Christian Classics," Vol. XXVIII [Philadelphia: Westminster Press, 1955]), pp. 29-32. Cf. WA, Br 5, 238-241. The father, Hans Luther, died on May 29, 1530.

[75] A renewed attack on Vienna was repulsed in August, 1532.

[76] John Faber was the Roman Catholic archbishop of Vienna. Cf. No. 1320, n. 36.

matter in such a wicked way. May Almighty God help us and be gracious to us! I fear a sure reverse and that Ferdinand [77] will lose his land. Very well, this is the way they want it. I am afraid that I will be a prophet, for I said that the emperor [78] was called to Germany for two purposes: first, to root out the Lutherans by force, and [second] if this does not succeed, to oppose the Turks and all of us in a massacre of Germany. This is probably the pope's intention. But I have confidence that God will destroy the Turks."

If Fugger Were God for a Day

April, 1532   *No. 216*

"I should be unwilling to take the whole world in return for having Fugger [79] or some other bigwig be our Lord God for a single day, for Satan would destroy us all in a moment."

The Character of Neighborly Love

April, 1532   *No. 217*

"One ought to love one's neighbor with a love as chaste as that of a bridegroom for his bride. In this case all faults are concealed and covered over and only the virtues are seen."

The Magistrate Needs God's Help

April, 1532   *No. 219*

"The magistrate is a minister of God. By himself he cannot maintain civil discipline. He is like a net placed in the water, and our Lord God chases the fish into the net. He drives wrongdoers into the net so that they do not slip away. It would be impossible if there were no divine judgment which declares, 'Either you repent

---

[77] Ferdinand, archduke of Austria, succeeded Charles V and reigned as emperor of Germany from 1556 to 1564. Luther here refers to the fact that the Turks were threatening to overrun Austria. See his earlier treatise, *On War Against the Turk.* LW 46, 155-205.

[78] Charles V, emperor of Germany from 1519 to 1556.

[79] Anton Fugger (d. 1560) had been the head of the famous family banking house in Augsburg since 1525. See V. von Klarwill (ed.), *The Fugger News-Letters* (2 vols.: New York: G. P. Putman, 1925, 1926).

or you are punished.' Likewise [it is written], 'There is a God who judges on earth' [Ps. 58:11]. Consequently nobody who does not repent will escape from the punishment of the magistrate. Even if you get away from me, you will not run away from the hangman."

Suicides Are Not Necessarily Damned
April 7, 1532   No. 222

"I don't share the opinion that suicides are certainly to be damned. My reason is that they do not wish to kill themselves but are overcome by the power of the devil. They are like a man who is murdered in the woods by a robber. However, this ought not be taught to the common people, lest Satan be given an opportunity to cause slaughter, and I recommend that the popular custom be strictly adhered to according to which it [the suicide's corpse] is not carried over the threshold, etc.[80] Such persons do not die by free choice or by law, but our Lord God will dispatch them as he executes a person through a robber. Magistrates should treat them quite strictly, although it is not plain that their souls are damned. However, they are examples by which our Lord God wishes to show that the devil is powerful and also that we should be diligent in prayer. But for these examples, we would not fear God. Hence he must teach us in this way."

A Prophecy Concerning Luther
April 7, 1532   No. 223

A certain old man from Meiningen had a son at Erfurt who was a friend of Luther's. He once said to Luther when he heard him complain of ill health, "Dear son,[81] don't worry, some day you'll be a great man." Luther said, "On that occasion I heard a prophet!"

---

[80] According to popular belief the corpse of a suicide was not to be carried out of the house "over the threshold." Cf. WA, TR 1, 95, n. 7.
[81] German: *Lieber Bacalarie*. The form of address indicates that Luther was still a student in the university in Erfurt at the time.

Luther "Excommunicated" Three Times
Between April 7 and 15, 1532   No. 225

"Three times have I been excommunicated. The first time was by Dr. Staupitz,[82] who absolved me from the observance and rule of the Augustinian Order so that, if the pope pressed him to imprison me or command me to be silent, he could excuse himself on the ground that I was not under his obedience. The second time was by the pope [83] and the third time was by the emperor.[84] Consequently I cannot be accused of laying aside my habit, and I am now silent by divine authority alone."

Impatience Is Not Necessarily a Sin
Between April 7 and 15, 1532   No. 228

When I[85] asked him about the passage in which Jeremiah cursed the day on which he had been born[86] and suggested that such impatience was a sin, he [Martin Luther] replied, "Sometimes one has to wake up our Lord God with such words. Otherwise he doesn't hear. It is a case of real murmuring on the part of Jeremiah. Christ spoke in this way, 'How long am I to be with you?' [Mark 9:19]. Moses went so far as to throw his keys at our Lord God's feet[87] when he asked, 'Did I conceive all this people?' [Num. 11:12]. It can't be otherwise. It's annoying when one has the best of intentions but things don't turn out well. Surely this is murmuring. I do the same, and I can't banish the thought from my mind when I wish that I had never started [this business].[88] So likewise when I wish I were dead rather than witness such contempt [for the Word of God and his faithful servants].[89] Accordingly it is only

---

[82] Cf. *LW* 31, 257; cf. also No. 94, n. 14.

[83] Cf. *LW* 32, 14, 15.

[84] At the Diet of Worms in 1521 Luther was declared an outlaw of the empire. Cf. *LW* 48, 210-212, 216.

[85] The recorder, Veit Dietrich.

[86] Cf. Jer. 20:14.

[87] I.e., give up his job.

[88] I.e., the Reformation. Text in brackets from later variant by John Aurifaber.

[89] Text in brackets by John Aurifaber.

speculative theologians who condemn such impatience and recommend patience. If they get down to the realm of practice, they will be aware of this. Cases of this kind are exceedingly important. One should not dispute about them in a speculative way.

"It is a great thing to set a true preacher in motion, and unless our Lord God himself gets him going, nothing will come of it. It requires a mighty spirit to serve people in body and soul and yet suffer extreme peril and the basest ingratitude for so serving. [Jesus] therefore asked Peter, 'Do you love me?' and then said, 'Feed my lambs' [John 21:15]. It is as if he would say, 'If you wish to be a true pastor, only the love with which you love me will do. Otherwise it is impossible, for who will suffer ingratitude and give up money and health to study, only to expose himself to the gravest danger?' Therefore he says, 'It is necessary that you love me.'"

An Auditor Is Encouraged to Marry
Between April 7 and 15, 1532   No. 233

"You can't be without a wife and remain without sin. After all, marriage is an ordinance and creation of God. Therefore it is not Satan's idea when a man desires to marry an honorable girl, for Satan hates this kind of life. So make the venture in the name of the Lord and on the strength of his blessing and institution!"[90]

A Preacher Should Vary His Style
Between April 7 and 15, 1532   No. 234

"A preacher is like a carpenter. His tool is the Word of God. Because the materials on which he works vary, he ought not always pursue the same course when he preaches. For the sake of the variety of his auditors he should sometimes console, sometimes frighten, sometimes scold, sometimes soothe," etc.[91]

---

[90] At the beginning of this entry is the annotation in Greek, *to emon*, which means "mine." That is, Luther directed these words to the writer, Veit Dietrich. Cf. No. 185, n. 66.

[91] The indicator *to emon* precedes this entry. See n. 90, above.

The Doctrine of the Trinity Attacked
Between April 7 and 15, 1532　　　　　　　　　*No. 237*

When an exceedingly virulent book was published in 1532 against the [doctrine of the] Trinity,[92] he [Martin Luther] said, "These people do not realize that others, too, have been assailed by doubts about this article. But to set my opinion over against the Word of God and the Holy Spirit is insupportable."

God Must Be a Devout Man
Between April 7 and 15, 1532　　　　　　　　　*No. 239*

"Our Lord God must be a devout man to be able to love knaves. I can't do it, although I am myself a knave."

The Omnipresence of God
Between April 7 and 15, 1532　　　　　　　　　*No. 240*

When we were debating whether God truly is in each and every minute creature, in the grass, in a tree, etc., he [Martin Luther] responded, "It is so, for God is excluded from no place and is confined to none. He is everywhere and he is nowhere."

The question was asked whether God is only potentially everywhere or is actually everywhere. He replied, "God is in every creature in both ways because although a creature acts through its properties, God acts not through his properties but through his being."

Thereupon somebody said, "I do not understand that."

He [Luther] countered, "Do you believe that Christ on the cross was God?"

"Yes."

"Do you believe that God was in the womb of the Virgin?"

"Yes."

"The principle here is the same, for it is equally impossible to man's reason in both cases, as impossible that God can be enclosed

---

[92] Probably Michael Servetus, *Dialogi de Trinitate* (Hagenau, 1532); English translation by Earl M. Wilbur, *The Two Treatises of Servetus on the Trinity* (Cambridge: Harvard, 1932).

in the womb of the Virgin as it is that he can be enclosed in every creature."

Thereupon the other person said, "Then he is in the devil too!"

"Yes, and essentially! He's in hell too, as it is written in II Thessalonians 1 [:9], 'They shall suffer the punishment of eternal destruction and exclusion from the presence of the Lord.'"

Challenge to Record a Remark of Luther
Between April 7 and 15, 1532   No. 246

When Master Philip[93] laughed at the astrologers for saying that if it had not been for the planet Saturn men would never die, our [Martin Luther] remarked, "If it had not been for Adam no man would die. If this were not so, though there were a thousand Saturns for one, I would beshit myself. Make a note of this! Write it down!" [94]

The Painfulness of Separation in Death
Between April 20 and May 16, 1532   No. 250

"There is no sweeter union than that in a good marriage. Nor is there any death more bitter than that which separates a married couple. Only the death of children comes close to this; how much this hurts I have myself experienced." [95]

Church Fathers Judged by the Gospel
Between April 20 and May 16, 1532   No. 252

"Jerome[96] can be read for the sake of history, but he has nothing at all to say about faith and the teaching of true religion. Origen[97] I have already banned. I have no use for Chrysostom[98] either,

---

[93] Philip Melanchthon. See No. 157, n. 59.
[94] A challenging aside to those who were recording every word that Luther said.
[95] Luther's daughter Elizabeth died in her first year on August 3, 1528. The occasion for the conversation here recorded was the death of John Zink, or Zinck, a young student. Cf. Tappert, *Luther: Letters of Spiritual Counsel*, pp. 64, 65.
[96] Cf. No. 51, n. 2.
[97] Cf. No. 153, n. 56.
[98] John Chrysostom (*ca.* 345-407), eloquent preacher and patriarch of Constantinople.

for he is only a gossip. Basil[99] doesn't amount to anything; he was a monk after all, and I wouldn't give a penny for him. Philip's apology[100] is superior to all the doctors of the church, even to Augustine[101] himself. Hilary[102] and Theophylact[103] are good, and so is Ambrose.[104] The last sometimes treats excellently of the forgiveness of sins, which is the chief article, namely, that the divine majesty pardons by grace. For our righteousness, or the righteousness of works, isn't worth anything. Sin doesn't harm us as much as our own righteousness.

"In the article of the forgiveness of sins we have the knowledge of Christ, which alone can comfort us and lift us up. Apart from the forgiveness of sins I can't stand a bad conscience at all; the devil hounds me about a single sin until the world becomes too small for me, and afterward I feel like spitting on myself for having been afraid of such a small thing. So only the knowledge of Christ preserves me. From this I conclude: The devil and God are two enemies. Therefore, while God loves life, the devil hates life. The knowledge of God can consequently be so pictured as if it is God's will to be angry, and one may be led to think that our Lord God and the devil are both intent on strangling us. To this one must reply, 'Life is God's aim, and so he will not slay you.' This is what knowledge of Christ means: by his death has been won the victory over death, etc."

Domestic and Ecclesiastical Wrath
Between April 20 and May 16, 1532   No. 255

"Domestic wrath is our Lord God's plaything; there only a slap or a cuff applies. Political wrath, on the other hand, carries away wife and child through carnage and war. Then there is also ecclesiastical wrath, which involves the soul and heaven. If I can endure conflict with the devil, sin, and a bad conscience, then

---

[99] Basil the Great (*ca.* 330-379), bishop of Caesarea in Cappadocia.
[100] Philip Melanchthon's *Augsburg Confession* (1530), often called an apology.
[101] Cf. No. 51, n. 4.
[102] Cf. No. 192, n. 70.
[103] Theophylactos, archbishop of Achrida in the eleventh century.
[104] Cf. No. 51, n. 6.

I can also put up with the irritations of Katy von Bora.[105] Nobody will get anything from me by force."

This he [Martin Luther] said when he happened to get involved in a quarrel with his wife about some trifling thing.

God Is Unknowable and Yet Known
Between April 20 and May 16, 1532   No. 257

"In his dialogue concerning being, Plato[106] disputes about God and declares that God is nothing and yet is everything. Eck[107] followed Plato, and other theologians also said that the affirmative definition is uncertain but the negative definition is absolute. Nobody has understood this. It ought to be put and can be understood thus: 'God is incomprehensible and invisible, and hence whatever is comprehended and seen is not God.' It can also be expressed in another way: 'God is both visible and invisible. He is visible through his Word and work. Apart from his Word and work one should not look for him.' These theologians have wished to apprehend God through speculations and have paid no attention to the Word. I recommend that speculation be laid aside, and I should like to have this rule adhered to after my death."

Heresies of the Ancient Church Revived
Between April 20 and May 16, 1532   No. 269

"I don't know of anything in our Lord Christ that the devil has not assailed. Accordingly he has to start again from the beginning and rake up the old errors and heresies. Sabellius[108] was the first; he said that Christ is God and that there is only one person in the Godhead. This is the earliest and most subtle heresy, that there is only one person, Father, Son, and Holy Spirit. Then followed

---

[105] Cf. No. 49, n. 1.
[106] Intended is probably Plato's *Timaeus*, 27. Edith Hamilton and H. Cairns (eds.), *The Selected Dialogues of Plato* (New York: Pantheon Books, 1961), p. 1161.
[107] John Eck (1486-1543), the Roman theologian with whom Luther locked horns in the Leipzig Debate (1519) and elsewhere. Cf. *LW* 31, 307-325.
[108] A heretic of the third century about whose life little is known.

the Patripassians,[109] who did not disagree particularly with the Sabellians. Afterward the Arians distinguished among the persons but declared that the Son was not God from eternity but was only called God, just as princes are called gods.[110] The Manicheans[111] followed by attacking the humanity of Christ and saying that he was a phantom who did not have a real body. Later the Photinians[112] appeared and said that Christ indeed had a real body but lacked a soul. Thus the devil assailed Christ from stem to stern. There was nothing left to attack, and so the devil has to start all over again from the beginning."

Did Paul Teach More Plainly Than Christ?
Between April 20 and May 16, 1532   No. 271

When somebody said that Paul taught many things more plainly than Christ, Luther used this example, "Sin came into the world through one man" [Rom. 5:12], and said, "But for this sentence it would be hard to defend original sin with irrefutable texts. I have said that the reason for this is that preaching about Christ began to be spread abroad more and more after his death and [the sending of] the Holy Spirit, who was to proclaim Christ more clearly." Luther also added that Christ taught with moderation on account of the fathers, so that when the law was abrogated this might be done with respect for and patience toward the fathers.

"I believe that Paul was not very well when he was in that ecstasy[113] and said that he couldn't tell in words [what he had heard]. That he couldn't tell is true. Such deep emotions don't permit expression in words. I can't say how I feel, although my feelings are insignificant in comparison. So he was unable to speak even if he wished to do so."

---

[109] In addition to Sabellius, men like Praxeas, Noetus, and Callistus in the third century.
[110] Cf. Ps. 82:6-7. The Arians were followers of Arius, leading heretic of the ancient church. Cf. No. 3695, n. 24.
[111] Followers of Mani, third-century founder of an Oriental religion based on dualism.
[112] Adherents of Photinus, bishop of Sirmium (d. 376).
[113] Cf. II Cor. 12:1-4.

Christ Allows His Ministers to Suffer
May 18, 1532   *No. 272*

"In this life Christ is incomprehensible. He rewards his best ministers in such a way that I must say I hardly know what I am about, whether I preach aright or not. This tormented St. Paul too. He didn't talk much about it to others, I think. He couldn't talk about it, for who can imagine what he meant when he said, 'I die every day' [I Cor. 15:31]. Christ, too, had his temptations."

This he [Martin Luther] said at dinner on May 18 after he had been laid low, early in the morning of May 16 at Torgau, by a spiritual assault of Satan. What the nature of the assault was can be gathered from his conversations at this time.[114]

Despair of Grace the Greatest Sin
May 18, 1532   *No. 273*

"The sin which Judas committed when he betrayed Christ[115] was a small sin because it could be forgiven. But to despair of grace is a greater sin because it cannot be forgiven, for God has determined for Christ's sake to forgive the sin of those who believe. This sin is so great and wicked that it leads either to despair or to presumption. Consequently one ought to be disposed to say, 'It is true. I have sinned. But I will not despair on this account or commit the sin again.' However, it's a calumny to conclude from these words of mine that it is permissible to sin and then to believe, for one can't believe in Christ unless one declares and resolves not to sin again. Sin carries us down to despair or up to presumption. In either case the sin is not repented of, for sin is either exaggerated or not acknowledged at all."

Dog Provides Example of Concentration
May 18, 1532   *No. 274*

When Luther's puppy[116] happened to be at the table, looked

---

[114] There is no other evidence that Luther was in Torgau at this time. Cf. Georg Buchwald, *Luther-Kalendarium* (Leipzig: M. Heinsius, 1939), p. 86.
[115] Cf. Matt. 26:47-50.
[116] Luther's dog Tölpel is mentioned again and again in the Table Talk.

for a morsel from his master, and watched with open mouth and motionless eyes, he [Martin Luther] said, "Oh, if I could only pray the way this dog watches the meat! All his thoughts are concentrated on the piece of meat. Otherwise he has no thought, wish, or hope."

Behold, the heart of the pious dog was also lacking in this, that he could not pray without thoughts.[117]

Subjects Remain Faithful Despite Prince
June 8, 1532   No. 275

"It is said that a mad dog doesn't live more than nine days. Accordingly our Lord God probably lets Duke George[118] remain mad for nine years or longer, for he is nothing but a mad dog. Well, I should like before my death to see him take the field against us and have his subjects refuse to join him. Then he would have to acknowledge that more depends on our Lord God than on him."

This he [Martin Luther] said on June 8, 1532, when nine citizens of Oschatz had written to Luther for advice. They were ordered by Duke George either to sell their goods or to stand publicly in the church in the presence of the bishop of Meissen[119] for three successive Sundays with white towels wrapped around them, renounce [their faith], and be absolved. They also wrote that they would rather give up their riches than Christ and would rather commit their bodies to brief suffering than their souls to endless torment. These were their words in German.[120]

An Opinion About Thomas Aquinas
Between June 8 and 28, 1532   No. 280

"Scotus has abbreviated Thomas.[121] On the *Four Books of*

---

[117] The last sentence probably represents the writer's (i.e., Veit Dietrich's) observation.
[118] Duke George of Albertine Saxony, a bitter opponent of Luther and the Reformation.
[119] John VII von Schleinitz was bishop from 1518 to 1537.
[120] The report in Latin, that is to say, corresponds to the German original, presumably written by Franz Köhler. Cf. *WA*, Br 6, 317-318.
[121] John Duns Scotus (d. 1308) and Thomas Aquinas (d. 1274) were leading scholastic theologians.

Sentences[122] Scotus is better than Thomas, although the latter is most esteemed. When I was a young theologian and was required to prepare nine corollaries from one question, I took these two words: 'God created.' Thomas gave me about a hundred questions on them. This is the procedure of Thomas: First he takes statements from Paul, Peter, John, Isaiah, etc. Afterward he concludes that Aristotle says so and so and he interprets Scripture according to Aristotle. The second question of Part II and the first question of Part I[123] were tolerable, but they were seldom read in the schools. What were read were the ridiculous books against the heathen, etc.[124] Christ has indeed had his hell here on earth. It is as Paul said with reference to Christians, namely, that according to their hearts they sit in heaven. An unhappy person is in hell, therefore, and a happy person is in heaven."

The Miracle at the Diet of Augsburg Between June 8 and 28, 1532　　　　　　*No. 284*

"Our faith is an odd thing—that I should believe that that man who was hanged is the Son of God, although I have never seen him, known him, or met him. He is to me like a stone placed in the middle of the sea, a stone about which I know nothing except what the gospel says: I am the Lord. Well, then, if he says so, so be it! He has also demonstrated it at the diet in Augsburg,[125] where the fury of all the kings and princes was arrayed against him. If we hadn't known who Christ is, he would have showed us his majesty there, so that in all fairness we ought to honor him. Two whole years have now passed since one was compelled to say, 'He

---

[122] By Peter Lombard. Cf. No. 192, n. 67.
[123] In Thomas Aquinas, *Summa Theologica*. English translation in 21 vols. (London: Burns, Oates and Washburn, 1920-1925).
[124] Thomas Aquinas also wrote *Summa contra gentiles*. English translation by Anton C. Pegis, *On the Truth of the Catholic Faith* (5 vols.; New York: Doubleday & Co., 1955-1957).
[125] It was at the diet in Augsburg in 1530 that the *Augsburg Confession* was presented as a declaration of faith to the emperor in the presence of the princes of the Holy Roman Empire of the German Nation. See M. Reu, *The Augsburg Confession* (Chicago: Wartburg, 1930).

is Christ!' And he will remain Christ a good deal longer. That great miracle at the diet is almost forgotten, as if it had never happened."

If Samson Would Deal with the Turks
June 28, 1532   *No. 289*

On that same day, June 28, 1532, he [Martin Luther] sat at table deep in thought. At length he said, "I have just been thinking about the Turks. If I were Samson I would give them something to think about. Every day I would kill a thousand Turks; in a year this would amount to 350,000 Turks."

When somebody suggested that he would not then have had cannons, he replied, "Instead I would have my special prayer!"

"The story of Samson is very astonishing. In defiance of the Philistines he lay with a whore in their city.[126] His strength wasn't in his hair. Although he lost his strength with his hair, it wasn't the cutting of his hair but the breaking of his vow that did it. Otherwise the hair wouldn't have done it. For he was a Nazirite,[127] and our Lord God wanted the law to be kept. This must always be said in addition, that the Spirit took possession of him, and when the soul is filled the body must become strong. These are great stories. In them one sees that God loved Abraham on account of the seed which He promised to give to the people. However, we see that immediately after the death of every ruler there was a political collapse, just as things will become different immediately after our age and as things changed in Bohemia soon after Huss."[128]

Moses Used Sources When He Wrote Genesis
Summer, 1532   *No. 291*

When somebody asked about Moses and how he could write about the creation and other things that happened so long before his time, he [Martin Luther] said, "I think many things had been

---
[126] Cf. Judg. 16:1-31.
[127] Cf. Num. 6:2.
[128] I.e., after John Huss was burned at the stake in 1415. The followers of Huss were divided after his death, Bohemia was torn by a long civil conflict, and eventually most of the Bohemians returned to Roman obedience.

written before Moses and that Moses took these things and added to them what God commanded him. No doubt he had the story of the creation from the tradition of the fathers. All in all, I believe that the preaching of the promised seed of Adam[129] was greater before the Flood than the preaching of Christ is now. There must have been heretics then, too. If Cain[130] had not resorted to bloodshed according to the covenant, he might have seduced the whole world and started a silly heresy, but God permitted him to fall into sin.

"The end of all heresy is the sword. We see this in the case of the pope, Münzer,[131] Zwingli,[132] the Arians,[133] etc. They all started out [with a certain show of piety],[134] but in the end they were driven to the sword. They were at first not wanting in the will [to carry out their intentions] but they didn't have the opportunity. Satan, as Paul said, can't deny himself.[135] He must show himself to be a liar and murderer.[136] Moreover, I think that Cain's death also caused a great outcry. They said, 'Behold, Lamech has killed our father,' etc." [137]

Some Conjectures About the Future Life
Summer, 1532   *No. 305*

"In the future life we'll have enjoyment of every kind and the whole earth will be adorned with many trees and all things that are pleasant to look at. If we have our Lord God we'll have enough. We'll be children of God. I don't believe that we shall all be of the same stature, and there will be no marriage; otherwise everybody will want to be a woman or a man."

---

[129] Cf. Gen. 3:15; 13:15-16.
[130] Cf. Gen. 4:8-15.
[131] Thomas Münzer, a radical reformer, was executed in 1525 for his role in the Peasants' War.
[132] Cf. No. 5005, n. 35.
[133] Cf. No. 3695, n. 24.
[134] Text in brackets from a variant. Cf. *WA*, TR 1, 121, n. 26.
[135] Cf. II Cor. 2:11.
[136] Cf. John 8:44.
[137] Cf. Gen. 4:23.

A Comparison of Proverbs and Ecclesiasticus
Summer, 1532 No. 311

"In Proverbs the eighth chapter is the best. Similar to this is the first chapter of Ecclesiasticus. In both, however, there is nothing about Christ, nor are there promises or prophecies. Therefore, the Psalter, Isaiah, Jeremiah, and even Daniel are far superior to the books of Solomon as far as prophecies are concerned. Those are the best books in the Bible which, like Daniel, devour the Turks and treat of the kingdoms of the world. So in neither [Proverbs nor Ecclesiasticus] is there anything about Christ or about promises or about the kingdoms of the world or about future events, but only about rules of life."

Now, then, the question is raised: Which of the two teaches better about rules of life and is superior to the other? "They have nothing theological except about wisdom, that is, about the Word of God, whence he is called wise who has the Word of God."

Two Rules for Translating the Bible
Summer or Fall, 1532 No. 312

"In translating the Holy Scriptures I follow two rules:

"First, if some passage is obscure I consider whether it treats of grace or of law, whether wrath or the forgiveness of sin [is contained in it], and with which of these it agrees better. By this procedure I have often understood the most obscure passages. Either the law or the gospel has made them meaningful, for God divides his teaching into law and gospel. The law, moreover, has to do either with civil government or with economic life or with the church. The church is above the earth in heaven, where there is no further division but only a mathematical point, and so principles cannot fail there. This is (and Gerson[138] said it is supreme wisdom) to reduce all things to the first principle, that is, to the most general genus. In theology there are law and gospel, and it must be one or the other. Gerson calls this reduction to the most

---

[138] Jean Gerson (1363-1429), learned French scholar to whose works Luther often appealed.

general genus. So every prophet either threatens and teaches, terrifies and judges things, or makes a promise. Everything ends with this, and it means that God is your gracious Lord. This is my first rule in translation.

"The second rule is that if the meaning is ambiguous I ask those who have a better knowledge of the language than I have whether the Hebrew words can bear this or that sense which seems to me to be especially fitting. And that is most fitting which is closest to the argument of the book. The Jews go astray so often in the Scriptures because they do not know the [true] contents of the books. But if one knows the contents, that sense ought to be chosen which is nearest to them."

Left-wing and Right-wing Positions
Summer or Fall, 1532   *No. 314*

"In their teaching about the sacraments the papists go too far to the left, for they ascribe too much to the sacraments and claim that they justify by their mere observance. On the other hand, the sacramentarians[139] go too far to the right because they take everything away from the sacraments. Whether one falls out of the ship in front or behind, therefore, one lands in the water."

Dissembling Is Necessary to Ruling
Summer or Fall, 1532   *No. 315*

"There must be law in the administration of the household and of the government, for sin should not be tolerated. But if sin is committed there should be forgiveness; otherwise everything is ruined. A husband ought to overlook many things in his wife and children, but he ought not give up the law. It is so in all stations of life. There is forgiveness of sins in all creatures. Not all the trees grow upright, not all the streams flow in a straight line, the soil is not the same everywhere, etc. The judgment is therefore

---

[139] Luther's favorite term for those (especially Anabaptists and Zwinglians) who denied that the sacraments are means of grace. Luther put on the right those who are today generally placed on the left. Cf. Roland H. Bainton, *Studies on the Reformation, Collected Papers* (Boston: Beacon Press, 1963), pp. 119, 120.

right: he who does not know how to dissemble does not know how to rule. This is clemency.[140] One must be tolerant without giving up all restraints. As they say, 'Neither everything nor nothing.' "

Melanchthon's Commentary on Romans
Summer or Fall, 1532   No. 316

Concerning Philip's commentary on Romans,[141] published in the year 1532, he [Martin Luther] said, "If he were now living, Augustine would enjoy reading this book, although Philip often reproached him. St. Jerome, if he were alive, would probably write against the book like any other Barefoot Friar. Unless there is some special forgiveness of sins beyond that which is common and which all of us stand in need of, he is lost. I don't ask that our Lord God should be as gracious to me as to him on account of our teaching, but I wish to say with Isaiah and Jeremiah: My teaching is true, and I do not expect to be forgiven for it because the teaching is not my teaching. So Christ also said, 'The words that I say to you I do not speak on my own authority' [John 14:10]. My teaching, if it be life, will continue as may be."

Many Things Not Recorded in Scripture
October, 1532   No. 319

"Moses wrote nothing about the creation of angels, first, because he wrote only about the creation of visible things and, second, because he didn't wish to give occasion for speculation. Our Lord God did well to leave many things unwritten. Besides, we would have belittled what we now have and would have sought after the things that are higher." October, 1532.

An Account of a Monstrous Birth
Summer or Fall, 1532   No. 323

When we were discussing monstrous beings to which women sometimes give birth, there was mention of an offspring which was

---

[140] Greek: *epieikeia*, "equity."
[141] Philip Melanchthon's *Commentary on St. Paul's Epistle to the Romans* appeared in September, 1532. Cf. No. 5511, n. 71.

like a mouse when it was born and tried to run under a stool into a mousehole in the wall. He [Martin Luther] said, "That is a demonstration that the power of the mind is so great that it can even change the body." When I said that I could not believe this, he answered, "You do not know what the power of the mind is." When somebody asked whether monstrosities of this kind ought to be baptized he replied, "No, because I hold that they are only animal life." Later somebody else asked whether they have souls, and he responded, "I don't know. I haven't asked God about it."

Administration of the Lord's Supper to Convicts
Summer or Fall, 1532   No. 325

When a certain Bohemian[142] said that the sacrament ought not to be given to those who have been convicted of a public crime and have been condemned in a public trial because there is danger that they might not believe, Luther responded, "This doesn't concern the one who administers. His only concern should be that he offer the true Word and the true sacrament. I don't worry about whether he [the communicant] has true faith. I give the sacrament on account of the confession which I have heard, the condition of his heart be what it may. I wager a thousand souls that the absolution and the sacrament are right. I must believe him when he says he is penitent. If he deceives me, he deceives himself. Nevertheless, the sacrament is true and the absolution is true. It is as if I were to give somebody ten pieces of gold and he took them to be only ten coppers. The gold is right in front of his eyes. If he doesn't know what he's taking, the fault is his and the loss is his."

Christ and Faith Must Be the Center
Summer or Fall, 1532   No. 327

"Under the papacy I was exposed to every error. The reason is that I had no faith. Faith is, as it were, the center of a circle. If anybody strays from the center, it is impossible for him to have the circle around him, and he must blunder. The center is Christ."

---

[142] Perhaps Martin Michalec, who was in Wittenberg in 1532. Cf. *WA*, TR 1, 134, n. 6.

The Turks and the End of the World
Summer or Fall, 1532 No. 332

"I hope our Lord God will do something against the Turks for his name's sake, not for the sake of Ferdinand.[143] All things in Scripture have now been fulfilled. Only Daniel 12 remains.[144] Daniel and the Revelation of St. John fit together well. I think Rome is the holy place between two seas.[145] There sits the pope in the temple of God.[146] But if the Turks go there everything is ruined. There is nothing left but the day of judgment. Then the world will come to its end."

Collapse of Wall Almost Crushes Luther
July 12, 1532 No. 333

At the fifth hour on the Friday after St. Kilian's Day (it was July 12) Luther was almost crushed with his wife under the collapse of a wall.[147] At the time he said that nature ought to be supported on account of the devil. "We took too much of a risk," he said, "when we left the wall standing thus without supports. If nothing else, supports would at least deprive the devil of an opportunity. After all, he can't make two out of three. One ought not build on air."

Luther Abandoned Early Allegorization
Summer or Fall, 1532 No. 335

"When I was a monk I was a master in the use of allegories. I allegorized everything. Afterward through the Epistle to the Romans I came to some knowledge of Christ. I recognized then that allegories are nothing, that it's not what Christ signifies but what Christ is that counts. Before I allegorized everything, even a chamber pot, but afterward I reflected on the histories and thought

---

[143] Cf. No. 206, n. 77.
[144] Cf. Dan. 11:36—12:13.
[145] Cf. Dan. 11:45.
[146] Cf. II Thess. 2:4.
[147] At the time a cellar was being constructed under the Black Cloister, which was Luther's home in Wittenberg.

how difficult it must have been for Gideon to fight with his enemies in the manner reported.[148] If I had been there I would have befouled my breeches for fear. It was not allegory, but it was the Spirit and faith that inflicted such havoc on the enemy with only three hundred men. Jerome[149] and Origen[150] contributed to the practice of searching only for allegories. God forgive them. In all of Origen there is not one word about Christ."

A Lie Is Like a Snowball
Summer or Fall, 1532 No. 340

"A lie is like a snowball. The longer it is rolled on the ground the larger it becomes."

Office and Person Must Be Distinguished
Summer or Fall, 1532 No. 342

"One ought to think as follows about ministers. The office does not belong to Judas but to Christ alone. When Christ said to Judas, 'Go, baptize,'[151] Christ was himself the baptizer and not Judas because the command comes from above even if it passes down through a stinking pipe. Nothing is taken from the office on account of the unworthiness of a minister. So when the prefect distributes grain in the name of our prince, the people get the whole grain despite the fact that the prefect is an adulterer.[152] Office and person must be distinguished. It is even so in the case of alms which I give through a thief, etc.

"Thus the pope has a true ministry, although he abuses it. He does not abolish the Word, baptism, or the sacrament [of the altar] but only misuses them. Accordingly the sacraments ought to be received from them [the papists], except for the sacrament of the

---

[148] Cf. Judg. 7:1-23. The report of Veit Dietrich reads "Joshua" instead of "Gideon."
[149] Cf. No. 51, n. 2.
[150] Cf. No. 153, n. 56.
[151] Cf. Matt. 28:19. The name "Judas" appears to be intended as a designation for any betrayer of Christ in the ministry.
[152] The town prefect in Wittenberg was Hans Metzsch, taken to task often by Luther for his profligate life. Cf. Tappert (ed.), *Luther: Letters of Spiritual Counsel*, pp. 279-282.

altar, which they still corrupt.[153] The Jews did not repudiate Moses, either, although they distorted him. Christ therefore said, 'Hear them!'[154] Nor does the pope forbid the Word but desires that it be understood as he understands it. He does not abolish the Word but only misuses it. The issue is use and abuse. To take a crude example, if somebody proposed to put on a crown like a pair of breeches, we would say that the crown ought to be placed on the head. It is not the thing that is rejected but the proper use of it. The thing is perverted. Instead of grasping a knife by the handle, it is grasped by the cutting blade. This is not what the spiritualists[155] do; they throw the knife away altogether and say that it is no knife. So the Anabaptists reject baptism almost entirely. The pope, who distorts it, nevertheless allows baptism to remain. The spiritualists take away the substance; the pope takes away only the accident.

"Likewise it is the true name of God that is used wrongly, for unless the godless misused the true name, why was it necessary to prohibit this? Therefore, anybody who misuses the name of God misuses the true name of God, as it is said, 'You have blasphemed my name,' and yet those who misuse God's name do not take the name away, but the name remains. So the pope can also misuse a sacrament, and yet true baptism and the true sacrament [of the altar] remain. Otherwise how could the pope sin unless he had the true name of God and the true sacraments? Even so, the seditious man sins against the magistrate and yet does not remove the magistrate himself. For the pope has the Word and the sacraments not for himself but because he is in the public ministry, and consequently those who hear him hear the true Word of God. So Judas says, 'Rise up in the name of Jesus Christ,' but he doesn't believe a word of it. The pope also baptizes. The pope occupies an office, and that's where you Bohemian Brethren[156] and we get our office too."

---

[153] The exception here made was expressly added by the reporter, Veit Dietrich, who wrote, "This I am adding."
[154] Cf. Luke 16:29.
[155] German: *Schwermer, Schwärmer*. Literally, "swarmers," i.e., enthusiasts, fanatics, or spiritualists.
[156] Luther was addressing Ignatius Perknowsky, adherent of the Bohemian Brethren, who was staying in Luther's house during a visit to Wittenberg.

No Compulsion to Observe Ceremonies
Summer or Fall, 1532   No. 344

When somebody[157] asked Martin Luther whether the sacrament [of the altar] ought to be adored, he replied, "One should not make an act of worship out of the sacrament. To be sure, I kneel, but I do so out of reverence. When I am lying in bed I receive it [the sacrament] without kneeling. It is a matter of freedom, just as one is at liberty to kiss the Bible or not. This might also be called adoration. If I do not do it, I have not sinned. But if anybody tries to compel me to do it as a thing necessary for salvation, I refuse and preserve my freedom."

Augustine at First Devoured, Then Put Aside
Summer or Fall, 1532   No. 347

"Ever since I came to an understanding of Paul, I have not been able to think well of any doctor [of the church]. They have become of little value to me. At first I devoured, not merely read, Augustine.[158] But when the door was opened for me in Paul, so that I understood what justification by faith is, it was all over with Augustine. There are only two notable assertions in all of Augustine. The first is that when sin is forgiven it does not cease to exist but ceases to damn and control us. The second is that the law is kept when that is forgiven which does not happen. The books of his *Confessions* teach nothing; they only incite the reader; they are made up merely of examples, but do not instruct. St. Augustine was a pious sinner, for he had only one concubine and one son by her.[159] He was not given much to anger. St. Jerome,[160] like the rest of us—Dr. Jonas,[161] Pomeranus,[162] and me—we are all much more inclined to angry outbursts. Nor do I know which of our

---

[157] Identified as Ignatius Perknowsky in a parallel text in *WA*, TR 2, No. 1745.
[158] Cf. No. 51, n. 4.
[159] Augustine, *Confessions*, IV, 2; VI, 25; IX, 14.
[160] Cf. No. 51, n. 2.
[161] Justus Jonas (1493-1555) was a colleague of Luther in the university in Wittenberg. See Martin Lehmann, *Justus Jonas* (Minneapolis: Augsburg, 1963).
[162] John Bugenhagen, of Pomerania. Cf. No. 122, n. 36.

doctors today has Augustine's temperament except Brenz[163] and Justus Menius."[164]

Difference Between Luther and Melanchthon
Summer or Fall, 1532   *No. 348*

"Philip[165] stabs, too, but only with pins and needles. The pricks are hard to heal and they hurt. But when I stab I do it with a heavy pike used to hunt boars."

Theology Is Not Quickly Learned
Fall, 1532   *No. 352*

"Clever men see that the church is despised and that others are exalted. They judge according to reason, without the Word of God, and thus reach this conclusion. Hence it comes to pass that they despise all religion and say that the article concerning the resurrection was only invented to terrify the common people. Peasants, however, seldom go so far as to despise God and religion, for they hardly think about such things. But clever people are interested in them, reflect upon them, and weigh them according to reason. Such a man is Erasmus.[166] Other very clever men support this epicurean. But we know that the Holy Scriptures are confirmed, as no other teaching can be, by such miracles as the raising of the dead, the expulsion of demons, etc. It is for this reason that our Lord God warns us so often to abide by the Holy Scriptures.

"I didn't learn my theology all at once. I had to ponder over it ever more deeply, and my spiritual trials[167] were of help to me in this, for one does not learn anything without practice. This is what the spiritualists[168] and sects lack. They don't have the right adversary, the devil. He would teach them well. None of the arts can

---

[163] John Brenz (1499-1570) contributed to the spread of the Reformation in southern Germany.
[164] Justus Menius (1499-1558), a student of Philip Melanchthon and reformer of the church in Erfurt and elsewhere.
[165] Philip Melanchthon. Cf. No. 157, n. 59.
[166] Desiderius Erasmus. Cf. No. 113, n. 25.
[167] Latin: *tentationes*, i.e., *Anfechtungen*.
[168] German: *Schwermer, Schwärmer*. Cf. No. 342, n. 155.

be learned without practice. What kind of physician would that be who stayed in school all the time? When he finally puts his medicine to use and deals more and more with nature, he will come to see that he hasn't as yet mastered the art. Why shouldn't this be so in the case of the Holy Scriptures, too, where God has provided a different adversary? It is therefore the greatest gift [of God] to have a text and to be able to say, 'This is right. I know it.' People think that they can know everything by simply listening to a sermon. Zwingli[169] also made the mistake of thinking that he knew everything, that theology is an easy art. But I know that I have yet to comprehend the Lord's Prayer. No one can be learned without practice. The peasant put it well: Armor is fine for a man who knows how to use it. To be sure, the Holy Scriptures are sufficient in themselves, but God grant that I find the right text. For when Satan disputes with me whether God is gracious to me, I dare not quote the passage, 'He who loves God will inherit the kingdom of God,'[170] because Satan will at once object, 'But you have not loved God!' Nor can I oppose this on the ground that I am a diligent reader [of the Scriptures] and a preacher. The shoe doesn't fit.[171] I should say, rather, that Jesus Christ died for me and should cite the article [of the Creed] concerning forgiveness of sin. That will do it!"

On the Observance of the Sabbath

Fall, 1532   *No. 356*

Against the new error concerning the necessity of the Sabbath,[172] namely, that it must be observed just as the other works

---

[169] Huldreich Zwingli. Cf. No. 5005, n. 35.
[170] Cf. I Cor. 2:9.
[171] Literally, the horseshoe is not attached properly. That is, this kind of argument does not meet the need.
[172] Andrew Karlstadt (*ca.* 1480-1541), a colleague of Luther in Wittenberg, was one of the early Sabbatarians with whom Luther came into conflict. Cf. also *LW* 26, 7. Unlike many contemporaries, Luther held that Christians are bound to observe only those parts of the Mosaic law that agree with natural law. The latter enjoins a day of rest. For the Jews Saturday was fixed as the day of rest, but Christians were not bound to this day. Cf. Luther's *Against the Heavenly Prophets*, 1525 (*LW* 40, 93-98) and this *Large Catechism*, 1529 (Theodore G. Tappert [ed], *The Book of Concord* [Philadelphia: Muhlenberg Press, 1959], pp. 375-379).

of the Decalogue, [Martin Luther said], "How do they propose to prove that Saturday is the seventh day? For the Jews themselves must take their appointed day from us Christians. It's nothing but spite and envy. Besides, it has not yet been established whether Christ died on a Saturday or a Friday. Pomeranus has written best about this matter,[173] yet it can't be settled or demonstrated. Accordingly one can reply thus:

"First, the Sabbath is only ceremonial.

"Second, it must be asked where they get the command that the Ten Commandments are to be applied to and imposed upon us Christians. For except as I keep the Decalogue for the sake of the common people, I mean to treat it differently. Moses doesn't belong to the Gentiles but only to the Jews. We don't accept Moses, because he was not sent to us. It is good to hold to Moses where he suits us, but to those who would make him our master we say No. For what Moses teaches is also taught by nature. To be sure, he expressed it better than the Gentiles, but they nevertheless taught the same thing.

"Third, those who insist on the Sabbath ought to be circumcised as well. It would be another matter if they wished for certain reasons to change the Lord's day into the Sabbath and otherwise left it free. But when they say, 'You must observe this,' we deny it and reply, 'Then go ahead and observe all of it!' Besides, the commandment concerning the Sabbath is different from the other commandments of the Decalogue. The others are general and are all taught by nature, just as a prince gives a general command to all his subjects and then gives special commands to his individual aides. So the Sabbath is special and applies only to the Jews."

Prayer and the Promise of God
Fall, 1532   *No. 358*

"When we pray we have the advantage [of the promise] that what we ask will be granted, although not according to our wish. If it weren't for the promise[174] I wouldn't pray. God does well,

---

[173] John Bugenhagen, *Historia des Leidens und Aufferstehung unsers Herrn, Jhesu Christi* (Wittenberg: Rhaw, 1530).
[174] Cf. Jas. 5:16.

moreover, that he doesn't give us everything as we wish, for otherwise we'd want to have everything on our own terms. That our Lord God is the same in life and death I have often experienced. If our prayer is earnest it will be heard, even if not as and when we wish. This must be so or our faith is vain. Consequently it's difficult to pray. I know well what a prayer requires of me. I haven't committed adultery, but I've broken the first table[175] against God's Word and honor. On account of my great sins [against the first table] I can't get to the others in the second table."

Medicine May Be Used to Cure Disease
Fall, 1532   *No. 360*

"I believe that in all grave illnesses the devil is present as the author and cause. First, he is the author of death. Second, Peter says in Acts that those who were oppressed by the devil were healed by Christ.[176] Moreover, Christ cured not only the oppressed but also the paralytics, the blind, etc.[177] Generally speaking, therefore, I think that all dangerous diseases are blows of the devil. For this, however, he employs the instruments of nature. So a thief dies by the sword, Satan corrupts the qualities and humors of the body, etc. God also employs means for the preservation of health, such as sleep, food, and drink, for he does nothing except through instruments. So the devil also injures through appropriate means. When a fence leans over a little, he knocks it all the way down to the ground.

"Accordingly a physician is our Lord God's mender of the body, as we theologians are his healers of the spirit; we are to restore what the devil has damaged. So a physician administers theriaca[178] when Satan gives poison. Healing comes from the application of nature to the creature, for medicine is divinely revealed and not derived from books, even as knowledge of law is not from

---

[175] I.e., the first table of the Decalogue, or the first three commandments.
[176] Cf. Acts 10:38.
[177] Cf. Mark 3:4-12; 8:22-25.
[178] An antidote for poison.

books but is drawn from nature. It's remarkable that a prince is sure to find effective the medicines which he administers to himself but finds ineffective what his physician prescribes. So both electors[179] have eye drops which help when they take them, no matter whether their affliction is caused by heat or cold, but a physician wouldn't dare prescribe the drops. It's so in theology too. Philip[180] lifts up my spirit with a mere word. If Eck[181] or Zwingli[182] said the same thing, it would dash me to the ground. It's our Lord God who created all things, and they are good. Wherefore it's permissible to use medicine, for it is a creature of God.

"Thus I replied to Hohndorf,[183] who inquired of me when he heard from Karlstadt[184] that it's not permissible to make use of medicine. I said to him, 'Do you eat when you're hungry?'"

Karlstadt Opposes the Granting of Degrees
Fall, 1532   *No. 361*

"[Andrew] Karlstadt conferred a degree on a certain student.[185] On this occasion he delivered an oration and said, 'I stand here and grant a degree to this learned man. I do this impiously for the sake of two florins.' He cited the passage, 'Neither be called masters,' etc. [Matt. 23:10]. However, in this passage Christ was warning against the sects and was admonishing that one should let him alone be master in spiritual matters. Otherwise a son should not call his parent 'father.' What will come of this? After he spoke thus Karlstadt suffered a decline, [fell into many errors, and has also remained in them]."[186]

---

[179] Electors Frederick and John of Ernestine Saxony.
[180] Philip Melanchthon. Cf. No. 157, n. 59.
[181] John Eck. Cf. No. 257, n. 107.
[182] Huldreich Zwingli. Cf. No. 5005, n. 35.
[183] John Hohndorf (d. 1534), mayor of Wittenberg.
[184] Andrew Karlstadt. Cf. No. 356, n. 172.
[185] On February 3, 1523, doctor's degrees were awarded to Johannes Westermann and Gottschalk Gropp in Wittenberg. Cf. Gerhard L. Belgum (ed.), *The Mature Luther* (Decorah, Iowa: Luther College Press, 1959), pp. 51, 52.
[186] Text in brackets from later variant by John Aurifaber.

RECORDED BY DIETRICH

The Word of God and the Sacraments
Fall, 1532   *No. 365*

"The text, '[Let the children come to me, . . . for] to such belongs the kingdom of God' [Mark 10:14], is the promise to Abraham. This text clearly speaks about children. One can't get around it. The text doesn't speak of adults, such as the apostles now were. Moreover, it says of children, 'to such belongs.' That is, 'I'm their Christ; I've been promised to them. I've also been promised to you adult Jews, but you've become too clever.' Thus we have a promise and command for the baptism of children, because Christ said, 'Preach to all nations,'[187] as if he would say, 'I wish to be the God of all.' Circumcision was only for Abraham and the Jews, but baptism is for all nations, large and small, young and old. Circumcision doesn't save, but it was attached to the future Christ. Even so, the promise which is added makes baptism. Abraham had the Word along with circumcision. Hence baptism is no more than water, but the water has been surrounded by the Word. Baptism offers as much as circumcision used to. It was proper for Abraham to say, 'I have been circumcised, and in that circumcision Christ was promised to me.' The promise does it. In the New Testament the promise is, 'I shall be your God,' and it is on this promise that you should be baptized. In itself circumcision was nothing. So it doesn't help the Turks when they are circumcised[188] because the promise is lost. If the promise were absent I would thumb my nose at the water. Accordingly the patriarchs received the promise, 'I will be your God,' and then they were circumcised. However, there is this difference between circumcision and baptism, namely, that circumcision was performed before Christ in anticipation of the very grace which is in baptism, while baptism is observed after Christ on the strength of the grace which he has secured. The grace is the same, and the only difference is between the past and future tense. However, both look to the last judgment when all will be revealed.

"The text about children ought not to be passed over lightly, but one ought to do what they say at court: The letter of a prince

---
[187] Cf. Matt. 28:19, 20.
[188] Circumcision was practiced in Islam.

should be read three times. What does 'I am your God' mean except that he wishes to save us? Therefore, be circumcised as a sign. But the text, 'To such belongs the kingdom of heaven,' means to say, 'You adults are sons of the devil and have lost your childlikeness.' So although certain persons have been baptized, when they grow up and don't believe they are nevertheless damned. The devil snatches them from their childlikeness.

"Children under the law accepted circumcision on account of that word, 'I am your God.' They didn't assent to it, yet those so circumcised were the people of God. Even so, a prince protects infants whom he hasn't known and who haven't known him. All this is accomplished by the covenant, the promised seed. Circumcision is no longer in full force now because it was intended to be performed only to the time of Christ. Signs have often been changed. In the time from Adam to Abraham people had only the sign of sacrifice, the burning of victims by fire.[189] That was a more magnificent sign than we have. Afterward Noah had a rainbow[190] and Abraham had circumcision.[191] I think that from that first sign of fire came the custom of the Chaldeans to worship fire. Circumcision lasted from Abraham to the time of Christ, and after the time of Christ baptism has been used. Thus the signs have become less and less, but the things and the deeds have grown increasingly.

"The sign and the promise should be tied to each other, not torn from each other. Those err who abandon the sign and say, 'God is the God of all nations and therefore I won't allow myself to be baptized.' For the promise always stands in such a way that the letter and the seal should be together. Neither avails without the other. One doesn't have faith in a seal which stands by itself, nor in a letter by itself. It is even so here. To be sure, it may be that if a person dies who was just baptized and stands upon the promise, he will be saved, but this is another question. Yet this remains firm, that signs are not to be neglected. And this is the reason we don't damn infants who die before they are baptized: the parents wish and intend to have them baptized. Consequently

---

[189] Cf. Gen. 4:4.
[190] Cf. Gen. 9:13.
[191] Cf. Gen. 17:23.

I don't judge such an infant but commend him to God. After baptism one should seek to do the same thing, for the Word and the sign are joined together. If you have the letter, let a seal be affixed to it. It would have availed nothing if a Jew had said, 'I am Abraham's son and therefore I don't want to be circumcised.'

"Because the objection is now raised that the day of circumcision was fixed—namely, the eighth day—but the time of baptism was not fixed, I reply: I'm not concerned about the work but about the Word. The eighth day adds nothing. Nor does either the command or the sign add anything, for Abraham was righteous before the circumcision. Learn to hold the Word high. It's true that circumcision was a command, a requirement, and was prescribed for the eighth day, but you should say, 'This day or that day, this command or that command—these aren't the important things. This is of central importance: that God is your God and the God of your seed. It's on the strength of this promise that you should be circumcised.' Even so, it doesn't matter whether one is baptized when young or old, but it matters that God is the God of young and old and that he gave his Son for them. It's on this that you should be baptized.

"No heathen could say, 'God is my God,' unless he heard the Word. Therefore, these statements are different: God is the Lord of all nations, and God is the God of all nations. For he's not the God of those who don't have his Word, just as he's not the God of the Jews who don't have his Word, even if they are circumcised. To be sure, he reveals himself to them, but they do not all accept him.

"As for the children, I think that all children who are baptized may be saved. With respect to predestination one should get so far as to say: If he doesn't have the Word, I commit him to God's judgment as to whether he gets it or not. If he doesn't he is lost. As far as we are concerned, we now have God's Word, and so we ought not have any doubt about our salvation. It's in this way that we should dispute about predestination, for it has already been settled: I have been baptized and I have the Word, and so I have no doubt about my salvation as long as I continue to cling to the Word. When we take our eyes off Christ we come upon predestination and start to dispute. Our Lord God says, 'Why don't you believe me? Yet you hear me when I say that you are beloved by me and your sins are forgiven.' This is our nature, that we are always running away from the Word.

"The papists have alarmed us with wicked thoughts about children who die. Here we must be careful. Women and their maids are thoughtless and strangle infants unintentionally. Often mothers and midwives abandon infants who are born unexpectedly and might become horrible monstrosities. It does no harm, therefore, to keep these women in fear, lest they thoughtlessly let the children die. There are enough accidents without these. Consequently we say and we warn that children be brought promptly for baptism."

[Somebody asked] whether the Lord's Supper should be given to children. "I reply: There is no urgency about the sacrament of the altar. So there's no command concerning prayer, but there's a precept that when we pray we should expect to be heard.[192] Nor is there a precept about afflictions, although those who are afflicted ought to be patient.[193] However, it doesn't follow that the children are damned who either do not pray or are not afflicted. When in I Corinthians [11:28] Paul said that a man should examine himself, he spoke only of adults because he was speaking about those who were quarreling among themselves. However, he doesn't here forbid that the sacrament of the altar be given even to children."

The Blessing of Women and Children
Fall, 1532   No. 374

When it was reported from the war against the Turks[194] that our soldiers were carrying various slips of paper inscribed with Turkish letters in the belief that the soldiers would thereby be protected against all arms, he [Martin Luther] said, "Even saintly men sin when they are in danger, and so it isn't to be wondered at that the heathen make use of magic. So Jephthah made a vow

---

[192] Cf. I John 5:14.
[193] Cf. II Cor. 6:4.
[194] Cf. No. 206, n. 75.

concerning his daughter, although he didn't have her in mind.[195] A wrong was done to his daughter, and so he sinned."

When I[196] asked about the passage in which it is written that she bewailed her virginity,[197] he [Martin Luther] replied that the reason for the lamentation was that she would die without offspring. "The Jews regarded this as the greatest calamity. So the mother of Samuel almost went mad because she was childless.[198] I did, too, when I was first married and God put me to the test,[199] for a child, as they say, is the best wool that one can shear from the sheep. It is written in Genesis [33:5] with reference to children, 'Those whom God has graciously given to me,' as in the psalm [119:29], 'Graciously teach me thy law.' Furthermore, from the first chapter of Genesis [1:28] comes this sentiment about children: 'God blessed them.' He says 'Blessed' and expects you to respond with 'Thanks be to God,' but this is generally forgotten. Where would we be if it were not for women? And afterward when some little mistake is made we are beside ourselves. It has been rightly said concerning the first chapter of Genesis that it's impossible to exhaust it in preaching. It's the greatest part of the Old Testament, and the New Testament is a revelation of the Old."

It Is Easier to Doubt Than to Believe
November 30, 1532   *No. 388*

A question was proposed by Master Ignatius,[200] a student of sacred literature, on the day before the Kalends of December, 1532: Why do we more readily believe Satan when he terrifies than Christ when he consoles? The question was answered by Dr. Martin Luther: "Because we are better equipped to doubt than to hope; because hope comes from the Spirit of God but despair comes from our own spirit. Accordingly God has forbidden it [despair] under severe penalty. That we more easily believe penalty than reward

---

[195] Cf. Judg. 11:30-39.
[196] Veit Dietrich, the reporter of this conversation.
[197] Cf. Judg. 11:38.
[198] Cf. I Sam. 1:2-18.
[199] Actually Luther's first child was born twelve months after his marriage.
[200] Ignatius Perknowsky. Cf. No. 342, n. 156.

is a product of the reason or spirit of man. Hoping and believing are different from thinking and speculating. Reason sees death before it, and it's impossible for reason not to be terrified by it. Likewise we can't be persuaded [by our reason] that God gives his Son and loves us so much, and hence we say, 'You have not allowed your Son to be crucified for nothing!' This is above reason. That God is so merciful, not on account of my works but on account of his Son, is incomprehensible.

"In this article all the sect leaders are wanting, even if they say they believe it. I think they all have a bad conscience, and I point out in proof of this that when they are up against it they become desperate. Arius[201] did this, and Münzer.[202] I hold, therefore, that they know they are wrong. Even so, the bishop of Mainz,[203] the margrave,[204] and Duke George[205] make a joke of the Word of God, as Adam also did in paradise and as nature always does. When a man sins, he says it isn't important. But from this sin he proceeds to the sin against the Holy Spirit, and God lets him fall into wilful sin. So Duke George fell into sin, and he recognizes that he's doing wrong, but not only doesn't he refrain from sin but he doesn't ask to be forgiven. This is the sin against the Holy Spirit, and here one passes from the second to the first table [of the law].[206] When you feel that something is wrong and you have a bad conscience about it, this is not the sin against the Holy Spirit, but when you sin and have a good conscience about it, this is the sin against the Holy Spirit. Such persons are Duke George, the margrave, Karlstadt,[207] Zwingli,[208] and Münzer, who rebuke our Lord God with wilful lies.

"Dear Lord God, it is enough to have sinned without trying to justify oneself! This isn't tolerated in a home. The father of a

---

[201] Cf. No. 3695, n. 24.
[202] Thomas Münzer. Cf. 291, n. 131.
[203] Cardinal Albrecht, archbishop of Mainz. Cf. No. 1362, n. 65.
[204] Margrave George of Brandenburg.
[205] Duke George of Albertine Saxony. Cf. No. 275, n. 118.
[206] Cf. No. 358, n. 175.
[207] Andrew Karlstadt. Cf. No. 356, n. 172.
[208] Huldreich Zwingli. Cf. No. 5005, n. 35.

household doesn't allow it. It burns in one's heart if a person who sins tries to justify himself. When you confess a sin and yet do not cease from it, it is a grievous sin and is contempt of God, but it's not the sin against the Holy Spirit. On the other hand, when you know you are wrong and nevertheless try to defend yourself, this is too much.

"Our Lord God can suffer it that no sin should be so great that it may not be forgiven when the sinner falls down before Christ. But Duke George relies on being forgiven by the Christian church, and so he goes on sinning, but he'll find out otherwise. One should have no doubt about a penitent sinner, even if he repeats his sin again and again, but one should also consider that if he dies in his sin he has had it.

"I think many of the kings of Israel, like Ahab, have been saved. About Solomon I have no doubt. So we see that all history presses toward the forgiveness of sins. Everything circles around the center, and that is Christ."

Prenatal Baptisms Are Ridiculed
December, 1532   No. 394

"[According to Aristotle][209] the whole soul is in each and every part of the body. On this basis they [the papists] baptize a fetus which has not yet been fully brought into the world. Augustine[210] treated of this at great length. If I prick my finger, my whole body feels it. Therefore, when I baptize a finger I baptize the whole body.

"I don't wish to be baptized thus. But I don't care about the element, whatever one may have. Indeed, it's enough to speak the words. Let the children be committed to our Lord God. The baptism itself is of no concern to me.[211] Besides, the Word is the principal part of baptism. If in an emergency there's no water at hand, it doesn't matter whether water or beer is used."

---

[209] Text in brackets from later version by John Aurifaber. Cf. Aristotle, *Ethics*, I, 6.
[210] Cf. No. 51, n. 4.
[211] I.e., this is God's business and not mine.

There Are Two Kinds of Offense
December, 1532   *No. 395*

"Offense is of two kinds, received and given. [An example of] offense received is that the Jews were offended by Christ because he spoke and acted according to the Word of God, just as God wished. This opinion needed to be uprooted. The pope is also offended because I teach Christian liberty, but what do I care? In fact, I preach against him so that it may be known that the doctrine of the papists is corrupt, but what I say and do is according to God. We belabor them, but for their own good, as Paul says.[212] I wish to offend them, not for their ruin but for their good. To defend error would be of the devil. If our Lord God lets a man fall so far that he doesn't think the Word is the Word, we don't wish to hold him but will let him go."

Katy Asks for the Meaning of a Passage
December, 1532   *No. 396*

When his wife inquired about the passage in Psalm 18 [:20, 24] in which David pleads his righteousness, he [Martin Luther] responded, "David is speaking even as I can now speak to you and say, 'Katy, I haven't done you any harm.' I can't say this to our Lord God, but it's proper to say it to other human beings. One who is below is judged, but not one who is above. When David wishes evil to some, therefore, he prays against his enemies not in their personal but in their official capacities."

Luther Explains His Vehement Writing
December, 1532   *No. 397*

When asked by the younger margrave[213] why he wrote with such vehemence, he [Martin Luther] said, "Our Lord God must precede a heavy shower with thunder and then let it rain in a very

---
[212] Cf. Rom. 10:19.
[213] Luther was with Elector Joachim II of Brandenburg (1538-1571) in November, 1532. Cf. WA, Br 6, 385.

gentle fashion so that the ground becomes soaked through. To put it differently, I can cut through a willow branch with a [bread]²¹⁴ knife, but to cut through tough oak requires an axe and wedge, and even with these one can hardly split it."

The Relation of Word, Spirit, and Faith
December, 1532   *No. 402*

"Faith and the Spirit go together, but the Spirit is not always revealed. So Cornelius had the Holy Spirit before Peter came to him, although he didn't know it.²¹⁵ Those in the book of Acts who said, 'We don't know the Holy Spirit,' also had the Spirit, just as the patriarchs in the Old Testament had Christ, although they didn't know him. They clung to the Word, and through it they received the Holy Spirit. Later in the book of Acts he was manifested to them outwardly. It's to be understood thus: The Word comes first, and with the Word the Spirit breathes upon my heart so that I believe. Then I feel that I have become a different person and I recognize that the Holy Spirit is there. Accordingly these are two things: to have the Holy Spirit and to know that you have him. When somebody speaks in your ear, you hardly hear his words before [you feel] his breath, so strong is the breath. Even so, when the Word is proclaimed, the Holy Spirit accompanies it and breathes upon your heart. The sophists²¹⁶ say that this is reflected knowledge, as an image is reflected in a mirror. When the Word is scattered abroad the Holy Spirit blows upon us, but he must also breathe upon us inwardly.

"Christ's saying concerning the Jews, 'They could not believe' [John 12:39], belongs in the box of secrets which it isn't given us to open. It's futile for anybody who is thus condemned to suppose that he would say to God, 'Why have you made me different?' For unbelievers will not come to the thought of asking, 'Why didn't you give me the Spirit?' But they will come to the thought, 'You had the law. Why didn't you keep it? You should have done so,'

---

²¹⁴ Word in brackets from later variant by John Aurifaber.
²¹⁵ Cf. Acts 10:1-48.
²¹⁶ Luther's usual term for the medieval scholastics.

etc. Such thoughts will gnaw at them. They won't be able to think of anything else. They won't be able to get around their conscience. The greatest gift is to have a conscience pacified by the Word. For this did God permit his Son to die, that we might have a good conscience."

Wicked Desire to Foresee the Future
December, 1532   *No. 403*

"Karlstadt[217] once said, 'If I knew that our Lord God was going to damn me, I would trot right along into hell.' This was wickedly said. God says, 'Do and believe what I tell you, and leave the rest to me.' They [Karlstadt and others like him] want to know beforehand, without and apart from the Word."

Youth, Not Age, Is Venturesome
December, 1532   *No. 406*

"No good work is undertaken or done with wise reflection. It must all happen in a half-sleep. This is how I was forced to take up the office of teaching. If I had known what I know now, ten horses wouldn't have driven me to it. Moses[218] and Jeremiah[219] also complained that they were deceived. Nor would any man take a wife if he first gave real thought [to what might happen in marriage and the household]." [220]

Here Philip[221] said that he had diligently observed that in history great deeds had never been done by old men. "This was so," said Luther, "when Alexander and Augustus[222] were young; afterward men become too wise. They didn't do great things by deliberate choice[223] but by a sort of impulse. If you young fellows

---

[217] Andrew Karlstadt. Cf. No. 356, n. 172.
[218] Cf. Num. 11:11-15.
[219] Cf. Jer. 20:7-12.
[220] Text in brackets from later version by John Aurifaber.
[221] Philip Melanchthon. Cf. No. 157, n. 59.
[222] Alexander the Great, king of Macedonia in the fourth century B.C., and Augustus, Roman emperor at the birth of Christ.
[223] Greek: *ek proaireseōs*.

were wise, the devil couldn't do anything to you; but since you aren't wise, you need us who are old. Our Lord God doesn't do great things except by violence, as they say. If old men were strong and young men were wise it would be worth something. The sect leaders are all young men like Icarus[224] and Phaeton.[225] Such are Zwingli[226] and Karlstadt.[227] They are novices in the sacred Scriptures."

To Be Glad to Die Is Unnatural
December, 1532 No. 408

"I don't like to see examples of joyful death. On the other hand, I like to see those who tremble and shake and grow pale when they face death and yet get through. It was so with the great saints; they were not glad to die. Fear is something natural because death is a punishment, and therefore something sad. According to the spirit one dies willingly, but according to the flesh the saying applies, 'Another will carry you where you do not wish to go' [John 21:18]. In the Psalms and other histories, as in Jeremiah, one sees how eager men were to escape death. 'Beware,' Jeremiah said, 'or you will bring innocent blood upon yourselves' [Jer. 26:15]. But when Christ said, 'Let this cup pass from me' [Matt. 26:39], the meaning was different, for this was the Same who said, 'I have life and death in my hand' [John 5:21, 24]. We are the ones who drew the bloody sweat from him."[228]

Cases of Conscience Pertaining to Marriage
December, 1532 No. 414

"Cases for the consolation of consciences belong in confession and not in books. A certain man took a wife, and after bearing several children she contracted syphilis[229] and was unable to fulfil

---

[224] A mythological character who, with his father Daedalus, flew on wings attached to his body with wax.
[225] A mythological character who presumptuously tried to drive the chariot of the sun across the heavens.
[226] Huldreich Zwingli. Cf. No. 5005, n. 35.
[227] Andrew Karlstadt. Cf. No. 356, n. 172.
[228] Cf. Luke 22:44.
[229] Latin: *morbum Gallicum*, "French disease."

her marital obligation. Thereupon the husband, troubled by the flesh, denied himself beyond his ability to sustain the burden of chastity. It is asked, Ought he to be allowed a second wife? I reply that one or the other of two things must happen: either he commits adultery or he takes another wife. It is my advice that he take a second wife; however, he should not abandon his first wife but should provide for her sufficiently to enable her to support her life.

"In short, there are many cases of this kind, from which it ought to be clearly seen and recognized that this is the law and that that is the gospel. The pope, who has heaped up laws, doesn't do this. He decrees thus: If a man has married two women, he should pay his nuptial obligation to the first, although she is not properly his wife, and sleep with the second. This is very bad advice to consciences. So the pope has revoked the imperial law concerning divorce without making another law, except only for a prohibition.

"I feel that judgments about marriages belong to the jurists. Since they make judgments concerning fathers, mothers, children, and servants, why shouldn't they also make decisions about the life of married people? When the papists oppose the imperial law concerning divorce, I reply that this doesn't follow from what is written, 'What God has joined together let no man put asunder,'[230] for the emperor puts asunder with his laws; it's not man who puts asunder, but God, for here 'man' signifies a private person. It is similar when it is written, 'You shall not kill' [Exod. 20:13], which is a command addressed to a private person and not to a magistrate.

"In such cases in which the conscience was troubled I have often offered counsel not according to the pope but according to my office, according to the gospel. Nevertheless, I warned the persons involved not to make this judgment of mine public. I said to them, 'Keep this to yourselves. If you can't keep it secret, take the consequences.' I won't make such judgments public because I don't have the authority to carry them out. It would therefore be useless. Moreover, others who are not troubled in conscience would take the judgments to be excuses for lust. But this judgment of mine is valid according to that saying of Christ, 'Whatever two or three say in my name,' etc. [Matt. 18:16-20]. Accordingly the

---

[230] Cf. Matt. 19:6.

statement, 'What God has joined together,' has this meaning: Here God doesn't mean God in heaven, but God's Word, and specifically that we obey our parents and magistrates.[231] God doesn't join together what happens without the consent of the father, and what I command and order my daughter is God's command to her. If there are no parents, then the closest blood relatives speak in God's stead. Consequently 'God' means God's Word, as in John [1:1], 'And the Word was God.' On the other hand, God puts asunder when my daughter marries against my will. If she knows my will she knows God's will, for God has said that what you do to anybody God does to him, as appears in many passages in Genesis, where the father is consulted and it is said that God is consulted. So Christ declares in Luke,[232] 'God said, The two shall become one flesh,' although it was Adam who had said it. For next to God the authority of parents is divine. But the world calls God 'luck,' as it does when it is said, 'what man has joined together,' that is, the foolish frenzy of love has joined together."

The Authority of Parents and of Rulers
December, 1532   *No. 415*

"It can be shown by proof that the magistracy is based on the Fourth Commandment. The reason is that obedience is necessary. The authority of parents is also necessary. If, then, the authority of parents vanishes and the obedience of children increases, it's according to natural law that the children have a guardian to help bring them up. Such guardians are the governing authorities, and the emperor is therefore the guardian of all parents.

"With his absolute power God could restrain disobedient children in some other way, but he uses his ordinate power, namely, the magistracy. The father should therefore remain father. If the authority of the father is lost, the magistrate takes his place. The magistrate's place (if he can't exercise discipline) is also taken by

---

[231] Cf. Exod. 20:12 and Luther's explanation of the Fourth Commandment in his *Small Catechism* and *Large Catechism* (1529). Tappert (ed.), *Book of Concord*, p. 343 and pp. 379-389. Cf. also in this volume, No. 415.
[232] Matt. 19:5.

the devil. Accordingly the proverb is true: The devil brings up all whom fathers and mothers can't.

"Here an objection may be raised: Since the father doesn't have the right to put his child to death, then the magistrate doesn't either. To this I reply: the magistrate is the servant of the parents, and the consent of the parents is the consent of God, who commands that disobedient children be put to death. The command is clear in Moses. God commands that such a child be put to death, even if the father does not wish it." [233]

Why the Bishops Let the Monks Alone
December, 1532   No. 416

"The bishops didn't dare touch a single monk because when a sow cries out the whole herd comes running."

Ceremonies and How They Are to Be Judged
December, 1532   No. 430

"Anybody who wants to attack ceremonies, no matter how insignificant they may be, must grasp his sword with both hands. He mustn't do like Erasmus,[234] who laughs at them merely because they are silly. If you object that God is foolish, too, and prescribed such silly things as circumcision, the sacrifice of Isaac,[235] etc., I must ask you: What if these silly things which you laugh at are pleasing to God? Erasmus never meets this argument because reason generally laughs at such things. When it comes to divine things reason despises them."

When we objected to this, he [Martin Luther] responded, "Well, my dear fellow, Erasmus doesn't know this principle, that Scripture is to be urged and followed. Only the article of justification must settle the matter, otherwise our thoughts will remain in the realm of reason. Perhaps a ceremony will be pleasing to God. Why, then, do you oppose it? Hasn't our Lord God commanded

---

[233] Cf. Exod. 21:15, 17.
[234] Desiderius Erasmus. Cf. No. 113, n. 25.
[235] Cf. Gen. 17:10; 22:1-13.

even sillier things? Nobody will hold his ground against such arguments unless he knows more than Erasmus. The argument [of the papists],[236] 'The church commands it,' knocks them all down.

"It isn't possible that a believing man could have written so many books as Erasmus without setting down a line about Christ."

Difference Between a Lawyer and a Theologian
December, 1532   *No. 431*

"The lawyer says: Let justice be done and the world be damned.[237] The theologian says: Let sin be forgiven and the world will be saved, for justice is not done but sin is always committed."

The Kind of God Men Think They Have
December, 1532   *No. 432*

"When an epicurean[238] thinks about God and observes how things happen in the world, he can't do otherwise than conclude: Either God can't stop these things, and then he must be very weak; he must not be omnipotent. Or else he doesn't want to stop them, and then he must be very wicked, for he delights in evils. Or again, he doesn't know what is happening, and then he must be very foolish. So God is unduly deprived of his power, his justice, and his wisdom. Erasmus[239] and others, like Mutianus,[240] think the same way.

Forgiveness of Sin Is Hard to Believe
Early in the year 1533   *No. 437*

"It's impossible for our adversaries to understand the forgive-

---

[236] Text in brackets from variant. On the subject under discussion, see U. S. Leupold (trans.), Vilmos Vajta, *Luther on Worship* (Philadelphia: Muhlenberg, 1958).

[237] Proverbial saying adopted by Emperor Ferdinand as his motto. Cf. No. 206, n. 77.

[238] By "epicurean" Luther meant a skeptic. Cf. No. 466, n. 267.

[239] Cf. No. 430.

[240] Conrad Muth (*ca.* 1471-1526), a German humanist who advocated concealing doubts under an appearance of loyalty to the church.

ness of sins because they are immersed in their notion of quality.[241] The Holy Scriptures call Christians saints and the people of God. It's a pity that it's forgotten that we are saints, for to forget this is to forget Christ and baptism. (In Psalm 86 [:2] the Hebrew for 'I am a saint,' *chasid*, means the opposite, 'I am cursed.') So it comes about that those who are truly sinners don't want to be considered sinners, and those who are saints don't want to be called saints either. The latter don't believe the gospel which comforts them and the former don't believe the law which accuses them.

"You say that the sins which we commit every day offend God, and therefore we are not saints. To this I reply: Mother love is stronger than the filth and scabbiness on a child, and so the love of God toward us is stronger than the dirt that clings to us. Accordingly, although we are sinners, we do not lose our filial relation on account of our filthiness, nor do we fall from grace on account of our sin.

"You object that we are always sinning, and where there are sins the Holy Spirit does not dwell; therefore we are not saints because the Spirit sanctifies. I reply: The text says, 'The Spirit will glorify me' [John 16:13, 14]. Therefore, where Christ is, there is the Holy Spirit also. Besides, sins do not separate Christ from sinners who believe. The God of the Turks helps only to the extent that one is godly. This is also true of the pope's God, but when a papist begins to doubt, as he must, that he has made enough satisfaction, he becomes alarmed. Such is the faith of the pope and the Turks. But the Christian says: I believe and cling to him who is in heaven as a Savior. If I fall into sin I rise again but don't continue to sin. I rise up and become the enemy of sin. Thus the Christian faith differs from other religions in this, that the Christian hopes even in the midst of evils and sins. Without the Holy Spirit natural man can't do this. He can only seek refuge in works. To say, 'I am a child of God,' is accordingly not to doubt even when good works are lacking, as they always are in all of us. This is so great a thing that one is startled by it. Such is its magnitude that one can't believe it."

---

[241] Variant reads: "their notion of the righteousness that remains in them."

The Right and Wrong Use of Reason
Early in the year 1533 No. 439

[The question was raised] whether the tools of the arts and nature are useful to theology. [Martin Luther answered:] "One knife cuts better than another. So good tools—for example, languages and the arts—can contribute to clearer teaching. Just as many, like Erasmus, are equipped with languages and the arts and nevertheless make damaging mistakes, so the same thing happens with weapons, most of which are made for slaughter. A thing must be distinguished from its misuse. Job distinguished thus when he said, 'You speak as one of the foolish women would speak' [Job 2:10]. This text has always pleased me on account of its proper distinction between the creature and its abuse."

[The question was asked,] Is the light of reason also useful [to theology]? [Martin Luther answered:] "I make a distinction. Reason that is under the devil's control is harmful, and the more clever and successful it is, the more harm it does. We see this in the case of learned men who on the basis of their reason disagree with the Word. On the other hand, when illuminated by the Holy Spirit, reason helps to interpret the Holy Scriptures. So Cochlaeus'[242] tongue speaks blasphemies while my tongue speaks God's praise. Nevertheless, it is the same instrument in both of us. It is a tongue, whether before or after faith. The tongue, as a tongue, doesn't contribute to faith, and yet it serves faith when the heart is illuminated. So reason, when illuminated [by the Spirit], helps faith by reflecting on something, but reason without faith isn't and can't be helpful. Without faith the tongue utters nothing but blasphemies, as we see in the case of Duke George.[243] But reason that's illuminated takes all its thoughts from the Word. The substance remains and the unreal disappears when reason is illuminated by the Spirit."

God Bestows His Gifts Even on the Wicked
Early in the year 1533 No. 443

Once when he was drinking some excellent wine he [Martin

---
[242] John Cochlaeus. Cf. No. 1320, n. 38.
[243] Cf. No. 275, n. 118.

Luther] said, "I don't believe our Lord God will ever give more than he has given to the peasants. He gives them such good wine, grain, eggs, chickens, etc. Indeed, he gives them all created things. One thing he doesn't give them, however, and that is himself. From the fact that he bestows such great gifts on the wicked and those who blaspheme him, we can conclude what he will give us."

More Learning in Aesop Than in Jerome
Early in the year 1533   *No. 445*

"I think Jerome[244] has somehow been saved by his faith in Christ. But God forgive him for the harm he has done through his teaching! I know very well that he has done me much harm. He scolded women and gossiped about other women who were not present. I wish he had had a wife, for then he would have written many things differently. It's a wonder that in so many books of his there isn't a word about Christ, although he censures this in his sixth book.[245] I know no doctor whom I hate so much, although I once loved him ardently and read him voraciously. Surely there's more learning in Aesop[246] than in all of Jerome. If only Jerome had encouraged the works of faith and the fruits of the gospel! But he spoke only of fasting, etc. My dear Staupitz[247] once said, 'I'd like to know how that man was saved!' And his predecessor Dr. Proles[248] said, 'I should not like to have had St. Jerome as my prior!'"

Sunrise Suggests the Existence of God
Early in the year 1533   *No. 447*

"That notion of the pope and of all the philosophers that if I am good I shall have a gracious God, and if not there is no God,

---

[244] Cf. No. 51, n. 2.

[245] Jerome, *Epistles,* 133 (to Ctesiphon).

[246] Luther had so high an opinion of Aesop's Fables that he published a German version. Cf. in this volume, No. 3490, and John W. Doberstein, "Luther and the Fables of Aesop," *The Lutheran Church Quarterly,* XIII (1940), 69-74.

[247] John Staupitz. Cf. No. 94, n. 14.

[248] Andrew Proles was vicar-general of the Augustinian Observantists in Germany before John Staupitz.

means that one makes oneself into God. But I can't understand what must be in a man's mind if he doesn't feel seriously that there is a God when he sees the sun rise. It must at times occur to him that there are eternal things, or else he must push his face into the dirt like a sow. For it's incredible that they [the planets] be observed to move without inquiring whether there isn't somebody who moves them. In other areas it's known that a house doesn't build itself, etc. I should be glad to know what Erasmus[249] and others think about this."

Erasmus Does Not Understand the Gospel
Early in the year 1533   No. 448

"Paul calls it a mystery of God [Col. 2:2] that Another bears our sin and says that he has committed it. Erasmus knows nothing about this. The Father says, 'What my Son promises you, I will do.' Only spiritual trial teaches what Christ is. I've often experienced how the name of Christ helps. God willing, nobody will drive me away from it. The Scriptures make me sure of this experience."

Comfort When Offenses Arise over Teaching
Early in the year 1533   No. 452

"Offenses arise from my teaching, but I comfort myself as Paul did when he wrote to Titus that this truth was revealed to further the faith of the elect [Titus 1:1]. For the sake of the elect it [the deed of Christ] was done. It is for their sake that we preach, for they are serious about it. I wouldn't lose a word over the rest. I've bitten into many a nut, believing it to be good, only to find it wormy. Zwingli[250] and Erasmus are nothing but wormy nuts that taste like crap in one's mouth."

The Trials of a Preacher and Reformer
Early in the year 1533   No. 453

"If I were to write about the burdens of the preacher as I have

---

[249] Desiderius Erasmus. Cf. No. 113, n. 25.
[250] Huldreich Zwingli. Cf. No. 5005, n. 35.

experienced them and as I know them, I would scare everybody off. For a good preacher must be committed to this, that nothing is dearer to him than Christ and the life to come, and that when this life is gone Christ will say to all, 'Come to me, son. [You have been my dear and faithful servant].'[251] I hope that on the last day he'll speak to me, too, in this way, for here he speaks to me in a very unfriendly way. I bear [the hatred of] the whole world, the emperor, and the pope, but since I got into this I must stand my ground and say, 'It's right.' Afterward the devil also speaks to me about this, and he has often tormented me with this argument, 'You haven't been called,' as if I had not been made a doctor."[252]

The Relation of Faith and Love in Paul
Early in the year 1533   *No. 458*

"Concerning the verse in Galatians [5:6], 'faith working through love,' we also say that faith doesn't exist without works. However, Paul's view is this: Faith is active in love, that is, that faith justifies which expresses itself in acts. Now, it is assumed by some that the fruits of faith make the faith to be faith, although Paul intends something different, namely, that faith makes the fruit to be fruit. Faith comes first and then love follows. This also happens in the case of God's works. Circumcision, in so far as it is a work by itself, is of no account. But this, he says, is what counts: 'Believe in me and be godly.'"

Beware of Melancholy and Trust God
February 19, 1533   *No. 461*

When on February 19, 1533, he [Martin Luther] was suffering exceedingly from pains in the head, he said, "I believe firmly that I don't have these headaches and stomach pains because I work too hard, although this contributes somewhat, but rather because of my thoughts in spiritual assaults. I think it is clear that I'm in

---

[251] Cf. Matt. 25:21. Text in brackets from later variant by John Aurifaber.
[252] Luther often appealed to his doctor's degree as the ground for his authority to instruct and reform the church. Cf. *LW* 13, 66.

a condition like David's, who as an old man couldn't be warmed by a maiden[253] because he was so exhausted by his temptations and thoughts. These so weakened him that he had to endure many a severe trial.

"Therefore I advise you young fellows (this he said to me[254] and Henry Schneidewein[255] and Peter Weller[256] in the presence of Pomeranus):[257] Beware of melancholy, for it is forbidden by God because it's so destructive to the body. Our Lord God has commanded us to be cheerful. In this world sadness generally springs from money, honor, study, etc. My temptation is this, that I think I don't have a gracious God. This is [because I am still caught up in] the law. It is the greatest grief, and, as Paul says, it produces death [II Cor. 7:10]. God hates it, and he comforts us by saying, 'I am your God.'[258] I know his promise, and yet should some thought that isn't worth a fart nevertheless overwhelm me, I have the advantage (that our Lord God gives me) of taking hold of his Word once again. God be praised, I grasp the First Commandment which declares, 'I am your God [Exod. 20:2]. I'm not going to devour you. I'm not going to be poison for you.' Although it may be a little disturbing to some, I have never in my life been tempted by money. However, it sometimes happens that I think, 'What if your teaching has been false?' This temptation Oecolampadius[259] could not bear, and he died over it. Zwingli[260] could not bear it either. In short, no men conquer it. We ought to know, however, that above all righteousness and above all sin stands the declaration, 'I am the Lord your God' [Exod. 20:2]. (But I preach to others what I don't do myself.) Then we ought also to know and consider what really are our sins, and we shouldn't annoy our Lord

---

[253] Cf. I Kings 1:1-4.
[254] Veit Dietrich, the recorder of this conversation.
[255] Henry Schneidewein (1510-1580), a lawyer in the service of the elector of Saxony.
[256] Peter Weller was a lawyer and the brother of Jerome Weller (1499-1572) and often a visitor in Luther's home.
[257] John Bugenhagen, of Pomerania. Cf. No. 122, n. 36.
[258] Cf. Ps. 50:7.
[259] John Oecolampadius. Cf. No. 94, n. 19.
[260] Huldreich Zwingli. Cf. No. 5005, n. 35.

God with little sins. It's true, he punishes us for these, too, but the sins of the first table[261] lead to desperation when God doesn't help us promptly. The other sins, those of the second table, produce contrition and the hope of penitence. In addition, they hold out the offer of mercy, that God is gracious. But the first table is not to be trifled with.

"When I was young, that saying in Proverbs [27:23], 'Know the condition of your flocks' (that is, a shepherd ought to know and understand his sheep) almost tortured me to death. I understood the verse this way: I had to bare myself so completely to my pastor, prior, etc., that he might know what I did every day of my life. So I told everything I had done from my youth up, with the result that my preceptor in the monastery finally reprimanded me for doing so. So you young fellows, even if you have physical troubles, suffer them gladly for the sake of that eternal punishment of the heart in the conscience. But if you are sad, seek whatever relief you can. I absolve you of all pastimes through which you seek recreation, except such as are manifest sins, no matter whether they are eating, drinking, dancing, gaming, or anything else.

"The appearance of the church under the papacy was exceedingly wretched. It has now revived again, and I am of the opinion that the three last woes in the Apocalypse[262] have now passed and better times are beginning. I know for sure that this age, in which we now are, is better than the age in which the Jews were living at the time of Christ. However, the saying of Christ, 'Then there will be great tribulation, such as has not been from the beginning' [Matt. 24:21], I understand to apply to the tribulation of the godly and not to the tribulation of the world when the pope persecuted the church. 'If those days had not been shortened,' the passage continues, 'no human being would be saved' [Matt. 24:22]. This means that if our Lord God hadn't intervened through the gospel, the pope would have destroyed everything, and the gospel and the sacraments would have been lost together with the Holy Scriptures. Although there were great scandals among the Jews, under the papacy it was worse. For in former times only one people was

---

[261] I.e., the first three of the Ten Commandments.
[262] Cf. Revelation 18.

thrown into confusion, but under the papacy the whole world was unsettled. 'He takes his seat in the temple of God' [II Thess. 2:4]. However, as I have said, the church is better off now than it was then."

Signs of the End of the World
February, 1533   *No. 462*

"The above passage[263] about the calamities of the last days I don't understand to refer to physical punishment, for the text is sure: at its end the world will be very happy, powerful, proud, and secure.[264] You see this now. I hardly have a better sign of the last day than this. Besides, the Word is also held in the greatest contempt. All these things are now happening. Blessed is he who understands them! But hardly anybody perceives them."

Luther's Estimate of Some Opponents
February, 1533   *No. 463*

"The papists and I write against each other in different ways. I enter the fray after careful reflection and in a sufficiently hostile frame of mind. For ten years I battled with the devil and established all my positions, and so I knew that they would stand up. But neither Erasmus[265] nor any of the others took the matters seriously. Only Latomus[266] has written excellently against me. Mark this well: Only Latomus wrote against Luther; all the rest, even Erasmus, were croaking toads."

Erasmus Condemned Out of His Own Mouth
March 2, 1533   *No. 466*

March 2. "Erasmus sticks to his own affairs, that is, to heathen business. He doesn't care about ours, that is, theological affairs. He gathers all the greatest philosophers, kings, and princes and their

---

[263] The passage cited in the previous piece, Matt. 24:21.
[264] Cf. Matt. 24:37, 38.
[265] Desiderius Erasmus. Cf. No. 113, n. 25.
[266] Jacobus Masson (or Latomus), of Louvain, wrote against Luther in 1521, and Luther replied in the same year. Cf. *LW* 32, 133-260.

opinions, words, and deeds. Then he collects the offenses in our teaching and says, like an inexperienced youth, that Christ censures them all—in fact, damns them. Finally he draws his necessary conclusion: If there were a God, he wouldn't tolerate such things. Therefore, he has a God who is called Nemesis, that is, luck or chance. In no other God does he believe.

"In support of this I have two proofs. First, in all his writings there is no statement anywhere about faith in Christ, about victory over sin, etc. Second, he persecutes our cause with choice scurrility and in doing so employs words and ideas which would not occur to a stupid fool, though they are carefully thought out. In defending his own cause, however, he shows his true colors, otherwise he wouldn't always be shielding Epicurus.[267] Here the words apply, 'I will condemn you out of your own mouth, you wicked servant' [Luke 19:22]!"

Do Not Debate with Satan When Alone
Spring, 1533   *No. 469*

"Almost every night when I wake up the devil is there and wants to dispute with me. I have come to this conclusion: When the argument that the Christian is without the law and above the law doesn't help, I instantly chase him away with a fart. The rogue wants to dispute about righteousness although he is himself a knave, for he kicked God out of heaven and crucified his Son. No man should be alone when he opposes Satan. The church and the ministry of the Word were instituted for this purpose, that hands may be joined together and one may help another. If the prayer of one doesn't help, the prayer of another will."

The Church in the Temptations of Christ
Spring, 1533   *No. 471*

"The dignified mother church acquired riches, and afterward the daughter lost her mother. Although the church possesses goods,

---

[267] The Greek philosopher (b. 341 B.C.) who denied divine providence and taught that happiness consists of the undisturbed enjoyment of life. Luther generally cited Epicurus and his adherents as examples of skepticism.

those who are unworthy take them. There is a picture of the church in the temptations of Christ in Matthew 4 [:1-11]. First, the church was tried by poverty and persecution under the Roman emperors. Second, by heresies, for Christ was led not into the temple but [to the pinnacle] above the temple, that is, beyond the Scriptures. Third, by wealth and power under the popes."

Luther held that it was in his body that Christ was led by Satan, but Philip[268] held that it was in his thoughts that all those things had occurred, that it was at a different time that he had climbed the steps of the temple, and that it was then that the thought came to him, "You can let yourself down here without danger," etc.

Difference Between Samson and Julius Caesar
Spring, 1533   *No. 473*

I[269] asked what the difference was between Samson,[270] who had great strength, which he got from the Spirit, and Caius [Julius] Caesar[271] or some other man who was strong in body and mind. To this he [Martin Luther] replied, "The spirit of Samson was the Holy Spirit, who makes holy and who produces actions which are obedient to God and serve him. We can also speak of the Spirit among the heathen; that is, God also acts among them, but this is not sanctifying action. I often wonder about the example of Samson. There must have been a strong forgiveness of sins in his case. Human strength couldn't do what he did."

On the Authorship of the Book of Job
Spring, 1533   *No. 475*

"Job didn't speak the way it is written [in his book], but he thought those things. One doesn't speak that way under temptation. Nevertheless, the things reported actually happened. They

---

[268] Philip Melanchthon. Cf. No. 157, n. 59.
[269] The recorder of this conversation, Veit Dietrich.
[270] Cf. Judges 14–16.
[271] Julius Caesar, Roman general and ruler in the century before Christ.

are like the plot of a story which a writer, like Terence,[272] adopts and to which he adds characters and circumstances. The author wished to paint a picture of patience. It's possible that Solomon himself wrote this book, for the style is not very different from his.[273] At the time of Solomon the story which he undertook to write was old and well known. It was as if I today were to take up the stories of Joseph or Rebekah. The Hebrew poet, whoever he was, saw and wrote about those temptations, as Vergil described Aeneas,[274] led him through all the seas and resting places, and made him a statesman and soldier. Whoever wrote Job, it appears that he was a great theologian."

What Is Involved in a Call to the Ministry
Spring, 1533   *No. 483*

"First of all, this is certain: young people must be brought up to learn the Scriptures. Later they will know that they are to be educated to be pastors. Afterward they will offer their services when some position is unoccupied. That is to say, they will not force their way in but will indicate that they are prepared, in case anybody should ask for them; thus they will know whether they should go. It is like a girl who is trained for marriage; if anybody asks her, she gets married. To force one's way in is to push somebody else out. But to offer one's service is to say, 'I'll be glad to accept if you can use me in this place.' If he is wanted, it is a true call. So Isaiah said, 'Here I am. Send me' [Isa. 6:8]. He went when he heard that a preacher was needed. This ought to be done.

"A young man should find out whether somebody is wanted, and then whether he is wanted. The latter must also be. What is to be said about talents is touched upon in the text that speaks about servants who are called.[275] It is written in Paul, 'If anyone aspires to the office of bishop, do not hinder him, for he desires a noble task' [I Tim. 3:1]. But to force one's way in is to do as

---
[272] Terence was a Roman playwright of the second century B.C.
[273] I.e., not very different from the style of other writings of the Old Testament ascribed to Solomon.
[274] The *Aeneid* by the Roman poet Vergilius Maro. See No. 116, n. 30.
[275] Cf. Luke 19:12-27.

Karlstadt did; during my absence he abandoned his citadel (that is, his pulpit), occupied my pulpit, changed the mass, etc.[276] All this he did on his own authority. So he did also in Orlamünde,[277] and he said he wanted to give the theologians some trouble."

Erasmus Ridicules Matters of Faith
Spring, 1533 *No. 484*

"If I were to cut open Erasmus'[278] heart I would find there nothing but ridicule about the Trinity, about the sacrament, etc. Everything is a laughing matter for him. He doesn't think that God is anything superior to a man or that God can speak beyond man's ability to understand. I know this for certain, for shouldn't I know what is characteristic of the heart of the wicked? Now, every part of the Holy Scriptures preaches faith. But what would faith be if it consisted only of things of reason? Faith is the daily death of the old Adam; but reason is restless—it tempts us continuously, and the devil has the knack of striking at this weakness."

The Revolt and the Prophecy of John Huss
Spring, 1533 *No. 488*

"Alexander III[279] published indulgences and ordered the angels to take away the souls of those who had died on the journey to Rome. John Huss[280] said at the time that this was avarice. He was accordingly summoned to Rome, but he sent his deputies there, and afterward a council was called. So the cause of Huss is also mine. He rebelled against the indulgence for St. Peter's Church,

---

[276] While Luther was absent in the Wartburg Castle in the fall of 1521 and the spring of 1522, Andrew Karlstadt took it upon himself to introduce changes in Wittenberg that confused the people. Cf. *LW* 51, 69-100.
[277] In 1524 Karlstadt introduced even more radical changes in the church in Orlamünde, near Wittenberg, and was expelled on account of them.
[278] Desiderius Erasmus. Cf. No. 113, n. 25.
[279] Alexander V, pope from 1409 to 1410.
[280] John Huss (1369-1415), Bohemian reformer, was burned at the stake during sessions of the Council of Constance. On his prophecies, see Jaroslav Pelikan, *Obedient Rebels* (New York: Harper and Row, 1964), p. 137.

and in the year 1415 he was put to death. His opposition lasted only two years. 'In another hundred years,' he said, 'you will have to pay attention and you won't be able to stop it.'"

Good and Evil Winds Caused by Spirits
Spring, 1533 *No. 489*

When Ignatius[281] wondered at the assertion that Satan could deceive men's eyes, he [Martin Luther] said, "If you don't believe this, behold how mightily the devil can deceive a man's reason, as he deceives Duke George's."[282]

At this point I[283] mentioned the storm which arose in the middle of the night in Nürnberg on February 18, 1533. It raged so furiously that it felled about four thousand trees in the woods near our city[284] and ripped off almost half the roof of the castle. For a mighty wind arose, attended by thunder and lightning, so that men thought the last day had come. The doctor responded, "The devil provokes such storms, but good winds are produced by good angels. Winds are nothing but spirits, either good or evil. The devil sits there and snorts, and so do the angels when the winds are salubrious."

How to Deal with Thoughts that Trouble You
April 6, 1533[285] *No. 491*

"When you are troubled by your thoughts, drive them away in any way you can—if not with some argument, then at least by conversation about something you find delight in."

When somebody objected that nothing great can be accomplished without weighty thoughts he [Martin Luther] replied,

---

[281] Ignatius Perknowsky. Cf. No. 342, n. 156.
[282] Duke George of Albertine Saxony. Cf. No. 275, n. 118.
[283] Veit Dietrich, the recorder of this conversation.
[284] The reporter was a native of Nürnberg; hence "our city." The text reads "forty thousand trees," but in John Aurifaber's variant the more likely number four thousand is given.
[285] Marginal note reads: "At breakfast on Palm Sunday, 1533; that is, April 6, 1533."

"Thoughts must be distinguished. Thoughts of the intellect do not make one sad, but considerations of the will do. They cause us to be vexed or pleased about something, and we have sad and melancholy thoughts when we sigh and complain.

"The intellect is not sad. So when I was writing against the pope I wasn't gloomy, because thoughts of my intellect were being worked out. I wrote with joy at that time, as the preceptor of Lichtenburg[286] said to me at supper, 'I am astonished that you can be so joyful; if I were involved in this business, I would have died.' The pope never hurt me, except at first when Sylvester[287] wrote against me and put this legend in the front of his book: 'master of the sacred palace.' Then I thought, 'Good God, has it come to this that the matter will go before the pope?' However, our Lord God was gracious to me, and the stupid dolt wrote such wretched stuff that I had to laugh. Since then I've never been frightened. Now, at my age, I'm not disturbed by such people. I have nothing to do with them. But the devil looks for me when I am at home in bed, and one or two devils constantly lie in wait for me. They are clever devils. If they can't get anywhere in my heart, they grab my head and torment me there, and when that becomes useless, I'll turn my behind upon them. That's where they belong.

"If I should die in bed, this would be a disgrace and offense to the pope, for our Lord God gives him as much as to understand, 'You should hate Luther, you pope and princes and lords, and yet you are not to do him any harm.' Nothing came of John Huss.[288] I hold that there has been nobody in a thousand years whom the world hated so much as me. I hate the world, too, and I know of nothing in all of life that attracts me any longer. I am quite tired of living. May our Lord God come soon and quickly take me away! Especially may he come with his last day! I shall await him. I shall gladly stretch out my neck so he can strike me to the ground with a thunderclap. Amen."

---

[286] Wolfgang Reissenbusch. See Tappert (ed.), *Luther: Letters of Spiritual Counsel*, p. 272.
[287] Sylvester Prierias (1456-1523), Dominican scholar who originally prepared the charges of heresy against Luther. Cf. *LW* 31, 255.
[288] Cf. No. 488.

Criterion for Worship Is Obedience, Not Beauty
Spring, 1533   *No. 493*

"Hear and obey [Christ]![289] This is the greatest service of God. Nothing else counts. For do what we will, what God has in heaven is better and more beautiful than anything we can do. Otherwise Saul would have delighted him,[290] but God said, 'Your worship is only an annoyance,' although it was a beautiful service. Elsewhere it is written, 'Sacrifice and offering I have not desired, but I wish to be obeyed.'[291] So Jeremiah declares that soldiers engaged in a war say that obedience is victory."[292]

How to Preach on the Annunciation of Mary
March 25, 1533   *No. 494*

On the festival of the Annunciation of Mary in 1533[293] he [Martin Luther] said, "When preaching on this day one should stick to the story, so that we may celebrate the incarnation of Christ, rejoice that we were made his brethren, and be glad that he who fills heaven and earth is in the womb of the maiden. Disputations stand in the way of joy because they bring forth doubts, and these produce sorrow, just as if the girl had not rejoiced until she knew that she was promised in marriage and her doubt vanished. Therefore, I hate Erasmus[294] from the bottom of my heart because he calls into question what ought to be our joy. Bernard[295] filled a whole sermon with praise of the Virgin Mary and in so doing forgot to mention what happened; so highly did he and Anselm[296] esteem Mary. But a Christian puts the questions aside and occupies

---

[289] Word in brackets from variant by John Aurifaber.
[290] Cf. I Sam. 15:22.
[291] Cf. Ps. 40:6-8.
[292] Cf. Jer. 7:23.
[293] Tuesday, March 25, 1533.
[294] Desiderius Erasmus. Cf. No. 113, n. 25.
[295] Bernard of Clairvaux (*ca.* 1091-1153); in *Opera omnia,* ed. J. Mabillon (Paris, 1719), I, 739.
[296] Anselm of Canterbury (1033-1109) is often called the father of medieval scholasticism.

himself with the effects [of the incarnation]. The incarnation, therefore, should be held high. Mary can't be sufficiently praised as a creature, but that the Creator himself comes to us and becomes our ransom—this is the reason for our rejoicing. I don't think the story can be told more simply than it was by Luke. Nobody could have invented the word 'sent.' " [297]

As a Monk Luther Observed Prayers Strictly
Spring, 1533　　　　　　　　　　　　　　　　*No. 495*

"When I was a monk I was unwilling to omit any of the prayers,[298] but when I was busy with public lecturing and writing I often accumulated my appointed prayers for a whole week, or even two or three weeks. Then I would take a Saturday off, or shut myself in for as long as three days without food and drink, until I had said the prescribed prayers. This made my head split, and as a consequence I couldn't close my eyes for five nights, lay sick unto death, and went out of my senses. Even after I had quickly recovered and I tried again to read, my head went 'round and 'round. Thus our Lord God drew me, as if by force, from that torment of prayers. To such an extent had I been captive [to human traditions]![299] Therefore I readily forgive those who can't at once assent to my teaching. You young fellows know nothing about such outrages. What is written applies to you: 'Others have labored and you have entered into their labor' [John 4:38].

"In the Dialogues of St. Gregory[300] there is a story to the effect that he had a very faithful steward who, because he had laid aside three gold coins without telling his brethren about them, was condemned. So it is here. When Christ is away the devil is present and says, 'You must do it to the very last detail.' But Christ overlooks all sins. God gives so that we may be thankful. He never bothers me about my having done wrong in my teaching, but this is unknown to those who were in monasteries a long time. Mün-

---

[297] Cf. Luke 1:26.
[298] Horary prayers, or prayers prescribed for monks at certain hours of the day.
[299] Text in brackets inserted by later hand.
[300] Gregory the Great, *Dialogues*, ed. Edmund G. Gardner (London: P. L. Warner, 1911), Book IV, chap. 55. Cf. No. 51, n. 5.

zer,[301] Oecolampadius,[302] and Zwingli[303] escaped early, but they didn't stand up very long. For the devil can find a person quickly, especially if Christ is not in his heart. The devil leads such a person into the Holy Scriptures without Christ, that is, to the law and to works. So it takes toil and trouble before Christ himself helps again."

Satan and a Christian Debate About Assurance
Spring, 1533   *No. 501*

"Christ wished to humble Peter, for he wasn't content to ask once but asked again and again, 'Peter, do you love me? Feed my sheep[304] and lift them up without the severity of the law. Toward others, however, employ the severity of the law because they are not sheep, for I suffer and do all things for humble sheep.'

"In the light of nature and reason the highest wisdom is the law. When Satan speaks according to the law and says to you in your heart, 'God doesn't want to forgive you,' how will you as a sinner cheer yourself, especially if signs of wrath, like illness, etc., are added?

"[The devil says,] 'Behold, you are weak. How do you know, therefore, that God is gracious to you?' Then the Christian must come and say, 'I have been baptized, and by the sacrament I have been incorporated [in Christ]; moreover, I have the Word.'

"The devil objects: 'This is nothing, for many are called, but few are chosen' [Matt. 22:14].

"Reply: 'They lose what they were baptized for. They don't accept it. They fall away again. They hold on to the law and forget Christ. Therefore, they are not of the elect.' So Duke George,[305] Margrave Joachim,[306] and the bishop of Mainz [307] were

---

[301] For a short time Thomas Münzer had been confessor in a monastery. Cf. No. 291, n. 131.
[302] John Oecolampadius held several ecclesiastical positions before he adopted Reformation views. Cf. No. 94, n. 19.
[303] Huldreich Zwingli was a parish priest when he came to his new understanding of the Christian faith. Cf. No. 5005, n. 35.
[304] Cf. John 21:15-17.
[305] Cf. No. 275, n. 118.
[306] Cf. No. 397, n. 213.
[307] Cardinal Albrecht, archbishop of Mainz. Cf. No. 1362, n. 65.

called and have baptism, the sacrament [of the altar], and Christ the same as we do, but when you get right down to it they rely on their cowls and other works.

"But a Christian remains firmly attached to Christ and says, 'If I'm not good, Peter wasn't either, but Christ is good.' Such are the elect. Others say, 'God is gracious to me because I hope to amend my ways,' but this is only a gallows repentance; the heart isn't in it. Although the wicked sometimes have compunctions (so they call them)—that is, promise themselves that they will be good—they soon depart from the straight path and seek to merit [a reward]. But a Christian says, 'I wish to do as much as I can, but Christ is the bishop of souls. To him will I cling, even if I sin.' It is thus that one has assurance."

Predestination Related to the Grace of God
Spring, 1533 No. 502

"Concerning the statement, 'It depends not upon man's will [or exertion, but upon God's mercy,' Rom. 9:16], I respond: In this passage Paul was doing nothing less than disputing about predestination, but he was speaking against the Jews and the righteousness of the law and he meant to say, 'You must despair, give God the glory, and confess that you didn't start it.' When I was a monk I depended on such willing and exertion, but the longer [I worked at it] the farther away I got. What I have now I have not from exertion but from God. So in this passage Paul was saying everything against presumption, so that we may say, 'Lord, whatever [good] there is in us exists by thy grace.'

"So he also appeals to that saying, 'I will have mercy on whom I have mercy' [Rom. 9:15], that is, 'you won't do it without my forgiveness.' In short, all this is spoken against those who are proud: 'He to whom I give it will have it; you are not to win it from me by your holiness.' What more should he do? He says, 'You are to have it. But when you seek it and insist on having it because of your righteousness, I won't suffer it. I would rather throw everything away—priesthood, kingdom, even my law. But expect grace from me, and you will have it.'"

When somebody inquired whether a person [under the papacy][308] would be saved if he had not embraced this teaching of ours, he [Martin Luther] replied, "I really don't know. God might have had regard for his baptism. This could do it. Even so, I have seen many [monks] die with a crucifix held before their eyes [as was then customary].[309] In spite of everything else, the name [of Christ] proved to be effective on their deathbed."

Christ Taught Only in a Corner of Judaea
Spring, 1533   No. 504

"The authority of Christ when he taught wasn't so great as ours is today. He himself said, 'Greater works than these will you do' [John 14:12]. He is the grain of mustard seed, but we are the bushes [Matt. 13:31, 32]. Accordingly he said, 'They were unwilling to bear me, although I taught in a corner, but you must bear me throughout all the world.' To preach Christ is to offend the flesh, but to preach the flesh is to offend Christ."

It Is God's Way to Speak to Men Through Others
Spring, 1533   No. 505

"At the time of Balaam there were true preachers and there were false. Where the text states that he would first go away and consult God [Num. 23:3], this is to be understood as meaning that he would consult true preachers and that these advised him not to do it.[310] Then Moses explained himself by saying that Balaam no longer went to the right persons (as before)[311] but to Zwingli,[312] etc. Accordingly this expression (namely, that he consulted God) indicates to us that those people esteemed the Word of God highly because they had regard for what was said and not for who was speaking. So it was said of Rebekah[313] that she did not inquire of God but of Shem or some other patriarch. For God always had

---

[308] Text in brackets from several variants.
[309] Text in brackets from several variants.
[310] An early variant reads: "not to undertake anything against God." Cf. WA, TR 1, 229, n. 7.
[311] Cf. Num. 24:1.
[312] Variant by Aurifaber reads: "but to false teachers."
[313] Cf. Gen. 25:22.

certain persons and places in the world. He sent Moses, and when Moses said something they had to concede, 'Not Moses, but God has spoken.'

"After Moses God sent Christ. His teaching is also certain and his person is sure, and so we are not mistaken in concluding, when we hear something from him, that it is God who has said it. For he said from heaven, 'This is my Son, listen to him' [Matt. 17:5]. Afterward, when Christ went away, he sent apostles and instituted sacraments (baptism and the Lord's Supper), so that when these are present and are heard and received we can truly say, 'God says this.' Often when I was troubled by something, Pomeranus[314] or Philip[315] or even my Katy[316] would speak to me, and I was comforted as I realized that God was saying this because a brother was saying it either out of duty or out of love. For God says that we should listen to Christ, but Christ says that we should listen to the apostles.

"This leads the sacramentarians[317] astray. They speak according to their own ideas, but we speak what God says. Before the world existed, God said, 'Let there be a world,' and the world was.[318] So he says here [in the Lord's Supper],[319] 'Let this be my body,' and it is, nor is it prevented by the scoffing of Bullinger,[320] who says that because the body of Christ isn't seen it isn't present. For in the former instance God created visible things but in the latter instance he created invisible, in such fashion as he wished."

One Should Not Pay Too Much Attention to Dreams
Spring, 1533   *No. 508*

"This is where dreams come from. Man's spirit can't rest, for Satan is there even when a man is asleep, though angels are also

---

[314] John Bugenhagen, of Pomerania. Cf. No. 122, n. 36.
[315] Philip Melanchthon. Cf. No. 157, n. 59.
[316] Luther's wife. Cf. No. 49, n. 1.
[317] Cf. No. 314, n. 139.
[318] Cf. Gen. 1:1-31.
[319] Text in brackets from variant by John Aurifaber. In the quotation that follows Luther was paraphrasing I Cor. 11:24.
[320] Henry Bullinger (1504-1575) became the leader of the German Reformed in Switzerland after Huldreich Zwingli's death in 1531.

present. The devil can so frighten me that sweat pours from me in my sleep.

"I don't pay attention to either dreams or signs. I have the Word, and that I let suffice. I don't want an angel to come to me. I wouldn't believe him now anyway, although the time may come when I would desire it in special circumstances. I don't say that dreams and signs are of value at other times, nor do I care, for we already have everything we should have in the Scriptures. Troubled dreams are of the devil, because everything that serves death and terror and murder and lies is the devil's handiwork.

"Satan has often distracted me from prayer and has put such thoughts into my head that I ran away from it. The most severe bouts I have had with him I had when I was in bed at my Katy's[321] side."

Authority of Minister Resides in Office, Not Person
Spring, 1533   No. 512

"From the passage, 'Receive the Holy Spirit. If you forgive,' etc. [John 20:22, 23], some conclude that therefore only those who personally have the Holy Spirit are able to forgive sins. But this isn't the meaning, for Christ gives the Spirit to the public office and not to a private person, as he had just said, 'As the Father has sent me, even so I send you' [John 20:21]. Consequently he was speaking about those who had been called and who had the authority to preach, administer the sacraments, etc. When somebody has the authority to preach he also has the authority to administer the sacraments, for we hold that the sacrament is less important than preaching. On this account, under the papacy none was admitted to the degree of bachelor of theology except priests, and they already had the right to administer sacraments."

Predestination Is an Impenetrable Mystery
Spring, 1533   No. 514

"Paul wasn't discussing predestination[322] with the Jews but was

---
[321] Cf. No. 505, n. 316.
[322] Cf. Rom. 9:15. See also No. 502.

disputing only with those who opposed it and said, 'We are the people of God, we have the fathers, the promises were given to us,' etc. He didn't touch upon predestination except to repudiate the righteousness of the law. Paul said that we should not preach as if we could become good by our works, our fathers, etc. These don't help. The others, those who believe, have it just as good as those who have fathers, etc. God has decreed it so from eternity. Hence Paul attacks only this.

"By grace alone are we saved. God doesn't want to be obligated to anybody. Once we believe, he tells us (and this, too, is by grace), 'Give, and it will be given to you [Luke 6:38]. You are bound to give in any case, whether out of pity for the Turks or some other unfortunates, so you may just as well do it when I command it.' We have no claim on him. So Esau and Jacob also testified to righteousness.[323]

"Otherwise one can't settle the deep questions of theology, but Paul simply argues that it is by grace alone that we are saved. He meant to stick to this. Think what it means that you are not saved by the law, etc., but the Jews have works! Nobody but Christ can solve this. Hence he [Paul] said, 'O the depth [of the riches and wisdom and knowledge of God,' Rom. 11:33]!"

Easy to Have Doubts About the Lord's Supper
Spring, 1533   *No. 515*

"If they[324] can prove to me that the word 'is' is the same in this passage[325] as 'signifies,' I will believe them. They haven't had the temptations I have had about the sacrament. I've often said before about this commotion begun by Karlstadt:[326] I know of no trials

---

[323] Cf. Gen. 24:1–35:29.

[324] The followers of Huldreich Zwingli or those whom Luther liked to call sacramentarians. Cf. No. 314, n. 139. On the subject under discussion, see Regin Prenter, *Spiritus Creator* (Philadelphia: Muhlenberg, 1953), pp. 101-172: C. J. F. Wisloff, *The Gift of Communion: Luther's Controversy with Rome* (Minneapolis: Augsburg, 1964); Hermann Sasse, *This Is My Body: Luther's Contention for the Real Presence* (Minneapolis: Augsburg, 1959).

[325] Cf. I Cor. 11:24.

[326] Andrew Karlstadt was one of the earliest representatives of a left-wing view of the sacrament. Cf. No. 356, n. 172.

of faith which have come from the sects except these two, rebaptism and the sacrament [of the altar], because I recognized that if one wishes to make the relation of the bread to God offensive one can do so."

When our Bohemian[327] interrupted to say that he still had doubts about baptism, he [Martin Luther] replied gently,[328] "When you first came here you were not at the stage which you have now attained. Continue to be patient. Give our Lord God time. Let the trees bloom before they bring forth fruit. Who was I before? I used to worship saints who hadn't even been born! The time hasn't come yet for me to speak otherwise [about baptism], I should now say, but wait and you'll see what the Word of God is and can be."

Christ in Sacrament Because He Is Ubiquitous
Spring, 1533   *No. 517*

"Christ is truly in our hearts. People don't understand that God can do more than create heaven and earth and all things. So, I say, when you hear that God said so, you should ask, 'What's this, if God can do even more?' If he could make the world he could have created more worlds. Why, then, don't I believe that it is God's Word that says, 'This is my body' [I Cor. 11:24]?

"They reply, 'I don't believe because heaven and earth are so constituted that they require space.'

"To this I respond, 'Our Lord God made a world for men and another world for spirits. What if he had added a third world? He could have.' Why, then, do they argue against us?

"According to his divinity Christ is everywhere. So I have written against Zwingli:[329] When I think of God I think of everything as a poppy seed in his eyes, and it is present wherever I am. Christ is God and man in one person. Where I seek God, there

---

[327] Ignatius Perknowsky. Cf. No. 342, n. 156.
[328] A marginal note here reads: "Observe with what moderation he bore this weakness."
[329] Huldreich Zwingli. Cf. No. 5005, n. 35. A typical expression of Luther's insistence on the ubiquity or omnipresence of Christ may be seen in *LW* 37, 56-66.

I'll find him. Accordingly when we think of divinity we must turn our eyes away from time and space because our Lord God and Creator must be beyond space and time and creature."

Temptations in the Monastery and Elsewhere
Spring, 1533   No. 518

"It would be better if I were to overthrow all the articles of faith than yield to the swarming sects [on the Lord's Supper]. I know they are true, and so I'll defend them against everybody. I've heard no argument from men that persuaded me, but the bouts I've engaged in during the night[330] have become much more bitter than those during the day. For my adversaries have only annoyed me, but the devil is able to confront me with arguments. Often he has offered an argument of such weight that I didn't know whether God exists or not. I shall now confess this to you so that you won't believe him. When I was without the Word of God and was thinking about the Turks, the pope, the princes, etc., he came and struck against me with weapons. But when I have taken hold of the Scriptures I have won.

"On the other hand, when the devil gets me off the track he tempts me more than I can say. External temptations only make me proud and arrogant—as you see in my books that I despise my adversaries. I take them for fools. But when the devil comes, he is the lord of the world and confronts me with strong objections, for Christ has set us not against flesh and blood but against the powers of the air.[331] I will defy Duke George[332] and all the lawyers and theologians, but when these knaves, the spirits of iniquity, come, the church must join in the fight. A Christian doesn't inquire about misfortune in this life, for he knows that Christ will help us here. Satan wants the life beyond, which is eternal. We must lose our life here in any case, and it is an insignificant loss.

"Let us therefore fight here against Satan. It is as that cardinal said, 'It wouldn't be good for us to know about the angels' fighting

---
[330] Cf. No. 491.
[331] Cf. Eph. 2:2.
[332] Cf. No. 275, n. 118.

for us because we would give up.' When the Hussites requested both kinds,[333] another cardinal said, 'Let the beasts eat and drink whatever they wish, but let us resist their efforts to reform us.' The devil can't have any other intention than to destroy us because he's the foe of Christ and doesn't worry about his punishment, which he knows is imminent. He is like Duke George, who can't stop until he has killed me. Satan is opposed to the church, and he is worse than Duke George to the extent that he is greater and stronger than him. The best thing we can do, therefore, is to put our fists together and pray. Even if we don't keep the Ten Commandments, but rather sin against them, we have the Lord's Prayer to set over against them. As for me, I fear no fanatic, for I know none who can oppose me with arguments that would put me to confusion. All their arguments I've already heard from the devil—in fact, more weighty ones—but I have overcome them through the Word of God. I don't think Cochlaeus[334] could stand my devil even as long as it takes me to say a single word. He and those like him know nothing about this.

"Let us put our trust in Christ. Whether God wishes to take me hence now or tomorrow, I want to leave this bequest, that I desire to acknowledge Christ as my Lord. This I have not only from the Scriptures but also from experience, for the name of Christ often helped me when nobody else could. So I've had words and deeds in my favor, Scriptures and experience, and God gave me both in abundance. It was hard for me during the temptations, yet it has been good for me.

"I often made confession to Staupitz,[335] not about women but about really serious sins. He said, 'I don't understand you.' This was real consolation! Afterward when I went to another confessor I had the same experience. In short, no confessor wanted to have anything to do with me. Then I thought, 'Nobody has this temptation except you,' and I became as dead as a corpse. Finally, when I was sad and downcast, Staupitz started to talk to me at table and

---

[333] Many followers of John Huss insisted on the distribution of the wine as well as the bread of the sacrament to the laity. Cf. No. 488, n. 280.
[334] John Cochlaeus. Cf. No. 1320, n. 38.
[335] John Staupitz. Cf. No. 94, n. 14.

asked, 'Why are you so sad?' I replied, 'Alas, what am I to do!' Then he said, 'You don't know how necessary this is for you; otherwise nothing good will come of you.' He himself didn't understand [what he said], for he thought I was too learned and that I would become haughty if I remained free from spiritual trials. But I took his words to be like Paul's, 'A thorn was given me in the flesh to keep me from being too elated; my power is made perfect in weakness' [II Cor. 12:7, 9]. Therefore I accepted his words as the voice of the Holy Spirit comforting me.

"I was very pious in the monastery, yet I was sad because I thought God was not gracious to me. I said mass and prayed and hardly saw or heard a woman as long as I was in the order. Now I have other temptations from the devil. He often throws this up to me: 'How many people must you have led astray!' A magistrate and a doctor must be sure that they are called by God, otherwise one is lost. This killed Oecolampadius.[336] One should be glad, therefore, to have a brother who says, 'Brother, do this, for it is the call of your superior or of God (which is a call of faith) or of an equal (which is a call of love).' Nobody realizes how great and how necessary a place is occupied by the calling, by saying to someone, 'Do this.' If a man is fitted for an office and waits to be called, he does well, and Paul says that he desires a noble task [I Tim. 3:1]."

Counsel for a Man Overtaken by Melancholy
Spring, 1533   *No. 522*

I[337] asked him [Martin Luther] about a certain man who, when he had a stomachache for several days and as a consequence had pain in his head and was confused in his thoughts, got the notion and was afraid that he was falling into a state of melancholy. He disclosed his anxiety to me and asked that I notify the doctor, whereupon he [Martin Luther] responded with these words: "When the devil can bring this about, it means that imagination

---

[336] John Oecolampadius. Cf. No. 94, n. 19.
[337] Veit Dietrich, the recorder of this conversation.

has produced the effect. On this account his thoughts ought to be changed. He ought to think about Christ. You should say to him, 'Christ lives. You have been baptized. God is not a God of sadness, death, etc., but the devil is. Christ is a God of joy, and so the Scriptures often say that we should rejoice, be glad, etc. This is Christ. Because you have a gracious God, he won't take you by the throat.'

"A Christian should and must be a cheerful person. If he isn't, the devil is tempting him. I have sometimes been grievously tempted while bathing in my garden, and then I have sung the hymn, 'Let us now praise Christ.' Otherwise I would have been lost then and there. Accordingly, when you notice that you have some such thoughts, say, 'This isn't Christ.' To be sure, he can hear the name of Christ, but it's a lie because Christ says, 'Let not your hearts be troubled [John 14:27]. Trust in me,' etc. This is a command of God: 'Rejoice!'[338] I now preach this, and I also write it, but I haven't as yet learned it. But it happens that we learn as we're tempted. If we were always glad, the devil would befoul us.[339] Christ knows that our hearts are troubled, and it is for this reason that he says and commands, 'Let not your hearts be troubled.'

"Thus we are like the holy fathers in our faith. The weaker we are than the fathers, the greater the victory Christ obtains for us. We are very inexperienced, very weak, and very proud over against the devil; he has a great advantage over us, for our wisdom, power, and holiness are not so great as our fathers' were. But our Lord God wants to put an end to the devil's extreme arrogance. Paul had to say, 'I alone have resisted all the derision of Satan.'"

Luther Worries over Results of His Teaching
Spring, 1533   *No. 525*

"The devil has often troubled me by saying, 'Who commanded you to teach against the monasteries?' Or again, 'Before there was glorious peace, but now you have disturbed it, and who ordered you to do so?'"

---

[338] Cf. Matt. 5:12.
[339] I.e., it would be more than we could bear.

Here I[340] interrupted his talk and said, "You didn't tell anybody either to leave the monastery or to disturb the peace. You only taught that it is in vain that people worship God with the precepts of men.[341] Then those things of which you have now spoken followed of their own accord under God's direction."

But he answered me thus, "Dear fellow, before it would have occurred to me to put it in this light I would have sweated anxiously over it."

Luther Expresses His Thanks for Staupitz
Spring, 1533   *No. 526*

"Our Lord God is our Lord. He calls us and therefore we must preach. Otherwise who would endure the hatred? For contempt and ingratitude have increased greatly. However, my good Staupitz[342] said, 'One must keep one's eyes fixed on that man who is called Christ.' Staupitz is the one who started the teaching [of the gospel in our time]."

Sacramentarians Stress Spirit Without Word
Spring, 1533   *No. 528*

"The devil has no better way to conquer us than by leading us away from the Word and to the Spirit. I have observed this as something remarkable in the sacramentarians[343] that they don't consider the Word but only the things added to the Word, namely, the bread and wine. But one should hold fast to the Word and not concede the Spirit to people apart from the Word. The sacramentarians see only bread and wine (and, in like manner, water) but not the Word. So they see only the serpent held up on a pole in Numbers 21 [:4-9],[344] and not the Word."

---

[340] Veit Dietrich, the recorder of this conversation.
[341] Cf. Matt. 15:9.
[342] John Staupitz. Cf. No. 94, n. 19.
[343] Cf. No. 314, n. 139.
[344] The text mistakenly reads: "Numbers 6."

Human Frailty in the Face of God's Demands
Summer or Fall, 1533   *No. 547*

"God makes fools of both theologians and princes, for he commits to us an impossible task which nobody would undertake if he knew about it beforehand but which he is not allowed to relinquish once it has been committed and undertaken. So it is with the rest of our work. We demand many things, but they aren't done except to a limited degree. We teach many things, but they are learned only to a modest extent. 'Nothing is successful,' as the preacher of Solomon says [Eccles. 1:1, 2].

"Why does God act so? Because he alone is wise and powerful. Because if our suggestions and ideas were carried out we would become presumptuous and would claim wisdom and power for ourselves. Because we surround the glory of wisdom and power with the defects which belong to our nature. We want to set things straight and make everything right. To this God says, 'Well, then, go ahead! Be clever and do a good job! Be a preacher and make the people godly! Be a lord and mend the people's ways! Get to it at once!'

"What a retrogression would occur! And the conclusion would be: 'Vanity of vanities' and 'Let wisdom be attributed to God alone' [Eccles: 1:2; 2:26]. We are fools and wretched bunglers in all we do and attempt."

Children Should Be Baptized on God's Command
Summer or Fall, 1533   *No. 549*

"You say you don't baptize children because they don't believe. Why do you preach the Word to adults who don't believe, unless perhaps in the hope that they may believe? You do it on the strength of God's command alone. For if you baptize me because I say I believe, then you baptize on account of me and in my name. Therefore, since you don't know whether I believe or don't believe, you do it only because of God's command. It isn't necessary to exclude children, since as a rule you baptize all, whether they believe or not.

"It would be a terrible thing if I were baptized on the strength of my confession. What would you do if you learned privately that a man who publicly desired baptism or the sacrament [of the altar] was an unbeliever? You couldn't deny it to him, and yet you would know that he is without faith. So Christ offered [the sacrament] to Judas.[345] Therefore, anybody at all should be baptized unless he has been publicly convicted of a crime, and let his faith and salvation be committed to God's keeping."

Good and Evil Are Used and Misused
Summer or Fall, 1533   No. 566

"See whether this is true: God uses all evil for good, but man and the devil use all good for evil. God drives man to marriage by means of sensual desire. Otherwise, if it were not for love, who would get married? Afterward man's appetite is curbed somewhat so that he doesn't commit adultery with other women.

"God snatches man by means of ambition to become a magistrate. Otherwise who would seek this office? After a while his ambition is kept within the bounds of his authority, he doesn't seek what belongs to others, and he doesn't injure his own people, but there must be an inclination and a desire there.

"God compels man to seek a better living by means of greed. Otherwise who would do anything if he wished for nothing or could keep none of his possessions? In a little while man's greed, too, is kept within limits.

"God drives man to faith by means of fear and despair. Except for pride and envy, which are simply devilish, God uses these evils for good by antiperistasis,[346] that is, he does not use the subjects in whom these qualities exist but he uses the objects that are persecuted by them. For so God troubles the saints through the devil and his followers. On the other hand, the devil uses God himself and all good things for evil: chastity and celibacy for hypocrisy, humility for pride, love for sects and sedition, poverty for luxury and idleness."

---

[345] It was often speculated, for want of contrary evidence in the New Testament, that Judas participated in the Last Supper.
[346] A word of Greek origin meaning the principle according to which opposition strengthens what is opposed.

Ordination to the Priesthood and to the Ministry
Summer or Fall, 1533 — No. 574

"Orders in the church were civil positions which were taken over and made into spiritual offices. Under the papacy, priests were called only to offer sacrifices. After every call by a bishop, a new call was therefore needed for preaching. Now it is asked, 'I was called to offer sacrifices and I no longer sacrifice, but I preach. This is as if I had been called to be a cobbler and was made king. The question is asked, first, whether my present call is proper. Second, do those who offer a sacrifice and make a wrong use of it (it was instituted for the church and not for the one who offers the sacrifice, but the papists usurp it for private use) have the true sacrament?'

"Here is a definition: A minister is one who is placed in the church for the preaching of the Word and the administration of the sacraments. But I was called to sacrifice, which is impious. Therefore I am not a true minister. To one or the other [of these questions] one can reply that the doctorate conferred general authority and that I would have been allowed to preach. Certainly this is the solution of one question or the other.

"I take the case of a minister who is quite a scoundrel, and even an epicurean,[347] and who believes that he administers nothing but bread and wine, although the entire church believes that it is body and blood. What should be done in this case? I answer: The mouth is deceived, but faith is not deceived. Nevertheless, if the minister should say the words [of institution] so that the church hears them, it is the unbelieving priest who is in peril and not the church which believes the words and receives what the words say and faith relies upon, so long as there is no public preaching against the sacrament, as there is today among the sacramentarians.[348] For where a church is taught that there is only bread and where it may be that there are one, two, or three persons who believe, the people don't receive the body of Christ. Only the mouth is deceived, but faith is not deceived. Faith doesn't sin. But if only one person is unbelieving, this doesn't take anything away from the sacrament.

---
[347] I.e., a skeptic or unbeliever. Cf. No. 466, n. 267.
[348] Cf. No. 314, n. 139.

For Christ established the sacrament on himself and not on the person of the minister. It rests on the Word. Accordingly, when there is a confession of the Word, no matter what kind of knave the minister may be, this detracts not at all from the sacrament. The reason is that a scoundrel, too, swears by the name of the Lord, and it is the true name of the Lord, for unless it is the true name of the Lord he commits no sin. God's name doesn't become the devil's name even when I sin, but I sin for the very reason that it is the true name of God. The pope also misuses the Word. One must assert the substance, and abuse doesn't remove it. The sacramentarians get rid of the substance and have nothing but bread and wine.

"I solve it this way. The Antichrist takes his seat in the temple of God [II Thess. 2:4], and the temple of God is the seat of the devil. These are times of stress, as he [the apostle] says [II Tim. 3:1]. Who can bring these things into harmony: that the devil should sit on the very throne of God and yet the throne should be said to remain the throne of God? Therefore, the temple of God continues to exist under the papacy; that is, the papacy will have the upper hand. The question is now asked, 'Inasmuch as I was made a priest under the dominion of the pope, am I still a priest of God?' I answer: Of course! Although I was a member of the Antichrist, I remained in the church, just as the pope remains in the church because he sits in the temple of God. That is, he has had the sacraments, the Bible, and the keys,[349] although he has at the same time opposed the temple of God. So Paul called him the adversary[350] who was to be in the temple of God and was to rule the church of Christ. It is on this account that Paul said, 'There will come times of stress' [II Tim. 3:1]. The pope has used not only the sacraments but all things against the church. In summary, one must arrive at the conclusion that one says, 'I haven't instituted the sacrament, but God has.' Otherwise there is no solution. One must say 'God,' and then everything will be right. The pope tosses people

---

[349] The power of keys, or the authority to absolve, preach, and administer sacraments.

[350] Cf. II Thess. 2:4. This word and the rest of the sentence are in Greek.

into the church with improper ordination. By antiperistasis[351] one might wish to resist this, and yet it is accomplished, and he introduces poor priests into the ministry. Pulpits and baptismal fonts are already there, and the pope tosses men into these. Hence the calling is legitimate."

Adoration and Service Related to Law and Gospel
Summer or Fall, 1533   No. 575

"First of all, adoration is of two kinds, true and false. Second, true adoration is of two kinds. On the one hand, it is external, as in bending the knee, bowing, uncovering the head, etc. On the other hand, it is internal, as in acknowledging the benefits of God, giving thanks, believing, etc. To serve, however, is to do something. So one adores with one's face turned toward the Lord, but when one serves [a neighbor] one's back is turned toward the Lord. Adoration [is related to] the gospel, and service [is related to] the law."

In His Practice the Physician Needs Forgiveness
Summer or Fall, 1533   No. 577

I[352] argued in this fashion against medicine. Major premise:[353] He who practices an uncertain art is imprudent. Minor premise: All medicine is uncertain.[354] Conclusion: All physicians are imprudent. I prove the minor premise (that all medicine is uncertain) by saying: First, our bodies are subject to the devil; he can alter and weaken them by his breath. Second, created things are also subject to Satan, and they can infect [our bodies] as if they were poison. Afterward the physician comes, gives the sick man something, and so the patient dies. This is imprudence and impiety.

[Martin Luther] replied, "It's the devil who kills, not the physician, although it is the physician who administers the medicine.

---

[351] Cf. No. 566, n. 346.
[352] Veit Dietrich, the recorder of this conversation.
[353] Major and minor premises are here interchanged to conform with the rules of logic and with some early variants.
[354] That is, medicine is not a precise science.

Food can spoil on the table, but it isn't the cook who therefore kills the man who eats.

"But what is to be said in answer to all this? Like the study of law, medicine is lacking in general rules and is on this account uncertain. When a physician visits a sick person, doesn't diagnose the illness well, prescribes a drug, and this kills the patient, the physician is certainly the author of his death and is guilty of manslaughter. Nor is it an excuse that, insofar as it was possible, he did with all diligence whatever he was able to do. I reply: It isn't possible for the physician to be excused except through the forgiveness of sins. He must go to this for help. Otherwise, if he acts by his own righteousness, he is of the devil. The same can be applied to lawyers. Only equity[355] can excuse them—or forgiveness of sins, as the theologian calls it. Otherwise it isn't possible for them to survive, for it's impossible to reach a mathematical point."

Lawyers, Theologians, and Natural Law
Summer or Fall, 1533   No. 581

"Lawyers don't properly define the natural law that is common to men and beasts, for it's necessary to distinguish between man as lord and the other animals, and a more excellent quality must be attributed to man. Accordingly the lawyers would express it better if they said that in one case natural law is brutish and in the other case it is rational. Besides, there is no law in the animal but only in man, and therefore they should not call it natural law, for law is what ought to happen. Five and three ought not to be eight but are eight.

"It is also improper to say that natural law is in the animal because it protects itself, for the animal does this of its own accord and because it is its nature to do so. Acts are therefore characteristic of animals, and not law, which exists only in man. To beget and to feed are acts and not laws. There has to be a 'must' in every law. One may not say to a sow, 'You must eat,' for it eats without being bidden. Properly speaking, therefore, lawyers have no natural law but only civil law, which flows out of human reason. Laws

---
[355] Cf. No. 315, n. 140.

are not things that are about to happen [of their own accord]. An apple tree bears fruit without my telling it to. In theology, however, natural law is not what happens but what ought to happen, while lawyers apply the term to what happens and not to what ought to happen or is demanded. Besides, if natural law is attributed to man, as lawyers hold, everything will be mixed up."

It Is Easier, Yet Harder, to Believe Than Formerly
Summer or Fall, 1533   No. 582

"In the church nobody can be absolved unless he promises to amend his life. Absolution consists, first, of belief in Christ and, second, of amendment of life. The sins which I confess are that I do not pray as often as I should, that I do not thank God as much as I ought, that I sometimes get angry and curse Duke George,[356] etc. Before our time confession was wretched torment. In contrast, what a noble life is ours now!

"I used to be a poor wretch, but now you have it good. Unless you acknowledge this, the devil will some day make you regret it. Now we can't even believe the man Jesus Christ, though I used to be able to believe all that rubbish. Flail away and slay us for being unwilling to believe that good man! Oh, I would be hurt if I were God!

"I used to believe everything about the pope and the monks. Now I can't or won't believe what Christ says. This is an unpleasant fact. We'll put it by until the last day."

Church Fathers to Be Honored for Their Faith
Summer or Fall, 1533   No. 584

"Although the fathers were often wrong, they ought nevertheless to be honored on account of their testimony to faith. So I venerate Jerome[357] and Gregory[358] and others inasmuch as one can sense [from their writings],[359] in spite of everything else, that they

---

[356] Cf. No. 275, n. 118.
[357] Cf. No. 51, n. 2.
[358] Cf. No. 51, n. 5.
[359] Text in brackets from variant by John Aurifaber.

believed as we do, as the church from the beginning believed, and as we believe. So Bernard[360] was magnificent when he taught and preached. However, when he engaged in disputation he assailed what he had before preached. Consequently the fathers aren't worth much for controversy, but on account of their testimony to faith they ought all to be honored. Bernard was superior to all the doctors in the church when he preached, but he became quite a different man in his disputations, for then he attributed too much to law and to free will. To dispute in the church is therefore bad."

God Appears to Be Too Severe and Too Lenient
Summer or Fall, 1533 No. 587

"Our Lord God is always in the wrong, no matter what he does. He condemned Adam for disobedience when he ate of the fruit of the tree.[361] Reason considers only the object of obedience, and so God is said to have gone too far. On the other hand, God freely forgives all sins, even the crucifixion of his Son, provided men believe, and this is also regarded as going too far. Who can bring these two into harmony—the greatest severity and the greatest liberty and indulgence (as it seems to reason)? Therefore it is said, 'Become like children' [Matt. 18:3]."

Devil Upsets Distinction Between Law and Gospel
Summer or Fall, 1533 No. 590

"In a conflict with the devil it isn't enough to say, 'This is the Word of God,' for it is the devil's greatest [trick] to take away one's weapon when fear suddenly strikes. He has done this to me. He knows that in my heart I am constantly praying, 'Our Father,' etc., but he often harasses me about my not praying. The devil is the kind of spirit who won't leave the weapon in a person's hand if our Lord God steps out even for a moment. Accordingly one must pray constantly, 'Father, help,' etc. Nobody should fight with the devil unless he first prays, 'Our Father.' It is a remarkable thing.

---
[360] Cf. No. 494, n. 295.
[361] Cf. Gen. 3:17.

He is hostile to us. We don't know a hundredth part of what he knows. He tempted Abraham, David, etc., and he knows how to get the upper hand. Judas was not tempted in his life, and so when his hour came he went ahead with self-assurance but without knowing what was before him.[362] We, who are at odds with the devil, know by God's grace how to resist him.

"It's the supreme art of the devil that he can make the law out of the gospel. If I can hold on to the distinction between law and gospel, I can say to him any and every time that he should kiss my backside. Even if I sinned I would say, 'Should I deny the gospel on this account?' It hasn't come to that yet. Once I debate about what I have done and left undone, I am finished. But if I reply on the basis of the gospel, 'The forgiveness of sins covers it all,' I have won. On the other hand, if the devil gets me involved in what I have done and left undone, he has won, unless God helps and says, 'Indeed! Even if you had not done anything, you would still have to be saved by forgiveness, for you have been baptized, communicated, etc.' But if I don't get this [help from God], it will be as it was in the case of Dr. Krause,[363] in Halle, who said, 'Alas, Christ accuses me.' There was the 'doing something.' If God had helped, he would have said, 'If you've done something, you've done it.' ('So you are mine,' says the devil.) It hasn't come to that yet, for above 'doing' is 'believing.' But before one gets to believe, one is done for.

"So don't be too daring. The distinction between law and gospel will do it. The devil turns the Word upside down. If one sticks to the law, one is lost. A good conscience won't set one free, but the distinction [between law and gospel] will. So you should say, 'The Word is twofold, on the one hand terrifying and on the other hand comforting.' Here Satan objects, 'But God says you are damned because you don't keep the law.' I respond, 'God also says that I shall live.' His mercy is greater than sin, and life is stronger than death. Hence if I have left this or that undone, our Lord God

---

[362] Cf. Matt. 26:47-50.
[363] When the Reformation had first been introduced in Halle, Saxony, John Krause, counselor of Archbishop Albrecht of Mainz, was inclined to favor it. Afterward he supported Albrecht in its suppression, whereupon he became troubled in conscience and committed suicide. Cf. *LW* 26, 195.

will tread it under foot with his grace. But who can get so far in the present temptation? It was a bitter experience even for Christ himself[364] [and it would be for us], except that he has promised that he won't let us be tempted beyond our strength [I Cor. 10:13]. However, he often lets things go so far that one can't keep up."

Some Observations About the Ministry
Summer or Fall, 1533   No. 600

"Christ gave the keys[365] to the church for the consolation of men, and he entrusts the keys to ministers or to Christians.

"Karlstadt[366] inferred from Paul's statement — that a bishop should be the husband of one wife [Titus 1:6]—that it isn't possible to be a bishop unless one has a wife.

"Osiander[367] holds this to be a necessary inference: God has given the keys, and therefore we are constrained to ask for them, but only ministers are so constrained, for it is written, 'Give to the brother as often as he asks.'[368] It looks as if papal rule is to be reintroduced. He wants to be free from the ministry and to compel the brother!"

Interpretation of the Betrayal of Christ by Judas
Summer or Fall, 1533   No. 604

"I wonder that nothing is written [in the Scriptures] about Judas' knavery against Christ.[369] I think he did this mostly with his tongue, as Christ complained about him in the psalm [41:6-9]. He must have gone to the Pharisees and spoken crossly about Christ,

---

[364] Cf. Matt. 26:36-46. On the subject under discussion, see Thomas M. McDonough, *The Law and the Gospel in Luther* (Oxford: University Press, 1963).
[365] Cf. No. 574, n. 349. See *The Keys* (1530). LW 40, 321-377.
[366] Andrew Karlstadt in his *Supra coelibatu, monachatu et viduitate* (1521). Cf. Hermann Barge, *Andreas Bodenstein von Karlstadt* (2 vols.; Leipzig, 1905), I, 275-277.
[367] Andrew Osiander (1498-1552) was a quarrelsome follower of Luther. On the matter at hand see Wilhelm Möller, *Andreas Osiander* (Elberfeld: Friderichs, 1870), pp. 174-184.
[368] Cf. Matt. 18:21-22.
[369] Cf. Matt. 26:47-50; John 13:21-30; 18:2-5.

saying, 'I baptize, too, but I see it's different,' etc. He was also a thief[370] and hoped to get a large sum from Christ. He was like Witzel[371] and Crotus,[372] who came to us at the beginning in the hope of getting something big. Judas must also have been a wicked man, because it is never without cause that the man [Jesus Christ] is as hostile to anybody as he was in Psalm 41. He must have laid in wait for Jesus. Otherwise, if he hadn't been so wicked, our Lord God would have forgiven him, as he did Peter, who also fell;[373] but it was on account of weakness that Peter couldn't stand."

There Is Much to Be Learned from Judas
Summer or Fall, 1533 No. 605

"Judas is as important in the company of the apostles as any other three of the apostles, and he throws light on countless arguments, like the article of justification against the Donatists, who said that one could baptize only those who had the Holy Spirit. There are many proofs that Judas was an apostle, that is, one of the Twelve. Accordingly what he did in his office was right, but when he was a thief he sinned. One must distinguish him from his office, for Christ did not commit theft to him but an office.

"Judas also throws light on the reproach that is heaped on us: 'There are many wicked people among you.' Very well! And Judas was an apostle! Undoubtedly he behaved better than the others; nobody charged him with making any mistakes at table. Judas was really the pope, therefore, for the pope also snatched the money box.[374] He appeared to confess Christ, but actually he had nothing but the name [of Christian]. He was called Judas, but in actual fact he was Iscariot." [375]

---

[370] Cf. John 12:6.
[371] George Witzel (1501-1573) was attracted to Luther's teaching but after 1531 turned against the Reformer under the influence of Desiderius Erasmus and a study of the church fathers.
[372] Crotus Rubeanus (*ca.* 1480-1539), humanist in Erfurt, veered from initial enthusiasm for Luther to opposition.
[373] Cf. Matt. 26:69-75; John 18:15-18, 25-27.
[374] Cf. John 13:29.
[375] Cf. John 6:71.

How Solomon Came to Have So Many Wives
Summer or Fall, 1533   *No. 611*

"Abraham must have been a man of the greatest integrity, for he was unwilling to take another wife except for the urging and consent of Sarah.[376] He had the right to take a virgin who was a freewoman, but he abstained from his right and took a maidservant, and one whom his wife chose. With respect to the law that is in Moses concerning the raising up of a brother's seed,[377] I think our Lord God wished to provide for that sex. Most of the males perished in war and other dangers, but the females were spared such dangers and survived. Consequently our Lord God wished to give them an advantage and made this provision for them, and if a man was unwilling to cohabit with his deceased brother's wife, he nevertheless supported her. It's from this, I think, that Solomon came to have so many wives."[378]

Father Criticizes Luther for Becoming Monk
Fall, 1533   *No. 623*

He [Martin Luther] became a monk against the will of his father. When he celebrated his first mass and asked his father why he was angry about the step he took, the father replied reproachfully, "Don't you know that it's written, Honor your father and your mother" [Exod. 20:12]? When he excused himself by saying that he was so frightened by a storm that he was compelled to become a monk, his father answered, "Just so it wasn't a phantom you saw!" Afterward it was his father who advised him to get married.

He [Martin Luther] was born in Eisleben and is a native of the district of Möhra, near Eisenach. His grandfather was Henricus Luder, and his father was Johannes Luder.

---

[376] Cf. Gen. 16:1-4.
[377] Cf. Deut. 25:5-10.
[378] Cf. I Kings 11:3.

The Central Issue Is Doctrine, Not Life

Fall, 1533   *No. 624*

"Doctrine and life must be distinguished. Life is bad among us, as it is among the papists, but we don't fight about life and condemn the papists on that account. Wycliffe[379] and Huss[380] didn't know this and attacked [the papacy] for its life. I don't scold myself into becoming good, but I fight over the Word and whether our adversaries teach it in its purity. That doctrine should be attacked—this has never before happened. This is my calling. Others have censured only life, but to treat doctrine is to strike at the most sensitive point, for surely the government and the ministry of the papists are bad. Once we've asserted this, it's easy to say and declare that the life is also bad.

"When the Word remains pure, then the life (even if there is something lacking in it) can be molded properly. Everything depends on the Word, and the pope has abolished the Word and created another one. With this I have won, and I have won nothing else than that I teach aright. Although we are better morally, this isn't anything to fight about. It's the teaching that breaks the pope's neck. Therefore Daniel[381] pictured the pope rightly when he stated that there will be a kingdom in which the king will act according to his will, that he will pay attention to neither civil nor spiritual matters but will simply say, 'I want that,' without offering any reason, even a natural one. When you ask, 'Is the papacy established by natural, divine, or human right?' you get the answer, 'No, it is a worship of the will.' [382] So the pope must say, 'Nobody has commanded us.' It is simply a religion of free will. Daniel calls God a god of '*maozim*' [383]—I almost said 'masses.'"

---

[379] John Wycliffe (*ca.* 1324-1384) was a medieval English theologian who became a sharp critic of the secularized papacy and church.
[380] Cf. No. 488, n. 280.
[381] Cf. Dan. 11:36.
[382] Greek: *ethelothrēskeia*.
[383] Hebrew for "forces" or "fortresses" in Dan. 11:38.

Heretics Provoke Theologian to Search Scriptures
Fall, 1533　　　　　　　　　　　　　　　　　　*No. 626*

"Anybody who wishes to be a theologian must have a fair mastery of the Scriptures, so that he may have an explanation for whatever can be alleged against any passage. That is to say, he must distinguish between law and gospel. If I were able to do this perfectly I would never again be sad. Whoever apprehends this has won.

"Whatever is Scripture is either law or gospel. One of the two must triumph: the law leads to despair, the gospel leads to salvation. I learn more about this every day, and Duke George[384] could too. The gospel is life. The pope drove me to this; he opened my eyes to it. It is as Augustine[385] said to himself: the heretics provoke us to search the Scriptures. Otherwise nobody would think about them."

The World Is Like a Drunken Peasant
Fall, 1533　　　　　　　　　　　　　　　　　　*No. 630*

"The world is like a drunken peasant. If you lift him into the saddle on one side, he will fall off on the other side. One can't help him, no matter how one tries. He wants to be the devil's."

A Question About Making the Miracles Known
Fall, 1533　　　　　　　　　　　　　　　　　　*No. 640*

When I[386] asked, with reference to a passage,[387] whether those sinned who had been forbidden by Christ to say anything and nevertheless made the miracles public, he [Martin Luther] replied, "When Christ spoke outside of his office he spoke as God, but when he spoke according to his office he spoke as a man and a servant.

---

[384] Cf. No. 275, n. 118. The editor of WA, TR (1, 297, n. 6) conjectures that an additional but obscure insertion in the text at this point refers to Huldreich Zwingli. Since Zwingli had died two years earlier, this reading seems unlikely.
[385] Augustine (cf. No. 51, n. 4), *Expositions on the Book of Psalms*, LV, 23.
[386] Veit Dietrich, the recorder of this conversation.
[387] Cf. Mark 1:44.

When he spoke about his person outside of his office he said, 'All that the Father has is mine' [John 16:15], 'Believe in God, believe also in me' [John 14:1]. But when he spoke according to his office and not about his person, he said, 'I have come to serve' [Matt. 20:28]. Thus it is according to his office that he forbids making the miracles public. Therefore they did well to preach the miracles which he showed them, and he also did well to prohibit this. This is evident from the fact that the evangelist boasts about them. In the whole gospel [of John] one can see that Christ wishes to glorify not himself but the Father. He [John] wrote this as an example for us preachers."

The Defects of Speculative or Mystical Theology
Fall, 1533   *No. 644*

"The speculative learning of the theologians is altogether worthless. I have read Bonaventure[388] on this, and he almost drove me mad because I desired to experience the union of God with my soul (about which he babbles) through a union of intellect and will. Such theologians are nothing but fanatics. This is the true speculative theology (and it's practical too): Believe in Christ and do what you ought. Likewise, the mystical theology of Dionysius[389] is nothing but trumpery, and Plato[390] prattles that everything is non-being and everything is being, and he leaves it at that. This is what mystical theology declares: Abandon your intellect and senses and rise up above being and non-being.

"Is being in such shadows? God is everything," etc.

Meaning of Words Used in the Lord's Supper
Fall, 1533   *No. 649*

"The question is asked, with reference to the words in the

---

[388] Bonaventure (1221-1274) was a Franciscan whose mystical and dialectical writings occupy an important place in the history of medieval thought.
[389] Dionysius the Areopagite was converted to Christianity by St. Paul, and it became customary in the Middle Ages to ascribe to him a number of mystical writings which probably originated in the fifth or sixth century.
[390] Cf. No. 257.

Lord's Supper, whether 'is given' [391] is to be understood as a present giving, when the sacrament is distributed, or as a [past] giving on the cross. I answer: I prefer that it be taken as a present giving. However, it can also be taken as a giving on the cross. This isn't prevented by the fact that Christ spoke in the present tense, 'which is given for you,' when he ought to have said, 'which will be given,' for Christ is the same yesterday and today [Heb. 13:8]. 'I am the one who does it,' he says, 'and nobody else.' Accordingly I prefer that 'is given' be understood as signifying the use of what has been done [on the cross]."

A Defense of the Baptism of Infants

Fall, 1533   *No. 650*

"The church has baptized infants for a thousand years, and God has given the Holy Spirit to those who have been baptized as infants. Moreover, this conclusion is valid *a posteriori*, for Peter also infers this in Acts 10 [:44-47], 'We have preached Christ among the Gentiles, and God gave his testimony by the Holy Spirit,' etc. This is an argument from the act, or *a posteriori*. God gave his blessing to the Gentiles without the law, and therefore they are without the law.

"Second, for more than a thousand years the church has baptized infants. Moreover, because the church never existed except among the baptized, and it was necessary that the church always exist, therefore infant baptism is true baptism. So I argue *a priori* that Christ commanded that all nations be taught and baptized,[392] and this included children. Again, it isn't the minister as a person who baptizes, but it's Christ who baptizes. Now, if an infant is baptized by Christ, how can I take this away and say that he isn't baptized?

"The pope unwittingly kept baptism and the [sacrament of the] altar, and through the pope's priests, as through men who were drowsy and drunk, God gave the sacraments. The Anabap-

---

[391] Cf. I Cor. 11:23.
[392] Cf. Matt. 28:19.

tists[393] and Waldensians[394] rest the sacraments on the faith of the person, and therefore they reject the baptism of infants, arguing that one ought first to teach and only afterward to baptize.[395] I respond: There Christ spoke not of the institution but of the effect [of baptism]. If I should hold that the baptism of children is without effect, it doesn't follow that they should be rebaptized when they grow up and believe, for if some at Mount [Sinai] hadn't believed in the law[396] (whether or not they believed in God), would it have been necessary to make a law again after they had come to believe? It's one thing to have the effect of a work and it's another to have the work. Everything depends on distinguishing between the work of God and the work of men. The work of God is unchangeable."

---

[393] Luther often used this term loosely, but here he had in mind those who practiced rebaptism.
[394] Religious dissenters in late medieval France and Italy, the Waldensians established connections with the Protestant Reformers in the sixteenth century. They practiced infant baptism, in spite of Luther's lumping them together with Anabaptists, but tended to be Donatistic. Cf. No. 2864b, n. 19.
[395] Cf. Mark 16:16.
[396] Cf. Exod. 19:17–20:17.

TABLE TALK RECORDED BY GEORGE RÖRER

1531-1535

INTRODUCTION

The few pieces numbered 657 to 684 in WA, TR 1 fall in the early years of the 1530's. When Ernst Kroker edited these notes he believed that they had been taken at Luther's table by Nicholas Medler (1502-1551), who had matriculated at Wittenberg in 1522 and after teaching for a few years had returned to study theology from 1531 to 1536. During these years he was at Luther's table often and was therefore in a position to have recorded the conversations in question. Investigations of Albert Freitag later persuaded Kroker that George Rörer rather than Nicholas Medler was responsible for these notes.[1]

Rörer, a Bavarian, had been born in 1492. After studying first in the university in Leipzig and then in Wittenberg, in 1525 he was made deacon in the city church of Wittenberg. He demonstrated great skill and faithfulness in taking shorthand notes of Luther's public lectures and sermons, and the Reformer also used him for private dictation. In 1537 the elector of Saxony freed Rörer from other duties, and he now devoted much of his time and strength to the commission for revising Luther's German translation of the Bible, of which commission he was secretary. After Luther's death Rörer went to Jena. He was called to Copenhagen in 1551 and then back to Jena in 1553. There he remained as librarian in the university library until his death in 1557. His loyalty to Luther is reflected in the work he did on both the Wittenberg and the Jena editions of Luther's works.

Rörer is mentioned again and again in the Table Talk as a guest in Luther's home. Because of his skill in taking shorthand notes it is not surprising that he, too, recorded what Luther said at table. However, of the many notes he took only these few can be attributed to him with a measure of assurance.

---

[1] See Kroker's acknowledgment and his reference to the pertinent literature in WA, TR 6, xvi-xviii.

TABLE TALK RECORDED BY GEORGE RÖRER

Ordination and the Administration of Sacraments
Early in the year 1535   No. 659

"1. Men are not ordained in order to make or produce anything but to administer what they find in the church, for they do not produce or make baptism or the Word but are to give and administer these.

"2. Baptism is water and the Word. How? Does the minister make it so? No, but because it's Christ's institution. Bread and wine also become the body of Christ because Christ so ordained.

"3. They [papal priests] haughtily arrogate to themselves the power to consecrate [and make the sacrament],[1] a power which neither saints, nor angels, nor Mary had and which the entire assembly of laymen does not boast of having had in primitive times.

"4. Rather, where the Word (which is the most important thing) is, there is the kingdom of God. Consequently all things are there: church, Christ, sacraments, ordination. So Christ said, 'Go and teach all nations to observe all I have commanded you' [Matt. 28:19, 20], namely, you who are to be ordained. Through the doctors he ordered the nations to observe his commandments. Moreover, he commanded them to take and eat [Matt. 26:26]. So Paul delivered this to the Corinthians and ordered suitable men to teach what had been delivered to them.[2] Note carefully that where it's conceded that the church and the Word exist, there it's conceded that the whole Christ exists and not merely some partial thing or part of Christ.

"The church can be excused thus [with respect to administering the Lord's Supper in one kind]:[3] Just as a person who desires

---

[1] Text in brackets from variant by John Aurifaber.
[2] Cf. I Cor. 1:1, 23-26.
[3] Text in brackets from variant by John Aurifaber.

baptism, but dies beforehand, is baptized in his faith at the time of death instead of with water, although we would otherwise baptize all unto death, so those who desire both kinds but can't get them are like persons unknowingly held in captivity who nevertheless are communicated in both kinds by faith. God could also preserve his own in other ways, unknown to us, as long as there remains in them the knowledge and certain faith that it is according to Christ's institution that his true body and blood are in the sacrament. Then they are communicated in this faith, and no sin can harm them unto damnation because they were deceived and uninformed, doing what they did unknowingly. Accordingly they are not damned if by chance the priest shows only the bread, for faith in Christ's institution swallows up everything. That people have kept this faith is evident from that hymn, 'With his flesh and his blood,' etc.[4] At the same time this hymn shows that both kinds were once in use among the laity. I'll leave it at that, lest they [the papists] prohibit this hymn, though it comes from their church and was not composed by Luther."

Children Are Examples of Guilelessness
April 5, 1533 *No. 660*

I[5] told him [Martin Luther] on April 5, 1533, that my daughter Anastasia, who was then five years old, often spoke with the greatest confidence about Christ, the angels, heavenly joys, etc. I once said to her, "Oh, if one could but believe such things!" and she asked with a certain childlike seriousness whether I didn't believe them. He [Martin Luther] replied that there is a remarkable innocence in children, and therefore Christ has set them before us as our teachers;[6] they know no sin of envy, avarice, unbelief, etc., and take an apple for a gold piece. Hence Peter wrote [I Pet. 2:2] that newborn babes long for nothing but [the pure spiritual milk], etc.

---

[4] From the first stanza of the hymn, "*Gott sey gelobet und gebenedeiet.*" See Philipp Wackernagel, *Das deutsche Kirchenlied* (5 vols.; Leipzig, 1864-1877), V, 949.

[5] The recorder of this conversation, probably George Rörer.

[6] Cf. Matt. 18:3.

How Adam Must Have Talked to Cain
Early in the 1530's No. 663

"'Why has your countenance fallen?' [Gen. 4:6]. Paul expressed the same thing when he said, 'Love is not rude' [I Cor. 13:5]. This ought to be referred not only to the countenance but to the whole carriage of the body.

"'At once your sin is lying at the door' [Gen. 4:7]. Adam touched upon the security of sinners and spoke with Cain as with the greatest hypocrite, the most venomous barefoot monk, as if he would say, 'What happened to me, poor devil, in paradise? I tried to conceal it with fig leaves and hid myself behind trees. But, dear fellow, our Lord God doesn't let himself be deceived. Fig leaves won't do.' It must have been very painful to Adam to drive out his firstborn son. He expelled and ejected him from his home and the church. 'Go away,' he must have said, 'and don't let me ever see you again! I know very well what I lost in paradise. I don't want to lose anything more on your account. I'll keep God's commandments now with more seriousness.' Adam must have preached Cain an earnest sermon."

Every Tree in Forest of Scriptures Shaken
Early in the 1530's No. 674

He [Martin Luther] once said to C[onrad] C[ordatus],[7] "The Scriptures are a vast forest, but there's no tree in it that I haven't shaken with my hand."

The occasion for his saying this was that he had just heard it stated that the passages in the Scriptures about works are always very closely associated with righteousness, that is, seem to attribute righteousness to works.

---

[7] Cf. No. 165, n. 62.

TABLE TALK RECORDED BY JOHN SCHLAGINHAUFEN

1531-1532

INTRODUCTION

The pieces numbered 1232 to 1889 in WA, TR 2 were recorded by John Schlaginhaufen and were published for the first time in 1888 by Wilhelm Preger.[1] They date from 1531 to 1532, years also covered by Veit Dietrich and Conrad Cordatus, and therefore only about one-seventh of the total number of entries were selected for inclusion in this edition.

John Schlaginhaufen, whom Luther sometimes addressed in the Latinized form of his name, Turbicida, seems to have been born in the Upper Palatinate and at an undetermined date. He was matriculated at Wittenberg in 1520, and so he was probably about the same age as Veit Dietrich. Nothing more is known about him until he appears in November, 1531, as one of the young men who lived in Luther's home and ate at his table. He seems often to have been despondent, and at such times he absented himself from the table or sat there in silence or timidly expressed what was troubling him. He was bothered by the thought that he might not be one of those elected by God for salvation, and he was reluctant to participate in the Lord's Supper when he felt that his faith was weak. Sometimes he walked with Luther in the garden outside of the Black Cloister in which the Reformer lived, and Luther tried to comfort and cheer him. Meanwhile it may be taken as a sign of Schlaginhaufen's standing in the eyes of Luther's wife that he was the first person she called when she was alarmed by her husband's sudden attack of illness (No. 1493).

The friendly relation between Luther and Schlaginhaufen continued after the latter left Wittenberg in the late fall of 1532 to become pastor in nearby Zahna and then, a year later, in somewhat remoter Cöthen. In the latter place he was soon made superintendent, and in this capacity he helped complete the introduction of the Reformation in Anhalt and became one of the signers of the *Smalcald Articles* in 1537. How long after this he may have lived is not known.

---

[1] *Tischreden Luthers aus den Jahren 1531 und 1532 nach den Aufzeichnungen von Johann Schlaginhaufen,* herausgegeben von Wilhelm Preger (Leipzig: Dörffling & Franks, 1888).

TABLE TALK RECORDED BY JOHN SCHLAGINHAUFEN

Nobody Knows Distinction Between Law and Gospel
Before December 14, 1531   No. 1234

"There's no man living on earth who knows how to distinguish between the law and the gospel. We may think we understand it when we are listening to a sermon, but we're far from it. Only the Holy Spirit knows this. Even the man Christ was so wanting in understanding when he was in the vineyard that an angel had to console him [John 12:27-29]; though he was a doctor from heaven he was strengthened by the angel. Because I've been writing so much and so long about it, you'd think I'd know the distinction, but when a crisis comes I recognize very well that I am far, far from understanding. So God alone should and must be our holy master."

God Is Friendlier to Us Than Katy to Her Child
Before December 14, 1531   No. 1237

"God must be much friendlier to me and speak to me in friendlier fashion than my Katy to little Martin.[1] Neither Katy nor I could intentionally gouge out the eye or tear off the head of our child. Nor could God. God must have patience with us. He has given evidence of it, and therefore he sent his Son into our flesh in order that we may look to him for the best.

"I think Paul himself was hostile to God because he couldn't believe as he wished he could.

"When I reflect on the magnitude of God's mercy and majesty, I am myself horrified at how far God has humbled himself."

Luther Taught to Prefer Fathers to Scriptures
Before December 14, 1531   No. 1240

"Dr. Usingen,[2] my teacher, said to me when I loved the Scrip-

---
[1] The son of Luther and his wife Katy was about a month old at this time.
[2] Bartholomew Arnoldi of Usingen (*ca.* 1465-1533) taught philosophy in Erfurt University when Luther was a student there.

tures so much, 'What is the Bible? One must read the ancient doctors, for they sucked the truth out of the Bible. The Bible is the cause of all sedition.' Psalm 2 [:10] says, 'Now therefore, O kings, be wise,' but they say No. So be it! They are ruined, like reckless tipplers."

Lawyers Should Not Be Arrogant Before God
Before December 14, 1531   No. 1241

"Before my time there was no lawyer who knew what was right. What they have they got from me. One doesn't read in the gospel that lawyers ought to be worshiped. It's nothing when one says, 'God and man.' When our Lord God wishes to judge, is he concerned about the lawyers? Before the world I'll let them be right, but before God they must be under me. If I can judge Moses and put him down, what must the standing of lawyers be? When our Lord God says, 'You are consul, emperor, lawyer,' they must say to themselves, 'Then I am not God.' Psalm 2 [:10] will be my psalm: 'Now therefore, O kings, be wise.' If one or the other must be lost, let the law be lost and Christ remain."

Moses and Luther at the Last Judgment
Before December 14, 1531   No. 1242

"I won't tolerate Moses because he is an enemy of Christ. If he appears with me before the judgment I'll turn him away in the name of the devil and say, 'Here stands Christ.'

"In the last judgment Moses will look at me and say, 'You have known and understood me correctly,' and he will be favorably disposed to me."

Satan Was Permitted by God to Test Job
Before December 14, 1531   No. 1252

"The devil has two things with which he goes about his work. These are murder and falsehood [John 8:44]. God commanded, 'You shall not kill' [Exod. 20:13] and 'You shall have no other gods'

[Exod. 20:3]. Against these two commandments Satan is constantly acting. He may and can do nothing else than lie and murder."

At this point I[3] asked him [Martin Luther] whether the devil uses his power by God's permission or by God's command. He replied, "Oh, no! The power he uses is not commanded. Good gracious, no! But our Lord God doesn't stop him. He looks through his fingers.[4] It's as if a great lord saw that somebody set his barn on fire, did nothing to prevent it, but merely winked at it. This is what God does to the devil."

Then I introduced contrary testimony from Job: "Behold, he is in your power; only spare his life" [Job 2:6].

"In the case of Job, [Luther replied,] the devil had power with God's permission. It was as if God said, 'This one time I'll make a concession to you, but spare his life.'"

Much Babbling Not Desirable for Real Prayer
Before December 14, 1531 *No. 1254*

"Our lay brothers in Erfurt[5] had to pray four hundred Our Fathers in one day for the canonical hours.[6] Once a certain brother said, 'If I were our Lord God I wouldn't like to hear what I alone must pray, to say nothing of having my ears filled with the babbling of all the brothers.' But when Moses cried out to God at the Red Sea[7] without using many words—that must have been a real prayer!"

The Gospel Is Preached Through Music
Before December 14, 1531 *No. 1258*

"What is law doesn't make progress, but what is gospel does. God has preached the gospel through music, too, as may be seen

---

[3] John Schlaginhaufen, the recorder of this conversation.
[4] I.e., acts as if he did not notice it.
[5] Augustinian lay brothers in Erfurt, where Luther first entered the monastery in 1505.
[6] According to John Schlaginhaufen's recording, this conversation follows one on Luther's experience with the prescribed prayers of monastic life, which is parallel to No. 495.
[7] Cf. Exod. 14:15.

in Josquin,[8] all of whose compositions flow freely, gently, and cheerfully, are not forced or cramped by rules, and are like the song of the finch."

Destroying as Well as Creating Occupies God
Before December 14, 1531   No. 1259

"I maintain that God is just as busy annihilating as creating." This he [Martin Luther] said when there was mention of excrement, and he added, "I marvel that man hasn't long since defecated the whole world full, up to the sky," etc.

Prophets Disbelieved and Lawyers Confused
Between December 14 and 28, 1531   No. 1269

"There is no prophet more vicious than Ezekiel. He surpasses all others in his abusive language. The sharp words with which the prophets provoked men drew blood, for when the prophets said that Jerusalem would be destroyed and would fall, this seemed to the Jews to be most heretical; the Jews couldn't stand it. So now that Luther declares that the church will be ruined and undone, nobody wants to believe and endure this. It's impossible to believe it because the article of the Creed states, 'I believe the catholic church.' In Judah many kings perished before Jerusalem—like Sennacherib, etc.[9]—and yet Jeremiah said that Jerusalem would be destroyed. If I had heard such a prophecy from Jeremiah, I would myself have knocked off his head. Nevertheless, the Holy Spirit spoke through Jeremiah, and it [what he prophesied] happened.

"If the pope had been able to bring up a single argument against me, as the Jews brought them up against Jeremiah and the other prophets, I couldn't have survived. The pope didn't argue with me *de jure* but *de facto*. If I had no other argument to advance against the pope than a *de facto* argument, I would hang myself

---

[8] Josquin de Prez (d. 1521), a church musician on the eve of the Reformation whose compositions were prized by Luther and often sung at his table. See Paul Nettl, *Luther and Music* (Philadelphia: Muhlenberg, 1948), pp. 1-104.

[9] Cf. Isa. 37:36, 37.

tomorrow. But my case rests on what is right. The Turk is emperor *de facto* but not *de jure*. Afterward divine right is divided into civil and *de facto* right. So God gave the right to Charles[10] and the fact to the Turk, but the fact is not converted into a right. He who has the right in fact will easily get the right legally, as the Turk has done.

"I'll be surprised if there's a lawyer in Germany, or even in the whole world, who knows what *de facto* and *de jure* rights are." (That is a strong oath that the doctor swore.) [11] "In short, unless the lawyers ask for forgiveness and crawl to the gospel, I'll addle them so much that they won't know the way out. I don't understand law, but I am an authority in matters of conscience. Then civil law is *de facto* law, and it's both the law of nations and civil law."

Claims Made for Relics Are Not True
Between December 14 and 28, 1531 No. 1272

"It is claimed that the head of St. John the Baptist is in Rome, although all histories show that the Saracens opened John's grave and burned everything to powder. Yet the pope is not ashamed of his lies. So with reference to other relics like the nails and the wood of the cross—they are the greatest lies."

Abundance of God's Gifts Taken for Granted
December 28, 1531 No. 1273

On the day of the Innocents[12] [Martin Luther said], "If God were to withhold our necessities from us for a year, what a cry there would be throughout the world! But now that he lavishes them upon us we're all ungrateful, and there is no one who gives thanks."

---

[10] Emperor Charles V. Cf. No. 206, n. 78.

[11] These words of Schlaginhaufen seem to refer to Luther's assertion in the preceding paragraph that he would hang himself.

[12] This was December 28, 1531.

Large Proportion of Grain Used to Make Beer
Between December 28 and 31, 1531   No. 1281

"Whoever it was who invented the brewing of beer has been a curse for Germany. Prices must be high in our lands. Horses devour the greatest part of the grain, for we grow more oats than rye. Then the good peasants and townspeople drink up almost as much of the grain in the form of beer. On this account the farmers in noble Thuringia, where the land is very fertile, have learned the rascality of growing woad[13] where good and noble grain used to be cultivated, and this has so burned and exhausted the soil that it is beyond all reason."

Complaint of a Preacher About Poverty
Between December 28 and 31, 1531   No. 1287

A certain parish minister came to Dr. Martin [Luther] and complained loudly to him about his wretchedness and poverty. Philip Melanchthon,[14] who was in the monastery[15] at the time, responded, "You have vowed poverty, chastity, and obedience.[16] Now keep your vows." Then Dr. Luther said, "I am now compelled to be obedient to my wife, to desperate knaves and rascals, and to thankless men."

Luther Offers Spiritual Counsel to an Auditor
Between December 28 and 31, 1531   No. 1288

Then, after Master Philip had departed,[17] he [Martin Luther] said to me,[18] "Be of good cheer. Things will surely be better with you, for I know that your trials contribute to the glory of God and

---

[13] A plant used for dyeing.
[14] Cf. No. 157, n. 59.
[15] The Black Cloister, which had been converted into Luther's home.
[16] It may be presumed that the visitor, like many other evangelical ministers, was a former monk.
[17] The presence of Philip Melanchthon had just been mentioned in the preceding entry.
[18] John Schlaginhaufen, the recorder of this entry.

to your profit and that of many others. I, too, suffered from such trials, and at the time I had nobody to console me. When I complained about such spiritual assaults to my good Staupitz, he replied, 'I don't understand this; I know nothing about it.'[19]

"You now have the advantage that you can come to me, to Philip [Melanchthon], or to Cordatus[20] to seek comfort, and you must believe with confidence that we speak God's Word to you. If you plead for help from me, how much greater help will befall you from Christ when you plead for help from him who is a thousand times better than Philip or Cordatus? Just hold out! Let the devil rage! He will surely meet with a rebuff."

Thereupon, when I spoke to Dr. Luther about my temptations on the left and on the right hand, he replied, "The devil can do this in a masterful way; if he couldn't he wouldn't be the devil. The dear apostles were sinners, too, and were great big knaves, like Paul, who said, 'I formerly blasphemed and persecuted and insulted him; but I received mercy.' So Peter betrayed him [Christ], which was a villainous trick. In short, Christ appointed the apostles for the forgiveness of sins, that in the apostles we may see the mercy of God in Christ. I believe that at times the prophets also played the fool. After all, they were human beings as much as we are."

Then I spoke about my temptation when I was approaching [the sacrament of][21] the altar. He responded, "Gerson[22] and other fathers have said that one should adhere to one's original intention. It was your original intention to get forgiveness."

Entrance on New Year with Expectation of End
January 1, 1532 *No. 1290*

In this year 1532 Luther was forty-eight years old and he said, "I have another year to preach, but I am afraid I won't live so long.

---

[19] The incident has been reported above, No. 518. On John Staupitz, see No. 94, n. 14.
[20] Cf. No. 674, n. 62.
[21] Words in brackets from variant by John Aurifaber.
[22] Cf. No. 312, n. 138.

I hope I'll experience the last day. Know that it's at the door. Then what is written will happen: 'He will wipe away every tear' [Rev. 21:4]."

Signs on Every Hand of the Last Day
January 1, 1532   *No. 1297*

"The last day is at hand. My calendar has run out. I know nothing more in my Scriptures. All the firmaments and the course of the heavens are slowing down and approaching the end. For a whole year the Elbe[23] has remained at the same level, and this, too, is a portent."

What If Your Teaching Should Be False?
Between January 1 and March 23, 1532   *No. 1310*

"Satan often said to me, 'What if your teaching by which you've overthrown the pope, the mass, and the monks should be false?' He often assailed me in such a way as to make me break out in sweat. Finally I answered, 'Go and speak with my God, who commanded us to listen to this Christ.' Christ must do everything. Accordingly we wish to be Christians and leave it to Christ to answer for this."

Nuns Leave Convent on Account of Luther
January 8, 1532   *No. 1313*

"God, who undermined monasticism through me, repays me very well. He gives me tithes from them [the monastics]. All of them have taken refuge with me." For on this day five nuns from Freiberg came to him.[24]

---

[23] Wittenberg is on the Elbe River. Luther often spoke of the imminence of the judgment day; see George W. Forell, *Faith Active in Love* (New York: American Press, 1954), pp. 156-185.

[24] On January 8, 1532, five nuns and two lay sisters left a convent in Freiberg. Cf. WA, TR 2, 38, n. 1.

Attempt to Dismiss Priests' Concubines Fails
Between January 8 and March 23, 1532   No. 1316

Mr. von Bünau[25] reported that a reform was introduced among the canons in Zeitz and Naumburg. The canons were forced to give up their whores.[26] This lasted two weeks. The canons were unable to contain themselves and had to take the women back, but the women were unwilling to return unless the canons first promised to keep them and defend them. Then they had to provide the women with new clothes, and so they no longer looked the same. A locksmith declared that for two weeks he was overworked day and night making nothing but keys, for every woman in town wanted to have a key to the rectory, now that the whores had been discarded.

Luther observed: "I wish that God were not mocked this way. One shouldn't treat God's institution and command so frivolously. If the godly can hardly exist, what will happen to the mockers and the godless blasphemers? The godless papists have their god in the pope. It's as a certain great doctor said: By serving the pope he would have enough for eternal salvation, and meanwhile he would be exceedingly fortunate."

Translation of the Psalms and the Prophets
Between January 8 and March 23, 1532   No. 1317

"By God's grace the Psalter and the Prophets have now been completed in a good translation,[27] so that we might get more from the bare text than from long commentaries. Hence I don't like my Psalter,[28] for it is made up of a great deal of idle chatter. I used to be so fluent that I almost talked the whole world to death. I couldn't

---

[25] Günther von Bünau, bailiff of Altenburg, was a sequestrator of the elector of Saxony.

[26] In the variant by John Aurifaber the word "cooks" is substituted.

[27] A revised translation of the Psalter was published in the spring of 1531, and the following year all the prophetical books of the Old Testament appeared together. The conversation of Luther here recorded probably occurred while the latter work was on the press. Cf. *LW* 35, 228, 229.

[28] The reference may be to Luther's extensive commentary, *Dictata super psalterium* (1515). WA 3, 1-652; 4, 1-462.

do this now. I have changed my mind about it. There was a time when I could ramble on at greater length about a little flower than I can now about a large field. I don't like verbosity."

Jonas[29] said in response, "It's from the Holy Spirit and it pleases me."

Another Criticism of Desiderius Erasmus
Between January 8 and March 23, 1532   No. 1319

"In his countenance and style Erasmus betrays craftiness," he [Martin Luther] said, for he had his portrait there.[30] "He mocks both God and religion. Although he utters very noble words—blessed Christ, sacred Word, holy sacraments—these words are really very chilling. He has spirit in his biting sarcasm, and his words are passionate, as in his *Moria*[31] and *Julius*,[32] but when he teaches he is very frosty. He can talk well, but his words are artificial, not natural. When a sermon is fabricated it sounds like a patchwork and is cold through and through. Therefore Cicero said, 'There is no better way to reach the hearts of others than first to be moved yourself.'[33]

"The godless papists only imitate our words. See how he [Erasmus] blabbers about the psalm, 'Blessed is the man who fears the Lord,' etc. [Ps. 112:1], and about the second psalm in his *Paraphrases on the Psalms*.[34] He never has anything to say about the article of justification. He mentions Christ for the sake of his stipends, but he doesn't care. If Christ doesn't want to be a king, let him be a beggar; it is all the same to Erasmus. He irritated and put down the papacy, and now he draws his head out of the noose."

---

[29] Justus Jonas. Cf. No. 347, n. 161.

[30] Ernst Kroker suggests that Luther might have had Holbein's woodcut of Desiderius Erasmus in his hand. On Erasmus, cf. No. 113, n. 25.

[31] *The Praise of Folly* (1509); English translation by Hoyt H. Hudson (Princeton: Princeton University Press, 1941).

[32] *Julius Excluded from Heaven* (1513), a satire on Pope Julius II ascribed to Erasmus.

[33] Cicero, *De finibus bonorum et malorum*, I, 68.

[34] Erasmus wrote *Paraphrase on St. Luke*, *Paraphrase on the Epistle to the Galatians*, etc., but not on the Psalms.

Roman Confutators of the Augsburg Confession
Between January 8 and March 23, 1532   No. 1320

"We had the greatest men to refute our apology:[35] Faber,[36] Eck,[37] and Cochlaeus.[38] Faber was to write against the article of justification, Eck to defend the pope and human traditions, Cochlaeus to argue against the marriage of priests and about the invocation of saints. They are the very ones who are now calling the mass a secret sacrifice.[39] Let them come! I'll grease their stilts [so they fall]. These windbags retract everything. Now they call the mass a secret sacrifice, which they never conceded to us, because hitherto they called the mass a real sacrifice that justifies, sanctifies, and propitiates and that can be sold. It's with this that they enticed money out of the people, but now they write that the mass is secret, that is, significative. If so, then it isn't a real sacrifice. So the people will have nothing to do with it and will demand the return of the money they paid for it on the ground that it isn't a real sacrifice. I'll give them a good description of what a secret sacrifice is."

The World Cannot Stand Faithful Preachers
Between January 8 and March 23, 1532   No. 1321

"The world can endure all preachers, but not us. It used to be able to endure the tyrannical papists, but it won't listen to us who attack the pope with divine authority. Therefore the world must collapse. We'll pass away on account of poverty. The papists will

---

[35] Luther's term for the *Augsburg Confession*. Cf. No. 252, n. 100. The so-called "Roman Confutation" was prepared at the Diet of Augsburg in 1530 to refute the *Augsburg Confession*. See Reu, *The Augsburg Confession*, pp. 114-127.

[36] John Faber (1478-1541), archbishop of Vienna and confessor of King Ferdinand I of Austria, was at first friendly toward the Reformation but later became one of its most vigorous opponents.

[37] John Eck. Cf. No. 257, n. 107.

[38] John Cochlaeus (1479-1552), a bitter critic of Luther whose polemical writings established the traditional Roman Catholic interpretation of the Reformer. See Adolf Herte, *Die Lutherkommentare des Johannes Cochläus* (Münster: Aschendorff, 1935).

[39] Latin: *Sacrificium mysteriale*. I.e., a sacrifice which is made in secrecy. Luther saw in this view an escape from reality into vague ambiguity.

vanish on account of misfortune, for their cause doesn't hold good. They see that God fights against them. The time will soon come when they'll give a large treasure for an upright preacher. What's more, they'll even worship and honor a liar. For this reason I'll help restore the papacy and exalt the monks, for the world can't exist without these masks."

A Sermon Should Be Relevant to Its Hearers
Between January 8 and March 23, 1532   No. 1322

"One should preach about things that are suited to a given place and given persons. A preacher once preached that it's wicked for a woman to have a wet nurse for her child, and he devoted his whole sermon to a treatment of this matter although he had nothing but poor spinning women in his parish to whom such an admonition didn't apply. Similar was the preacher who gave an exhortation in praise of marriage when he preached to some aged women in an infirmary."

Some Recollections of the Diet of Augsburg
Between January 8 and March 23, 1532   No. 1324

"When Dr. Zoch[40] read my books against the sacramentarians[41] he said, 'Now I see that he was illuminated by the Holy Spirit; none of the papists could have done this.' And so it was to the profit of the gospel. I say that the papists with all their strength couldn't have refuted the sacramentarians either by authority or from the Scriptures. They haven't thanked me as yet. I'll speak to them about it when I've died. I've made a sufficiently friendly advance to them in my exhortation,[42] where I wrote that for Christ's sake I was willing to labor and suffer, if only they would tolerate us, but it didn't help."

Dr. Jonas[43] responded, "That was a great book. At first it

---
[40] Lorenz Zoch, chancellor in Magdeburg.
[41] Cf. No. 314, n. 139.
[42] Luther's *Exhortation to All Clergy Assembled at Augsburg* (1530). LW 34, 3-61.
[43] Justus Jonas. Cf. No. 347, n. 161.

deeply moved the papists in Augsburg who said, 'Why should we deliberate? Everything is already settled.' Yet within a week they forgot that book entirely and became very sure of themselves. Then the second psalm arrived,[44] and this angered them again. Oh, how long those days seemed to us! How we sighed! And your letters were the greatest refreshment to us, especially the one[45] about the clouds and the sun shining through them and your allegories about these."

No Concession on the Sacrifice of the Mass
Between January 8 and March 23, 1532   No. 1325

"At the diet [of Augsburg] the papists tried to frighten and threaten us. They wished us to agree that the mass is a sacrifice of praise merely to provide themselves with a subterfuge in the term 'sacrifice.' I'm ready to concede to them that the mass is a sacrifice of praise, provided they on their part concede that it's not only the priest at the altar but every communicant who 'sacrifices.'"

Sudden Deaths Ascribed to God's Disfavor
Between January 8 and March 23, 1532   No. 1326

"Nobody pays attention to God's miracles. Look how the papists perish! After the coronation of Ferdinand,[46] the bishop of Trier[47] died with great trepidation after one drink. Count Ernest of Mansfeld,[48] who with great zeal called the emperor a savior, died without cross and candle, without confession and sacrament. Count von Werdenberg[49] died a sudden death in Augsburg; he had wished

---

[44] The reference is to Luther's letter of July 6, 1530, to Archbishop Albrecht of Mainz with an exposition of Psalm 2. Cf. *WA* 30^{II}, 391-412.
[45] Luther's letter to Gregory Brück dated August 5, 1530. English translation in Tappert (ed.), *Luther: Letters of Spiritual Counsel,* pp. 155-158.
[46] Ferdinand I was crowned in Cologne as king of the Romans on January 11, 1532.
[47] Richard von Greifenklau, archbishop of Trier, died on March 13, 1531.
[48] Died on May 9, 1531.
[49] Count Felix von Werdenberg died prematurely in Augsburg during the night of July 11-12, 1530.

to die in battle against Luther. Dr. Matthias, son of Hungius,[50] who celebrated his first mass in Erfurt before the diet [of Augsburg], died wretchedly as a model of papistic truth. For the people of Erfurt led his three whores with him into a brothel and defiled them in his presence; they took him in in a long cloak, and there he wasted away and finally, in one year, died."

Report About the Unbelief of Italians
Between January 8 and March 23, 1532   *No. 1327*

"The Italians laugh at us because we believe everything in the Scriptures. The pope[51] says that Christ was a bastard because he was born of a virgin, and a virgin who bears a child is a harlot. The Italians say that if we put our trust in God we'll be poor people who'll never again be able to be cheerful; one must rather put on a good appearance and not believe everything. This is what the pope does, they say.

"When there was a dispute whether the soul is mortal or immortal, the pope held to the former on the ground that it would be terrible to believe in a future life, for conscience, he said, is an evil beast that makes a man take a stand against himself."

Not Solitude but Social Intercourse Advised
Between January 8 and March 23, 1532   *No. 1329*

"The papists and Anabaptists teach: If you wish to know Christ, try to be alone, don't associate with men, become a separatist.[52] This is plainly diabolical advice which is in conflict with the first and the second table [of the Decalogue]. The first table requires faith and fear [of God]. According to the second commandment, this is to be preached and publicly praised before men and is to be discussed among men. One must not flee into a corner. So the

---

[50] Several variants read "son of Henning," suggesting that Henning Göde might have been intended.

[51] Pope Clement VII (1523-1534) is named in a parallel recorded by Conrad Cordatus. *WA, TR* 2, No. 2429.

[52] German: *Niclos bruder*. Luther probably had in mind the Nicolaitans, a gnostic sect of the second century.

second table teaches that one must do good to one's neighbor. We ought not to isolate ourselves but enter into companionship with our neighbor. Likewise it [this notion] is in conflict with marriage, economic life, and political existence and is contrary to the life of Christ, who didn't choose solitude. Christ's life was very turbulent, for people were always moving about him. He was never alone, except when he prayed. Away with those who say, 'Be glad to be alone and your heart will be pure.'"

Printers and Their Profits from Books
Between January 8 and March 23, 1532   No. 1343

"God blesses a moderate and just profit, but a wicked and intolerable profit is cursed. It was so with Melchior Lotther,[53] who got a very large return from his books; every penny earned a penny. At first the profits were so very large that Hans Grünenberg[54] had conscientious scruples and said, 'Dear Doctor, the yield is too great; I don't like to have such books.' He was a godly man and was blessed. But Lotther is now cursed for a second time on account of his unspeakable profit."

Laws Governing the Marriage of Priests
Between January 8 and March 23, 1532   No. 1346

"The marriage of priests is forbidden by canonical and civil law, and a penalty is added, namely, that a priest who marries is suspended from his office; he thus becomes a layman, like a husband, and his children have the right of inheritance. Away with the tyrants who separate and kill us married people! The pope, the maddest tyrant of all, has abrogated the old canons with new ones, and he has taken good care of himself, for he has subjected imperial laws to his canons, so that in his laws the emperor doesn't dare to decide anything that conflicts with the pope's canons. Yet nobody can endure the rigor of the canons less than the pope. Therefore, the pope in his shrewdness boasts that he is lord over Scripture and

---

[53] Melchior Lotther, Jr., had a printing shop and a wine store in Wittenberg.
[54] Hans Grünenberg was the oldest printer in Wittenberg.

council. He insists that he himself, and nobody else, may expound the Scriptures, and with this he has won.

"However, we conclude that the pope is under the Scriptures, and with that he is defeated. Gerson[55] wrote three books to show that by divine authority the pope is subject to the Scriptures. But that foolish ass of a pope has promoted his claim so crudely that even if we didn't have the Scriptures, it [our contention] might be coaxed out of arguments of reason. The pope has said, 'As I will it, so I command it; let my will serve in lieu of a reason.'[56] We, however, subject him to the Scriptures and say No to him. Let him prove from the Scriptures that he is above the Scriptures! This he can't do. Thus all his adherents are routed.

"In short, the marriage of priests is permitted by civil law but with the addition of the penalty that a priest who marries is suspended [from his office]. So he remains a married man and his children have the right of inheritance because he is no longer in office. But we poor monks and nuns,[57] as persons under vows, must put up with it, for the law says that whoever violates a nun is liable to death. So according to civil law Pomeranus[58] should be relieved of his office, but since that law hasn't been enforced as yet, one may ask whether his children have the right of inheritance even if he is in office. By law, although not in fact, they have been deprived of their inheritance. The papacy couldn't exist while there is sacerdotal marriage."

Luther's Child Offers Occasion for Remarks
Between January 8 and March 23, 1532   No. 1348

Then he played with his infant child and said, "Oh, this is the best of God's blessings. The peasants don't deserve it. They ought to have sows."

---

[55] Jean Gerson (1363-1429), professor at the Sorbonne in Paris, wrote several works on the authority of the pope during the great schism in the papacy. Cf. Matthew Spinka (ed.), *Advocates of Reform from Wyclif to Erasmus* (Philadelphia: Westminster Press, 1953).

[56] Latin: *sic volo, sic iubeo, sit pro ratione voluntas*. The quotation appears in Juvenal, *Satires*, 6, 223.

[57] Luther, a former monk, had married a former nun.

[58] John Bugenhagen, of Pomerania, had been a Roman priest. Cf. No. 122, n. 36.

We Trust Man More Than We Trust Christ
Between January 8 and March 23, 1532 No. 1353

"The principal lesson of theology is that Christ can be known. Here the teacher shouldn't be ashamed of learning from his student, nor the student of learning from his teacher. Christ is friendlier than we are. If I can be good to a friend, how much more will Christ be good to us! When Satan leads me to the law I am damned, but if I can take hold of the promise I am free. Peter said, 'Grow in the knowledge of Christ' [II Pet. 3:18]. This isn't a knowledge of the law, of dialectical skill, or of some other art, but it's the knowledge that Christ is the most just and the most merciful One, in whom alone we dwell. Satan clouds this basic knowledge in our hearts in a remarkable way and causes us to trust an earthly friend more than Christ."

An Estimate of Pope Clement VII
Between January 8 and March 23, 1532 No. 1359

"The present Pope Clement[59] is the wealthiest of all men and yet the most unhappy. He's a thorough scoundrel. He has plotted many wicked things. So he said that before he'd stop [persecuting us Lutherans],[60] he'd rather put the Turks on our necks. He'll do it too. Pray diligently, therefore, and remember this when I'm dead.

"The pope employs most wicked tricks, but they won't be successful for him any more than for King Ferdinand.[61] Next to Satan there is no greater rascal than the pope. He has plotted evil things against me, but he'll be the last. He isn't afraid of resorting to terror, and in fact he plans misfortunes. He wanted to kill the king of France.[62] When he was defeated at Pavia he made a treaty with the Roman emperor.[63] Now he wants to invite the Turks to be our guest. But he'll fail. He is a Florentine bastard."[64]

---

[59] Cf. No. 1327, n. 51.
[60] Words in brackets from variant by John Aurifaber.
[61] Cf. No. 206, n. 77.
[62] Francis I (1515-1547).
[63] Immediately after the Battle of Pavia (1525) Clement VII concluded a treaty with Emperor Charles V.
[64] German: *florentzisch hurnkindt*.

Observations on Pluralism and Canon Law
Between January 8 and March 23, 1532   No. 1362

"To be the pope is to do as one pleases. To be the emperor is to keep the laws.

"The bishop of Mainz[65] can't say with a good conscience, 'I can occupy three sees.' The bishop of Mainz says, 'I do this by papal authority.' But Satan would say, 'That authority isn't enough.' What will he answer? For two episcopal sees are two incompatible things.

"You lawyers, don't tread us under foot. If you do we'll bite your heels.

"If the consciences of the jurists are suppressed, they won't know what they ought to do. Münzer[66] took to the sword, and he was a fool.

"Civil law is what commends itself to human reason. Canon law is whatever the pope publishes. I'd give my left hand if the papists had to observe their own canons. I think they'd cry out about this more than about Luther."

Lawyers and Theologians in Similar Position
Between January 8 and March 23, 1532   No. 1364

"Lawyers will have the same experience that we theologians have. Because we theologians tell the truth, people are hostile to us and persecute us. If you lawyers would also speak to the nobles about their virtues, their usury, etc., your lot would be the same as ours. Lawyers now tend to despise us, though they got from us whatever they know. In short, we say that the lawyers are incompetent, and so they say that we theologians are incompetent."

The Great Saints Were Also Great Sinners
Between January 8 and March 23, 1532   No. 1370

"Let David be a prominent example of divine mercy. He tore

---

[65] Albrecht (1490-1545) was made archbishop of Magdeburg in 1513, administrator of Halberstadt in the same year, archbishop of Mainz in 1514, and cardinal in 1518.
[66] Cf. No. 291, n. 131.

apart a lion, he choked a devil when he slew Goliath, and he enjoyed God's favor, but afterward he tripped over a couple of pigtails.[67] Shame on you! He was also a murderer and became haughty. I think he canceled out his achievements. He almost was the greatest of all.

"John the Baptist was the holiest, for he had Christ's testimony. Next was Moses, then David, Elijah, etc. I think Moses, Aaron, and his sister also canceled out the good they did. When God said, 'You shall not enter . . . because you broke faith with me at the waters of Meribathkadesh' [Deut. 32:51, 52], he would have died quickly if he hadn't taken hold of the forgiveness of sins."

Angry Reaction to Troubles in Zwickau
Between January 8 and March 23, 1532 No. 1372

"I'd give this ring, and my finger too, to know as much as those people in Zwickau presume to know about theology.[68] But if some day a misfortune should overtake them, they would at once befoul their breeches and cause such a stink that nobody would be able to stay near them."

Death Is Caused by Satan, Not by God
Between January 8 and March 23, 1532 No. 1379

"The devil slays us all, for the Scripture states that he causes death and is the author of death [John 8:44]. Satan put God's Son to death."

The doctor's wife[69] said, "Oh, no, my dear Doctor! I don't believe it!"

Then the doctor said, "Who would love our Lord God if he himself had a mind to kill us? He won't be a murderer because he commanded, 'You shall not kill' [Exod. 20:13]. If our Lord God

---

[67] I.e., over a woman (Bathsheba). Cf. II Sam. 11:2–12:25.
[68] In 1531 there had been serious friction in Zwickau, a town near Wittenberg, between the town council and the ministers (including Luther's friends Nicholas Hausmann and Conrad Cordatus), during which Luther charged the councilmen with interfering in ecclesiastical affairs.
[69] The wife of Martin Luther. Cf. No. 49, n. 1.

wanted to kill me, it wouldn't matter inasmuch as I can expect good neither in heaven nor on earth. Besides, snakes, adders, toads, wolves, bears, lions—they all kill. What am I to expect?

"Everything that God makes he creates for life. He created things that they might be, and he called into being things that didn't exist, as if they did [Rom. 4:17]. This means that life belongs to God's purpose. But death has been introduced into the world through the devil's envy, and on this account the devil is called the author of death. For what else does Satan do than seduce from true religion, provoke sedition, cause wars, pestilence, etc., and bring about every evil?"

Christ's Power Is Hidden to the World
Between January 8 and March 23, 1532   No. 1385

"Christ governs his kingdom in a remarkable way. He hides himself so that none of his power may be seen, and yet he confounds kings and emperors. Not even the pope can resist this power. Full assurance about this is necessary. To be sure, I know that even Paul had weakness in his faith. Hence those boasts of his: 'I am a servant of God, an apostle of Jesus Christ' [Titus 1:1]. When he was on the sea an angel appeared to him and consoled him,[70] and when the brethren who were on their way to Rome met him he took courage.[71] So you see what the fellowship of the godly does. The Lord wishes them to stay together and comfort one another, for he knows that they will have adversaries."

The Manna of the Israelites and Manna Grass
Between January 8 and March 23, 1532   No. 1396

"I am persuaded and firmly believe that manna grass is the bread from heaven. It's so dainty that when one touches it with a finger it's broken. This is the glory of its reputation. In order to cook it one must have a clean pot. It's gathered in a sieve early in the morning, when the dew falls. It doesn't grow but comes from

---

[70] Cf. Acts 27:23, 24.
[71] Cf. Acts 28:14, 15.

the dew of heaven. It's bedewed bread, as Prudentius[72] says in his hymn. When the sun rises it melts away. All physicians call it manna. It doesn't grow on a bush but is grass that falls with the dew. It can be baked or cooked according to one's pleasure, as it is written in the text [Exod. 16:23]. It's neither begotten nor sowed nor raised but comes from the dew of heaven. It falls off when a sprig is shaken.

"Manna is something provided. Look, is it there? Do I find it here? It's like coriander, and is white as the dew. Manna is manna, a thrush is a thrush, water is water. How do they get here? God wishes to create manna where it doesn't exist, just as water is water and yet it flows from a rock.

"Early in the morning it lay on the ground like dew, said Moses [Exod. 16:14, 21], and by midday it had begun to melt away. It won't endure touch; if a maid[73] touches it, it will not remain unspoiled. The Word of God will not suffer any addition."

The Gospel Accomplished Much in a Decade
Between January 8 and March 23, 1532 No. 1400

"Erasmus,[74] Oecolampadius,[75] Zwingli,[76] and Karlstadt[77] want to measure everything by their wisdom and so they become confused. I thank God that I know and believe that God knows more than I do. He can do what is above my ability to comprehend. From invisible things he can make visible, for everything that is now happening through the light of the gospel is making visible things out of invisible. Who a decade ago would ever have dared hope for such an outcome? But the flesh is very godless.

"God in his grace promises us the forgiveness of sins, and he adds threats and punishments: 'If you don't believe you will perish'

---

[72] Aurelius Clemens Prudentius (b. 348), an early Christian poet.
[73] A variant text recorded by Veit Dietrich and Nicholas Medler (*WA*, TR 1, No. 731) reads, "if a cook touches it."
[74] Cf. No. 113, n. 25.
[75] Cf. No. 94, n. 19.
[76] Cf. No. 5005, n. 35.
[77] Cf. No. 356, n. 172.

[John 8:24]. Before we believed this and accepted it as a free gift, we preferred to torment ourselves to death and went in full armor to St. James.[78] In short, truth and life don't belong to this world, but falsehood and murder belong to it, of which the pope is one and the Turk is the other."

Talk About the Turks and the German Princes
March 24, 1532 No. 1405

On Palm Sunday[79] there was much talk about the Turks and about the German princes who think that when they take counsel they will also have success. "But God says that both are his" [said Martin Luther], "as if he would say, 'My dear princes, let me do the fighting, for both the counsel and the success are mine.' And we observe this from experience. So the Turks move against us with the greatest assurance, with uncommonly large forces, and with contempt for the terms of peace. They come, and this is a real coming!

"God is then in a mood to fight such fellows. He proved it to them before Vienna, where the Turks withdrew with ignominy on account of the pestilence. Now God can burn them with the fire of hell. When the Turks have plundered us they will be destroyed, for God will fight against them; he himself likes to fight against such arrogant fellows. He did this against the king of Ethiopia, who advanced against Judah with ten times a hundred thousand men, and the king of Judah fell upon the Ethiopian, who was overcome with nothing but talk (II Chronicles 14 [:9-12]). I wonder where they got so many men—sixteen hundred times a thousand! Through an angel the Lord also slew a hundred and eighty-five thousand Assyrians, and afterward the king of the Assyrians was himself slain by his own sons [II Kings 19:35-37]."

---

[78] I.e., went with the full burden of sin to Compostella (Santiago), in Spain, where St. James was alleged to have been buried. Compostella was a popular destination for pilgrimages at the close of the Middle Ages.

[79] March 24, 1532.

Explanation of Why the Disciples Were Afraid
April 7, 1532 No. 1416

Then I[80] asked the doctor about that fear of the disciples which the evangelist mentioned, "the doors being shut for fear of the Jews" [John 20:19], inasmuch as we don't read in the gospel that the Jews had at that time undertaken any action against them. The doctor replied to this question, "The apostles had seen what had happened to their Lord Christ, and so they were afraid that the same thing might happen to them as had happened to their master. They were also fearful because they could hardly believe that he had risen from the dead, for they said on the way to Emmaus, 'We had hoped that he was the one to redeem Israel' [Luke 24:21], just as if it was all over."

Then I said, "But they didn't preach until the coming of the Holy Spirit."

He replied, "He was promised to them in today's Gospel,[81] when Christ said to them, 'Receive the Holy Spirit' [John 20:22]. But it's written in Luke [24:49], 'Stay until you are clothed with power from on high.' It's as if he would say, 'I'll place armor on you that will withstand every shot.'"

God Must Help to End the Turkish Threat
Between April 7 and May 1, 1532 No. 1420

When the conversation turned to the Turks he [Martin Luther] said, "It doesn't matter how large an army is assembled. He must do it who is in heaven. Jonathan said, 'The Lord can save with many or with few' [I Sam. 14:6]. God can so bewilder an army that the soldiers hack one another to pieces."

The doctor's wife said, "God defend us against the Turks!"

The doctor added, "Yes, one of these days God will have to delouse our hides."

---

[80] John Schlaginhaufen, the recorder.
[81] The appointed lesson for the first Sunday after Easter was John 20:19-31. Consequently this conversation must have taken place on April 7, 1532.

Observations About Lawyers and Theologians
Between April 7 and May 1, 1532   No. 1421

Godliness befits theologians, not lawyers. When Weller[82] and the doctor disputed about uprightness, he [Martin Luther] said, "Master George Rörer[83] is a good and upright theologian, and so is Amsdorf.[84] On the other hand, there is only one upright, prudent, and wise lawyer, and that is Brück.[85]

"Lawyers are against God in fact, not by right. Put all the lawyers of the whole world together and see if they praise theology the way I have praised law. We talk favorably about you, but you don't do the same about us. No lawyers magnify the Word of God the way we magnify them. Brück renders to God and to Caesar what belongs to God and to the emperor, but lawyers don't give anything to God but only to themselves. Brück is a man who wants to be sure about his cause and therefore he reads in the Bible every day. Jerome [Schurff][86] is an Ovid[87] and Brück is a Vergil.[88] Be this as it may, our life consists of the forgiveness of sins. Otherwise it's no good. Theology has to do with God; it can't carry on with God the way a jurist can with temporal matters. So lawyers also speculate more."

Luther Admonishes Son Not to Be a Lawyer
Between April 7 and May 1, 1532   No. 1422

The doctor took his child[89] in his hands and said, "If you should

---

[82] Peter Weller was a lawyer. Cf. No. 461, n. 256.

[83] George Rörer was a frequent and diligent transcriber of Luther's sermons and lectures. See, e.g., LW 22, xi, and in this volume, p. 117.

[84] Nicholas Amsdorf (1488-1565) was an early adherent of Luther and remained faithful to the Reformation until his death.

[85] Gregory Brück (ca. 1484-1557) was chancellor to the elector of Saxony and played an important part in the Diet of Augsburg in 1530 and in the Smalcald League afterward.

[86] Jerome Schurff (1481-1554), conservative professor of law in Wittenberg, often had differences with Luther.

[87] Ovid (43 B.C.-A.D. 17?) was a Roman poet.

[88] Cf. No. 116, n. 30.

[89] Luther's son Martin, who eventually studied theology but never occupied a pulpit. Cf. No. 1237, n. 1.

become a lawyer, I'd hang you on the gallows. You must be a preacher and must baptize, preach, administer the sacrament, visit the sick, and comfort the sorrowful."

Germans Despised by Other Nationalities
Between April 7 and May 1, 1532   No. 1428

"There is no nation that is so despised as the German. Italians call us beasts. The French and the English and all other nationalities mock us. Who knows what God intends to do and will do with the Germans, though in God's eyes we've undoubtedly deserved a beating."

Story of the Devil Breaking Up a Marriage
Between April 7 and May 1, 1532   No. 1429

"When I was a boy the story was once told about Satan's inability to start a quarrel between a man and his wife who loved each other deeply. He achieved his purpose through an old woman, who placed a sharp knife under the pillow of each of them. Then she told each [about the knife under the other's pillow]. The man found the knife [under his wife's pillow] and killed his wife. Then Satan approached the old woman and held out a pair of shoes to her on a long stick. When she asked why he didn't come closer Satan replied, 'You're worse than I am, for you've done to the man and his wife what I couldn't do.'

"So we see that the devil is always hostile to whatever our Lord God does."

A Dead Luther May Give More Trouble
Between April 7 and May 1, 1532   No. 1442

"When I die I want to be a ghost and pester the bishops, priests, and godless monks so that they have more trouble with a dead Luther than they could have had before with a thousand living ones."

Whether Anabaptists May Be Saved
Between April 7 and May 1, 1532   *No. 1444*

Then there was talk about the blood of the Anabaptists that Ferdinand[90] had spilled and about the constancy of the Anabaptists. Peter Weller[91] asked whether they would be saved. The doctor [Martin Luther] replied, "We judge according to the gospel: he who doesn't believe in Christ can't be saved [John 3:18]. Therefore we must be sure that they are in error, etc. However, God can also act outside the prescribed rule, although we can't judge otherwise."

Zwingli, Too, May Be Saved by God
Between April 7 and May 1, 1532   *No. 1451*

"Zwingli[92] drew his sword. Therefore he has received the reward that Christ spoke of, 'All who take the sword will perish by the sword' [Matt. 26:52]. If God has saved him, he has done so above and beyond the rule."

Experience with the Pestilence in Wittenberg
Between April 7 and May 1, 1532   *No. 1455*

"During the pestilence here[93] no peasant was willing to bring in any wood, eggs, butter, cheese, grain, or anything else. This was going too far! We had to endure hunger as well as pestilence. But when they had the pestilence out there [in the country], they came into town here to buy and sell, and we had to catch the sickness from them."

In His Illness Luther Thinks of Death
Between April 7 and May 1, 1532   *No. 1456*

"One of these days, before I know it, I'll pass away," [94] [Martin

---

[90] Cf. No. 206, n. 77.
[91] Cf. No. 461, n. 256.
[92] Cf. No. 5005, n. 35.
[93] Probably the pestilence in Wittenberg in 1527.
[94] Many entries at this time allude to Luther's illness. For example, he was

Luther said]. Philip[95] said, "God will help, so that you will get well again." To this the doctor replied, "The Lord God has more trouble on his hands to devise a way of raising me up from the dead than I have to worry about dying."

Luther Leaves His Debts to His Wife
Between April 7 and May 1, 1532   No. 1457

"I'm rich," said Luther. "My God has given me a nun and has added three children.[96] I don't worry about my debts, for when my Katy has paid them there will be more."

Luther Jests with His Wife About Monogamy
Between April 7 and May 1, 1532   No. 1461

[Martin Luther said,] "The time will come when a man will take more than one wife."

The doctor's wife responded, "Let the devil believe that!"

The doctor said, "The reason, Katy, is that a woman can bear a child only once a year while her husband can beget many."

Katy responded, "Paul said that each man should have his own wife" [I Cor. 7:2].

To this the doctor replied, "Yes, 'his own wife' and not 'only one wife,' for the latter isn't what Paul wrote."

The doctor spoke thus in jest for a long time, and finally the doctor's wife said, "Before I put up with this, I'd rather go back to the convent[97] and leave you and all our children."

Lucas Cranach Tells Some Stories at Table
Between April 7 and May 1, 1532   No. 1464

The painter Lucas[98] told this story about a certain man whose

---

reported as saying, "Nothing I eat or drink tastes good to me any more; I'm already dead." WA, TR 2, Nos. 1404, 1436.
[95] Philip Melanchthon. Cf. No. 157, n. 59.
[96] Luther's wife Katherine von Bora and (at this time) three living children: John, Magdalene, and Martin.
[97] Cf. No. 49, n. 1.
[98] Lucas Cranach the Younger (1515-1586) was an occasional guest at Luther's table.

wife died in Torgau. A neighbor, who visited him to console him on the death of his wife, said, "Dear neighbor, I'm sorry that your wife died." To this he replied, "No matter how sorry you may be, she's dead anyhow."

There was another story about a husband who had died. A woman said to the widow by way of consoling her, "The Lord will give you another good husband." "But when?" she asked. "We're just in Lent, and nothing can come of it before Easter!" [99]

Christ Reproached as Adulterer
Between April 7 and May 1, 1532   No. 1472

[Martin Luther said,] "Christ was an adulterer for the first time with the woman at the well, for it was said, 'Nobody knows what he's doing with her' [John 4:27]. Again [he was an adulterer] with Magdalene, and still again with the adulterous woman in John 8 [:2-11], whom he let off so easily. So the good Christ had to become an adulterer before he died." [100]

Luther Overtaken by a Spell of Dizziness
May 1, 1532   No. 1493

When Licentiate Melchior[101] was elected on the fourth day after Cantate Sunday,[102] I[103] was present at the election. There Dr. Martin [Luther] began to feel dizzy. The doctor's wife sent a girl to fetch me. I went at once and saw that he was better. Then

---

[99] Lent was a *tempus clausum* during which weddings were forbidden by ecclesiastical law.

[100] This entry has been cited against Luther, among others by Arnold Lunn in *The Revolt Against Reason* (New York: Sheed & Ward, 1951), pp. 45, 257, 258. What Luther meant might have been made clearer if John Schlaginhaufen had indicated the context of the Reformer's remarks. The probable context is suggested in a sermon of 1536 (*WA* 41, 647) in which Luther asserted that Christ was *reproached by the world* as a glutton, a winebibber, and even an adulterer.

[101] Melchior Fend was elected rector of the university in Wittenberg for the summer semester.

[102] May 1, 1532.

[103] John Schlaginhaufen, recorder of this entry.

Dr. Jonas[104] and Philip[105] also arrived. Dr. Martin said to Jonas, "Dr. Jonas, let's make an exchange. I'll take your stone,[106] and you take my weak head." Then Master Philip said, "If the sicknesses of all men were exchanged, it would probably be as Herodotus[107] said: every man would want to have his own sickness again, and no man would be willing to exchange it."

Widow Asks Luther to Find Husband for Her
Between May 7 and 13, 1532   No. 1525

When the doctor had gone to bed a man came who had been sent by the widow of the pastor in Belgern[108] to ask for a husband. He [Martin Luther] said, "Give [her a husband]? She's over seven years of age! Let her find her own husband! I can't provide one for her."

When the messenger had departed he said to me, laughing, "For God's sake I'll inquire. Write this down, Schlaginhaufen! What a bother! Am I to furnish husbands for these women? They must take me for a pimp! Fie on the world! Write it down, dear fellow, make a note of this!"

God May Be Known Only in Christ Jesus
May 20, 1532   No. 1543

At dinner on the day after Pentecost [Martin Luther said], "One shouldn't think of any other God than Christ; whoever doesn't speak through the mouth of Christ is not God. God wants to be heard through the Propitiator, and so he'll listen to nobody except through Christ. Though the Jews called and cried out, 'Lord, who livest,' etc., they looked for God in many places, but not in the Propitiator, where he promised to hear them. So it is in our case. Those who don't seek God or the Lord in Christ won't find him."

---

[104] Justus Jonas. Cf. No. 347, n. 161.
[105] Philip Melanchthon. Cf. No. 157, n. 59.
[106] Jonas often suffered kidney stone attacks, as Luther also did later in his life.
[107] Herodotus was a Greek historian (d. 425 B.C.).
[108] Balthasar Zeiger, pastor in Belgern, died February 24, 1532.

Estimate of Philip Melanchthon's Work
May 20, 1532   *No. 1545*

"Philip[109] has done in dialectics what nobody else has done in a thousand years. I knew dialectics before, but Philip taught me to apply dialectics to the concrete. Nobody can repay Philip for his work. He has to live in a poor house.[110] He'll have great value for the advancement of the gospel. He is a modest man. God help him! He'll get to heaven, and so he'll be well repaid; the world shouldn't pay for his effort and labor."

Luther's Account of His First Mass as Priest
May 20, 1532   *No. 1558*

"Christ must be a better man than Philip [Melanchthon] or Pomeranus[111] to be able to make us such a gift, that we have offered him thus as a sacrifice."

When all the others[112] had left he stood with me[113] in the court and said to me, "When I was about to hold my first mass,[114] my father sent twenty gulden for food and came with twenty persons, all of whom he put up. Somebody said to him, 'You must have a good friend here that you should come to visit him with such a large company,' etc.

"When at length I stood before the altar and was to consecrate, I was so terrified by the words *aeterno vivo vero Deo*[115] that I thought of running away from the altar and said to my prior, 'Reverend Father, I'm afraid I must leave the altar.' He shouted to me, 'Go ahead, faster, faster!'

---

[109] Philip Melanchthon. Cf. No. 157, n. 59.
[110] In 1537 Melanchthon and his family moved to a new and more satisfactory house.
[111] John Bugenhagen, of Pomerania. Cf. No. 122, n. 36.
[112] Caspar von Teutleben, Mrs. Stephen Wild, and Veit Dietrich were specifically mentioned in preceding entries of the same date.
[113] John Schlaginhaufen, the recorder of this entry.
[114] On May 2, 1507.
[115] Latin: "to Thee, the eternal, living, and true God." Part of the canon of the mass.

"So terrified was I by those words! Already I had forebodings that something was wrong, but God didn't give me an understanding of this until later."

Severe Whipping Makes Children Resentful
Between May 20 and 27, 1532 *No. 1559*

"One shouldn't whip children too hard. My father once whipped me so severely that I ran away from him, and he was worried that he might not win me back again. I wouldn't like to strike my little Hans[116] very much, lest he should become shy and hate me. I know nothing that would give me greater sorrow. God acts like this [for he says], 'I'll chastise you, my children, but through another—through Satan or the world—but if you cry out and run to me, I'll rescue you and raise you up again.' For God doesn't want us to hate him."

The Tempted and Afflicted Understand the Gospel
Between May 20 and 27, 1532 *No. 1583*

"There is only one article and one rule of theology, and this is true faith or trust in Christ. Whoever doesn't hold this article and this rule is no theologian. All other articles flow into and out of this one; without it the others are meaningless. The devil has tried from the very beginning to deride this article and to put his own wisdom in its place. However, this article has a good savor for all who are afflicted, downcast, troubled, and tempted, and these are the ones who understand the gospel."

How to Go About the Task of Preaching
Between May 20 and 27, 1532 *No. 1590*

He [Martin Luther] said to Anthony Lauterbach,[117] "When you are to preach, speak with God and say, 'Dear Lord God, I wish

---

[116] John Luther was almost six years old at this time.
[117] Anthony Lauterbach was a frequent guest at Luther's table during the 1530's, when he served as deacon in Wittenberg. Cf. pp. 253-254.

to preach in thine honor. I wish to speak about thee, glorify thee, praise thy name. Although I can't do this well of myself, I pray that thou mayest make it good.' When you preach, don't look at Philip[118] or Pomeranus[119] or me or any other learned man, but think of yourself as the most learned man when you are speaking from the pulpit.

"I have never been troubled by my inability to preach well, but I have often been alarmed and frightened to think that I was obliged to speak thus in God's presence about his mighty majesty and divine nature. So be of good courage and pray."

Each Age Has Its Own Peculiar Temptations
Between May 27 and 31, 1532   *No. 1601*

"Young fellows are tempted by girls, men who are thirty years old are tempted by gold, when they are forty years old they are tempted by honor and glory, and those who are sixty years old say to themselves, 'What a pious man I have become!'"

Pope Deprived of the Blessing of Offspring
Between May 27 and 31, 1532   *No. 1607*

"That God has hated the pope appears from this, that God has deprived him of the fruit of his body. We wouldn't have received the blessing [of children] if the Lord hadn't planted the desire in us. The ardor is in both [men and women], and children are engendered as a consequence. Even if a child is unattractive when it is born, we nevertheless love it."

We Must Often Try God's Patience
Between May 27 and 31, 1532   *No. 1615*

The doctor took his son[120] on his lap, and the child befouled him. Thereupon he [Martin Luther] said, "How our Lord God has

---

[118] Philip Melanchthon. Cf. No. 157, n. 59.
[119] John Bugenhagen, of Pomerania. Cf. No. 122, n. 36.
[120] Presumably Martin, then six months old.

to put up with many a murmur and stink from us, worse than a mother must endure from her child!"

Infant Is Example of Trust in God
June 8 or 9, 1532   No. 1631

When his infant son Martin was being suckled at his mother's breast, the doctor said, "The pope, the bishops, Duke George,[121] Ferdinand,[122] and all the demons hate this child, yet the little child isn't afraid of all of them put together. He sucks with pleasure at those breasts, is cheerful, is unconcerned about all his enemies, and lets them rage as long as they wish. Christ said truly, 'Unless you become like children,' etc. [Matt. 18:3]."

First Words of Genesis Hard to Understand
June 8 or 9, 1532   No. 1634

In the evening [Martin Luther said] in the garden, "Before a man learns the first words in Moses, 'God created the heavens and the earth' [Gen. 1:1], he is dead. Even if he lived to be a thousand years old, he wouldn't understand them fully. The Creator was so completely forgotten that God had to send his Son into the world to remind the world of the Father's benefaction and grace in the creation and in the sending of his Son," etc.

A Fornicator Excluded from the Sacrament
Between June 12 and July 12, 1532   No. 1646

"I have excommunicated my prefect Hans Metzsch[123] on account of his fornicating and I don't want him to participate in our sacraments. Since I've had him excluded, he has refrained from participation, nor shall he be admitted again unless he repents and comes to his senses."

---

[121] Cf. No. 275, n. 118.
[122] Cf. No. 206, n. 77.
[123] Hans Metzsch. Cf. No. 342, n. 152.

Fornication and Adultery Are Both Sinful
Between June 12 and July 12, 1532   No. 1647

Then Ignatius[124] inquired, "Dear Doctor, is fornication also a sin if I don't take another man's wife but an unattached wench, as long as I am myself free too?" The doctor [Martin Luther] replied by citing Paul, "Neither the immoral [. . . nor adulterers . . . will inherit the kingdom of God, I Cor. 6:9]." "Paul," he added, "made no distinction between fornication and adultery. I can't make a law for you. I simply point to the Scriptures. There it is written. Read it for yourself. I don't know what more I can do."

Some Suggestions Concerning Preaching
Between June 12 and July 12, 1532   No. 1650

"In my preaching I take pains to treat a verse [of the Scriptures], to stick to it, and so to instruct the people that they can say, 'That's what the sermon was about.'

"When Christ preached he proceeded quickly to a parable and spoke about sheep, shepherds, wolves, vineyards, fig trees, seeds, fields, plowing. The poor lay people were able to comprehend these things."

Luther's Career Was Not Planned by Him
Between June 12 and July 12, 1532   No. 1654

"God knows, I never thought of going so far as I did. I intended only to attack indulgences.[125] If anybody had said to me when I was at the Diet of Worms,[126] 'In a few years you'll have a wife and your own household,' I wouldn't have believed it."

Men Cannot Get Along Without Women
Between June 12 and July 12, 1532   No. 1658

"Many good things may be perceived in a wife. First, there is

---
[124] Ignatius Perknowsky. Cf. No. 342, n. 156.
[125] On Luther's attack on indulgences in 1517, see *LW* 31, 17-33, 77-252.
[126] Luther was at the Diet of Worms in 1521 (see *LW* 32, 101-131) and was married in 1525.

the Lord's blessing, namely, offspring. Then there is community of property. These are some of the pre-eminently good things that can overwhelm a man.

"Imagine what it would be like without this sex. The home, cities, economic life, and government would virtually disappear. Men can't do without women. Even if it were possible for men to beget and bear children, they still couldn't do without women."

Marriage and Cohabitation Are God's Creation
Between June 12 and July 12, 1532   No. 1659

"When one looks back upon it, marriage isn't so bad as when one looks forward to it. We see that our mothers and our fathers were saints and that we have the divine commandment, 'Honor your father and your mother' [Exod. 20:12]. When I look beside myself, I see my brothers and sisters and friends, and I find that there's nothing but godliness in marriage. To be sure, when I consider marriage, only the flesh seems to be there. Yet my father must have slept with my mother and made love to her, and they were nevertheless godly people. All the patriarchs and prophets did likewise. The longing of a man for a woman is God's creation—that is to say, when nature's sound, not when it's corrupted as it is among Italians and Turks."

The Abomination of the Roman Mass
Between June 12 and July 12, 1532   No. 1673

"No tongue can express and no heart can grasp the abomination of the mass. It's a wonder that God hasn't destroyed the world long ago on account of it, as he will undoubtedly destroy it with fire.

"The papacy relies on the mass in two ways: spiritually because the papacy regards the mass as worship, and corporeally because the princes of this world maintain the papacy.

"The mass is the rock of the papists. In spirit it's now overthrown. In the flesh God will also break this rock to pieces in a short time."

Sacramentarians Do Not Agree with Luther
Between June 12 and July 12, 1532   *No. 1680*

"Everybody wants to adorn his frauds with the cloak of the gospel. It has been reported that the sacramentarian[127] preachers in Augsburg are crying out and thundering against the evangelicals, 'We share the views of Luther and Philip.[128] They assent to our teaching. You don't know what fault you're finding in our teaching.' Thus because they don't want to be our friends in God's name, they are our friends in the name of all the demons, as Judas was Christ's enemy."

The Name of Christ Used as a Pretext
Between June 12 and July 12, 1532   *No. 1684*

"All Jews boasted that they were sons of Abraham. That was once high praise. It's like the rich man who, when he was buried and in hell, called, 'Father Abraham!' and Abraham replied, 'My son' [Luke 16:24, 25]. But our Lord God can distinguish these children nicely. To some he gives a reward here, and in the case of others he keeps the reward for the future. The Jews boasted that they were of Abraham, not on account of Abraham but on account of their own glory, just as the papists now boast of Christ in order that they may thereby get large fees."

Katy Nurses One Son, Has Another on the Way
Between June 12 and July 12, 1532   *No. 1697*

"It's difficult to feed two guests, one in the house and the other at the door." This he [Martin Luther] said when he saw his son Martin[129] being nursed at his mother's breast at the same time that Katy, the doctor's wife, had become pregnant.[130]

---

[127] A variant by John Aurifaber reads: "adherents of Zwingli." On the term "sacramentarian," see No. 314, n. 139.
[128] Philip Melanchthon. Cf. No. 157, n. 59.
[129] Martin was about seven months old at this time.
[130] Paul Luther was born January 28, 1533.

Wine for Old People, Milk for Children

Between June 12 and July 12, 1532   No. 1706

Dr. Martin Luther [said], "Old people should be given wine. Young children should slake their thirst with milk. Before the age of eight years no child should be given wine to drink."

The Wicked Prosper, the Righteous Suffer Want

Between June 12 and July 12, 1532   No. 1707

"Lucullus[131] was the first to introduce currency into Italy.

"Wicked knaves enjoy our Lord God's possessions the most. Tyrants have the power, usurers have the money, and peasants have the cheese, eggs, butter, oats, barley, apples, pears, etc. Christians must sit in prison, where neither sun nor moon shines on them. Very well! It'll surely be different some day!"

The World Becomes Weary of the Word of God

Between July 12 and August 12, 1532   No. 1727

"The world has now become very sure of itself. It relies on books and thinks that if these are read it knows everything. The devil almost succeeded in getting me, too, to become lazy and secure and to think: 'Here you have the books. If you read them you'll have the answers.' So the fanatics[132] and sacramentarians[133] suppose that because they have read only one little book they know everything. Against such security I pray the catechism[134] every day like my little Hans[135] and ask God to keep me in his dear, holy Word, lest I grow weary of it."

---

[131] Presumably Lucius Licinius Lucullus, Roman consul who died about the year 57 B.C.
[132] A variant by George Rörer reads: "Anabaptists."
[133] Cf. No. 314, n. 139.
[134] The traditional parts of the catechism that were taken up in Luther's *Small Catechism*: the Ten Commandments, Apostles' Creed, and Lord's Prayer.
[135] Luther's oldest son John was six years old.

TABLE TALK

Death of Elector John Frederick of Saxony
August 18, 1532 No. 1738

"The ringing of bells sounds different than usual when one knows that the deceased is somebody one loves.[136] Our good-for-nothing windbags have been wanting to rule. Now they have their chance.

"This prince was distinguished by the greatest clemency, Frederick[137] by the greatest prudence. If the qualities of the two princes had been united in one person, we would have had a prodigy. Duke Frederick seated himself, asked for counsel, closed his eyes, made note of what was said by one after another, and finally he spoke, saying, 'This or that won't stand up,' 'This or that will be the consequence.'

"How forsaken this great prince was when he died! Neither a son, nor a cousin, nor any relative was there. Physicians say that he died of a heart seizure."

Conversation After the Elector's Funeral
August 18, 1532 No. 1747

"It's hard to get away from thinking about works, for God wants them and commands them. But he doesn't want us to rely on them and record them. He says, 'I'll repay you well for them. Don't give the matter a thought and don't demand a reward for them.'"

This I[138] wrote while eating breakfast after the funeral ceremonies on the twelfth Sunday [after Trinity], which was August 18, when we laid to rest Elector John of Saxony, whose soul was committed to God. He died in Schweinitz on August 15 of an apoplectic spasm.

---

[136] Elector John Frederick of Saxony, who had succeeded his brother Frederick in 1525, died on August 16, 1532, in his hunting lodge in Schweinitz and was laid to rest two days later in the Castle Church in Wittenberg.
[137] Frederick the Wise, elector of Saxony from 1486 to 1525, protected Luther during the early years of the Reformation.
[138] John Schlaginhaufen, the recorder.

RECORDED BY SCHLAGINHAUFEN

Death May Come Quickly to Anybody
August 18, 1532   No. 1751

"Now that the princes have died as they have,[139] I almost hope that the same may happen to me."

Mistress Katy[140] responded, "God keep you from this!"

Then the doctor said, "Ah, dear Katy, it happens to a person quickly, as we've seen in the case of our prince."

Luther Reads Through Bible Twice a Year
October 21, 1532   No. 1877

"For some years now," the doctor said, "I have read through the Bible twice every year. If you picture the Bible to be a mighty tree and every word a little branch, I have shaken every one of these branches because I wanted to know what it was and what it meant."[141]

---

[139] See No. 1738.
[140] Latin: *Domina Ketha*, Luther's wife.
[141] For a similar analogy, see No. 674.

TABLE TALK COLLECTED BY CONRAD CORDATUS

1532-1533

INTRODUCTION

The pieces numbered 1950 to 3416 in WA, TR 2 and 3 belong to the years 1532 and 1533 and were collected, though not necessarily recorded, by Conrad Cordatus. As a matter of fact, Cordatus claimed to have been the first to take notes at Luther's table. "I always knew," he wrote, "that it was an audacious offense to write down everything I heard when I stood before the table or sat at it as a guest, but the usefulness of the practice overcame my shame. Besides, the doctor never indicated by as much as a word that what I did displeased him. What is more, I prepared the way for others who ventured to do the same thing, especially Master Veit Dietrich and John Schlaginhaufen. . . . Let whoever copies these notes, even against my will, at least do so with the same simple, candid spirit in which I have written, and let him extol Luther's words, as I do, more than the oracles of Apollo—not only, I say, the words that are serious and theological but also those that, for the sake of glitter, are playful and light."[1]

Cordatus was an Austrian by birth, having been born in 1476 to Hussite parents. He studied theology in Vienna, Ferrara, and Rome, receiving the degree of doctor of theology in Ferrara. He returned to his native land, but when he began to adopt Reformation teachings he was imprisoned. Finally he fled to Wittenberg, where he appeared as an impecunious refugee. After a year he went back to his homeland as an evangelical preacher only to be arrested and imprisoned once again. He escaped with the help of a compassionate guard. He reappeared in Wittenberg in 1528. From then until 1537 Luther tried to find suitable positions for Cordatus, who was a guest in the Reformer's home between periods of temporary employment. Then from 1537 to 1540 he was pastor in Eisleben, and from 1540 to his death in 1546 he was superintendent in Brandenburg.

---

[1] *Tagebuch über Dr. Martin Luther geführt von Dr. Conrad Cordatus, 1537.* Zum ersten Male herausgegeben von H. Wrampelmeyer (Halle: Max Niemeyer, 1885), No. 133a. Cf. WA, TR 2, No. 2068.

TABLE TALK

In addition to taking notes of his own at Luther's table, Cordatus assembled notes made by others and incorporated them into his own collection. Later he revised all the notes in his possession for the purpose of making stylistic improvements. Unfortunately this removed them a step further from what was actually said at table, and on this account a relatively small sampling was selected from the Cordatus collection for this edition. It will be observed that the notes do not always appear in chronological order. From April, 1533, the notes go back to May, 1532. This order, which is that of the manuscripts, may be accounted for by the later revisions which Cordatus made and by his incorporation of others' notes into his collection; he seems not to have been concerned at all about chronology.

TABLE TALK COLLECTED BY CONRAD CORDATUS

Women Are by Nature God's Creation
Between November 24 and December 8, 1532   No. 2807b

[Martin Luther said,] "Crotus[1] wrote blasphemously about the marriage of priests, declaring that the most holy bishop of Mainz[2] was irritated by no annoyances more than by the stinking, putrid, private parts of women. That godless knave, forgetful of his mother and his sister, dares to blaspheme God's creature through whom he was himself born. It would be tolerable if he were to find fault with the behavior of women, but to defile their creation and nature is most godless. As if I were to ridicule man's face on account of his nose! For the nose is the latrine of man's head and stands above his mouth. As a matter of fact, God himself must allow all prayer and worship to take place under this privy."[3]

Cicero in Comparison with the Scriptures
Between November 24 and December 8, 1532   No. 2808b

"Experience demonstrates the efficacy of divine truth. The more it's read, the more it works. With all his wisdom and eloquence Cicero[4] couldn't achieve this, although he was supreme in human wisdom. Such wisdom can't rise above its own level but must remain under it. Cicero was the wisest man. He wrote more than all the philosophers and also read all the books of the Greeks. I marvel at this man who, amid such great labors, read and wrote so much."

---

[1] Crotus Rubeanus. Cf. No. 604, n. 372.

[2] Cardinal Albrecht, archbishop of Mainz.

[3] I.e., all prayer and worship occurs through a man's lips, and these lips are under his nose.

[4] Cf. No. 3528, n. 84.

Adam Must Have Lived a Simple Life
Between November 24 and December 8, 1532   No. 2810b

"Adam was a very simple and unassuming man, [said Luther]. I don't think he lighted candles. He didn't know that the ox has suet in his body, for he wasn't as yet slaughtering cattle. I wonder where he got the hides. Beyond this, Adam was undoubtedly a handsome man. He lived so long that he saw the eighth generation of his descendants, up to the time of Noah. No doubt he was a very sensible man and well practiced in a variety of trials. He lived most temperately and drank neither wine nor beer.

"I wish the brewing of beer had never been invented, for a great deal of grain is consumed to make it, and nothing good is brewed."

Protective Angels and Destructive Demons
Between November 24 and December 8, 1532   No. 2829

"The angels are very close to us and protect us and other creatures of God at his command. To be able to protect us they have long arms, and so they can easily chase Satan away when he tries to harm us. They stand before the face of the Father, next to the sun, but without effort they swiftly come to our aid. The devils, too, are very near to us. Every moment they are plotting against our life and welfare, but the angels prevent them from harming us. Hence it is that they don't always harm us although they always want to harm us.

"There are many demons in the woods, water, swamps, and deserted places who may not injure people. Others are in dense clouds and cause storms, lightning, thunder, and hail and poison the air. Philosophers and physicians attribute these things to nature and I don't know what other causes," etc.

A Difference of Opinion About Astrology
December 8, 1532   No. 2834b

Wolfgang Minkwitz[5] spoke warmly in praise of astrology. When

---
[5] A former student in Wittenberg who is not otherwise identifiable.

he poked fun at the passage in Jeremiah 10 [:2], "Be not dismayed at the signs of the heavens," as if it were not against astrology but spoke about the visions of the heathen, Luther responded that this was jesting about such passages and not refuting them, for this passage, as well as Moses,[6] speaks about all the signs in the heavens, on the earth, and at sea. "For the heathen were not so silly [he said] that they feared the sun and the moon, but they feared and worshiped portents and supernatural events. Besides, astrology is not a science because it has no principles and proofs. On the contrary, astrologers judge everything by the outcome and by individual cases and say, 'This happened once and twice, and therefore it will always happen so.' They base their judgment on the results that suit them and prudently don't talk about those that don't suit.

"My Philip[7] has devoted much attention to this business, but he has never been able to persuade me to accept it, for he himself confesses, 'There is science in it, but nobody has mastered it, for astrologers have neither principles nor knowledge gained from experience, unless they wish to call something that happens experience.' But knowledge gained from experience is derived by induction from many individual instances, as in the case of this fire:[8] this fire burns, therefore all fire burns. Astrology doesn't have such knowledge but judges only on the basis of uncertain events."

The Anabaptists and Their Presumption Between December 8 and 11, 1532 No. 2838b

Then Master Heineck,[9] a Bohemian, said that Oecolampadius[10] and Zwingli[11] had boasted that they made peace with Luther because it was through him that God had first made the gospel known, but when Luther was dead they would bring their opinions to light. They did not know that they would not outlive Luther.[12]

---

[6] Possibly a reference to Exod. 22:18.
[7] Philip Melanchthon. Cf. No. 157, n. 59.
[8] It may be supposed that on this December day Luther pointed to the fire in a stove nearby.
[9] Ignatius Perknowsky. Cf. No. 342, n. 156.
[10] John Oecolampadius. Cf. No. 94, n. 19.
[11] Huldreich Zwingli. Cf. No. 5005, n. 35.
[12] Both Zwingli and Oecolampadius had died in 1531.

Then he spoke of a certain remarkable Anabaptist who, after wandering about in the wilderness for three days without eating or drinking, returned to the city. When all the inhabitants were assembled, the literate and the illiterate, he put the literate in one place and the common people in another. He sharply assailed the wisdom of the world and, turning to the common people, accepted and praised the simple. Luther responded, "The Anabaptists have written nothing against me because they have no learned men nor any eminent man. They are only a seditious mob. However, there were more than thirty doctors among this rabble who wanted to refute me."

Then he [Luther] spoke at length about Karlstadt:[13] "He ambitiously tried everything, for he imagined that there was nobody on earth more learned than he was. Whatever I wrote he altered by giving it another color. He wanted to be the only man. I would gladly have given way to him if this could have been done without injury to God. I would never have undertaken such great things so rashly. When at the beginning I wrote against indulgences,[14] I thought that I might remain still while I humbly sought the opinions of others. I assumed that afterward other people would appear who could carry on better than I could. This is what I thought to myself, I who by God's grace am more learned than the sophists and theologians," etc.

When Women Try to Run Everything
Between December 11, 1532, and January 2, 1533 No. 2847b

When he [Martin Luther] was arguing with his wife he said, "You convince me of whatever you please. You have complete control. I concede to you the control of the household, provided my rights are preserved. Female government has never done any good. God made Adam master over all creatures, to rule over all living things, but when Eve persuaded him that he was lord even

---

[13] Andrew Karlstadt. Cf. No. 356, n. 172.
[14] In 1517. Cf. LW 31, 19-23, 25.

over God she spoiled everything.[15] We have you women to thank for that! With tricks and cunning women deceive men, as I, too, have experienced."

A Dog Suggests a Topic for Comment
Between December 11, 1532, and January 2, 1533   *No. 2849b*

Dr. Martin Luther played with his dog[16] and said, "The dog is a very faithful animal and is held in high esteem if he isn't too ordinary. Our Lord God has made the best gifts most common. The pre-eminent gift given to all living things is the eye. Small birds have very bright eyes, like little stars, and can see a fly a room-length away. But we don't acknowledge such everyday gifts. We are stupid clods. In the future life we'll see them, however; there we ourselves will make birds with pretty, shining eyes."

Adam Would Be Astonished by Our Life
Between December 11, 1532, and January 2, 1533   *No. 2861b*

"If Adam were to return and see our life, food, drink, dress, etc., oh, how he would wonder about it! He would say, 'I have never been in this world. Perhaps some other Adam has been in this world first.' [So he would think] because he drank water, ate of the fruit of the trees, put up a hut with four gable walls, had no knife and no iron, and put on a covering made of hides. Now, however, there are immense expenditures for food and drink and we have palatial houses and highly ornamented garments. The ancients lived frugally. It was as Boaz said, 'Dip your bread in vinegar. Strengthen your heart with bread.'[17] The lands were populous, as we see in the book of Joshua,[18] and therefore the multitude of people produced thrift."

---

[15] Cf. Gen. 1:28; 3:1-7.
[16] This dog may have been the one referred to elsewhere as Tölpel. Cf. No. 274, n. 116.
[17] A conflation of altered quotations from Ruth 2:14 and Judg. 19:5.
[18] Cf. Josh. 17:14-18.

The Good Life of the Waldensians
Between December 11, 1532, and January 2, 1533   No. 2864b

Luther commended the life of the Waldensians[19] as the most upright of all: 'Outwardly they live very honorably. They keep their passions within bounds as much as possible. They're not arrogant. They attribute righteousness to others, for they don't claim to be the only righteous persons. They reject the abomination of the mass, purgatory, the invocation of saints, etc. They have ministers of the Word who are celibate; these they permit to marry, but on condition that they give up their office. They don't condemn marriage and openly confess that they wouldn't shun married ministers if they couldn't have unmarried ones. This is the way it will be with us too; if we want to have ministers, we'll have to take burghers.

"Likewise the Waldensians are not lazy or given to drunkenness. They have the best pedagogy. But they don't have the article of justification in its purity; they confess indeed that men are saved by faith and grace, but they understand faith as a quality that produces regeneration. They don't ascribe [everything] to faith alone in Christ. They explain faith and grace differently from us, and at the same time they attribute righteousness to works when they say, 'Faith apart from works is barren' [Jas. 2:20]. If this passage is applied to morals and the preaching of the law, it is excellent, but if we connect it with the article of justification, it's not so much inappropriate as it is ungodly."

A Eunuch Regrets His Castration
Between December 11, 1532, and January 2, 1533   No. 2865b

Master Forstemius[20] said that a certain brother named Law-

---

[19] The Waldensians (Waldenses), late medieval dissenters in Europe, owed their origin (*ca.* 1108) to Peter Waldo, a merchant in Lyons who had the Scriptures translated into the vernacular, advocated an ascetic life, and sharply criticized the priests of his day.

[20] This man is not identifiable.

rence, a Waldensian minister, had had himself castrated in his youth and confessed that in his old age he regretted it, for he burned more with desire then than before. Dr. Martin [Luther] replied, "Yes, indeed, eunuchs are more ardent than anybody else, for the passion doesn't disappear but only the power. For my part I'd rather have two pair [of testicles] added than one pair cut off."

Annoyances and Blessings in Marriage
January 2, 1533   *No. 2867b*

On the day after the Circumcision[21] Dr. Martin [Luther's] infant child[22] cried so that nobody could pacify him. The doctor and his wife sat there sadly for a whole hour. Afterward the doctor said, "These are the annoyances of marriage, and on their account everybody avoids marriage. We all fear the caprice of wives, the crying of children, bad neighbors. So we want to be free, not bound, in order that we may remain free lords and seek after whoredom.

"None of the fathers, furthermore, wrote anything memorable about marriage. Jerome[23] was a real monk's warden. He wrote in a quite ungodly fashion about marriage; he paid attention only to the sensual pleasures in marriage. In truth, the fathers fled to it for no reason except the trials of the flesh. They wished to avoid a drop of voluptuousness and fell into an ocean of sensual pleasures. Only Augustine[24] wrote a [good] statement about marriage. He said, 'If anybody can't live chastely, let him take a wife and go in security to the judgment of the Lord.' Likewise, 'If anybody is devoted to marriage not for the sake of children but on account of necessity, this belongs to the forgiveness of sin and fidelity in marriage.' The good father couldn't say, 'on account of faith in the Word.'

"By his grace and through his Word, God has restored marriage, the magistracy, and the ministry of the Word in order that

---

[21] The festival of the Circumcision of our Lord is on January 1.
[22] Martin Luther, Jr., was about fourteen months old.
[23] Cf. No. 51, n. 2.
[24] Cf. No. 51, n. 4.

we may see that these are divine ordinances, although they used to be regarded as mere masks. Married couples used to think that their being tied to each other was more a custom than an ordinance of God. Similarly civil rulers didn't know that they were serving God but thought they were bound to ceremonies. Thus the ministry of the Word was only a mask in cowls, tonsures, and unctions."

Fasting Was Made Easy by Gorging
January 2, 1533 *No. 2868b*

"Under the papacy everything was pleasant and without annoyances. Fasting then was easier than eating is to us now. To every day of fasting belonged three days of gorging. For a collation one got two pots of good beer, one small jug of wine, and some gingercake or salted bread to stimulate the thirst. The poor brothers then left like fiery angels, so red were they in the face."

The Last Will of a Man of the World
Between January 2 and 26, 1533 *No. 2883a*

"It's a remarkable and very offensive thing that the world is constantly degenerating more and more, though the gospel has been preached often. Everybody interprets the spiritual liberty of Christ as if it were carnal pleasure. In external matters, therefore, the kingdom of Satan and the kingdom of the pope are best for the world, for the world wishes to be governed by laws, the lies of superstition, and tyranny and is only made worse by the doctrine of grace because it doesn't believe that there is any future life after this one. This was demonstrated by the man who, when he was dying, set down his written will and testament in a letter in which nothing was read but these words: 'As long as I could I robbed. Rob as long as you can!'"

Luther's Parents Were Poor and Worked Hard
Between January 2 and 26, 1533 *No. 2888a*

"In his youth my father was a poor miner. My mother carried all her wood home on her back. It was in this way that they brought us up."

A Suggestion for Students on Reading
Between January 2 and 26, 1533 *No. 2894a*

"A student who doesn't want his work to go for nothing ought to read and reread some good author until the author becomes part, as it were, of his flesh and blood. Scattered reading confuses more than it teaches. Many books, even good ones, have the same effect on the student. So he is like the man who dwells everywhere and therefore dwells nowhere. Just as in human society we don't enjoy the fellowship of every friend every day, but only of a few chosen ones, so we ought to do in our studies."

The Long Sermons of John Bugenhagen
January 26, 1533 *No. 2898*

"Every high priest should have his private sacrifices. Accordingly Pomeranus[25] sacrifices his hearers with his long sermons, for we are his victims. And today[26] he sacrificed us in a singular manner."

Civil Rulers Must Enforce the Law
Between January 26 and 29, 1533 *No. 2910b*

"It's only right that every government should embrace the gospel, for the gospel has so advanced civil authority that everybody should know how to fulfil the duties of his calling with a good conscience. Formerly, under the papacy, men were very timid about condemning the guilty because they were unable to distinguish between the private and the public person. Hence they were afraid to pronounce a sentence. The hangman had to take responsibility and ask the condemned man's pardon for what he was about to do to him, as if those who judged and sentenced the guilty committed a sin, while in fact this was their proper duty. Paul said, 'He does not bear the sword in vain; he is the servant of God' [Rom. 13:4]. God does it himself. It is as if I entrusted

---

[25] John Bugenhagen, of Pomerania. Cf. No. 122, n. 36.
[26] The Third Sunday after Epiphany, which was January 26, 1533.

my son to a teacher. If the teacher beat him with a rod it would please me and would be as if I did it myself. But if anybody else tried to strike my son without my commission, I wouldn't stand for it.

"Elector Frederick[27] was timid about punishing and said, 'It's easy to take a life, but one can't restore it.' And Elector John[28] always winked at the wicked and said, 'Aye, he'll be a good fellow in time!' By sparing the evildoers in this way the land is filled with scoundrels. But the prince or magistrate shouldn't be mild, for look what a sharp law the supremely gracious God gave when he declared, 'Whoever curses his father or his mother shall be put to death' [Exod. 21:17], even near the altar! Off with his head at once! Away with his head! Lest the earth be filled with the godless! So you'll be a just magistrate. In fact, the lawyers themselves slay when they teach, read, and pronounce sentence. The hangman has to leave them [the criminals] alone unless they are first judged guilty. Dr. Jerome[29] is an excellent jurist and a good Christian, but he hasn't reached the point where he can sentence anybody to death with a good conscience."

Responsibility for Curbing the Peasants
Between January 26 and 29, 1533 No. 2911b

"Preachers are the greatest murderers because they admonish the ruler to do his duty and punish the guilty. I, Martin Luther, slew all the peasants in the uprising,[30] for I ordered that they be put to death; all their blood is on my neck. But I refer it all to our Lord God, who commanded me to speak as I did. The devil and the ungodly kill, but they have no right to. Accordingly priests and official persons must be distinguished well, so that we may see that magistrates can condemn by law and can put to death by

---

[27] Frederick the Wise of Saxony. Cf. No. 131, n. 44.
[28] Elector John of Saxony. Cf. No. 3507, n. 55.
[29] Jerome Schurff; cf. No. 1421, n. 86. On the subject of this conversation, see F. Edward Cranz, *An Essay on the Development of Luther's Thought on Justice, Law, and Society* (Cambridge: Harvard, 1959).
[30] The Peasants' War in 1525. Cf. *LW* 46, 3-85.

virtue of their office. Today, by the grace of God, they have learned this well. Now they abuse their power against the gospel, but they won't get fat from it."

The Expulsion of Priests who Marry
Between January 26 and 29, 1533   No. 2925b

"That the papists hate me doesn't astonish me. I've probably deserved it from them. Christ censured the Jews with more civility than did the papists, yet the Jews put him to death. According to their law the papists are right in persecuting me, but according to God's law and will they'll see whom they stabbed. On the last day I'm going to talk with the pope, who assails the Word of God and his sacraments. The pope strangles the priests who marry and accept the sacrament (namely, matrimony), although all the laws require only that they be suspended from office. So Duke George[31] expelled people on account of the Word and the sacraments. In Oschatz he drove out ten housefathers[32] with twenty-seven children. The groaning will cry out against him; as the Preacher says, 'Do not the tears of the widow run down her cheeks and also rise up?' [Ecclus. 35:15]."

Luther Spends More Than He Receives
Between January 26 and 29, 1533   No. 2931

"God is the guardian and steward of the poor. I know this for certain from my experience, for I spend far more than I get from my stipend. So far I've not written anything, lectured, or preached for compensation. The two hundred gulden that I get from the prince[33] I have and receive by his indulgence. He who has Christ has enough. I have not wanted to do anything for money, although I might have become rich. I wanted to scrape the money together," etc.

---

[31] Cf. No. 275, n. 118.

[32] I.e., ten priests who had wives and children.

[33] Elector John Frederick of Saxony (1532-1547) gave Luther the annual gift he here refers to in addition to the house (the former Black Cloister) in which he lived.

The Firmness of the Elector in Augsburg
Between January 26 and 29, 1533   No. 2934a

"I believe Elector John[34] had the Holy Spirit, for in Augsburg[35] he was unwilling to yield a finger's breadth. He often said, 'Tell my scholars to do what is right without consideration of me.' If he hadn't stood so firm many of our doctors would have yielded. He held fast like a hero. He didn't want to submit to the emperor's command that preaching should cease,[36] and when I urged[37] him to submit because it was in his [the emperor's] city he replied to my letter, 'I don't know if I'm the fool or my scholars!' He was more ready to leave Augsburg than give up the preaching."

Trust in God or One's Own Goodness
Between January 26 and 29, 1533   No. 2935a

"It's the Holy Spirit alone who attains to certainty of faith in Christ without any doubting. The adherents of the sects always utter some words from which their doubting spirit becomes manifest: 'I hope I'm godly,' 'I hope I'm righteous.' The Christian, on the other hand, says, 'I do what I can. What I don't get done the suffering of Christ will pay for me. I'm saved in Christ. Nobody shall take this confidence from me. Jesus is my Savior.' There's nothing else by which our God and our conscience may be put at rest. Those who put their trust not in Christ but in their own righteousness are always in doubt.

"When [as a monk] I had prayed and said my mass I was very presumptuous. I didn't see the scoundrel behind it all[38] because I didn't put my trust in God but in my own righteousness, and I didn't thank God for the sacrament but expected him to thank me and be glad that I had sacrificed his Son to him. We [monks] had a saying when we went to mass, 'I'll go and get the Virgin a child.'"

---

[34] Elector John of Saxony. Cf. No. 3507, n. 55.
[35] At the Diet of Augsburg in 1530. Cf. No. 2974b, n. 46.
[36] Emperor Charles V ordered that evangelical preaching should cease.
[37] In a letter of May 15, 1530. WA, Br 5, 319-320.
[38] I.e., I was unsuspecting.

The Place of Reason in Christian Life
Between January 26 and 29, 1533   No. 2938b

Dr. [Luther] was asked[39] whether, since it is necessary to exclude reason from articles of faith, reason has any value at all for Christians. He replied, "Prior to faith and a knowledge of God, reason is darkness, but in believers it's an excellent instrument. Just as all gifts and instruments of nature are evil in godless men, so they are good in believers. Faith is now furthered by reason, speech, and eloquence, whereas these were only impediments prior to faith. Enlightened reason, taken captive by faith, receives life from faith, for it is slain and given life again. As our body will rise [from the dead] glorified, so our reason is different in believers than it was before, for it doesn't fight against faith but promotes it. Our speech, which used to be godless and blasphemous, now preaches, praises God, and gives him thanks. Thus my speech is different from what it once was; now it's enlightened. So iron which glows from fire is different from iron that doesn't glow. This is regeneration through the Word and occurs while the person and the members remain the same.

"Reason is subject to vanity, as all of God's creatures are subject to vanity, that is, to folly. But faith separates the vanity from the substance. David used a bow, a sword, and weapons and he said, 'Not in my bow do I trust' [Ps. 44:6], but he didn't spurn the weapons. So believers say, 'My wife, children, gold, etc., won't help in heaven,' but they don't throw them away; they separate vanity from substance. Gold remains gold, even on the neck of a whore. The body of a whore is just as much God's creation as the body of an honorable matron. So vanity is to be put aside, not substance. When Job criticized his wife he called her foolish; although women are foolish for the most part, Job spared the sex and said, 'You talk like a fool.'[40] The common people can't do this; they want to throw

---

[39] By Ignatius Perknowsky, a Bohemian, according to a variant. Cf. No. 342, n. 156. On the subject under discussion, see B. A. Gerrish, *Grace and Reason: A Study in the Theology of Luther* (Oxford: Clarendon Press, 1962). Cf. also Nos. 439, 5015.

[40] Cf. Job 2:10. The meaning is that Job did not say, "You talk foolishly like a woman."

away the substance with the vanity. But this is impossible, for unless there were something good, there couldn't be something bad, as Aristotle said; the bad can't be of itself but is the good that's been spoiled. So vanities exist in good substances. Reason, speech, and all gifts and created things are therefore different in believers and Christians than in unbelievers."

Preparation for Baptism of Son Paul
January 29, 1533   *No. 2946a*

"Gracious Lord,[41] I wish to impose on Your Grace once more. A son was just born to me, and I am a father again. Please help the poor fellow get where he belongs.[42] He was born the first hour during the night of January 28 in the year 1533, and he was named Paul. I've had him named Paul because St. Paul furnished me with many a good passage and argument, and so I wish to honor him by naming a son after him. God grant my son grace!

"I intend to send my children away [when they're grown]. Any of them who wants to be a soldier I'll send to Hans Loeser. Dr. Jonas and Philip[43] will have any of them who may want to study. And if one wants to toil I'll dispatch him to a peasant."

Protest Against an Outrageous Deal
February 9, 1533   *No. 2958b*

A certain citizen of Wittenberg, an old bachelor, bought a house for thirty florins. After he had it in his possession for a long time without building anything on it, he wished to sell it for four hundred florins, basing his estimate on the fact that he rented four bathrooms in it for twenty florins a year. [When he was told about this] Luther said, "Does that simpleton estimate that rotten timbers

---

[41] Hans Loeser, marshal of the elector of Saxony, was here asked to be a sponsor at Luther's son's baptism. It appears that this piece was dictated by Luther as a note to Loeser.

[42] I.e., by baptism into the fellowship of the church.

[43] Justus Jonas (cf. No. 347, n. 161) and Philip Melanchthon (cf. No. 157, n. 59) were also asked to be sponsors.

have the same value as desirable goods? If he continues obstinately in his demand he should be excommunicated from the Christian community and should by no means suppose that he belongs in heaven. It would be more than enough if he sold the house for one hundred fifty florins. If he still tries to sell it to some buyer [at the higher price], I'll excommunicate him.

"Excommunication must be restored again."

The Pope and the Ecclesiological Problem
Between February 9 and 12, 1533   No. 2962b

"The issue in the controversy over the papacy is that the pope boasts that he's the head of the church and condemns all who don't live under his power, for he says that although Christ is the [spiritual] head of the church, there must nevertheless also be a bodily head on earth. (I would gladly have conceded this to the pope if he had only taught the gospel.) In addition, he claims for himself authority over the church and the Scriptures. No one may expound the Scriptures except the pope alone, who does it as he pleases. He boasts that he is lord over the church, and the church in turn is mistress over the Scriptures, and so everybody must submit to him. This was intolerable to me and provoked me to write against the papacy. Our opponents still admit today that our teaching's true, but they defend themselves by saying that it's not yet approved by the pope.

"Duke George,[44] our bitterest foe, admits the same thing. On the day of judgment I intend to speak candidly to him like this: 'Listen, Duke George, do you believe that you are baptized? Do you believe that the Lord's Supper was instituted by Christ in both kinds? Do you believe that our doctrine is true?'

"Then he will reply, 'I believe, but because the pope hasn't approved,' etc.

"'Begone to your own god, for you have been unwilling to give honor to God.'

"Those who thus put their reliance on the church, contrary to

---

[44] Duke George of Saxony. Cf. No. 275, n. 118.

the plain Word, are very silly. It's as if one were to say, 'I'd like to love the son, but I must first kill the mother.' They attribute more to the church that is created than to the Word that creates. But, thank God, we have the testimony that we are not heretics but only schismatics, and they are to blame for our separation."

Schwenckfeld Misinterprets Scripture

February 12, 1533   *No. 2971a*

"It's extraordinary to what an extent the fanatics despise the oral Word. Even Christ, when he appeared to the apostles after his resurrection, was regarded as a mere specter until he comforted them with his words. The devil attaches importance only to unbuckling our sword. But the Scripture says, 'Gird your sword upon your thigh, O mighty one' [Ps. 45:3]. Draw it and strike about you!

"After he had disputed with me for a long time Swinefield[45] said, 'Doctor, you must take your eyes off the words, This is my body, and then we'll agree.' It's certain that the pope did this very thing at first, before he arrogated to himself the sole power to interpret the Scriptures. In so doing he crucified Christ. Let's pay attention to the Word alone or we'll crucify him again."

The Augsburg Confession and Its Apology

Between February 12 and March 3, 1533   *No. 2974b*

"So great are the effectiveness and the power of the Word of God that the more it is persecuted the more it flourishes and grows. Consider the Diet of Augsburg,[46] which is truly the last trump before the day of judgment. How the whole world raged against the Word! Oh, how we had to pray then that Christ might be

---

[45] Caspar Schwenckfeld (1490-1561), a Silesian, was first attracted to and then estranged from Luther. The two men differed, among other things, in their interpretation of the Lord's Supper. Luther often altered Schwenckfeld's name in order to ridicule him; here he called him Schweinsfeld (Swinefield).

[46] The diet of the empire that met in Augsburg in 1530, at which the *Augsburg Confession*, a statement of Lutheran faith and practice, was officially presented. Cf. Tappert (ed.), *Book of Concord*, pp. 23-96.

safe from the papists in heaven! Yet by means of our *Confession* our doctrine and faith were so brought to light that in a very short time the *Confession* was sent at the emperor's command to all kings and princes. In their courts were many distinguished and talented men who took to this teaching like tinder and afterward set fire [to others] everywhere. Thus our *Confession* and *Apology*[47] were made known with great honor, while the *Confutation*[48] gathers dust in the dark.

"Oh, how I wish that their [the papists'] *Confutation* were better known! How we'd like to fall upon that old, ragged parchment and shake it so that the pieces would be scattered to and fro! But they hate the light and won't come out. We offered them sufficient peace and unity there, but in their arrogance they were unwilling to assent. Accordingly they must be allowed to perish without mercy. So one reads in Joshua[49] that Joshua offered peace to all the cities, that none except Gibeon accepted it, and that all the others perished without mercy.

"That diet [in Augsburg] is therefore deserving of all praise. Nobody should regret what it cost because the Word of God was spread abroad contrary to the intention of all people, of the emperor, of the pope, etc. They wanted to extinguish it, but the blaze grew and spread," etc.

Girls Grow Up More Quickly Than Boys
Between February 12 and March 13, 1533   No. 2980b

"Girls begin to talk and to stand on their feet sooner than boys because weeds always grow up more quickly than good crops. So girls who are fourteen years old are nubile while boys of that age are not mature enough for marriage."

---

[47] *The Apology of the Augsburg Confession* was written by Philip Melanchthon and published in its final form in 1531. Cf. *ibid.*, pp. 97-285.
[48] The so-called *Roman Confutation* was a reply (1530) by Roman theologians to the *Augsburg Confession* and evoked Melanchthon's *Apology*.
[49] Joshua 9.

The Mayor's Story About a Butcher
Between February 12 and March 13, 1533 No. 2981b

"Cloistered women [said Luther] are called nuns because in German sterilized swine are so called.[50] Similarly, monks are named after horses, but they are not completely castrated; they have to wear breeches and pants just like other men."

Thereupon Burgomaster Hohndorf[51] told the story of a certain butcher who, when he was slaughtering, washed the animal's intestines near a body of water. He did this without putting on his breeches. The dog, looking for his due and seeing the man's testicles move back and forth, mistook them for the intestines, lay hold of them, and devoured them. "The good fellow came off a bad loser," he said. "He would have done better to have given the dog the whole ox instead."

Recollection of Witchcraft from His Youth
Between February 12 and March 13, 1533 No. 2982b

Luther said many things about witchcraft, about asthma and nightmares, and how his mother had been tormented by a neighbor woman who was a witch: "She was compelled to treat her neighbor with deference and try to conciliate her, for the neighbor had through witchcraft caused her own children such sharp pain that they cried themselves to death. A certain preacher taxed her for this, though in general terms; he, too, was poisoned and had to die, for nothing could restore his health. She had taken the soil from his footsteps, had cast a spell over it, and had thrown it into the water; without this soil he couldn't be healed."

Then Luther was asked whether such things can also happen to godly people. He answered, "Yes, indeed. Our soul is subject to a lie. When it's freed, the body remains subject to murder. I believe that my illnesses aren't natural but are pure sorcery. However, may God liberate his chosen ones from such evils!"

---

[50] Spayed sows were called *Nonnen*, or nuns. Gelded horses were called *Mönche*, or monks. Actually, of course, the animals were so called after monks and nuns and not vice versa.

[51] John Hohndorf. Cf. No. 360, n. 183.

Complaint of Dizziness and Ringing Ears
March 13, 1533   *No. 3006a*

"Nobody believes me when I complain what great pain vertigo and the ringing and buzzing in my ears give me.[52] I don't dare read for an hour without interruption. I can't pursue some thought to its manifest conclusion or think diligently about it. For at once the ringing is there and I'm forced to lie down.

"Itching purifies the body,[53] which is also purified by defecation and sweating. Itching's best suited to the health of the head. But I don't want to find fault with my head. It has faithfully ventured into battle with me. It has deserved my best thanks."

Prefaces to the New Testament by Erasmus
April 1, 1533   *No. 3033b*

On April 1 Martin Luther spent almost the whole day reading Erasmus' prefaces to the New Testament.[54] He said excitedly, "Even if this snake is so slippery that he can't be caught, we'll nevertheless condemn him with his writings, we and our church. Although many wise people in the church may be offended, yet it's better that we lose them than deny Christ, the Savior. I've had more experience with this Savior than I can ever say and thank him for.

"Erasmus has indeed put out very disgraceful prefaces, even if he did soften them, because he makes no distinction between Christ and Solon.[55] Moreover, as the prefaces to Romans and to the canonical First Epistle of John show, he obscures the authority of Paul and John, as if these writings were of no moment, as if the Epistle to the Romans had no relevance for our time, as if the difficulty in this epistle outweighed its value, etc. Is this praise for the book's author? For shame!"

---

[52] For over a month Luther had been complaining at table about headaches, giddiness, and buzzing in his ears.

[53] According to a variant somebody at table "complained that he was annoyed by itching day and night" and Luther offered to take the itch in exchange for his own headache.

[54] The reference is probably to Desiderius Erasmus' *Paraphrases* on books of the New Testament which he had begun in 1517.

[55] The most famous Greek lawmaker (*ca.* 639-559 B.C.).

Christians and Heathen Face Death

May 15, 1532   *No. 3140a*

"Christians could easily suffer death if they didn't know that God's wrath is connected with it. This circumstance makes death a bitter thing for us. The heathen, on the contrary, die confidently; they don't see God's wrath but think death is the end of man. They say, 'It doesn't amount to anything but a bad moment.' But Cicero[56] put it excellently, 'Afterward we'll be nothing or we'll be altogether blessed.' It's as if he would say, 'Nothing bad can happen to us as a consequence of death.'"

Every Seventh Year Brings a Change

June 5, 1532   *No. 3161a*

"My Hans is about to enter upon his seventh year,[57] which is always climacteric, that is, a time of change. People always change every seventh year. The first period of seven years is childhood, and at the second change—say, in the fourteenth year—boys begin to look out into the world; this is the time of boyhood, when the foundations are laid in the arts. At the age of twenty-one youths desire marriage, in the twenty-eighth year young men are householders and heads of families, while at the age of thirty-five men have civil and ecclesiastical positions. This continues to the age of forty-two, when we are kings. Soon after this men begin to lose their sense. So every seventh year always brings to man some new condition and way of life. This has happened to me, and it happens to everybody."

Part of City Destroyed in a Great Fire

June, 1532   *No. 3170*

"The fire in Naumburg[58] is a sign of the great wrath of God, for inhabitants say that within two hours everything that had been

---

[56] Cf. No. 3528, n. 84.
[57] Luther's oldest son, John, was born June 7, 1526.
[58] A suburb of Naumburg was burned to the ground on April 8, 1532.

standing was consumed and destroyed. They say that the conflagration was as if three soldiers had been stationed in each building and had set fire to it with gunpowder, though the fire couldn't have been started this way.

"The papists aren't affected by this. In contempt of the gospel they are rebuilding their church[59] at very great cost, as if their cultus were everlasting and the gospel were about to fall. The people in Erfurt who are repairing two towers of an enduring building are doing the same thing. But they'll see that their impudence will submit to the gospel."

Much Adjustment Required in Marriage
June, 1532 *No. 3178a*

"Man has strange thoughts the first year of marriage. When sitting at table he thinks, 'Before I was alone; now there are two.' Or in bed, when he wakes up, he sees a pair of pigtails lying beside him which he hadn't seen there before. On the other hand, wives bring to their husbands, no matter how busy they may be, a multitude of trivial matters. So my Katy used to sit next to me at first while I was studying hard and would spin and ask, 'Doctor, is the grandmaster[60] the margrave's brother?'"

Weddings Should Follow Engagements Quickly
June, 1532 *No. 3179a*

"It's always my advice that after an engagement is announced one should proceed as quickly as possible to the wedding. Postponement is dangerous on account of foul-mouthed people who are incited by Satan. Friends of both parties generally start unseemly rumors. I know what happened to me in the case of Philip's marriage[61] and also Eisleben's.[62] Only get together swiftly! If I hadn't

---

[59] The city and diocese were still Catholic at this time.
[60] The grandmaster of the Teutonic Order in Prussia was Margrave Albrecht of Brandenburg.
[61] On Philip Melanchthon's marriage, see No. 3538.
[62] John Agricola (1494-1566), a native of Eisleben and later head of a Latin school there, developed antinomian views which eventually brought him into conflict with Luther, who often interceded in his behalf.

married secretly,[63] all my friends would have cried, 'Not this woman but somebody else!'"

A Prayer for Rain in a Dry Season
June 9, 1532   No. 3222a

It was a time of drought, and lifting up his eyes to heaven he [Martin Luther] said, "Lord God, thou hast said through the lips of thy servant David, 'The Lord is near to all who call upon him in truth. He fulfils the desire of all who fear him, etc., and saves them' [Ps. 145:18, 19]. How is it, then, that thou art unwilling to give us rain? If thou dost not give us rain, at least give us something better, like tranquillity, life, and peace. But what will the ungodly say to these words, 'If you ask anything of the Father [he will give it to you] in my name' [John 16:23]? I know that we groan and cry unto thee from our hearts," etc.

That same night rain fell.

A Lesson Drawn from Timid Birds
June 9, 1532   No. 3223a

When some birds built a nest in his garden and always flew away when we passed by, he [Martin Luther] said, "Dear little bird, don't fly away. I wish you nothing but good. If only you'd believe me! [Then he turned away from the nest and said,] This is how we should believe God—that he wishes us well with his whole heart. He who has given his Son for me certainly doesn't want to kill us."

We Do Not Make God's Word True or Untrue
Between June 9 and 12, 1532   No. 3229b

"The objectivity and certainty of the Word remain even if it isn't believed. Everything depends on one's having the true sacrament of the altar, likewise true baptism, and also on my preaching

---

[63] For a description of the circumstances, see William H. Lazareth, *Luther on the Christian Home* (Philadelphia: Muhlenberg Press, 1960), pp. 11-27.

the true Word of God. I stake my soul on it and am ready to die for it. If you believe without doubting, you'll be saved; if not, you'll be damned. I put my confidence in no other faith, but in the Word of God.

"Let me give an example. If I gave you one hundred florins and hid them from you under the table and you believed and said that they were merely lead or a lead alloy, what difference would that make to me, who offered you gold? It's your fault that you don't believe. The gold's gold, even if you don't think so. God doesn't lie when he promises eternal life. Only let us be sure that we appropriate it for ourselves in faith. For our unbelief doesn't make God's promise empty. On the contrary, poverty is the companion of truth."

Description of Luther's "Tower Experience" Between June 9 and July 21, 1532   No. 3232c

"The words 'righteous' and 'righteousness of God' struck my conscience like lightning. When I heard them I was exceedingly terrified. If God is righteous[64] [I thought], he must punish. But when by God's grace I pondered, in the tower and heated room of this building,[65] over the words, 'He who through faith is righteous shall live' [Rom. 1:17] and 'the righteousness of God' [Rom. 3:21], I soon came to the conclusion that if we, as righteous men,

---

[64] The Latin word *justus* can be translated either by "righteous" or by "just."
[65] The "tower experience" of Luther is so called because it occurred in the tower of the Black Cloister in Wittenberg (later Luther's home) at an undetermined date between 1508 and 1518. This report of a conversation at table also indicates that Luther's exegetical discovery took place in a heated room (*hypocaustum*), which a variant (No. 3232a) calls "the secret place of the monks" and other variants (No. 3232b; cf. also No. 1681 in WA, TR 2) appear to call the lavatory (*cloaca*). Here the meaning of the abbreviation *cl.* has been the subject of debate, some arguing that it meant "cell" or "chapter" rather than *cloaca*. Roman Catholic and Protestant historians who have debated about these accounts have hardly been warranted in their glee or their outrage at the place where Luther's experience may have occurred. A compact summary of conflicting views with reference to the pertinent literature is available in Otto Scheel, *Martin Luther, vom Katholizismus zur Reformation* (2 vols.; Tübingen: J. C. B. Mohr, 1916-1917), II, 320, 435. For a debatable psychological interpretation, see Erik H. Erikson, *Young Man Luther* (New York: W. W. Norton & Co., 1958), pp. 170-222.

ought to live from faith and if the righteousness of God should contribute to the salvation of all who believe, then salvation won't be our merit but God's mercy. My spirit was thereby cheered. For it's by the righteousness of God that we're justified and saved through Christ. These words [which had before terrified me] now became more pleasing to me. The Holy Spirit unveiled the Scriptures for me in this tower."

Legal Problems Pertaining to Marriage
Summer, 1532   *No. 3267*

"The pastor in Zwickau[66] wrote me [about] marriage cases. I'll give him something to remember me by for implicating me in such matters that belong to the government! These are external things that are concerned with dowries and inheritances. What do they have to do with us? We advise people only in matters of conscience, and now the government wants to impose these other matters on us. What's more, when our counsels and opinions displease them, they don't carry them out, no matter how good they may be. We're shepherds of consciences, not of bodies and bodily matters. Nobody ought to subject himself to the burdens of others; they'll take care of them all right without us."

High Praise for Elector Frederick the Wise
Spring, 1533   *No. 3287a*

"It's a great gift to have a good and wise prince, such as Elector Frederick,[67] who was truly the father of his country. He governed excellently. He could fill barns and haylofts, and he had large trenches dug in the fields to store provisions. Every year he spent twelve thousand florins on building." And here he [Luther] counted about nine castles that had been built by the elector.

"Still the elector had enough money, for he was his own tax collector (on the advice of the jester Claus)[68] and required exact

---

[66] Leonard Beyer was minister there at this time.
[67] Cf. No. 131, n. 44.
[68] The court jester Claus died in 1515.

accounts of his officials and servants. Even when he entered one of his castles, he ate, drank, and fed his horses like any other guest and paid for everything right away, so that the stewards might not make the excuse that so much had been consumed by the prince. Consequently he left a very large treasure to his country. He had a heroic and thrifty spirit, but now the storehouses and trenches have become quite empty.

"He was very shrewd; he gave six hundred florins to Karl von Miltitz,[69] who brought a golden rose[70] as a gift from the pope, although the rose itself was scarcely worth two hundred. He was born on St. Anthony's Day in the year 1462, and every year on this day he offered his chaplain as many pieces of gold as there were years in his age. For a long time George Spalatin[71] got this amount, and in addition one hundred florins were assigned to him annually, so that he had an annual income of about four hundred florins for his straitened household; I wouldn't want to meet my expenses so closely.

"The elector died in his sixty-third year on May 16, 1525, at the most perilous time in the peasants' uprising. He was succeeded by his brother John."[72]

The Church Not Built by Ceremonies

Spring, 1533   *No. 3323b*

"The papists, the fanatics, and whoever they may be who set their own opinions against the gospel are already condemned with all their wisdom, holiness, and beliefs. For our wiseacres do nothing except to slander us and say, 'Luther has indeed destroyed the papacy but he can't build a new church,' that is, can't introduce a new form of worship and new ceremonies. These wretched men think that building up the church consists of the introduction of some sort of new ceremonies. They don't realize that building up

---

[69] A Saxon nobleman who was a chamberlain in the papal court after 1514.
[70] Since the eleventh century an ornament of gold, shaped like a rose spray, had been from time to time blessed by the pope and conferred on a sovereign or other person in recognition of distinguished service.
[71] Cf. No. 131, n. 45.
[72] Elector John of Saxony ruled from 1525 to 1532.

the church means to lead consciences from doubt and murmuring to faith, to knowledge, and to certainty."

No Frankness in Discussion of Differences
May 9, 1533   *No. 3327b*

On May 9 John Cellarius,[73] preacher in Bautzen, approached Luther and related many things about his acquaintances in Frankfurt who, even when they replied, said nothing sincerely. Their only answer was "Mm! Mm!"[74] Luther replied, "It's true. They don't answer frankly. They are such cursed knaves that they don't dare confess what they believe. It's plain that they're Erasmians[75] and double-dealers. I, too, can jest, drink, laugh, and be gay, but in matters like this let no one trifle with me!

"Martin Bucer acted humbly in his letter and in his personal appearance in Coburg.[76] However, I turned down his approach three times by saying, 'Martin, are you really serious? It's better for you to have us as your enemies than to set up a merely fictitious fellowship.' See what that little scoundrel is doing now! Yesterday I got two letters from a certain man who indicated that he had attended a mass in a Strassburg church where the words of Christ were sung, 'The Lord Jesus on the night when he was betrayed,' etc. [I Cor. 11:23], but the words, 'This is my body, this is my blood' [Matt. 26:26, 27], were omitted. This is the way they are said to act!"

One Must Stick to the Issue in a Debate
May or June, 1533   *No. 3329a*

"Up to now I've never had an opponent who fought with me on the same ground. They've always run off on a tangent and

---

[73] John Cellarius had just terminated his ministry in Frankfurt-am-Main and had moved to Bautzen.

[74] I.e., the answer was mumbled, so that it could not be understood.

[75] People who act like Desiderius Erasmus, with duplicity. Cf. No. 131.

[76] In 1530, during the Diet of Augsburg, Luther was in Castle Coburg, where Martin Bucer (cf. No. 184, n. 64) tried to reach an agreement with him about the Lord's Supper. The report of the conversation at table suggests the extent to which rumors and reports influenced theological and personal relationships.

haven't stayed on the field of battle. I have the knack of standing on firm ground. From it I argue. This is the point from which to strike. I don't run after anybody, for he who pursues somebody also gets tired.

"So I put the squeeze on Eck[77] when he tried to prove the primacy of Peter. Peter, he said, walked on the water:[78] the body of water is the world; therefore Peter is the prince of the apostles. I laughed at Eck for following Bernard[79] in calling the apostles the world. Driven into a corner Eck exclaimed, 'See, he doesn't acknowledge the authority of St. Bernard!' But I stuck to it, let Bernard be Bernard, and exposed the interpretation that the water on which Peter walked is the world.

"In order that you may remain in your position you must always remember that it isn't necessary for anybody who wants to win a duel to run over hills and byways, but he ought to stay on the spot, in the designated area, if he's not to be beaten in the duel.

"Mistakes should be acknowledged. For what is more human than to err? I frankly confess that I have erred in many things, but in things that are outside of faith. Concerning faith and grace I have taught consistently. Others wish to have unity with us and yet they teach differently."

Dependence on External Word of God

May or June, 1533   *No. 3330a*

"We'll stick to the oral Word. The devil can't stay where this means [of grace] is. So, for example, there are people who can't stand a bodily God, as God became flesh for us.[80] They want to have a spiritual God and boast of their use [of the Word], though the use without the fact is a figment of the imagination. God's sending [of his Son into the flesh] is a fact. The sacrament of baptism is a fact. Those people don't distinguish between the

---

[77] The reference here is to John Eck and the Leipzig Debate in 1519. Cf. No. 257, n. 107.
[78] Cf. Matt. 14:25-32.
[79] Bernard of Clairvaux. Cf. No. 494, n. 295.
[80] Cf. John 1:14.

fact and the use of the sacrament. Water, they say, is water, and they don't see that it's God's water. On the other hand, many people have the fact but not the use, that is, the fruit. So the pope has the forgiveness of sins, the Word, and the sacraments but he doesn't have the use [or fruit]. Accordingly one must distinguish between the use and the fact.

"I'd like to ask a fanatic how he becomes certain from his thoughts and the arguments of his own heart apart from the Word. We have the Scriptures, miracles, sacraments, testimonies. God sent his Son into the flesh, and of him it was said that men saw him, touched him, etc.[81] We intend to stick to this. If they don't hear us in God's name, they may hear others who speak in their own names.[82] Let him who doesn't want the truth believe a lie. This is what will happen to the world."

Effect of the Fall on Snakes and Fleas
Between June and September, 1533 No. 3345

"When God saw all the good things he had made, it was fitting that they should all be good, and therefore they were good.[83] Consequently we might have played with snakes as we do with little dogs. After the fall, however, many things, like fleas and gnats, became harmful to us. Therefore God also said, 'The ground shall bring forth to you thorns and thistles' [Gen. 3:18]. Power was then withdrawn from all men, and the annoyances that were permitted, and even the commands, were to many a reminder of disobedience. Instead of serving [creatures] men were commanded to rule over them."

Wrong to Postpone Sacrament Until Dying
Between June and September, 1533 No. 3355

"The thief [on the cross][84] sinned unknowingly and not in defiance of God's mercy or out of contempt for the Word, which he

---

[81] Cf. I John 1:1.
[82] Cf. John 5:43.
[83] Cf. Gen. 1:31.
[84] Cf. Luke 23:39-43.

hadn't heard until he was crucified. Consequently this example doesn't support those who have contempt in our time or those who postpone participating in the sacrament of Christ until the hour of death."

Difference Between the Two Kingdoms
Fall, 1533 *No. 3388b*

"Our Lord God has reserved the best rule for himself and his church, where one proceeds not in the exercise of law but in voluntary freedom. For Christ says, 'I baptize you, I catechize you, I absolve you, I preach to you, I comfort you. If you believe, you have this treasure. If you don't believe, the loss is yours. I don't forfeit anything as a consequence.'

"On the other hand, civil rule proceeds by demand: 'Do this, don't do that!' 'If you don't obey,' says the magistrate, 'and you do me an injury, I'll punish you. However, if you obey me, it will be of benefit to me.'

"Thus the civil government seeks its advantage with certain rigid demands. Christ's rule, however, looks to our benefit and allows us pleasing discretion. This works out well in the case of the elect. But in the case of civil rulers, the more they demand with their rigorous laws, 'Thus and so it must be done,' the less well it works out."

Fishing and Eating Fish with Pleasure
Fall, 1533 *No. 3390b*

Dr. Luther went out with his wife into the garden to fish in the pond and on the bank of the river. There they caught pike, loach, trout, blacktail, carp. Some of them we ate at the table with great delight and thanksgiving. The doctor said, "Katy, you are more pleased over these few fish than many a nobleman when he fishes in several large ponds and catches thousands of fish. Alas, greed and ambition prevent us from enjoying things. Many a skinflint sits in the midst of the greatest luxuries and yet can't enjoy them with pleasure. It's said that the ungodly won't see the glory of God; in fact, they can't even recognize present gifts because God overwhelms us so much with them. If they were rare, we might esteem them more highly. But we can't reflect on the pleasure which the creatures give.

"See how well a little fish multiplies, for one produces probably a thousand! It happens this way, that the male strikes with his tail, deposits sperm in the water, and from it the female conceives. Consider the birds, how chastely their reproduction takes place! The rooster pecks the hen's head, the hen lays a little egg nicely in the nest, sits on it, and soon the young chick peeps out. Look how the little chick is hidden in the egg! If we had never seen such an egg and one were brought from Shangri-la,[85] we'd all be startled and amazed. And all the philosophers couldn't offer an explanation for these creatures. Only Moses gives an explanation: 'God said, and it was so' [Gen. 1:9]. He commanded, and they were made. 'Be fruitful and multiply' [Gen. 1:22]. And so it goes on."

---

[85] German: *Calekutte,* a legendary place far away.

TABLE TALK RECORDED BY ANTHONY LAUTERBACH AND JEROME WELLER

1536-1537

INTRODUCTION

The pieces numbered 3465 to 3659 in *WA, TR* 3 are attributed to Anthony Lauterbach and Jerome Weller and belong to the years 1536 and 1537. About half of these have been selected for inclusion in this edition.

Inasmuch as Weller gathered some notes from others, notably from Lauterbach, it is not possible to determine with any degree of certainty which pieces were originally Weller's and which were Lauterbach's. Here we need to concern ourselves only with Weller since Lauterbach will be treated in the introduction to the next section.

Jerome Weller was born in 1499 in Freiberg, Saxony. He was matriculated at Wittenberg in 1525 and under Luther's influence turned from the study of law to the study of theology. From 1527 to 1536, when he was married and established his own household, Weller lived in Luther's house and ate at his table, in return for which he tutored Luther's children. In 1538 he left Wittenberg to serve for a year as chaplain at the court of the count of Anhalt in Dessau. In 1539 he was called back to his native Freiberg, where he was a teacher of theology until his death in 1572.

By temperament Weller was timid, squeamish, and given to melancholy. Luther rebuked him for avoiding people and urged him to seek out acquaintances and talk to them (cf. No. 3798). On another occasion Luther, who was absent from home at the time, wrote to Weller, "By all means flee solitude, for the devil watches and lies in wait for you most of all when you are alone. ... If the devil should say, 'Do not drink,' you should reply to him, 'On this very account, because you forbid it, I shall drink, and what is more, I shall drink a generous amount!'"[1]

---

[1] Tappert (ed.), *Luther: Letters of Spiritual Counsel*, pp. 84-87.

TABLE TALK RECORDED BY ANTHONY LAUTERBACH AND JEROME WELLER

The Coloring of Women Is Misplaced
October 27, 1536   No. 3467

He [Martin Luther] then spoke of female beauty and recalled what Martin Bucer[1] had said, "'Doctor, our women would be beautiful if their coloring were not misplaced. They have fine red eyes, pale white lips, yellow teeth, and black necks whereas they ought to have red cheeks, white faces, and black eyebrows.'"

Drunkenness at the Saxon Court and Elsewhere
October 27, 1536   No. 3468

While he was saying this, three young men, among whom was George Kaufmann,[2] came in. They had been drinking too much, were holding goblets in their hands, and were toasting the lute players and other youths who preceded them. Dr. Martin Luther looked at them severely and said, "Drink until misfortune overtakes you! People like you won't reach old age, for the best part of mankind perishes from too much drink.

"I was recently at court,[3] where I preached quite sternly against drunkenness, but it doesn't do any good. Taubenheim[4] and von Minkwitz[5] said it couldn't be otherwise at court; since music and jousting have declined, only drinking is left to honor a guest.

---

[1] Martin Bucer was a visitor at the end of May, 1536, when the Wittenberg Concord was drafted and subscribed in an attempt to overcome the differences between the Reformed and Lutherans. Cf. No. 184, n. 64.

[2] Luther's orphaned nephew, who was then living in the Reformer's home together with several brothers and sisters.

[3] Luther had been at the court of the elector of Saxony, in Torgau, at the end of September, 1536.

[4] Hans von Taubenheim was the elector of Saxony's collector of revenues.

[5] Probably George von Minkwitz.

Our elector,[6] who is quite a robust man, can stand a great deal of drinking. What he needs to satisfy himself is enough to make his neighbor drunk, for he's a man with a very strong body. Were he given to venery, it wouldn't be surprising if he worked his wenches to death. If I go again to see the elector I'll only ask him to order all his subjects everywhere to swill themselves full. Perhaps they'll refrain from what they're required to do, for 'we strive for what is forbidden and always desire what is denied us.'"[7]

Revival of Music and Gymnastics Proposed
October 27, 1536   *No. 3470*

"Excellent was the arrangement of the ancients that required men to exercise, lest they fall into debauchery, drunkenness, and gambling. I especially admire these two noble exercises, music and gymnastics. The first of these pertains to the spirit and serves to drive away care, while the second pertains to the body and practices the limbs by jumping and wrestling. The most important reason [for engaging in these exercises] is that we don't fall into other habits of drink, lust, and gambling such as we now, alas, see at the courts and in the cities. There one hears nothing but 'Here's to you! Drink it down!' Then one plays for a hundred florins. This is what happens when noble exercises are despised."

The Extent of Luther's Correspondence
Between October 27 and December 4, 1536   *No. 3472*

"I've preached here for twenty-four years.[8] I've walked to church so often that it wouldn't be at all surprising if I had not only worn out my shoes on the pavement but even my feet. I've done my part. I discipline myself.

"If I had kept only the letters that have been sent to me I could have filled a large building.[9] The many letters are witnesses

---

[6] John Frederick was elector of Saxony from 1532 to 1547.

[7] Ovid, *Ars amatoria*, 3, 4, 17.

[8] The reference here may be to the number of years Luther had been preaching in the city church of Wittenberg.

[9] On Luther's correspondence, see *LW* 48, xiii-xvi.

to my labor. But nothing has exhausted me more than cares, especially at night."

Noah's Drunkenness and that of the Germans
Between October 27 and December 4, 1536   No. 3476

"Tomorrow I have to lecture on the drunkenness of Noah,[10] so I should drink enough this evening to be able to talk about that wickedness as one who knows by experience."

Dr. Cordatus[11] said, "By no means; you ought to do the opposite!"

To this Luther responded, "One must make the best of the vices that are peculiar to each land. The Bohemians gorge themselves, the Wends[12] steal, the Germans swill without stopping. How would you outdo a German, dear Cordatus, except by making him drunk — especially a German who doesn't love music and women?"[13]

The Way in Which Italians Dance
Between October 27 and December 4, 1536   No. 3477

When he beheld some girls and boys who were dancing, he [Martin Luther] said, "In spite of everything, that is a remarkably pleasant pastime. Although the Italians intend to be chaste in their dancing, their carriage is nevertheless lascivious. They don't embrace each other. They don't even touch hands, but the one holds the other by means of a kerchief, and yet the motion of dancing is very wanton.

"Italians are extremely jealous. Woe to the man who speaks to another man's wife!"

---

[10] Cf. Gen. 9:20-27. For Luther's lectures on Genesis, see *LW* 1, IX-XII.
[11] Conrad Cordatus. Cf. No. 165, n. 62.
[12] Early Slavic settlers in Saxony. There were old Slavic enclaves in various parts of Germany.
[13] This jesting remark is as close as Luther ever got to the couplet which used to be attributed to him:
>He who loves not women, wine, and song
>Remains a fool his whole life long.

Rome Had a Reputation for Wickedness
Between October 27 and December 4, 1536　　No. 3478

He [Martin Luther] mentioned the city of Rome and observed: "Since our Lord God has put me into this disagreeable and horrible business [of writing against the pope],[14] I wouldn't take a hundred thousand gulden in exchange for what I saw and heard in Rome,[15] for otherwise I'd always be afraid that I was doing him an injustice. I speak of what I've seen.

"After he had carefully inspected Rome, that very learned man Bembo[16] said that Rome is the dregs of the worst people on all the earth. Another man[17] wrote, 'If you wish to live a holy life, depart from Rome; everything is permitted there except to be a virtuous man.' In earlier times, before the recovery of the gospel, there were often men in Rome itself who reproached the city for its wickedness. One was the Franciscan Ludovicus.[18] Another was the Augustinian Aegidius.[19] There were two other preachers[20] who, after they had censured papal conduct, were found the next morning with their tongues cut out. The pope's motto is 'Touch me not' [John 20:17]."

A Jew Is Baptized After Seeing Rome
Between October 27 and December 4, 1536　　No. 3479

Then he [Martin Luther] told the story[21] of a certain Jew who wished to embrace the Christian faith. The Jew confessed to the priest who was catechizing him that he would like to see Rome and observe the head of Christendom before he was baptized. The priest tried hard to counteract this plan for fear that an inspection

---

[14] Text in brackets from an early variant.
[15] In the winter of 1510-1511 Luther had visited Rome on business of his order.
[16] Pietro Bembo (1470-1547) was an Italian scholar and cardinal.
[17] One manuscript has on the margin: Mantuanus.
[18] Perhaps Ludovicus of Bologna.
[19] Perhaps Aegidius of Viterbo.
[20] Or "preaching friars," i.e., Dominicans.
[21] This story was current in the late Middle Ages and appears, e.g., in Boccacio's *Decameron*, first day, story 2.

of the scandalous conditions in Rome might dissuade the Jew [from being baptized]. But the Jew went to Rome, and after he had witnessed enough to cause his hair to stand on end he returned to the priest and requested baptism, saying, "Now I am glad to worship the God of the Christians, for he is sufficiently long-suffering. If he can endure such knavery in Rome he can easily endure all the wickedness in the world. For our God is angry enough to punish us, his people, in various ways."

Report on the Ruins of Ancient Rome
Between October 27 and December 4, 1536   No. 3479a

Then there was mention of the location of Rome. He [Martin Luther] had walked through the city for four weeks at great risk to himself, he said, and in that place, in ancient Rome, the best buildings had been completely leveled to the ground by the Goths. On Capitoline Hill is a Franciscan monastery, and the Tarpeian peak is higher than the Aventine, the Capitoline, and the Quirinal Hills.[22] The theater had been round in construction, he said; it had had a height of fifteen rows of seats arranged in a circle, and it had had a capacity of two hundred thousand people. Its walls and foundation are still standing. Next to it is the cemetery of Callixtus[23] in which many thousands of martyrs were buried, etc.

Increased Cost of Living in Wittenberg
Between October 27 and December 4, 1536   No. 3482

Master Philip[24] spoke about the high cost of living in this town[25] and said that a student requires twice as much money now as ten years ago. Dr. Martin Luther replied, "We see by experience. When farmers hear the pastors complaining about a shortage of food, they say, 'Oho, but they were able to make out before!' To this I have often responded, 'Yes, when one could buy fifteen eggs for four pieces of copper and a bushel of rye for two pieces of

---
[22] The elevations here reported are not correct.
[23] The catacombs of St. Callistus on the Appian Road.
[24] Philip Melanchthon. Cf. No. 157, n. 59.
[25] In Wittenberg.

silver, they were able to manage. But now that everything sells for three times as much, the cost of living has tripled while the pay is still the same.' Truly the farmer has now learned arithmetic; he knows how to double his cubic numbers."

Why Does the First Drink Taste Best?
Between October 27 and December 4, 1536   No. 3483

"How is it that the first drink from a tankard tastes best?[26] Perhaps it's on account of sin, because our flesh and our lips are sinful."

The Future Life and the Joys of the Godly
Between October 27 and December 4, 1536   No. 3484

He [Martin Luther] spoke of the marvels of the future life and its joys, although these things are indescribable: "It takes great faith to believe that our frail [and heavy][27] bodies will move about. I believe feebly on account of the infirmity of my flesh. The pope and the whole world don't believe this but laugh at it. However, we who are godly will see the Creator of heaven and earth. That will give us so much joy that we won't think about eating, drinking, sleeping, etc. Life will be quite different then. We'll spit on coins of silver and copper. For if we have such delight and pleasure in creatures—namely, in gold, the sun, stars, etc.—what will it be like when we see God?"

High Recommendation of Aesop's Fables
Between October 27 and December 4, 1536   No. 3490

Luther praised the fables of Aesop[28] highly: "They are worthy of translation and of being put into a proper order and arrange-

---

[26] It may be surmised that this question was suggested when beer was brought to the table. Perhaps this in turn led to remarks about joy on earth and in heaven, the subject of the following entry.

[27] Text in brackets from an early variant.

[28] Aesop's Fables are animal stories with attached morals for human beings. They are presumed to have been recorded in Greece about 600 B.C., although the existence of an author named Aesop is doubtful. In 1530 Luther had himself altered some of the fables, put them into German, and prepared a foreword for them. See WA 50, 432-460, and in this volume, No. 445, n. 246.

ment. It is not a book that was written by one man only, but it was diligently assembled by many men in different centuries. It would be very useful therefore if somebody would translate the book well and put it into proper order. The important fables that are pithy, smack of antiquity, and are useful to the commonwealth ought to be gathered into a first book; then those that are more elegant ought to be placed apart in a second book, and the rest ought to be reserved for a third.

"It is a result of God's providence that the writings of Cato[29] and Aesop have remained in the schools, for both are significant books. Cato contains the most useful sayings and precepts. Aesop contains the most delightful stories and descriptions. Moral teachings, if offered to young people, will contribute much to their edification. In short, next to the Bible the writings of Cato and Aesop are in my opinion the best, better than the mangled utterances of all the philosophers and jurists, just as Donatus[30] is the best grammarian."

Then he [Martin Luther] told some of the serious fables.

1. The Wolf and the Lamb

"The wolf said to the lamb, 'You have muddied the water for me.' Answer: 'By no means; you are standing above me [in the brook].' So he excused himself by simply referring to the circumstances.

"[Wolf:] 'You have nibbled off my meadow near the woods.' Answer: 'But I have no teeth, for I am still young.'

"For the third time [the wolf said], 'Your father once did this to me.' Answer: 'What does it have to do with me?'

"The wolf nevertheless burst forth, 'No matter how smart you try to be in excusing yourself, I'm going to devour you anyhow.'"

2. Another Example, About Gratitude
The Wolf and the Crane

"While the wolf was devouring the lamb a bone got stuck in

---

[29] Dionysius Cato probably lived in the third century and was the author of a collection of moral adages.
[30] Aelius Donatus, who lived in the middle of the fourth century, wrote the Latin grammar that was commonly used in schools in Luther's youth.

his throat. He implored a crane with his long neck to remove the bone from his throat. When this was done the crane asked for a reward. The wolf replied, 'Am I supposed to reward you? The fever take you! You ought rather thank me that I didn't bite off your neck!'"

3. Another Fable, Where Might Is Right
About Leonine Society

"The lion, allied with a wolf, an ass, and a dog, captured a deer. The lion asked for his share. The wolf, being famished, divided the game into four equal parts. For this he had his throat cut by the lion, who pulled the wolf's hide off over his ears. Seeing this, the ass gave all four parts to the lion. The lion asked, 'Who taught you to divide this way?'

"The ass replied, 'That doctor over there with the red biretta,' as he pointed to the mangled wolf.

"Happy is he who is made wary by the peril of another."

4. Another Fable
Everything Should Not Be Said Everywhere

"The lion invited all animals to his evil-smelling cave. He asked the wolf how it smelled, and the wolf replied, 'It stinks.'

"Then the ass, desiring to flatter the lion, said, 'It smells good.'

"When asked in the third place the fox said, 'I have a cold in my head.' Isn't this proverbial reply fitting? 'I have a cold in my head' means 'I am not at liberty to say anything.'"

5. Another Fable
Against Presumption and Temerity

"A certain merchant was buying bearskins from a hunter. Although the hunter had only twelve bearskins he sold the merchant thirteen. When he was to deliver the thirteenth, he took the merchant to a bear and said, 'Here it is.'

"The merchant answered, 'Give it to me.'

"When the hunter tried to stab the bear, the bear took hold of him, pulled his skin off over his head, and bit him in the ear as he left. When the hunter returned from the woods the merchant asked, 'What did the bear whisper into your ear?'

"Answer: 'He advised me not to sell twelve bearskins for thirteen today.'"

God Governs His World Through Frail Men
Between October 27 and December 4, 1536   No. 3492

"It is remarkable that God has committed to us preachers the ministry of the Word for the ruling of men's hearts, which we can't look into. But this is the office of God, who says to us, 'Preach! I shall give the increase. I know the hearts of men.' This should be our comfort, even when the world laughs at our office. So it is said that Maximilian[31] once burst out in hearty laughter at himself, and he explained it the next day: 'I laugh to think that God has committed his rule to a drunk and nasty cleric and to a goatlike climber.'"[32]

Luther Disparages His Earliest Writings
Between October 27 and December 4, 1536   No. 3493

When he [Martin Luther] heard that his books were in the library of the prince[33] he said, "My books ought by no means to be placed in that library, especially not the earliest books which I wrote at the beginning, for they are offensive not only to my adversaries but also to me."

The Preacher and the Notes of His Sermon
Between October 27 and December 4, 1536   No. 3494

"Our Lord God wishes himself to be the preacher, for preachers often go astray in their notes so that they can't go on with what they have begun. It has often happened to me that my best outline came undone. On the other hand, when I was least prepared my words flowed during the sermon."

---

[31] German emperor from 1493 to 1519.
[32] A later variant amplifies: ". . . that God has committed his spiritual rule to such a drunk and nasty cleric as Pope Julius and his civil rule to such a goatlike climber as I am."
[33] Presumably the elector of Saxony.

Amsdorf[34] also confessed that this had happened to him. Then Martin Luther said, "Oh, it isn't like a lawsuit. But many are casual and careless and pay no heed to what and how they preach. Dr. Pomeranus[35] is sufficiently full and solid in his sermons. On the other hand, I am thin and dry. When I hear Pomeranus, he gives me many commonplaces on which my thoughts may roam, and therefore he is a very good preacher."

Martin Luther said that he is often troubled in his sleep by the suggestion that he has to preach but doesn't have an outline.

Some Banter Between Lawyers and Theologians
December 4, 1536   *No. 3496*

Licentiate Amsdorf,[36] Licentiate Blank,[37] Master Philip Melanchthon,[38] and Dr. Melchior[39] were present in the evening.[40] At this time Dr. Martin Luther complained about the poverty of the theologians, oppressed on every hand, especially by noblemen who watched them with sharp eyes and rejoiced in their destruction and confusion. Turning to Dr. Melchior he said, "You lawyers also contribute to this and oppress us with a vengeance. I would advise you not to do this, not to lend your hands to the nobility, for the ruin of lawyers will follow the ruin of theologians."

When Dr. Melchior began to defend himself and his whole faculty, Dr. Martin Luther replied, "I exhort you not to push us, or you'll pay for it."

Then Blank said, "I'm a lawyer, too, but an innocent one. It cost me one thousand five hundred florins to study law, and in my practice I get only a few Brandenburger groschen. I feel it's

---

[34] Nicholas Amsdorf. See No. 1421, n. 84.
[35] John Bugenhagen, of Pomerania. See No. 122, n. 36.
[36] Cf. No. 1421, n. 84. There is some uncertainty about Amsdorf's presence in Wittenberg at this time. The reference may be to somebody else, or the dating may be wrong.
[37] Christopher Blank was a lawyer in Wittenberg.
[38] Cf. No. 157, n. 59.
[39] Melchior Kling, a member of the law faculty in Wittenberg.
[40] Here an early variant supplies the date, December 4.

my duty to do so." He made this ironical statement with a serious face.

Constance and the Council Called to Mantua
December 12, 1536   No. 3502

On December 12 Dr. Pomeranus[41] brought Martin Luther a book on the Council of Constance[42] which reported how its sessions were held and what was done in each of these. That evening Martin Luther read the book with concentrated attention, and among other things he found in it the decree that a safe-conduct given to a heretic is not to be observed.[43] Then our Father Luther said, "If we should be summoned and should appear,[44] it would be best to assail them [the papists] at our first meeting. It is all the same whether wrath comes at the beginning or at the end. Let us therefore attack the papacy with the article of justification: I believe in Jesus Christ; the just shall live through his faith.[45] With this thunderbolt the whole papacy would be shattered—namely, private masses, justifying works, purgatory, monastic life, invocation of saints, pilgrimages.[46] If we took our stand on this article, all other articles we might concede would have no effect.

"Campeggio[47] said that before he'd allow the mass to be taken from him, he'd let himself be broken on the wheel. To this I'll reply: Before I'd defend that mass, I'd let myself be turned to ashes, and more than ashes. If we proceed at the council in this manner, it will soon come to an end, for the two heads, Christ and the devil, must clash against each other; they can never be recon-

---

[41] John Bugenhagen, of Pomerania. Cf. No. 122, n. 36.
[42] The book has been identified as Ulrich von Richenthal, *Das Concilium, so zu Constantz gehalten ist worden* (2nd ed.; Augsburg, 1536).
[43] The decree adopted in the nineteenth session. J. D. Mansi, *Sacrorum conciliorum nova et amplissima collectio*, XXVII (Graz, 1961), 799.
[44] At the council called by the pope to meet in Mantua in 1537. The council did not meet until 1545, and then in Trent.
[45] Cf. Rom. 1:17.
[46] These topics are highlighted in the *Smalcald Articles* (1537), which Luther was at this time working on.
[47] Cardinal Lorenzo Campeggi, or Campeggio (1474-1539), was a papal nuncio who spent some time in Germany to negotiate a settlement of the religious problems resulting from the Reformation.

ciled. Consequently no concord is to be hoped for from this council because they [the papists] go not to yield to Christ but rashly to judge and condemn."

Then Dr. Pomeranus said, "Doctor, when you get to Mantua, the pope will be pleased with you, will welcome you, will not let you go, will take care of you the rest of your life." This he said ironically.

Luther Would Refuse Pope's Citation to Council
Between December 12 and 16, 1536   No. 3504

He [Martin Luther] made further reference to the council,[48] saying, "If the pope summoned me I wouldn't go. I'd scoff at his summons because he's our adversary. But if the council publicly asked me I'd comply, for I'd be welcome and I'd be received in a friendly fashion. He [the pope] damned me dreadfully in his *Bulla Coenae Domini*,[49] so that he excommunicated all who were attached to me. If you, my dear Katy,[50] went with me and acknowledged that you were Luther's wife, you'd be burned to death even if in other respects you honored the whole papacy. The Lord keep me in his Word! For I have very bitter enemies."

Signs in Nature and Their Interpretation
December 16, 1536   No. 3507

Between six and seven o'clock on December 16 a mighty crash of thunder was heard, preceded by a flash of lightning, following a week of bitterly cold weather. The mathematicians call this a chasm, and it indicates dryness in the air. Both Luther and Pomeranus[51] saw [and heard] it when they were at supper in their homes. [Afterward] they discussed these remarkable and rather menacing portents because it is not at all according to nature that we in the

---

[48] Cf. No. 3502, n. 44.
[49] Luther was included in the catalogue of heretics censured by the pope in the traditional Maundy Thursday "Lord's Supper Bull." In 1522 Luther republished the bull with a preface and annotations. Cf. WA 8, 688-720.
[50] Here Luther addressed his wife. Cf. No. 49, n. 1.
[51] John Bugenhagen, of Pomerania. Cf. No. 122, n. 36.

arctic circle should have such phenomena as often occur in Africa, in Asia, and among those who live in the torrid zone or the tropical circles. So it is plainly satanic.

[Martin Luther said,] "I think the devils wanted to start a disputation and that some angel stopped it with this chasm. The angel tore a hole in the devils' arguments. But the world pays no heed to frequent signs of this sort. When Francis von Sickingen[52] was about to die, something similar was seen by Philip Melanchthon.[53] When Adolf, a helper of the painter Lucas,[54] was traveling to Torgau at night with a peasant, he beheld a horrible sight: a great star in the sky, surrounded by beating drums, and the lord of a heavily armed body of men engaged in conflict with another army. In the year 1516 Elector John,[55] when he was in Weimar, saw 1) a large red star, 2) the star turned into a candle, 3) into a cross, 4) into a yellow star, and again 5) into the likeness of a broken star. This was observed in the year before the gospel.[56] I applied the vision to the business of the gospel which at that time occupied me and which rose at first like a reddish star. Then it burned, producing the cross of persecution, and finally it was obscured by sects and sedition. Yet it remains a fixed star. However, I attribute nothing certain to signs like these, for many are signs that Satan uses to deceive. Many such signs have been observed during the past fifteen years, but they have been singularly despised by the epicureans,[57] who await God's judgment without concern. So our neighbor,[58] who is enough of an epicurean, said, 'I know nothing. I haven't learned anything. But flaying people and amassing money are things I can do uncommonly well.'"

---

[52] Francis von Sickingen (1481-1523) was a "robber knight" on the eve of the Reformation who offered to help and protect Luther.

[53] Philip Melanchthon. Cf. No. 157, n. 59.

[54] Lucas Cranach the Elder (d. 1553) used his skill as an artist to support the Reformation.

[55] John the Steadfast was elector of Saxony from 1525 to 1532.

[56] I.e., before the recovery of the gospel, here dated from the posting of the *Ninety-five Theses* in 1517. Cf. *LW* 31, 19-23.

[57] Cf. No. 466, n. 267.

[58] A marginal note suggests that Duke Henry of Braunschweig/Wolfenbüttel was here intended.

Troubles Outside of Marriage and Inside
Between December 16 and 18, 1536   No. 3508

"He who takes a wife is not idle, for marriage keeps him busy. To remain continent in celibacy confronts one with temptations that are not trivial, as the experienced know. On the other hand, the annoyances of married life are [almost] unbearable to men. Accordingly Socrates is reported to have given a good answer to a man who was contemplating marriage: Whatever you may do, you'll regret it. In paradise, where there was no such ardor and raging passion, marriage must have been very pleasant. Flesh and blood were different then. But we have become so infected with original sin that there's no kind of life which, once undertaken, isn't a matter of regret at times. This is the fault of our original sin, which has defiled and deformed all human nature. It seems to me that it is the pleasantest kind of life to have a moderate household, to live with an obedient wife, and to be content with little." He [Martin Luther] looked up to heaven [and sighed], "Dear God, how art thou to arrange things so as to please us?"

Two Kinds of Adultery in the Sight of God
Between December 16 and 18, 1536   No. 3510

In God's sight adultery is of two kinds. The first is Matthew 5 [:27-28], which nobody escapes. [The second is] John 8 [:3-11] and is horrible. Yet it is praised, so that a prominent man said to Luther, "I didn't think adultery was such a great sin." But it is a sin against God, against the Holy Spirit, against civil authority, against domestic life. For an adulteress puts a stranger into the home as heir and cheats her husband.

Princes who Are Examples to Their Subjects
December 18, 1536   No. 3514

"The elector[59] and Landgrave Philip[60] are men with distinguished talents. They occupy themselves with public rather than private problems. If they live ten years longer (for men of affairs

---
[59] John Frederick was elector of Saxony from 1532 to 1547.
[60] Philip was landgrave of Hesse from 1509 to 1567.

like this can't live long) much that is of value to posterity will happen.

"He [the elector] is the right man for the job. He himself works from early morning until noon, for he has a calloused finger from writing. He is no drunkard, fornicator, gamester, or avaricious man, but is diligent, godly, and generous. May our dear Lord God preserve this prince! He is cutting down on his drinking. When I was in Torgau recently,[61] in the presence of the bishop[62] and the margrave,[63] I sharply reproached the drunkenness which is unworthy of the court, in which subjects ought to be able to find examples of respectability."

Rumors of the Pope's Death and Plans in Rome
Between January 1 and 14, 1537   No. 3518

Amsdorf[64] mentioned that Pope Paul III was dead[65] and that four patriarchs from Antioch, Constantinople, etc., have entered Rome with many others to prepare for a council. Dr. Martin Luther replied, "The papists know our heart, our advice, our teaching. We, on the other hand, know their intentions. God alone has secret plans, and what he'll do we'll find out when it happens. We'll leave things in his hands and cast all our cares on him, for it's his cause that is at stake, and he will advance it. We'll eat, drink, and sleep. If we appear to be fearful, the pope's courage will presently increase. Let the papists hold consultations and consider their treacheries. Christ lives, and before Christ died the betrayer Judas had to die, distracted and confessing his own guilt."

Melanchthon Deluded by Dependence on Astrology
Between January 1 and 14, 1537   No. 3520

"I regret that Philip Melanchthon[66] adheres so strongly to

---

[61] Luther was in Torgau at the end of September, 1536.
[62] Perhaps Matthias Jagow, bishop of Brandenburg.
[63] Joachim II, elector of Brandenburg from 1535 to 1571.
[64] Nicholas Amsdorf; cf. No. 1421, n. 84. There is question about Amsdorf's presence in Wittenberg at this time.
[65] The rumor of the pope's death was premature.
[66] Philip Melanchthon. Cf. No. 157, n. 59.

astrology. He's very much deluded, for he's easily affected by signs in the sky and he's deceived by his own thoughts. He has often been mistaken, but he can't be dissuaded. Some time ago when I came from Torgau feeling quite weak, he said that I was fated to die then. I was never willing to believe that he was so serious about this business. I don't fear celestial signs, for our creation is above all the stars and can't be subject to them, though our bodies may be. I'm not afraid of a chasm.[67] I'll leave it to the clever philosophers to hold it in esteem. Let Hans Metzsch[68] fear it!"

John Huss Remembered with Gratitude
Between January 1 and 14, 1537   No. 3522

Master Eisleben[69] read aloud some letters of John Huss[70] which he had himself translated.[71] They breathed the noblest spirit, patience, and prayer. They reported that while in prison Huss suffered excruciatingly from stone[72] and from the contempt of King Sigismund. Luther then spoke in admiration of the great spirit of John Huss, who wrote things like this with such firmness. "He was a man to be cherished," said Luther. "His death was properly avenged, for shortly afterward Sigismund[73] was plunged into great misfortune. His wife became the whore of the entire court. The Bohemians laid waste to Germany far and wide, Nürnberg had to pay tribute to them, and they got as far as Zeitz. Several times the Germans had to take to their heels."

---

[67] Cf. No. 3507.

[68] Cf. No. 342, n. 152.

[69] John Agricola of Eisleben. At this time Agricola was, with his whole family, a guest in Luther's home. Cf. No. 3179a, n. 62.

[70] Cf. No. 488, n. 280. Luther became acquainted with the writings of Huss only after his own proposals of reform had been developed.

[71] In 1536 three letters of Huss had been published in Latin with a preface by Luther, and Agricola had now started work on a German edition. Cf. WA 50, 23-34, 676-688.

[72] Kidney stones, from which Luther was now suffering.

[73] Sigismund, German emperor from 1410 to 1437, was partly responsible for the death of Huss. His second wife, here mentioned, was Barbara von Cilli.

Luther Explodes at Lampoon Against Women
January 14, 1537   No. 3523

Luther complained quite angrily in a public assembly about a few unknown students who had put together some infamous pamphlets against virgins and who deserved capital punishment according to imperial law, for they intended to defile others with their wickedness. "Anybody who lampoons priests and virgins will surely go to the dogs." [74]

Afterward he was quite angry at table in his home. He said that such scoundrels would not go unpunished, whoever they might be. If they were of the nobility, they were not by nature noble but were bastards who had degenerated from noblemen and inquired about neither their mothers nor their sisters. Then he [Luther] turned away and said, "Let us speak about good things and godly matters. Our Lord Christ is the one about whom one can never say enough that's good. Girls and women ought not to be censured in public pamphlets, even if there is reason to suspect them, but ought to be rebuked in private or reported to the magistrate. There are many imperfections in the female sex—as the proverb puts it, 'If all girls are good, where do wicked women come from?'" Then he [Luther] sang:

"A red apple may look good and inviting,
   And yet worminess hide;
So a girl with the worst disposition
   May be pretty outside." [75]

"There are defects everywhere, as the poets, instructed by experience, lament. St. Peter says by [divine] authority that woman is a weak vessel [I Pet. 3:7]."

Changed Attitude Toward Play and Games
Between January 14 and 31, 1537   No. 3526a

"Games with cards and dice are common, for our age has invented many games. Surely there has been a reaction. In my youth

---

[74] A proverbial saying.
[75] These lines are from a popular song of the day.

all games were prohibited; makers of cards and musicians at dances weren't admitted to the sacraments, and people were required to make confession of their gaming, dancing, and jousting. Today these things are the vogue, and they are defended as exercises for the mind."

The Court Needs the Law, Not the Gospel
Between January 14 and 31, 1537   No. 3527

"At court[76] this rule is to be observed, that one should swiftly cry out and complain. If one gets no hearing at first, one should plead and demand again. Modesty and the gospel don't belong at court. Rather, one must be shameless and querulous there. Moses with his horns must be brought to court, not Christ, who is gentle. Consequently I advise my pastors that they complain at court about the injustices they suffer. I have myself preached publicly in the presence of the elector and have said that he is a godly and upright prince but that the court officials do what they please."

When those present asked Jonas[77] and Philip[78] about this statement, they replied, "Dr. Martin is old enough to know very well what he ought to preach."

In Praise of Women and Marriage
Between January 14 and 31, 1537   No. 3528

Martin Luther looked admiringly at a painting of his wife[79] and said, "I think I'll have a husband added to that painting, send it to Mantua,[80] and inquire whether they prefer marriage [to celibacy]."[81]

---

[76] That is, at the court of a ruler.
[77] Justus Jonas. Cf. No. 347, n. 161.
[78] Philip Melanchthon. Cf. No. 157, n. 59.
[79] Lucas Cranach had done a portrait of Luther's wife, and it was probably hanging on a wall where it could be seen from the table at which Luther was seated.
[80] I.e., to the council called to meet in Mantua. Cf. No. 3502, n. 44.
[81] Text in brackets from a later variant.

Then he began to speak in praise of marriage, the divine institution from which everything proceeds and without which the whole world would have remained empty and all creatures would have been meaningless and of no account, since they were created for the sake of man. "So Eve and her breasts would not have existed, and none of the other ordinances would have followed. It was for this reason that, in the power of the Holy Spirit, Adam called his wife by that admirable name Eve, which means mother.[82] He didn't say 'wife' but 'mother,' and he added 'of all living.' Here you have the ornament that distinguishes woman, namely, that she is the fount of all living human beings. These words were very few, but neither Demosthenes[83] nor Cicero[84] ever composed such an oration. This is the oration of the very eloquent Holy Spirit, fitted to our first parent. He is the one who declaims here, and since this orator defines and praises [marriage] it is only right that we put a charitable construction on everything that may be frail in a woman. For Christ, our Savior, did not hold woman in contempt but entered the womb of a woman. Paul also reflected on this [when he wrote], 'Woman will be saved through bearing children,' etc. [I Tim. 2:15]. This is admirable praise, except that he uses the little word 'woman' and not 'mother.'"

Marriage Followed by Love or Regret

Between January 14 and 31, 1537   *No. 3530*

"It's the greatest blessing of God when love continues to flower in marriage. The first love is ardent, an intoxicated love which dazzles us and leads us on. When the intoxication has been slept off, the connubial love of the godly is genuine, while the ungodly have regrets."

---

[82] Cf. Gen. 3:20.

[83] Demosthenes (*ca.* 383-322 B.C.) was a Greek statesman whose name became a synonym for eloquence.

[84] M. Tullius Cicero (106-43 B.C.), eloquent Roman orator and statesman, was a model of Latin style.

Things Might Have Been Different

Between January 14 and 31, 1537   *No. 3533*

"Oh, how wonderful, beyond anything imaginable, our condition would have been if Adam hadn't fallen! Everything would have turned out according to God's command and Word. Adam would have said to Eve, 'God said that I am male and you are female.' They wouldn't have had to milk a cow or whistle to a dog. Everything would have happened according to God's Word. But now we do everything by habit without giving thanks."

A Letter from the Elector in His Own Hand

Between January 14 and 31, 1537   *No. 3537*

He [Martin Luther] read aloud a rather long letter that the elector had written to him[85] in his own handwriting. Its script was so irregular that the letters and characters could not be deciphered by many,[86] and for the most part they had to divine rather than read the meaning. Appropriate is the proverb, "The letter of a prince should be read three times."[87] Certainly this one needed to be!

There Are Dangers in Matchmaking

Between January 14 and 31, 1537   *No. 3538*

"Today I arranged a marriage. God grant that it may turn out well! It is well to pray, for the devil is hostile to this estate and quickly assails a marriage with poisonous tongues. I remember what happened to me in the case of Master Philip and his bride[88] when, after the wedding, he was told that she wasn't a virgin but had a tainted body. Oh, how I suffered with Philip for a whole

---

[85] Not, as has been supposed, the letter from Elector John the Steadfast of Saxony under date of January 7, 1537. Cf. WA, Br 8, 4.

[86] It appears that the letter was circulated at the table and that many examined it.

[87] This proverb was quoted in other contexts too. For example, cf. No. 365.

[88] Philip Melanchthon was married to Katharine Krapp, daughter of the mayor of Wittenberg, in November, 1520.

week! I resolved never again to be a matchmaker. So I advise all good people who contemplate marriage not to be dissuaded by the slanders of men—that is, not to believe Satan, who is bitterly hostile to this estate."

Gravely Ill, Luther Prepares for His Death
February, 1537   *No. 3543A*

When[89] Philip[90] looked at him [Martin Luther] he was dissolved in tears, and Luther said, "John Loeser[91] is accustomed to speak thus, 'It's no art to drink good wine, but to be able to drink bad wine is a real art.' So now you are thinking of teaching me to practice this art in order that I may be able to accept with resignation these pains of mine and this despair of life. If we accept good from the Lord's hands, why don't we submit to evil?[92] The Lord gave, and the Lord has taken away; blessed be the name of the Lord.[93] Long enough now have I played this game against the pope and the devil, and the Lord has wonderfully protected and comforted me. Why shouldn't I now bear with equanimity what he does with me according to his will? In any case our death is nothing compared with the death of the Son of God. Besides, so many very saintly men have been buried before us whose company we are not worthy of; if we desire to be with them, as we really do desire, it's necessary that we die. We ought to reach out for this with an eager spirit because our Lord is the Lord of life who holds us in his hand.

"Of course, a great change has taken place as far as I am concerned: Yesterday I was quite resolute in spirit and strong in body, while today, as you see, I am pitiably broken in my strength. How much I am changed from what I was yesterday!

---

[89] A variant inserts the date February 25, 1537. While in Smalcald to attend a meeting of the Smalcald League, Luther had become gravely ill with a kidney stone. This account is obviously not the record of a conversation at table; it is the report of an eyewitness in Smalcald, Veit Dietrich.
[90] Philip Melanchthon. Cf. No. 157, n. 59.
[91] Hans Loeser was godfather of Luther's son Paul. Cf. No. 2946a, n. 41.
[92] Cf. Job 2:10.
[93] Cf. Job 1:21.

Yesterday I felt exuberant and light as a bird. But, O God, we are nothing, and all that is ours is nothing, even when we are everything! I might have prayed to our Lord God, or at least grumbled at him, that he'd let me die in the land of my prince.[94] But if that's not to be, I'll be ready at whatever hour and place the Lord calls me. I'll be and I'll die an enemy of all the enemies of my Christ, and if I die under the excommunication of the pope, may he himself also die under the ban of my Christ."

The next day—that is, on February 26—he said when he vomited as a result of his sickness, "Ah, dear Father, take this dear soul into thy hand. I give thee thanks and bless thee, and let all thy creatures bless thee. Grant that I may speedily be gathered to the fathers."

Later, when the vomiting ceased, he said, "Go, my dear soul, go in God's name. How poor and wretched we human beings are! I have almost no strength left, and yet how Satan troubles and disturbs what little strength I have! Give me constancy and patience in thy faithfulness, my Father, that I may overcome [Satan].

"To you, my dear Amsdorf,[95] I commend Katy, my wife. I have no doubt that Satan produces and sharpens these pains. There's an obstruction in my body that prevents the stone and urine from following their course. But by God's grace I'll have it better after this life. So nothing that I now suffer from the devil will hurt me. I'll gladly go to pieces; only let Satan not have his way in the church after my death. I'm very much afraid of this because contempt of the gospel and ingratitude toward it are so great."

Hereupon he shed many bitter tears, sighed deeply, and folded his hands amid many sobs. "I'm concerned," he said, "lest the precious gospel may be lost, for it seems to me that I now observe some who first fall into strife and then yield to passions and forget that which is the chief thing in doctrine, with the result that the Word and the glory of God are lost to sight. How hard it became for us under the papacy! We read and did everything, and yet we found nothing. The more we looked, the further we were from

---

[94] In the land of Elector John Frederick of Saxony.
[95] Nicholas Amsdorf. Cf. No. 1421, n. 84.

our goal. I'm afraid the same thing will happen after I'm gone. The world doesn't care, but the pope knows that all his [utterances] are lies and trumpery."

At this point he again wept copiously [and continued], "Dear God, I am thy little creature, and thou art the Creator. I am thy clay, and thou art my potter.[96] If only the end will come for me and thou mayest preserve the Word longer! But I have reason to fear the opposite. I observe that the more we are enlightened, the more we suffer."

Then he sipped some almond broth and said, "Dear God, may it be blest for me either in time or for eternity! If this illness lasts longer, I'll surely go mad. Even if this should happen, I know that my God remains skilful and wise. Good God, how subject to death this wretched little body is! Except that I have faith in Jesus Christ, it wouldn't be surprising if I took my own life with a sword. The devil hates me, and so he increases my pain. He's got me in his claws, and no doubt I've deserved this from him. But avenge thyself, O Christ, against thy foe! I've done right to pick the pope to pieces, and I must hold him in check now once more. If anything good is to come of it, this should be done not in order that my health may be restored but in order that the power of the devil may be smashed forever. It hurts us, but God doesn't forsake us; he renders to each according to his works. So let God only take me away, and pay the devil as he has deserved. Amen."

On the same day he [Martin Luther] spoke as follows in the presence of Ponikau,[97] a nobleman and chamberlain of the elector: "I'm obliged to be stoned to death like Stephen[98] and to give the pope an occasion for pleasure, but I hope he won't laugh very long. My epitaph shall remain true: 'While alive I was your plague, when dead I'll be your death, O pope.'"[99]

Afterward he gave thanks to God for preserving him in the faith and confession of God's Word and name. Finally he asked

---

[96] Cf. Isa. 29:16.

[97] John von Ponikau, chamberlain of the elector of Saxony.

[98] Cf. Acts 7:54-60. Luther makes a play on words with the stones that struck and killed Stephen and the kidney stones that were causing him pain internally.

[99] Luther mentioned this "epitaph" several times. For example, cf. *LW* 34, 49.

Ponikau to commend his [Luther's] wife and children to the prince[100] and to thank the prince for his kindness.

The next day he said the same to the prince himself. First he committed to him the care of the church and afterward the care of his home. On that occasion the prince said that he hoped our Lord God would not do such a bad thing to his land and people [as to allow Luther to die], but if he did die, he promised to take care of the doctor's wife and children as if they were his own.

He [Martin Luther] ordered the ministers to report the following to the chancellor[101] of the duke of Saxony: "Tell my good friend the chancellor that I wish he might learn to know the pope as well as I know him. Then he'll be as hostile to him as I am."

He raised himself up and, after making the sign of the cross with his hand, he said to us who were standing around him, "The Lord fill you with his benediction and with hatred of the pope!"

A Legate of the Pope Rebuked in Smalcald
March 18, 1537   No. 3545

The pope's legate[102] was not admitted to the presence either of the elector or of Dr. Luther,[103] but they sharply rebuked him [and demanded to know] by what authority he had dared to confirm some children in Erfurt, in the domains of the elector. But when he put before them the reasons for his authority as legate—he asserted, first, that the pope is the head of the whole earth by human right; second, that the pope bears both swords by divine right; and third, that it is necessary for salvation to believe this—they openly ridiculed these claims without deigning to reply. However, they refuted these three claims.

---

[100] The elector of Saxony.
[101] Gregory Brück was a supporter of Luther and the Reformation at the court of the electors of Saxony. Cf. No. 1421, n. 85.
[102] Peter Vorstius, bishop of Aix.
[103] Vorstius seems to have had a private meeting with Elector John of Saxony in Smalcald, but not an official reception. Since Luther was ill, he did not meet Vorstius personally in Smalcald but learned about his conversation with the elector and was able to report it here after his return to Wittenberg.

Tyrannical Claims and Actions of the Pope
March 18, 1537 No. 3547

"One shouldn't remain silent about such unspeakable tyrannies of the pope, although young people aren't acquainted with them any more," [said Martin Luther]. "With the help of these tyrannies he's ventured everything that he's wished. He has impudently boasted about this in canon 22, which he's accustomed to cite often in support of his authority: 'Even if the pope destroys countless souls, one should not say to him, Why do you do this?'[104] Such horrible things are taught by the canons and decrees, which nobody could understand before our time. Truly terrible is the wrath of God, which can't be turned aside and which [through the pope] filled all Italy with abomination, factiousness, and poison; all that the pope couldn't accomplish by force of arms he subdued with poison. This is truly the day of wrath, calamity, and wretchedness for Italy. God preserve Germany for us! I'm afraid the pope, the bishops, and the Spaniards will lead our dear emperor into a land in which he'll die."[105]

The Scandalous Lives of Popes and Bishops
March 18, 1537 No. 3548

"Very great is the impudence and blindness of the papists, who remain impenitent in their errors. So all cardinals, bishops, and [other] papists know that they are wrong, but because they are papists they show what kind of persons they are, think they may do everything by their personal authority, and when their masks are down are nothing but epicureans.[106] They engage in lewd fornications.

"So Paul III[107] [before he held the papal office][108] prostituted

---

[104] *Decreti Magistri Gratiani Prima Pars*, dist. XXII, II. CIC 1, 73-74.
[105] Luther expresses the fear that Emperor Charles V may be drawn again into a war in Italy.
[106] Cf. No. 466, n. 267.
[107] Alessandro Farnese was Pope Paul III from 1534 to 1549. On his sister Giulia, see Ludwig Pastor, *The History of the Popes*, Vol. V (St. Louis, 1923), p. 417.
[108] Text in brackets from variants.

his beautiful sister to the pope[109] and was rewarded for this with the cardinalate. Soon afterward he abandoned his wife, for he had before been married and had a son, who is now a cardinal. So monstrous is the abomination of the pope that it exceeds all human imagination. He was not ashamed of being a procurer and accepting fees from the concubines of priests: [when they had a child] one florin (which was called a milk penny) from the child and one florin from the mother as well. It came to such a pass that all priests wanted to keep concubines in their houses without public disgrace, but when I was a young man concubines shunned priests. In Erfurt[110] the concubines of priests were held in honor, and at weddings and in public baths they were called Mrs. Dean, Mrs. Provost, etc. Dr. Staupitz[111] jestingly accused the bishop of Mainz[112] of being the biggest procurer in Germany, for no procurer in the richest brothel earned fifty gold pieces a year, he said, while the bishop received five hundred and more. The bishop replied, laughing, 'From this we pay the wages of the notaries in the chancellery.'"

A Response to the Calling of the Council
March 19, 1537   *No. 3550*

When asked what reply he had given to the pope and the emperor with reference to the council,[113] he [Martin Luther] responded, "Nothing but intrigues are set up against us. The pope ordered the council to oppose the harmful Lutheran heresy and summons us to kiss the emperor's sword that slays us. Thus we are called upon to surrender our own life and blood and concede that they are right. Surely this is too insolent and too much! It exceeds all imagination and utterance. Well, then, we'll defend ourselves with an Our Father and the Creed, but by no means with the Decalogue, for we're too weak in that. It isn't good."

---

[109] Pope Alexander VI (1492-1503) was notoriously immoral.
[110] Presumably as a student and monk in Erfurt Luther had heard what he here reported.
[111] John Staupitz. Cf. No. 94, n. 14.
[112] Cardinal Albrecht. Cf. No. 1362, n. 65.
[113] The council called to convene in Mantua. Cf. No. 3502, n. 44.

Pomeranus[114] said, "The expression, 'The Decalogue isn't good,' reminds me of a certain pastor who asked a boy, 'Can you pray?' 'No,' he replied. 'That's not good' [said the pastor, and to this the boy responded], 'That's why I didn't want to learn how.'"

Papists Fear What Happened in Smalcald

March 19, 1537 *No. 3551*

"The pope doesn't want reformation in his council,[115] for it's said that in Rome the word 'reformation' is hated more than thunder in the heavens or the last judgment. It's as a cardinal said, 'Let them eat and drink both kinds, etc.[116] What's that to us? But if they wish to reform us we'll fight.' We Lutherans won't be satisfied even if they should concede the eucharist in both kinds and the marriage of priests. We also wish to have the pure doctrine of faith and justification which banishes all idolatry. When idolatry is expelled the foundation of the papacy will collapse. The pope feels and fears such a reformation. Meanwhile the papists in Germany are very fearful, for the canons in Erfurt[117] asked what had been decided in Smalcald, whether it had been for their safety or their ruin. [Philip Melanchthon] said to them in reply, 'Remember the example of Augsburg.'[118] Moreover, the canons in Würzburg are making friends for themselves by means of unrighteous mammon; that is to say, they are in league with the landgrave."[119]

---

[114] John Bugenhagen, of Pomerania. Cf. No. 122, n. 36.

[115] See above, n. 113.

[116] Both bread and wine in the Lord's Supper. This was a secondary issue in the Reformation.

[117] The convalescing Luther and Philip Melanchthon had been in Erfurt on March 4-5, 1537, while returning from the meeting of the Smalcald League in Smalcald.

[118] I.e., the example of Lutheran forthrightness at the Diet of Augsburg in 1530, when the *Augsburg Confession* was presented.

[119] The reference seems to be a proposed alliance of Franconian and Hessian princes.

TABLE TALK

Modern Instruments of War Deplored
March 19, 1537   No. 3552

Afterward he [Martin Luther] spoke of firearms and cannons,[120] those most inhuman devices which smash walls and rocks and slay men in battle. "I think these things were invented by Satan himself, for they can't be defended against with [ordinary] weapons and fists. All human strength vanishes when confronted with firearms. A man is dead before he sees what's coming. If Adam had seen such devices as his descendants have constructed to fight one another, he would have died of grief."

Additional Comment on Illness in Smalcald
March 21, 1537   No. 3553

On March 21 he [Martin Luther] mentioned his mortal illness, or rather his death, for everybody had given up hope of his survival.[121] Restitution of his health was not looked for from man, and so his recovery was miraculous.

"After I requested that I be taken away from Smalcald in order that I might not die and be buried there in the presence of that monster,[122] I arrived in Tambach, where I drank a little red wine in the inn. Soon afterward by God's grace my bladder was opened, and so I wrote on the wall,[123] 'Tambach is my Phanuel,'[124] for the Lord appeared to me there. If I'd died there, my death might have brought complete disaster to the papists, for when I die they'll see what they've had in me; other preachers, like Zwingli[125] and Karlstadt,[126] wouldn't have observed the reasonableness that I did, and there's reason to fear that this would also be true of many others."

---

[120] Latin: *de machinis bellicis et de bombardis.*
[121] The reference is to Luther's kidney stone attack when he was in Smalcald. Cf. No. 3543A, n. 89.
[122] The papal legate Peter Vorstius. Cf. No. 3545, n. 103.
[123] A later variant adds: "with chalk."
[124] Cf. Luke 2:36.
[125] Huldreich Zwingli. Cf. No. 5005, n. 35.
[126] Andrew Karlstadt. Cf. No. 356, n. 172.

A Blast Against Agricola's Antinomianism
March 21, 1537   *No. 3554*

After this conversation Master Jobst[127] showed him [Martin Luther] statements which declared that the law should not be preached in the church because it does not justify. Deeply moved, he [Martin Luther] said, "To think that this should be said by our own people even in our lifetime! This is the opinion of Agricola,[128] who is driven by hatred and ambition. Would that we might pay heed to Master Philip! [129] Philip teaches clearly and eloquently about the function of the law. I am inferior to him, although I have also treated this topic clearly in my Galatians.[130]

"The prophecy that was written to me by Count Albrecht[131] is being fulfilled, namely, that there's something of a Münzer behind this.[132] For anybody who abolishes the teaching of the law in a political context abolishes government and domestic life, and anybody who abolishes the law in an ecclesiastical context ceases to have a knowledge of sin. The gospel doesn't expose sin except through the law, which is spiritual and which defines sin as opposition to God's will. Away with him who claims that transgressors don't sin against the law but only dishonor the Son of God! Such speculative theologians are the bane of the churches. Without a conscience, without knowledge, and without logical discrimination they teach everything confusedly and say things like this, 'Love is the fulfilment of the law,[133] and therefore we have no need of the law.' But those wretched fellows neglect the minor premise: that

---

[127] Probably Jodocus Neuheler, a guest at Luther's table.

[128] John Agricola was the originator of the antinomian controversy and had expressed antinomian views in Wittenberg during Luther's absence at the meeting of the Smalcald League. Cf. also No. 3179a, n. 62.

[129] Philip Melanchthon. Cf. No. 157, n. 59.

[130] *Lectures on Galatians* (1535). LW 26–28.

[131] The matter was discussed in a letter of January 27, 1537, which Count Albrecht of Mansfeld had written to Elector John Frederick of Saxony and which Luther may have read.

[132] I.e., there is something fanatical about this, as there was in the teaching of Thomas Münzer, who advocated rebellion against the princes and became a leader in the Peasants' War, in which he lost his life.

[133] Cf. Rom. 13:10.

this fulfilment (namely, love) is weak in our flesh, that we must struggle daily against the flesh with the help of the Spirit, and this belongs under the law."

Luther's Experience at His First Mass
Between March 21 and 28, 1537   No. 3556A

"I, Martin Luther, entered the monastery against the will of my father and lost favor with him, for he saw through the knavery of the monks very well. On the day on which I sang my first mass[134] he said to me, 'Son, don't you know that you ought to honor your father? Just so it wasn't a phantom you saw!'[135] Later when I stood there during the mass and began the canon,[136] I was so frightened that I would have fled[137] if I hadn't been admonished by the prior. For when I read the words, 'Thee, therefore, most merciful Father,' etc., and thought I had to speak to God without a Mediator, I felt like fleeing from the world like Judas. Who can bear the majesty of God without Christ as Mediator? In short, as a monk I experienced such horrors; I had to experience them before I could fight them."[138]

Children Must Be Disciplined with Understanding
Between March 28 and May 27, 1537   No. 3566A

"Stealing is no art. It's deception, manual dexterity. Presto, and the stuff is gone! That's how the gypsies were."

Then he [Martin Luther] spoke about children and said that they should not be allowed to commit thefts. "However, one ought

---

[134] On May 2, 1507.

[135] The meaning of these words is brought out in a parallel entry above, No. 623. Luther often recounted this experience, and usually with somewhat different nuances. Cf. No. 4574.

[136] The canon of the mass, the central action of the Roman sacrament in which bread and wine were believed to be transubstantiated and offered to God as a sacrifice, was said inaudibly by the priest.

[137] The variant No. 3556B here inserts: "from the altar."

[138] This conversation of Luther has been subjected to elaborate psychological analysis in Erikson, *Young Man Luther,* chap. V, and in earlier studies cited by Erikson. For a similar account, see *LW* 4, 341.

to observe reasonableness. If only cherries, apples, and the like are involved, such childish pranks ought not to be punished so severely; but if money, clothing, or coffers have been seized it is time to punish. My parents kept me under very strict discipline, even to the point of making me timid. For the sake of a mere nut my mother beat me until the blood flowed. By such strict discipline they finally forced me into the monastery; though they meant it heartily well, I was only made timid by it. They weren't able to keep a right balance between temperament and punishment. One must punish in such a way that the rod is accompanied by the apple. It's a bad thing if children and pupils lose their spirit on account of their parents and teachers. There have been bungling schoolmasters who spoiled many excellent talents by their rudeness. Ah, what a time we had on Fridays with the *lupus*[139] and on Thursdays with the parts of Donatus! [140] Then they asked each pupil to parse precisely, according to Donatus, *legeris, legere, legitur,* and even *lecti mei ars.*[141] These tests were nothing short of torture. Whatever the method that's used, it ought to pay attention to the difference in aptitudes and teach in such a way that all children are treated with equal love."

Preach to the Simple and Not to the Learned Between March 28 and May 27, 1537 No. 3573

Rector Bernard von Dölen,[142] minister in Herzberg, complained bitterly about his arrogant auditors who despised the reading of the catechism. Dr. Martin [Luther] was greatly disturbed and fell silent. Then he said, "Cursed be every preacher who aims at lofty topics in the church, looking for his own glory and selfishly desiring to please one individual or another. When I preach here[143]

---

[139] A *lupus* (Latin: "wolf") was a student monitor who reported such infractions of the rules by his fellow pupils as speaking in German instead of Latin.
[140] Cf. No. 3490, n. 30.
[141] Probably a common example of dog Latin in which schoolboys disguised German words so as to make them appear to be Latin.
[142] Bernard von Dölen moved to Freiberg in 1537 and was probably between pastorates when he visited Luther.
[143] In Wittenberg.

I adapt myself to the circumstances of the common people. I don't look at the doctors and masters, of whom scarcely forty are present, but at the hundred or the thousand young people and children. It's to them that I preach, to them that I devote myself, for they, too, need to understand. If the others don't want to listen they can leave. Therefore, my dear Bernard, take pains to be simple and direct; don't consider those who claim to be learned but be a preacher to unschooled youth and sucklings."

A Discussion of Lawyers and Lawsuits Between March 28 and May 27, 1537   No. 3575

He [Martin Luther] spoke at length about people who were in a perilous condition and confessed that he had often said to lawyers, "If I had a hundred sons I wouldn't bring up one of them to be a lawyer." [144]

[Then he went on,] "Dr. Jerome Schurff[145] frankly confessed to me in words like these: 'If a party comes to me and proposes a lawsuit, I first advise him to undertake a reconciliation. If he persists and lets the suit proceed I tell him that if he has a good case he'll win, but if not he'll take a loss. Then he leaves and takes his money with him.' Dr. Schurff is a godly man and until now has had a conscience; otherwise he would be much richer. But other lawyers are greedy, so that they can't recognize a genuine case, and they rob their clients blind."

Koeckeritz[146] responded, "Formerly both parties were required to pledge, before the suit began, as much as was at stake. Then a man was compelled to lose his living."

[Luther replied,] "This would scare off many a man. But the lawyers urge them on, take their money, and consume their substance."

---

[144] Actually Luther's oldest son John later studied law.
[145] Cf. No. 1421, n. 86.
[146] Caspar von Koeckeritz (d. 1567), a member of the Saxon nobility and a friend of Luther, had just settled in Wittenberg in this year 1537. In 1530 Luther had dedicated to Koeckeritz an exposition of Psalm 111; cf. WA 31¹, 391-426.

Luther's Illness and Comment on Medicine
Between March 28 and May 27, 1537   No. 3580

Dr. Martin [Luther] left the church when he felt faint during communion, and on his way he said, "Yesterday I felt fine, but today my condition is completely changed. It is due to change in the weather. Men are the best and most natural mathematicians, for they quickly feel in their limbs any opposition or conjunction [of stars] and any change of weather.

"The devil's also a fellow who can cause sickness. As Peter said in the book of Acts, the sick are oppressed by the devil [Acts 10:38]. Disease doesn't spring only from men's constitutions, and we observe that various medicines have been found to treat one sickness. Although these medicines have helped once or twice, soon they are ineffective. So powerful is the devil that he can alter all medicines and drugs and change what's in the boxes. Accordingly let us pray to the true physician, Christ. When the hour comes, as it must, in which we breathe our last breath, God grant that we may have a cheerful end. Amen."

Further Recollection of Journey to Rome
Between March 28 and May 27, 1537   No. 3582A

"I wouldn't have missed being in Rome[147] for a great deal of money. I wouldn't have believed it if I hadn't seen it for myself. For so great and shameless is the godlessness and wickedness there that neither God nor man, neither sin nor disgrace are taken seriously. All godly persons who've been there testify to this, and this is the witness of all the ungodly who have returned from Italy worse than they had been before. My chief concern when I departed for Rome was that I might make a full confession [of my sins] from my youth up and might become pious, although I had twice made such a confession in Erfurt. In Rome I encountered the most unlearned men. Dear God, what could the cardinals be expected to know when they were so overloaded with business and political affairs? We who study every day and are occupied every hour have trouble enough."

---
[147] Cf. Nos. 3478, 3479.

TABLE TALK

The Nature of Pilgrimage Then and Now
Between March 28 and May 27, 1537   No. 3588

"In former times saints made many pilgrimages to Rome, Jerusalem, and Compostella[148] in order to make satisfaction for sins. Now, however, we can go on true pilgrimages in faith, namely, when we diligently read the psalms, prophets, gospels, etc. Rather than walk about holy places we can thus pause at our thoughts, examine our heart, and visit the real promised land and paradise of eternal life."

Response to a False Report of His Death
Between May 27 and June 18, 1537   No. 3595

A certain messenger came from Hall, in the valley of the Inn in the Alps. He informed Dr. Martin [Luther] about a very common rumor in Italy, which is received with joy by the papists, to the effect that Martin Luther was dead and buried[149] and that his epitaph was written in Hebrew, Greek, and Latin letters. Many godly people were saddened by this rumor, the messenger said, and requested him to bring them a copy of the epitaph. "Since I find Your Reverence still alive," he said, "I beg you to give me a letter from your grave in order that with it I may comfort the godly people who have been grieving."

Dr. Martin [Luther] smiled and said, "This is an extraordinary request. Never before in my life have I written anything from my grave!" Nevertheless he wrote the following lines: "I, Dr. Martin Luther, testify herewith in my own hand that I am of one mind with the devil, the pope, and all my enemies, for they wish to rejoice over my death. I begrudge them their joy from the bottom of my heart and would willingly have died in Smalcald,[150] but God was not yet ready to sanction such joy. He will do this, however, sooner than they think, and it will be their misfortune,

---

[148] The tomb of St. James was alleged to be in Compostella (Santiago), Spain.
[149] For Luther's comment on a later report of his death, see *An Italian Lie Concerning Dr. Martin Luther's Death* (1545). LW 34, 361-366.
[150] Cf. No. 3543A.

for they will then say, 'Would that Luther were still alive!' This is a transcript in German, Greek, Latin, and Hebrew from my grave."

The Petition of a Jew Is Refused
Between May 27 and June 18, 1537   No. 3597

A letter was delivered to Dr. Martin [Luther] from a certain Jew[151] who requested and pleaded (as he had often written to the doctor before) that permission be obtained from the elector[152] to grant him [the Jew] safe entrance into and passage through the elector's principality. Dr. Martin [Luther] responded, "Why should these rascals, who injure people in body and property and who withdraw many Christians to their superstitions, be given permission? In Moravia they have circumcised many Christians and call them by the new name of Sabbatarians. This is what happens in those regions from which preachers of the gospel are expelled; there people are compelled to tolerate the Jews. It is said that Duke George[153] declared with an oath that before he would tolerate the Lutherans he would lay waste all churches, baptism, and sacraments. As if we didn't preach the same service of Christ and the same sacraments! In short, the world wants to be deceived. However, I'll write this Jew not to return."

Development of the Holy Year in Rome
June 18, 1537   No. 3597b

"Pope Boniface VIII introduced the jubilee year.[154] When the

---

[151] Josel Rosheim, i.e., Joseph Ben Gerson Lorchans, of Rosheim in lower Alsatia.
[152] John Frederick of Saxony. Cf. No. 3468, n. 6. For more information about the Jews during the Reformation, see Armas K. E. Holmio, *The Lutheran Reformation and the Jews* (Hancock, Mich.: Finnish Lutheran Book Concern, 1949).
[153] Cf. No. 275, n. 118.
[154] Boniface VIII, who was pope from 1294 to 1303, proclaimed a plenary indulgence for all pilgrims in Rome in the year 1300, the alleged thirteenth centennial of the birth of Jesus. Although according to a legend the holy year was to be observed again every hundred years, it was found expedient to shorten the intervals to fifty years in 1350 and to twenty-five years in 1475.

pope saw that in the jubilee year great throngs of people crowded Rome and offered very great treasures, a hundred years seemed too long, for many people would have to miss the opportunity inasmuch as very few live to be a hundred years old. Accordingly he chose to have it every fifty years. Afterward another pope, greedy for money, made it every twenty-five years. Then a jubilee year was instituted in Germany, at Aachen, where it rained money. Dear God, who can fully describe the lies and the knavery? Yet the papists wish to be very fair," etc.

Justification Explained by an Analogy
June 18, 1537 No. 3600

Martin Luther gave a very clear and apt explanation of the article of justification by showing its resemblance to the relation of a father and a son in this way: "A son is born an heir, is not made one, and inherits his father's goods without any work or merit. Meanwhile, however, the father commands and exhorts his son to be diligent in doing this or that. He promises him a reward or a gift in order that in return for it he may obey more readily and freely: 'If you're good and listen, if you study diligently, I'll buy you a nice coat. Come here to me and I'll give you a beautiful apple.' In this way the father helps his son in his weakness, although the inheritance belongs to him on other grounds. This is done for the sake of pedagogy.

"God also deals with us in this way. He coaxes us with promises of spiritual and physical things, although eternal life is given freely to those who believe in Christ as children of adoption, etc. So it ought to be taught in the church that God will repay good works, save in the article of justification, which is the origin and source of all other promises. One should say, 'Believe and you will be saved; do what you will, it won't help you [to be saved].' Accordingly we should remember that those promises and rewards are the pedagogy by which God, as a very gentle father, invites and entices us to do good, serve our neighbor," etc.

Incredible Tales of Sorcery and Magic
Between June 18 and July 28, 1537   *No. 3601*

There was mention of sorcerers and the art of magic and of how Satan blinds men.

"Much has been said of Faustus,[155] who called the devil his brother-in-law and let himself be heard from. If I, Martin Luther, had done no more than extend my hand to him, he would have destroyed me. But I would not have wanted to shy away from him. I would have stretched out my hand to him in the name of the Lord, God being my protector, for I believe that many poisons were prepared to harm me.

"So there was a certain man in Nordhausen by the name of Wildfever who devoured a peasant together with his horse and wagon, and later, after several hours, the peasant lay with his horse and wagon in a mud hole a few country roads away.

"Again, a certain monk haggled with a peasant about how much the peasant would charge to let the monk eat all the hay he could from a wagonload. The farmer demanded a penny. The monk devoured more than half the wagonload of hay, and so he was forcibly driven away by the farmer.

"Again, a debtor caused a Jew's leg to be torn out, and as a consequence the Jew fled [without collecting what was owed him].

"You see, such is the power of Satan to delude man's outward senses. What must he do to their souls?"

Interpretation of the Inheritance of Widows
Between June 18 and July 28, 1537   *No. 3604A*

"The greatest right is the greatest wrong.[156] Consequently there is need of a good interpreter, as in the case of that law in

---

[155] Johannes Faustus (Faust) was a magician who traveled about in Germany at the beginning of the sixteenth century. Even during his lifetime fabulous legends accumulated around him, and later he became the subject of literary exploitation. For example, at the end of the sixteenth century Christopher Marlowe wrote *The Tragical History of Dr. Faustus*.

[156] A common saying and a quotation from Cicero, *De officiis*, I, 10, 33: *Summum ius summa iniuria est*.

the Saxon code, 'After a man dies his widow should be given a stool and a coat.' Many a woman has worked in her household for thirty or forty years; if she ought to get what is according to the letter of the law, should it be worth only a penny? After all, servants must be paid better than this. Even an unknown beggar who stops at the door is given this much at a time. The word 'stool' must therefore be interpreted to mean house and home, and the word 'coat' should mean the sustenance by means of which she may maintain herself in her old age. This is the intention of that law, yet here and there some men wish to observe it literally and kick widows out as they would dogs."

An Argument for the Baptism of Infants
Between June 18 and July 28, 1537   No. 3608

Luther spoke about the baptism of infants and said that there was a time when many postponed baptism in the case of infants because they thought, when they observed that children of Christian parents degenerated from religion to an evil life, that it was safer to defer baptism until adolescence, lest it be contaminated and in order that it might rather be honored when received by those who were more mature. What appeared to be mistaken piety became the occasion for something bad, for St. Augustine and many others proceeded from postponement of baptism to such contempt of it that they were unwilling to be baptized.

Luther then related a story from Augustine's *Confessions*[157] according to which a certain unbaptized companion of Augustine was baptized by his parents when he was in the agony of death. When Augustine, who was then still a youth, visited him and scoffed at the baptism, the companion responded, "Be still, my dear Augustine, and do not attack holy baptism, God's covenant, in this way. I have been baptized, and on this I will die." With these words he discouraged Augustine from his frivolous objection. It is therefore safer to baptize infants.

Then he [Luther] proposed a syllogism concerning the baptism of infants: "Either there has been no church or baptism had

---
[157] Augustine, *Confessions*, IV, 4.

no effect. But it is impossible that there has been no church for fourteen hundred years. Therefore the baptism of infants has been effective."

A Comparison of Aristotle and Cicero
Between June 18 and July 28, 1537   No. 3608e

"I once read the writings of Aristotle[158] diligently," Dr. Luther said, "and since he observes the [scholarly] method precisely he should be esteemed. Otherwise he doesn't treat of significant things, for he knew nothing about the soul, about God, and about the immortality of the soul." And he read some passages aloud. "In short, Cicero[159] far excels Aristotle, for in his *Tusculan Disputations* and his *Nature of the Gods* Cicero wrote excellently about the soul and its immortality. Aristotle's *Ethics* is fair, but Cicero's *Offices* is better. His [Aristotle's] *Nature of Animals* has some value."

Comment on the Digamy of Priests
Between June 18 and July 28, 1537   No. 3609B

"I'm astonished that the lawyers, and especially the canonists, are so deeply offended by the digamy[160] of priests and maintain that such priests no longer have the right to preach and administer sacraments although Solomon, who had a hundred, even a thousand, wives,[161] wrote a better book than all the lawyers can. They want to tie the Word of God to persons, and yet when we were under the papacy we could put up with mass-priests and chaplains who had sixty concubines, twenty pederasts, and sodomists. Lawyers interpret digamy in an astonishing way if somebody marries a widow, etc. Oh, how vast is the ignorance of God in man's heart

---

[158] While he was a university student Luther began his acquaintance with the writings of this Greek philosopher. Among his works were the *Nicomachean Ethics* (on which Luther had lectured in 1508), the *Eudemian Ethics*, and the *Historia animalium*, here mentioned by Luther.
[159] The works of the Roman orator and statesman which Luther mentions are the *Tusculanae Disputationes*, the *De deorum natura*, and the *De officiis*. Cf. No. 3528, n. 84.
[160] The state of being married twice, whether successively or simultaneously.
[161] See No. 611.

that he can't distinguish between a commandment of God and a tradition of men! To have one, two, three, or four wives in succession is [in every case] a marriage and isn't contrary to God, but what's to prevent fornication and adultery, which are against God's command? The poor people don't know what digamy is. Lamech was the first man who had two wives at the same time,[162] and Jacob had four,[163] yet they were holy ministers of God."

Proper and Improper Uses of Consecration
Between June 18 and July 28, 1537   No. 3610

Master Gabriel,[164] pastor in Torgau, asked Dr. Martin Luther about that passage of Paul to Timothy [I Tim. 4:5], "For it is consecrated by the word of God and prayer."

Dr. Martin Luther replied, "Godly men acknowledge that all things are of God and consecrate them through the Word of God when they pray. To them all things are pure when they are used according to God's will. This passage doesn't support the papists who argue thus: Water that's been blessed has the Word of God; you despise holy water; therefore you despise the Word of God.

"I answer: This isn't the will and command of God. Rather, it's an abomination to suppose that we cause water to be above nature and to become something beneficial to the soul. We don't say grace to make our food better than it had been before; if we think the food is health-bringing on this account it is an abuse of the Word of God. This abuse is accordingly to be carefully distinguished from a true use of the Word of God according to divine command. One shouldn't rely on the first word of God that comes along, for every abuse, error, and impiety has its origin in the Lord's name. Consecration is a pure and permitted practice, as in the letter to the Corinthians, 'The unbelieving husband is consecrated through his believing wife' [I Cor. 7:14], that is, sexual intercourse is in such a case pure and permitted."

---

[162] Cf. Gen. 4:19.
[163] Cf. Gen. 29:21—30:13.
[164] Gabriel Didymus, called Zwilling (1487-1558), appears to have visited Wittenberg in the summer of 1537 according to a letter which Luther wrote to the town council in Torgau under date of August 21, 1537. WA, Br 8, 112.

Acknowledging God's Gifts in the Cherry Season
Between June 18 and July 28, 1537[165] *No. 3613*

Dr. Justus Jonas[166] praised the glorious blessing which God grants in fruit. "I have a branch with cherries on it hanging over my table," he said, "in order that when I look at it I may learn the article about divine creation."

Dr. Martin Luther responded, "Why don't you learn it daily by looking at your children, the fruit of your body? They're there every day, and surely they amount to much more than all the fruit of the trees! There you may see the providence of God, who created them from nothing. In half a year he gave them body, life, and limb, and he will also sustain them. Yet we overlook them, as if those gifts of God made us blind and greedy, as it usually happens that men become worse and more greedy when they have offspring; they don't realize that every child is apportioned his lot according to the saying, 'The more children the more luck.' Dear God, how great are the ignorance and the wickedness of man, who doesn't think about the best gifts of God but does just the opposite."

Luther Evaluates Some Contemporaries
August 1, 1537 *No. 3619*

On the first day of August he sat at the table after breakfast, and after some reflection he wrote on the table with chalk: "Subtance and words—Philip.[167] Words without substance—Erasmus.[168] Substance without words—Luther. Neither substance nor words—Karlstadt."[169]

When he had written this Master Philip and Master Basil[170] happened to come in, and the former said that this is true as far as Erasmus and Karlstadt are concerned, but too much is attributed to him, and "words" must also be attributed to Luther.

---

[165] Some early manuscripts indicate that this entry belongs in the year 1536.
[166] Cf. No. 347, n. 161.
[167] Philip Melanchthon. Cf. No. 157, n. 59.
[168] Cf. No. 113, n. 25.
[169] Cf. No. 356, n. 172.
[170] Basilius Monner (d. 1566), a former Augustinian friar, was a lawyer at the court of the elector of Saxony and later professor in Jena.

Why Court Cases Are Often Protracted
Between August 1 and 24, 1537   No. 3622

He [Martin Luther] said many things about the opinions of lawyers, who govern the world by opinions rather than by law. "For this reason many cases and controversies are prolonged for ten years and more," he said. "If they ruled according to fixed laws, decisions would be reached more promptly. What is called law is something that has been a) decided, b) made public, and c) accepted by the use of people, so that a whole city and its neighbors know it. Consequently Dr. Henning[171] and Jerome Schurff[172] say they are unwilling to recommend that anybody study for their profession, not even their own sons. God keep my sons from it!"

The Use and Abuse of Music
Between August 31 and October 11, 1537   No. 3633

He [Martin Luther] asked somebody if he was a musician. When the latter replied that he knew nothing about music, he [Martin Luther] responded, "Oh, the art is a noble commodity. One shouldn't use it for pay, for purse or coffer. The art is easy to practice, is esteemed everywhere, benefits all people, and nevertheless preserves its own integrity. Yet nobody wants to learn or love it."

Difference Between Speaking and Saying Something
November 1, 1537   No. 3637

He [Martin Luther] said that there are many fluent preachers who speak at length but say nothing, who have words without substance. Philip Melanchthon said, "Every age has had such Thrasos,[173] for Cicero[174] was reported to have said when he heard

---

[171] Henning Göde was a lawyer in Wittenberg.
[172] Cf. No. 1421, n. 86.
[173] Thraso, or Thrason, was a loud-mouthed soldier in Terence's play *The Eunuch*, first produced in 161 B.C.
[174] Cf. No. 3528, n. 84.

an exceptionally loquacious man orate, 'I have never heard anybody say nothing with such authority.' And Erasmus of Rotterdam,[175] when he heard a certain man in Bologna exult in his oration and was afterward asked what he thought of it, is said to have replied, 'Very good, for he far exceeded my expectation.'

"'How?'

"'Because I did not think there was so much stupidity in that man.'

"To speak is not an art, therefore, but it is given to only a few to speak aptly. Nobody ought to take anything upon himself unless it has been given to him from on high. Julius Caesar,[176] an eloquent man, was reported to have said that whenever he read what Brutus had written he thought he was eloquent but if he read the orations of Cicero he was convinced that he had no gift of speech."

Some Astonishing Relics of Saints
Between November 1 and December 21, 1537   No. 3637b

"Certain men have impudently boasted that they possess a feather from the holy angel St. Michael. The bishop of Mainz claims to have a flame from the bush of Moses.[177] So in Compostella[178] the banner is exhibited that Christ had in hell, and likewise the crown of thorns, the nails, etc., and also some of Mary's milk."

A Story Serves as Parable of the World
Between November 1 and December 21, 1537   No. 3645

"A man once rented an ass to ride on. The owner of the ass went on foot next to the rider. When it got too hot for the rider on the ass, he asked the owner to ride so that he might walk in the shade alongside. The owner of the ass was unwilling to do

---

[175] Cf. No. 113, n. 25.
[176] Julius Caesar (d. 44 B.C.), Roman general and statesman, was assassinated by Marcus Junius Brutus and others.
[177] Cardinal Albrecht, archbishop of Mainz. Cf. No. 1362, n. 65. Cf. also Exod. 3:2-4.
[178] Cf. No. 3588, n. 148.

this because he had rented the ass to him for riding and not the ass's shadow. For the latter he would have to pay extra.

"This is a picture of the world, which doesn't give anything for nothing, not even a shadow."

A Public Disputation on Antinomianism
Between November 1 and December 21, 1537   No. 3650a

"My best friends want to grind me under foot and throw the gospel into confusion. On that account I shall arrange a disputation to challenge my adversaries.[179] Perhaps they'll put on humility, but I won't be content with this appearance of theirs. I'll call them by name so that they answer to their positions publicly. The matter isn't to be treated in a frivolous manner. At stake is the glory of Christ, not our reputation."

Thereupon he [Martin Luther] said with a deep sob, "How painful it is to lose a good friend, one who is cherished with a great love! I've had him[180] at my table, he has laughed with me, and yet he opposes me behind my back. I won't stand for it. Nor can he maintain his position, for it's the crassest error to reject the law. It would be more tolerable if only it were other errors and offenses that were at issue. But to reject the law, without which neither church nor civil authority nor home nor any individual can exist, is to kick the bottom out of the barrel. It's time to resist. I can't and I won't stand for it."

Then he [Martin Luther] related with what gentleness he had rebuked him and with what cunning he [Agricola] responded.

Reflections on the Gospel for Christmas
December 25, 1537   No. 3654b

On the day of the Nativity [of our Lord] Dr. Martin Luther

---

[179] For some time John Agricola had been embracing and making public views which were opposed by Luther as antinomian. Although Luther had before been kind and conciliatory toward Agricola (cf. No. 3179a, n. 62), the latter's preparation of a series of antinomian theses led Luther to prepare some countertheses, and on December 18, 1537, a public disputation was held in Wittenberg. Also cf. No. 3554, and WA 39^I, 345–347.

[180] John Agricola.

said many things about this remarkable festival which offers godly people the greatest pleasure and consolation, for the dear angels themselves preach and accompany their preaching with their singing.[181]

"Those are true witnesses to the Messiah who declare, 'Rejoice, be glad! Here you have the real Prince and a child of heaven and earth!' They sing the best song: Glory be to God (that is, religion and faith), peace on earth (namely, in civil life), good will[182] (that we feel right and are well pleased). It isn't known, however, whether the angels were prophesying or expressing a wish, whether these words are to be understood indicatively or optatively. In his *Harmonia*[183] Osiander attaches "good will" grammatically to a disposition, just as the sophists[184] have interpreted it to mean a good purpose, as if they were to say, 'They have glory and peace who have devotion and purpose.' So Osiander speaks of being equipped with good will as if it were a disposition and not a feeling of joy, as if it meant being pleased with everything. They [the sophists] sweat over the grammar and the words, not over the substance, while they ought to make the words subject to the things and not the things to the words. When I proceed from the things I can use various words, as Horace said, 'Not unwillingly the words follow the thing foreseen.'"[185]

Speculations About Predestination Unhealthy

December 25, 1537 No. 3655b

He [Martin Luther] spoke at length about the idle people who occupy themselves with disputation about predestination beyond the limits of Scripture. It is the most ungodly and dangerous business to abandon the certain and revealed will of God in order to search into the hidden mysteries of God."

---

[181] Cf. Luke 2:8-14.
[182] Greek: *eudokia*.
[183] Andrew Osiander (1498-1552), an early supporter of Luther, wrote *Harmoniae evangelicae libri IIII* (Basel, 1537). Cf. No. 600, n. 367.
[184] The scholastic theologians of the late Middle Ages.
[185] Horace was a Latin poet (65-8 B.C.); the quotation is from his *Ars Poetica*, 311.

TABLE TALK RECORDED BY ANTHONY LAUTERBACH

1538-1539

INTRODUCTION

The pieces numbered 3683 to 4719 in WA, TR 3 and 4 date from 1538 and 1539 and represent notes taken by Anthony Lauterbach. It has been customary to refer to these notes as a "diary" because Lauterbach was more careful than others to set down in chronological order the precise date of each conversation or group of conversations and because it has been supposed that Lauterbach intended his notes as a record of his own life and activity. However true this is, what we have here is really not an account of Lauterbach's personal life but a reproduction of what Luther said and did. It is accordingly not a diary in our customary use of this term, and for this reason the misleading title (which is also used by Ernst Kroker in the Weimar edition) is not employed here.

It is interesting to observe that Lauterbach's notes cover almost half of all the days from January, 1538, to July, 1539. The selection in this edition includes about one-sixth of Lauterbach's entries.

Anthony Lauterbach was born in Stolpen, near Dresden, in 1502 as the son of the mayor there.[1] He matriculated in the university in Leipzig in 1517, and twelve years later he was enrolled as a student in Wittenberg, where he took his master's degree. In 1533 he was made deacon in Leisnig, but when friction developed there between him and his superior, Luther helped him in 1537 to secure a post as deacon in the city church of Wittenberg. There he was married the same year to a former nun, and despite the fact that he now had a home of his own, he was a frequent guest in Luther's home, as his notes indicate. As a matter of fact, Luther's wife once complained that Lauterbach took more notes at the Reformer's table than anybody else (cf. No. 5187). In July, 1539, he was called to Pirna as pastor and remained there to his death in 1569. According to his own statement, he left Witten-

---

[1] *M. Anton Lauterbach's Tagebuch auf das Jahr 1538.* . . . Aus der Handschrift herausgegeben von Johann Karl Seidemann (Dresden: Justus Naumann, 1872), v-ix.

berg reluctantly: "On July 23 I was called by the driver and a senator from Pirna to set out on the journey. When I said farewell to my very dear teachers and asked them to dismiss me with a blessing but to keep the position of deacon open for me, this was promised. The Rev. Father Martin Luther gave me this consolation when I wept: 'It has pleased God to call you to be pastor in Pirna, and you do well to obey. Although we would be glad to keep you here, nevertheless we must act according to God's will and not against his will. Depart therefore in peace! The Lord will be with you with his great power, and we shall pray for you and your church. Don't be sorrowful. He who is with you is stronger than he who is in the world [I John 4:4].'" [2]

---

[2] WA, TR 4, No. 4713.

TABLE TALK RECORDED BY ANTHONY LAUTERBACH

Presumptuous Opinion of a Young Preacher

January 1, 1538   *No. 3683*

How good, joyful, and auspicious is the beginning of a new year for the glory of Christ, the salvation of his church, and the confusion of Satan and his adherents!

On the first day of January in the year 1538 Dr. Martin [Luther] sharply interrogated George Karg,[1] who had been summoned to the sacristy in the church, about an oath which with astonishing presumption he had uttered in a letter to his best friend [and in which he declared that] if Christ offered him the kingdom of heaven he would not accept it at this time because he did not wish to agree with Luther on that matter. When this letter was transmitted to the elector[2] by George Karg's friend, the elector handed it over to Dr. Luther with a stern command that Karg be incarcerated in the citadel. But Dr. Luther first gave him a hearing in the sacristy; then he was arrested by the magistrate and put into prison, contrary to all the privileges of the university. Afterward, on February 1, he was released from prison, where he had been shackled in its steam room, when Martin Luther interceded in his behalf.[3]

Later on, when he had returned to his home, Dr. Luther sighed and said, "How great is the presumption and security of the world! Whoever thinks he's something dares to scoff at Christ and lift his foot against him. It'll get even worse; epicureanism[4] will make

---

[1] George Karg (1512-1576) had begun to preach before permission was granted by the faculty in Wittenberg and as an inexperienced young man had embraced some questionable opinions.

[2] Elector John Frederick of Saxony. Cf. No. 3468, n. 6.

[3] The last sentence, and perhaps the whole paragraph, was probably rewritten by Anthony Lauterbach at a later date.

[4] I.e., skepticism. Cf. No. 466, n. 267.

great headway. For contempt of the Word, which is characteristic of this world and believes neither in God nor in a life to come, is nothing else than a preparation for epicureanism before the last day. Isn't it a terrible thing that there should be such epicureans among the people of God? Not merely private and secret epicureans, but public ones in the ministry of the church, such as the Sadducees were who taught thus among the Jews and who exercised authority in religion and yet believed nothing about a future life! Such today are our papists, who know the Scriptures and yet take them to be foolishness. The bishop of Mainz[5] says and does whatever he pleases.

"Leipzig is so immersed in greed that forty-five florins are taken annually from every one hundred florins under the pretense of piety, for it's deemed charity to lend a person one hundred florins and justice to take forty-five florins from them.[6] In ten years one hundred florins will yield one thousand florins. Isn't this epicureanism? Leipzig is submerged in a sea of avarice that's deeper than the mountains of Arabia during the Flood.[7] The mountains were submerged only fifteen cubits under the waves, but Leipzig lies fifteen miles under the waves of avarice. All the others[8] are the same.

"Alas, bad times are yet to come. Our epicureans are worse than the Italian cardinals who say, 'Let the others be godly; we don't want to.'"

A Catholic Dean Becomes an Evangelical
January 2, 1538   *No. 3685*

On that day[9] George Roschütz,[10] of Wurzen, came to see Dr.

---

[5] Cardinal Albrecht, archbishop of Mainz. Cf. No. 1362, n. 65.
[6] For interest on the loan.
[7] Cf. Gen. 7:20.
[8] Perhaps this means "all the other cities," although Aurifaber later rendered this "all the other usurers and skinflints."
[9] According to the preceding entry, not translated here, this was January 2, 1538.
[10] Usually written Gregory Rossig (d. 1547), who was dean of the cathedral in Wurzen until 1538, when he became an evangelical minister.

Martin [Luther] for counsel. He said that for reasons of conscience he could no longer adhere to the papacy and asked whether he could with good conscience preach in Wurzen in accordance with his call or ought he give up his stipend there and live here in Wittenberg. Luther replied that it was permissible for him to preach the Word of God according to his call, but if he wished to study here Luther could perhaps make arrangements with the elector[11] that a position be given to him in lieu of his stipend.

Then he said to me,[12] "Everybody wants to ask me for advice, but I don't know whether they do this to learn from me or to spy on me. The ancients gave excellent counsel when they said that one shouldn't marry a foreigner or prescribe medicine or offer advice at a distance, for this is dangerous."

On the same day he [Martin Luther] wrote a letter to Dr. Pomeranus[13] and addressed it "to the bishop of the church in Wittenberg and to the ambassador of Christ in Denmark, sent from the heart and face of his less distinguished lord and brother." Thereupon he said, "The pope boasts of the cardinals sent from his side. I glory in godly preachers sent from my face and my heart."[14]

Greedy Men Are Concerned About Themselves
January 9, 1538   *No. 3692*

On January 9 Melanchthon[15] ate supper with Luther and spoke at length about events in the world, about how men are variously disposed, and about Master Veit, of Windsheim,[16] who had given himself up to avarice and possessed the best judgment about good and bad money.

---

[11] Elector John Frederick of Saxony. Cf. No. 3468, n. 6.
[12] Anthony Lauterbach, the recorder of this conversation.
[13] John Bugenhagen, of Pomerania, was at this time in Denmark to reorganize the church there after the introduction of the Reformation. Cf. No. 122, n. 36, and Walter M. Ruccius, *John Bugenhagen* (Philadelphia: United Lutheran Publication House, 1926), pp. 96-105.
[14] The contrast is between the Latin *a latere* and *a facie et a corde*. A legate *a latere* (from the pope's side) was the highest of the pope's representatives.
[15] Philip Melanchthon. Cf. No. 157, n. 59.
[16] Veit Oertel (b. 1501) had been matriculated in Wittenberg in 1523.

The wife of Doctor [Martin Luther] said, "If my husband had been disposed in this way he would have become a very wealthy man."

To this Philip [Melanchthon] rejoined, "That's impossible, for those whose hearts are occupied with public cares can't attend to private ones."

Counseling a Boy who Saw a Ghost
January 10, 1538   No. 3694

January 10. A certain youth, [apprenticed to] a blacksmith, had been deceived and frightened by nocturnal apparitions and had been led about all the streets from six o'clock to eight o'clock in the evening. Then he was interrogated by the specter as to whether he knew the catechism and was told that he had recently acted in an impious way, that he had received the sacrament in both kinds.[17] Finally he was told, "If you go back to your master's house I'll break your neck." Accordingly he did not enter that house for several days.

We took the youth to Doctor [Luther] and gave him an account of the case. Luther then said that one should not be too quick to believe any and everybody, for many fabricate such things; even if he saw a ghost he should not leave his calling. Thereupon Luther questioned the youth about his conversation with Satan and said to him, "See to it that you don't lie. Fear God, hear God's Word, return to your master's house, and do the work of your calling. If Satan comes back, say to him, 'I won't obey you. I'll obey God, who has called me to this work. Even if an angel should come from heaven [and tell me otherwise], I'll remain in my calling.'"

Questions About Purgatory, Prayer, Free Will
January 10, 1538   No. 3695

On that day a certain student came to him [Martin Luther] to ask his opinion about some doubts of his. He read aloud, from

---

[17] I.e., had consumed wine as well as bread in the evangelical rather than the Roman fashion.

Eck's *Commonplaces*,[18] the first section on purgatory, where Eck tried to prove his doctrine from the fathers. Luther replied that neither Ambrose[19] nor Augustine[20] nor Jerome[21] had anything to say about purgatory, but Gregory,[22] who was deceived by visions, taught something about purgatory, although God has forbidden that anything should be searched out with the help of spirits and has commanded that Moses and the prophets be heard.[23] On this subject, therefore, no authority is to be attributed to St. Jerome. Eck and others interpret the passage in Paul's letter to the Corinthians, "for the Day [will disclose it, because it will be revealed with fire, and the fire will test what sort of work each one has done," I Cor. 3:13], as referring to purgatory, although this passage has nothing to say about purgatory but about doctrine and the good and the evil life of the godly and heretics. Arius[24] had his day and all heretics have had their day and judgment, but the fire of faith revealed it, as the last day will reveal all things. In short, God has set before us two ways in his Word, the way to salvation through faith and the way to damnation through unbelief. There is no mention of purgatory. Nor should purgatory be admitted because it obscures the benefits and grace of Christ. However, it may be admitted to the sphere of the world [where true Christians are winnowed and purged].[25]

Another question was raised about the intercession of saints, whether the dead pray for us. Luther replied, "Let's permit them to pray! Yet both their life and their prayer are unknown to us. We can't understand how their death is life. If it should be objected that St. Ambrose made an entreaty in behalf of Emperor

---

[18] John Eck, *Enchiridion locorum communium adversos Lutheranos* (1525). On Eck, cf. No. 257, n. 107.
[19] Cf. No. 51, n. 6.
[20] Cf. No. 51, n. 4.
[21] Cf. No. 51, n. 2.
[22] Cf. No. 51, n. 5.
[23] Cf. Luke 16:29.
[24] Arius (*ca.* 256-336), one of the most notorious of heretics, was condemned by the Council of Nicaea (325) on account of his teaching about the person of Christ.
[25] Text in brackets from later version.

Theodosius[26] after the latter's death, this was an invention of his. If it should be objected that Augustine prayed for his mother Monica [after her death], this proves nothing, nor did he wish his writings to be adhered to unless they agreed with the Holy Scriptures, for he wrote, 'I do not wish that my writings,' etc.[27] In short, it's necessary to stick to the clear Word of God and not to human opinions."

There was a third question concerning free will, whether man has it. Luther replied, "This expression 'free will' was very odious to all the fathers, although they conceded, as we do too, that God gave man a free will. But the question here is whether this freedom is in our power. One ought properly call it a changeable, mutable will because God works in us and we are passive; like a potter, from the same material he can make a vessel either for honor or dishonor [Rom. 9:21]. Accordingly our free will is passive, not active, because it doesn't lie in our power."

Thereupon he instructed him [the student] to read the Bible and Philip's *Loci Communes*.[28]

Evaluation of Peter Lombard and His Work
January 10, 1538 No. 3698

"Peter Lombard[29] was a very diligent man with a superior mind. He wrote many excellent things. He would really have been a great doctor of the church if he had given himself wholly and truly to the Holy Scriptures, but he confuses the Scriptures with many useless questions. There were very great intellects in those days, but the times were not like ours. The scholastics got so far as to teach that man is uncorrupted, only slightly wounded,

---

[26] Roman emperor from A.D. 379 to 395.
[27] Augustine, *Epistles*, 82; 148.
[28] Philip Melanchthon's *Loci communes rerum theologicarum* (Wittenberg, 1521), intended as a key to the interpretation of the Scriptures, was published in several editions and was expanded from an originally brief manual to a large book. Cf. Charles L. Hill (trans.), *The Loci Communes of Philip Melanchthon* (Boston: Meador, 1944); Clyde L. Manschreck (trans.), *Melanchthon: On Christian Doctrine* (New York: Oxford University Press, 1965).
[29] Peter, called "the Lombard" from his birthplace. Cf. No. 192, n. 67.

and so he can keep the law by his own strength, without grace, although a man who has attained grace can keep the law more easily than would be possible by his own strength. Such monstrous things did they teach—without paying attention to the fall of Adam, without recognizing that the law of God is spiritual."

The Folly of the Dominicans and Others
January 14, 1538   *No. 3701*

On January 14 he [Martin Luther] spoke a great deal about the kingdom of the pope and how it has been founded not on laws but on superstition: "In fact, the Dominicans and Franciscans have been the chief auxiliaries of the pope, for the Dominicans, or Order of Preachers,[30] were the famous Atlantans[31] who tried to become illustrious at the expense of the dishonor of others and couldn't tolerate learned men. I think they made great fools of themselves in their controversy with Reuchlin.[32] Against me, too, they engaged in many machinations, but not without injury to themselves. In a future council they and the rest of the papists will take many liberties with their clamor. Their chief cry is and has been: 'What are the Bible and the Scriptures worth? One must obey the church and the councils!' They'll try to silence us with this cry, for they arrogate to themselves the right and the oversight of all men and they'll claim to be judges of the believers. This also happened to the prophets, who had to succumb, as it is written in Jeremiah 29 [:26-27], where the writer speaks against the priest Zephaniah: 'The Lord has appointed you to have charge in your house over every madman who prophesies. Why have you not rebuked Jeremiah of Anathoth?' From this passage it's clear that the priests who were put in high office abused their authority against the

---

[30] Along with the Franciscans, the Dominicans were the leading mendicant order in the late Middle Ages and called themselves the Order of Preachers.

[31] In Greek mythology Atlas had the task of carrying the world on his shoulders.

[32] The distinguished Hebrew scholar John Reuchlin (1455-1522) fought for the preservation of Jewish literature at a time when the Dominicans in Cologne were bent on its destruction. The Dominicans suffered in prestige from the satirical *Letters of Obscure Men*, which made them out to be stupid. Cf. F. G. Stokes (ed.), *Epistolae Obscurorum Virorum* (New York: Harper & Row, 1964).

godly prophets. So it comes about that the ungodly in the world revile the godly under a pretense of piety. Blessed is he who isn't offended by this!"

The Form of the Church Is a Servant Form
January 17, 1538   *No. 3709*

Jerome Schurff[33] and the philosophers are offended by the form of the church, which is subject to scandals and sects, because they think of the church as pure, holy, unspotted, and the dove of God. It's true that the church has this appearance in God's sight, but in the eyes of the world the church is like its bridegroom Christ: hacked to pieces, marked with scratches, despised, crucified, mocked [Isa. 53:2, 3]. The image of the church and of Christ is a sheep. The image of hypocrites is a serpent, a viper, an adder. We're experiencing this in the very bitter hatred of religion which far exceeds every hatred of men and beasts, and we've encountered it in Oecolampadius,[34] Zwingli,[35] and Bucer.[36] At first Cochlaeus[37] wrote to me in a very gentle way, admonishing me to hold to the gospel, but afterward he became a viper."

The Authority of Popes and Councils
January 31, 1538   *No. 3720*

On the last day of January Luther discussed many things with the licentiate of Magdeburg[38] about the casual haughtiness of the Italians. "Although they have been convicted by the very plain Word of God," said Luther, "it's intolerable to them to be reformed by the Germans. I've often thought to myself, 'What if you went to the council[39] after all in order to establish some sort of harmony?'

---

[33] Cf. No. 1421, n. 86.
[34] John Oecolampadius. Cf. No. 94, n. 19.
[35] Huldreich Zwingli. Cf. No. 5005, n. 35.
[36] Martin Bucer. Cf. No. 184, n. 64.
[37] John Cochlaeus. Cf. No. 1320, n. 38.
[38] Liborius Magdeburg was pastor in Orlamünde from 1538 to his death in 1539.
[39] Cf. Nos. 3502, 3504, 3550.

But no means to this end can be found, for if the pope were willing to acknowledge manifest articles of faith and his gross and palpable errors and were willing to submit to the council, he would lose his authority because he boasts that he's the head of the church and that all its members owe him obedience. Accordingly the Council of Constance is accused of arrogating to itself authority over the pope.[40] If the papists made a concession to us in the most insignificant point, everything else would be put into question. Everybody would cry out, 'Hasn't it been said that the pope is the head of the church and can't err?' This is the foundation and chief claim of the papacy. Sylvester Prierias,[41] the master of the sacred palace, tried to frighten me with such a thunderbolt when he said, 'Whoever questions a word or act of the Roman church is a heretic.' At that time I was still weak. I didn't want to attack the church. I had respect for such arguments. Now, however, I write about the council and offer the emperor this advice: that he give the Roman pontiff the liberty and power to decide and decree whatever he pleases. This is the best way to solve the problem. Little as the pope can concede anything, so little can I relax what is demanded by the Word of God."

Rejection of the Medieval Scholastics
February 2, 1538　　　　　　　　　　　　　　　　No. 3722

On February 2 the elector of Saxony,[42] Duke Henry of Saxony,[43] the landgrave,[44] and Margrave Joachim[45] arrived in Wittenberg and did Luther the honor of asking him to preach the follow-

---

[40] At the Council of Constance (1414-1418) it had been decided on April 6, 1415, that the highest authority in the church belongs to the council rather than the pope. Cf. Hans J. Margull (ed.), *The Councils of the Church* (Philadelphia: Fortress Press, 1966), pp. 192-206; cf. also E. F. Jacob, *Essays in the Conciliar Epoch* (Manchester, University Press, 1943).
[41] Sylvester Prierias was *magister sacri palatii* and as such censor of books and inquisitor in cases of suspected heresy. Cf. No. 491, n. 287.
[42] Elector John Frederick. Cf. No. 3468, n. 6.
[43] Perhaps intended here was the Duke Henry who later (1539-1541) ruled over Albertine Saxony.
[44] Landgrave Philip of Hesse. Cf. No. 3514, n. 60.
[45] Margrave John of Küstrin (1535-1571).

ing day, which he did in praise of the Lord's Prayer. That evening Luther talked cheerfully with Amsdorf.[46] They spoke at length about studies in the previous age, when the most gifted men had to occupy themselves with fruitless investigations. To students of our time the sophistical terminology of that age is altogether unfamiliar and seems barbarous. When the papacy was flourishing Scotus,[47] Bonaventure,[48] Gabriel,[49] and Thomas[50] had to embroider their thoughts with fantasies because they had no serious tasks to perform.

"Gabriel [Biel] wrote a book on the canon of the mass[51] which I once thought was the best [on the subject]. When I read it my heart bled. The authority of the Scriptures meant nothing to Gabriel. I still have the books that used to torment me so. Scotus wrote best on the third book of the *Sentences*.[52] Occam[53] was very clever in his devotion to method; he had a fondness for enlarging upon and amplifying things into infinity, but Thomas was most loquacious because he was seduced by metaphysics.

"God led us away from all this in a wonderful way; without my quite being aware of it he took me away from that game more than twenty years ago. How difficult it was at first when we journeyed toward Kemberg[54] after All Saints' Day[55] in the year 1517, when I first made up my mind to write against the crass errors of indulgences! Dr. Jerome Schurff[56] advised against this: 'You wish to write against the pope? What are you trying to do? It won't be tolerated!' I replied, 'And if they have to tolerate it?'

---

[46] Nicholas Amsdorf. Cf. No. 1421, n. 84.
[47] John Duns Scotus (d. 1308), called "the subtile doctor," was one of the leading scholastic theologians.
[48] Bonaventure (1221-1274), called "the seraphic doctor," was, like Scotus, a Franciscan theologian.
[49] Gabriel Biel (d. 1495) was a German disciple of William of Occam.
[50] Thomas Aquinas. Cf. No. 96, n. 22.
[51] *Expositio canonis missae* (Tübingen, 1499).
[52] John Duns Scotus, *Opus Oxoniense*, so called because it was written in Oxford.
[53] William of Occam, called "the invincible doctor," was a nominalist theologian. Cf. No. 5135, n. 125.
[54] A monastery near Wittenberg.
[55] November 1.
[56] Jerome Schurff. Cf. No. 1421, n. 86.

Presently Sylvester,[57] master of the sacred palace, entered the arena, fulminating against me with this syllogism: 'Whoever questions what the Roman church says and does is heretical. Luther questions what the Roman church says and does, and therefore [he is a heretic].' So it all began.

"The pope speaks of the church in three distinct ways: essentially it is the body of the church itself, representatively it is the college of cardinals, virtually it is the pope himself. There is no mention of the council, for the pope wishes to be the virtual church, above the Scriptures and the authority of councils. Duke George[58] is so zealous in behalf of the essential church because he wishes himself to be the church. He hates the pope, and so he wants to act as reformer of the church and reform him; as the bishop of Mainz should have only one bishopric and ride with fourteen horses, and as the bishop of Merseburg should ride with three horses, so the pope should cease from his acts of simony. For all the papists hold that the bishops should remain but should be reformed. However, the papists don't want to risk being found in error during a reform.

"Italy has often been humiliated before, but it has always been proud. Now, however, it is afraid and acknowledges its wickedness, but it doesn't wish to be punished by us Germans because we are a barbarous nation in its eyes. Nevertheless, if somebody were to arise in Italy who had authority and protection, he would be able to accomplish something."

The Mass Not of Primary Importance
February 2, 1538   *No. 3723*

Dr. Schneidewein[59] said that on many points the Italians are Lutheran and would commend him [Luther] without hesitation. "If you had not attacked the mass," they said, "you would have a large following in Italy." To reject the mass is the most horrible

---
[57] Sylvester Prierias. Cf. No. 491, n. 287.
[58] Cf. No. 275, n. 118.
[59] Henry Schneidewein, a lawyer and later professor of law in Jena, returned from a trip to Italy in January, 1537. Cf. No. 461, n. 255.

thing in their eyes. They are so attached to this cultus that they think that anybody who has attended mass will on that day be free from danger and unable to sin. It is on this account that the greatest sins and murders occur after the hearing of masses; long lasting hate and feuds lead to homicide after mass. A certain man, who plotted against his enemy in hate and animosity for two years, was unable to catch up with him until he took him by surprise in church after mass, killed him, and fled.

Then Luther responded, "My book on the abrogation of the mass[60] is quite harsh. It was written against blaspheming opponents and not for beginners who are offended by it. If twenty years ago anybody had taken away the mass from me he would have had a fight on his hands with me, for at that time I adored it with my whole heart. And yet the mass and the entire papacy are based on nothing else than gain and profit."

Luther Recalls His Illness in Smalcald
February 5, 1538 *No. 3733*

On February 5 Luther spoke about the perilous times and sighed: "Dear God, if I had died of stone in Smalcald[61] I would now have been in heaven, freed from all evil, for a year. I was at that time sufficiently annoyed by the physicians. They gave me as much to drink as if I had been a big ox. They worked over my body until all my members, even my private parts, became lifeless. I had to obey the physicians. I did what I did from necessity, lest I appear to neglect my body. Wretched is the man who relies on the help of physicians. I don't deny that medicine is a gift of God and I don't reject this knowledge, but where are the physicians who are perfect? A good regimen is worth a great deal. So if I feel tired and nevertheless adhere to my regimen, go to bed by the ninth hour, and have a restful night, I will be refreshed. When I get up from my rest I can't work very long. My time has just about come anyhow."

---

[60] *The Misuse of the Mass* (1521). LW 36, 127-230.
[61] Cf. No. 3543A.

RECORDED BY LAUTERBACH

Reflections on Washing Before Supper
February 13, 1538   *No. 3742*

On this day,[62] when he [Martin Luther] came out of the bath[63] and washed his hands before the evening meal, he said, "How dirty the water gets after a bath! Well, I have forgotten that our skin and flesh are made of dirt. It is as the Scripture says, 'You are dust and ashes' [Gen. 3:19]. How proud you are, O man!"

Fish on the Table Evokes Comment
February 13, 1538   *No. 3743*

Thereupon, when he saw that fish had been placed on the table, he [Martin Luther] spoke at length about God's power in generation, and especially about reproduction in streams and the sea, where one fish can bring many thousands to life, as one can see from the roe. "One can fish in the Elbe River all day, and yet it remains full of fish. The number and the reproduction of fish, especially at sea, is incredible, for it is said that the ocean near Antwerp produces a new kind of fish every week."

Ten Children Cannot Support One Father
February 17, 1538   *No. 3751*

The artist and mayor Lucas[64] said that this is a perilous time, that there is widespread disobedience and ingratitude, so that a magistrate is very much occupied with cases involving the relation of parents and children. Luther responded, "There is an old proverb, 'A father can support ten children better than ten children can support one father.' It is not for nothing, therefore, that God urges the Fourth Commandment upon us, 'Honor [your father and your mother] that your days may be long in the land' [Exod. 20:12]."

---

[62] February 13, 1538, as indicated in preceding untranslated entries.

[63] There had presumably been a bathroom in the Black Cloister in Wittenberg even before Luther planned one in 1541.

[64] The artist Lucas Cranach the Elder was mayor of Wittenberg in 1537 and again in 1540.

TABLE TALK

The Downcast Should Avoid Solitude
February 18, 1538   *No. 3754*

On February 18 Philip[65] was very sad and downcast on account of the disobedience of his son-in-law,[66] who would not permit his daughter[67] to come to Wittenberg, although the mother and her children[68] were to go to Halle in order to bring the daughter back for the father's consolation. This impudent disobedience of Sabinus so disturbed the father-in-law that he was inaccessible to any comfort and lived to himself, apart from the companionship of others. Luther pitied him and spoke at length with Dr. Cruciger,[69] Zoch,[70] and Milich[71] about Philip's wretchedness and melancholy and why it was that in his affliction he liked solitude when he ought rather to seek companionship.

"He is gnawing at his own heart," said Luther. "I, too, often suffer from severe trials and sorrows. At such times I seek the fellowship of men, for the humblest maid has often comforted me. A man doesn't have control of himself when he is downcast and alone, even if he is well equipped with a knowledge of the Scriptures. It is not for nothing that Christ gathers his church around the Word and the sacraments[72] and is unwilling to let these be hidden in a corner. Away with monks and hermits! These are inventions of Satan because they exist apart from all the godly ordinances and arrangements of God. According to the plan of creation every man is either a domestic or a political or an ecclesiastical person. Outside of these ordinances he is not a man, unless he is miraculously exempted. Accordingly a solitary life should be avoided as much as possible."

---

[65] Philip Melanchthon. Cf. No. 157, n. 59.
[66] George Sabinus.
[67] Melanchthon's daughter Anna had at the age of fifteen years in 1536 married George Sabinus.
[68] That is, Mrs. Philip Melanchthon and her younger children Philip and Magdalene.
[69] Caspar Cruciger (1504-1548) was a colleague of Luther on the faculty in Wittenberg and served often as the Reformer's secretary.
[70] Lorenz Zoch the Younger was a lawyer in Wittenberg.
[71] Jacob Milich (1501-1559) was professor of medicine in Wittenberg.
[72] An early variant adds: "and around prayers and hymns."

RECORDED BY LAUTERBACH

A Wedding and a Bridegroom's Authority
February 18, 1538   *No. 3755*

That evening Luther attended the wedding of Hans Lufft's daughter.[73] Before the evening meal Luther escorted the bride to the bedroom and said to the bridegroom that he should be content with the general custom and be lord in his house whenever his wife is not at home! And as a symbol of such retention of lordship Luther took off one of the bridegroom's shoes and placed it on the canopy bed.

Reflections on a Defeat by the Turks
February 21, 1538   *No. 3765*

Then there was talk about the noblemen who were prisoners of the Turks.[74] "Good God!" said Luther. "What a disgrace it is for our nation to advance in such a disorderly and womanish fashion against the army of the enemy where there wasn't a single Turkish soldier! Those are wretched prisoners. Nobody has pity on them or prays for them. In imagined security we drink, play games, incite one another to hatred, and thus prepare a way for the Turks to enter our land. Let us cry out to God, pray, and mend our ways according to God's Word so that, if we are to die, we may be put to death by Turks or Spaniards, may be killed in the profession of the faith, and may not become Turkish or Spanish!"

Our Ways Are Not God's Ways
February 22, 1538   *No. 3769*

The question was raised, How can the omnipotent God permit Satan and the ungodly to have so much power? He [Luther] answered, "Why is God wiser than men? Because what doesn't please us is right in his sight. So Henning[75] once remonstrated with Elec-

---

[73] A daughter of the printer Hans Lufft was married to a physician, Andrew Aurifaber.
[74] This conversation concerned the defeat of the imperial army under King Ferdinand I in Hungary on December 2, 1537.
[75] Henning Göde. Cf. No. 3622, n. 171.

tor Frederick[76] for burning green wood at court inasmuch as this would be detrimental if done in his own home. The elector replied, 'What is expedient in your house is inexpedient in mine.'"

Luther's Wife Complains About the Servants
February 22, 1538   *No. 3771*

The doctor's wife complained about the disobedience of the servants in the household. He [Luther] responded, "They are so bad that they need to be put under the yoke of a Turk. He would be able to deal with such persons and measure out to them, day by day, a quantity of work and food, as Pharaoh did to the children of Israel in the Exodus.[77] Such disobedience provokes God's wrath and invites misfortune at the hands of the Turks."

The Tyranny and Burden of Celibacy
February 24, 1538   *No. 3777*

Then he [Luther] spoke at length about the tyranny of celibacy, how great a burden celibacy was. "When he was quite old, Augustine[78] still complained about nocturnal pollutions. When he was goaded by desire Jerome[79] beat his breast with stones but was unable to drive the girl[80] out of his heart. Francis[81] made snowballs and Benedict[82] lay down on thorns. Bernard[83] macerated his harassed body until it stank horribly. I believe that virgins also have temptations and enticements, but if there are fluxes and pollutions the gift of virginity is no longer there; then the remedy of marriage which God has given should be taken hold of.

"People who occupied stations at least as high as ours lived

---

[76] John Frederick of Saxony. Cf. No. 3468, n. 6.
[77] Cf. Exod. 1:11-14; 5:7-19.
[78] Augustine, *Sermons*, 292 ("Of Conjugal Chastity"), 5.
[79] Cf. No. 51, n. 2.
[80] A later version adds: "whom he had seen dancing in Rome."
[81] Francis of Assisi (1182-1226) was the founder of the Franciscan Order.
[82] Benedict of Nursia (d. early in the sixth century) was the founder of the Benedictine Order of monks.
[83] Cf. No. 494, n. 295.

in the estate of marriage. Peter had a mother-in-law,[84] and therefore had a wife too. So James, the brother of the Lord, and all the apostles were married, except John. Paul counted himself among the unmarried and widowers,[85] but it appears that he was married in his youth according to the custom of the Jews. Spyridion, bishop of Cyprus,[86] was married. Bishop Hilary[87] had a wife, for when he was in exile he wrote a letter to his little daughter in which he urged her to be obedient and to learn to pray. He wrote that he had been at the home of a rich man who promised that if Hilary's daughter behaved he would send her a golden cloak. In such a childlike way Hilary wrote to his little daughter. I marvel that the holy fathers contended with such juvenile temptations and did not feel the loftier ones when they occupied such high offices."

Danish King Asks Bugenhagen to Stay
February 26, 1538 No. 3780

On this day a letter reached Luther from King Christian of Denmark[88] in which the king requested that Dr. Pomeranus[89] be permitted to remain for a longer time because Norway, which has more than four thousand parishes, has also accepted the gospel and because the departure of Pomeranus would be inopportune. He begged Luther to attend the meeting in Braunschweig[90] in person, for there were many who eagerly desired to see him face to face.

Large Churches Unsuitable for Preaching
February 26, 1538 No. 3781

Afterward there was mention of large churches which are not suited to preaching. "Cologne has a cathedral [Martin Luther said]

---

[84] Cf. Mark 1:30.
[85] Cf. I Cor. 7:8.
[86] Spyridion, bishop of Trimithus, on Cyprus, in the fourth century.
[87] Cf. No. 192, n. 70.
[88] Christian III (1536-1559). The letter is not extant.
[89] John Bugenhagen, of Pomerania. Cf. No. 122, n. 36.
[90] A meeting of princes was scheduled to be held in Braunschweig especially to receive the king of Denmark into the Smalcald League.

that is so large that it has four rows of columns, each row consisting of twenty columns. These are extraordinary buildings, but they aren't suitable for listening to sermons. Good, modest churches with low arches are the best for preachers and for listeners, for the ultimate object of these buildings is not the bellowing and bawling of choristers but the Word of God and its proclamation. The cathedral of St. Peter in Rome and the cathedrals in Cologne and Ulm are very large but inappropriate."

Hope that an Opponent Will See Light
February 26, 1538   *No. 3783*

On February 26 the elector[91] departed again, and on that day Count Hoyer[92] invited Luther to breakfast. Although he had hitherto been an opponent of the gospel, the count conducted himself quite courteously toward our father. Luther said, "God grant him knowledge that is above the wisdom of our flesh in order that he may acknowledge Christ, for his name prevents many in the church from embracing the truth of the gospel. I know what it cost me when I was disturbed by daily strife. But it is the work of God who makes the last to be first.[93] It would be very easy for God to choose this fellow in place of his brother Albrecht,[94] who is otherwise quite evangelical as far as his profession is concerned and who is not without faults."

The Chamber Pots of Eleven Thousand Virgins
February 28, 1538   *No. 3785*

On the last day of February Luther spoke of the mildness of Count Hoyer of Mansfeld.[95] This remarkable papist had laughed

---

[91] Elector John Frederick of Saxony. Cf. No. 3468, n. 6.
[92] Count Hoyer of Mansfeld belonged to the Catholic side of his family.
[93] Cf. Matt. 19:30.
[94] Count Albrecht of Mansfeld had been friendly to Luther and his cause from early times but the Reformer had frequent occasion to criticize him for being oppressive to his subjects and for feuding with his brothers and his Catholic cousins. See No. 3793.
[95] Cf. No. 3783, n. 92.

at papistic abominations and had related that in a certain place the chamber pots of eleven thousand virgins[96] had been exhibited as relics. When Luther had breakfast with the count[97] the latter was reported to have said that he hoped to live until the next council met[98] in order that he might observe how Duke George[99] would reform the papists according to the law of the [council's] decrees. The papists, he said, would prefer Luther's reformation to the severe reforms of Duke George.

Practice Teaches More Than Theory
March 25, 1538   No. 3793

On March 25 a certain citizen of Wittenberg consulted Luther with reference to his case against Count Albrecht of Mansfeld.[100] Luther responded, "You have a good case, but what you are lacking is judges. For in all trials there are two impediments especially. The first is that a man is right but can't prove that he's right (and this is the situation in which both of you find yourselves). The second impediment is the judge and executor (and both of you are wanting in this respect).

"Truth and right are set forth very well in books, but in practice they are nothing. Accordingly Dr. Jerome Schurff[101] said, 'Let the devil take me if things turn out the way the books say!' Alas, truth, right, and justice are odious things in this world. It is as Pilate replied to Christ, ['What is truth?' John 18:38]. Nobody submits to the law unless he despairs of defending himself in some other way. In one's strength lies right, or let this be transposed: right is might. If the adversaries are powerful they will delay the case with endless circumlocutions, and then great injury

---

[96] According to legend eleven thousand maidens, including St. Ursula, had been martyred at Cologne during or before the fifth century. At the close of the Middle Ages one of many associations for the encouragement of prayer was named after these alleged martyrs and called the Brotherhood of the Eleven Thousand Virgins or also, more popularly, St. Ursula's Little Ship.

[97] Cf. No. 3783.

[98] On the proposed council, see No. 3502.

[99] Cf. No. 275, n. 118.

[100] Cf. No. 3783.

[101] Cf. No. 1421, n. 86.

results. Lawyers' craftiness is dangerous business. A godly man ought to know the law only for the sake of defense, to enable him to understand and prevent the wicked tricks of the world. Such a man is Dr. Pontanus.[102] Other lawyers are godless; they seek only their own advantage and have the law in their control."

Afterward he [Luther] spoke about lawyers at court: "If they are bright and moderately well acquainted with the law, their minds are sharpened by daily exercise, and so practice makes them excel more than lecturing does the men who are occupied only with theory. Important things happen at court; practical wisdom is learned from these things, and it's such wisdom rather than books that rules the world. It's so in all fields that activity and practice make men better informed than mere knowledge. The reading of the Bible would never have led me to the understanding I have unless I had been instructed by the actions of my adversaries. In the beginning I defended the mass and monasticism with my life and body, but the circumstances taught me otherwise. So in my relations with the sacramentarians[103] the situation taught me to hold fast to the words, 'This is my body'; I didn't allow myself to be disturbed by their digressions but rested in this passage."

Proposal to Publish Luther's Works
March 29, 1538　　　　　　　　　　　　　　　　*No. 3797*

On March 29 the Strassburgers asked for permission to publish the collected works of Luther with a reliable index to the same.[104] Luther replied, "I'd like all my books to be destroyed so that only the sacred writings in the Bible would be diligently read. For one is referred from one book to another, as it happened in the ancient church, when one turned from a reading of the Bible to a reading of Eusebius,[105] then of Jerome,[106] then of Gregory,[107] and finally

---

[102] Gregory Brück. Cf. No. 1421, n. 85.
[103] Cf. No. 314, n. 139.
[104] The first volume of Luther's German writings appeared on September 29, 1539. Cf. *LW* 34, 281-284.
[105] Probably Eusebius of Caesarea (*ca.* 275-339), bishop, church historian, and biblical exegete.
[106] Cf. No. 51, n. 2.
[107] Cf. No. 51, n. 5.

of the scholastics and philosophers. This will happen to us too. I'd like them [my books] to be preserved for the sake of history, in order that men may observe the course of events and the conflict with the pope, who once seemed formidable but is now regarded with disdain."

Consolation for a Depressed Friend
March 29, 1538　　　　　　　　　　　　　　　　*No. 3798*

Thereupon Dr. Weller[108] arrived very troubled and depressed. Luther comforted him and told him to give his heart to the Lord and seek fellowship with men. Luther asked whether he was angry with God or with Luther or with himself.

Weller replied, "I confess that I am murmuring against God."

To this Luther said, "God will give up nothing. I, too, often honor God in this way. When I should procure good incense for him I bring him the stinking pitch and fetid dung of mumuring and impatience. If we didn't have the article concerning the forgiveness of sins (which God has promised surely to keep) we'd be in a bad way."

Weller said, "The devil is a master at taking hold of us where it hurts most."

Luther: "Yes, he doesn't learn this from us. He is quite agile. If he hasn't exempted the patriarchs, the prophets, and the prince of prophets, Christ, he will not spare us. He can make the oddest syllogisms: 'You have sinned. God is angry with sinners. Therefore despair!' Accordingly we must proceed from the law to the gospel and grasp the article concerning the forgiveness of sins. You are not the only one, dear brother, who suffers from such anguish. Peter admonishes us not to be surprised when the same experience of suffering is required of the brotherhood.[109] Moses, David, and Isaiah suffered much and often. What kind of trials do you suppose David was going through when he composed the psalm, 'O Lord, rebuke me not in thy anger' [Ps. 6:1]? He would rather have died

---

[108] Jerome Weller was professor of theology in Freiberg from 1539 to his death. Cf. p. 203.
[109] Cf. I Pet. 5:9.

by the sword than to have experienced these horrible feelings against God and of God against him. I believe that confessors have to endure more than martyrs, for day after day they see idolatries, offenses, and sins, the prosperity and security of the godless, and on the other hand the anxieties of the godly who are accounted as sheep for the slaughter." [110]

Continuation of the Consolation

March 29, 1538   *No. 3799*

Thereupon[111] he entreated Weller to cultivate the company of men when he is afflicted with such melancholy and not live alone. "'Woe to him who is alone,' the preacher says [Eccles. 4:10]. When I'm morose I flee above all from solitude. Christ was himself tempted by Satan when our Lord was alone in the wilderness.[112] On the other hand, the wilderness of John the Baptist[113] was inhabited like Düben,[114] Jessen,[115] and other places; he was among men. In short, spiritual anguish exceeds bodily suffering by far. The anguish of Judas—"you have betrayed innocent blood"[116]—became for him the most awful death.

"This is especially so when the devil turns the gospel into law. The teachings of law and gospel are altogether necessary, but they must be distinguished even when they are conjoined, otherwise men will despair or become presumptuous. Consequently Moses describes these teachings well when he speaks of an upper and lower millstone.[117] The upper millstone rumbles and pounds. This is the law. It's very well set up by God so that it grinds. On the other hand, the lower millstone is quiet, and this is the gospel. Our Lord God has suspended the upper millstone in

---

[110] Cf. Ps. 44:22.
[111] This conversation is obviously a continuation of what precedes in No. 3798.
[112] Cf. Matt. 4:1-11.
[113] Cf. Matt. 3:1.
[114] A small village on the heath south of Wittenberg. Cf. No. 3928, n. 194.
[115] A small village east of Wittenberg.
[116] Cf. Matt. 27:4.
[117] Cf. Deut. 24:6.

such a way that the grain is crushed and ground only on the lower stone.

"This is my only and my best advice: Don't remain alone when you are assailed! Flee solitude! Do as that monk did who, when he felt tempted in his cell, said, 'I won't stay here; I'll run out of the cell to my brethren.' So it's reported of Paul in the book of Acts [27:33; 28:15] that he suffered for fourteen days from severe hunger and from shipwreck and afterward was received by his brethren and took courage. This is what I do too. I'd rather go to my swineherd John, or even to the pigs themselves, than remain alone."

The Diets Prescribed by Physicians
April 2, 1538 *No. 3801*

On April 2 he [Martin Luther] sat at home and mentioned the rigid diet prescribed by physicians as a consequence of which many men are debilitated. "It's true [he said] that a good diet is the best medicine when it suits the individual, but to live medically is to live wretchedly." Then he related some examples of deceased persons who starved themselves to death on the advice of their physicians. "I eat what I like and will die when God wills it. The times fade away, and we grow old with the silent years.[118] When I now think of my contemporaries who are fifty years old, oh, how few they are. About every thirty years a new generation arises. We all belong in the ground; there's no way around it."

The Germans as Tacitus Described Them
April 3, 1538 *No. 3803*

On April 3 Luther and Philip traveled to Torgau.[119] Various things were touched upon in the conversations that took place then. Philip praised the cosmography of Cornelius Tacitus,[120] who is

---

[118] Ovid, *Fasti*, 6, 771.
[119] Luther and Philip Melanchthon visited the court of the elector of Saxony in Torgau. Since this conversation during the trip was reported by Anthony Lauterbach, it is to be assumed that he accompanied them.
[120] Tacitus (A.D. 55 - *ca.* 117) was a Roman historian and author of *Germania*, an account of Germany and its people.

said to have lived in the time of Emperor Caligula.[121] Tacitus, he said, described Germany and commended its people highly for their constancy and loyalty and especially for their chastity and marital fidelity. In this respect the Germans excelled all other nations; but in these last times, alas, this highly praised people is degenerating.

[Luther said,] "Nobody doubts that the best age was before the Flood. Then men lived to an advanced age in great moderation, without drunkenness, war, and strife. They served only God and fellow-men, and in an admirable way they contemplated God's heavenly and earthly creatures. A spring of fresh water was more pleasing to them then than all the malmsey wine is to us now." Thereupon he vehemently damned drunkenness and gluttony. "The Germans [he added] are the best nation, and I think the *h* has been changed to *g* and that they used to be called Hermans."

Comparisons of Germans and Italians
April 3, 1538 *No. 3807*

In the cart[122] he [Martin Luther] then spoke about Italian marriages.[123] "These [he said] exceed by far all the lewdness and the adulteries of the Germans. The latter are nevertheless sins, but the former uncleannesses are satanic. God protect us from this devil! By God's grace none of the native tongues in Germany was at all acquainted with this heinous offense."

Rival Claims for Ecclesiastical Property
April 3, 1538 *No. 3810*

Afterward the question was raised whether it is permissible to defend oneself if the emperor takes up arms against us. He [Martin Luther] responded, "This is not a theological matter but a legal one.

---

[121] Caligula (A.D. 12-41) was Roman emperor after Augustus and Tiberius.
[122] The cart on which Luther and Melanchthon traveled to Torgau. Cf. No. 3803.
[123] The expression refers to pederasty. Italy, especially the Italy of the Renaissance, was notorious for sexual immorality. See Will Durant, *The Renaissance* ("The Story of Civilization," Vol. VI [New York: Simon and Schuster, 1957]), pp. 760-761.

If the emperor undertakes war he will be a tyrant and will oppose our ministry and religion, and then he will also oppose our civil and domestic life. Here there is no question whether it's permissible to fight for one's faith. On the contrary, it's necessary to fight for one's children and family. If I'm able, I'll write an admonition to the whole world in defense of such people. This is my prophecy, however: Our princes will keep the peace, and I don't think it will come to a religious war, but they will sin against civil and domestic justice and thereby provoke punishment. The quarrel will start over episcopal and monastic endowments. For the emperor has already occupied three bishoprics—Utrecht, Lüttich, Hildesheim— the last of which he has offered to Braunschweig.[124] He has an appetite for and devours ecclesiastical property. Our princes won't tolerate this, and so the pounding and jostling will begin over the property."

A Prince Invites Luther to Hunt
April 3, 1538 No. 3811

In the evening the prince of Anhalt, as deputy of the elector,[125] invited Luther to join him in the hunt the following day and then to have supper with him. Luther replied, "I have indeed been sent here for this purpose, but I'm not a hunter of wild game. I give chase to the pope, the cardinals, the bishops, the canons, and the monks."

How to Deal with Specters and Poltergeists
April 5, 1538 No. 3814

On April 5 a pastor came from the church in Süptitz, near Torgau,[126] to complain of apparitions and disturbances caused by Satan. He said that Satan disturbed his peace with nocturnal tumults and the smashing of all the utensils in his house. Satan

---

[124] To Duke Henry of Braunschweig/Wolfenbüttel. Cf. No. 4887, n. 13.
[125] John of Anhalt served as deputy of Elector John Frederick of Saxony during the latter's absence at a meeting in Braunschweig.
[126] Probably James Osterlandt. Luther was at this time still in Torgau. See No. 3803.

hurled pots and dishes close to his head, so that they broke in pieces, and Satan annoyed him by laughing outloud, although he saw nothing of him. For a whole year, the pastor said, he had endured these and many other trials, so that his wife and children wished to leave [the house].

Luther responded, "Dear Brother, be strong in the Lord and firm in your faith! Don't give in to that robber! Suffer the outward things and the minor damage that comes from the breaking of pots, for it can't harm you in body and soul, as you have found, for the angel of the Lord is with you. Let Satan play with the pots. Meanwhile pray to God with your wife and children [and say], 'Be off, Satan! I'm lord in this house, not you. By divine authority I'm head of this household, and I have a call from heaven to be pastor of this church. I have testimony from heaven and earth, and this is what I rely on. You enter this house as a thief and robber. You are a murderer and a scoundrel. Why don't you stay in heaven? Who invited you to come here?' In this way you should sing him his litany and his legend[127] and let him play as long as he pleases.

"I was often pestered [by the devil] when I was imprisoned in my Patmos, high up in the fortress in the kingdom of the birds.[128] I resisted him in faith and confronted him with this verse: God, who created man, is mine, and all things are under his feet.[129] If you have any power over him, try it!"

Then he told a story about a woman in Magdeburg who, when Satan disturbed her, drove him away by breaking wind. "This example is not always to be followed and is dangerous," Luther said, "because Satan, who is the spirit and author of presumption, is not easily mocked and put to flight. Reliance on such an example can prove that it's not at all appropriate for somebody else. So it once happened that a horned specter of Satan lost his horn when a godly man boasted of his baptism, but when another man foolishly tried to imitate this example, he was killed by Satan."

---

[127] I.e., you should recite who Satan is and what he has done.
[128] Luther referred to the Wartburg, the castle to which he was taken for his protection after the Diet of Worms in 1521, as his Patmos and as the kingdom of the birds. Cf. *LW* 48, 210-213.
[129] Cf. Ps. 8:6.

Monks Steal from Dying People
April 8, 1538 No. 3826

On April 8 the excellent matron, Mrs. Hohndorf,[130] complained about the fraud of the Minorite monks[131] who annoyed her dying father and mother with respect to a last will. When at her father's behest she had committed four hundred florins to the keeping of a monk, she said she had been compelled to swear not to tell anybody. On her father's death the monk retained this money contrary to the rights of the children and infants. Persuaded at length by the magistrates, she confessed and revealed the theft of the monks.

Luther responded that many such examples of imposture and fraud are exceedingly odious, but that nobody dared to accuse the monks. Then he told the story of a certain monk who demanded of a dying nobleman, "Sir, are you willing to give this and that to the monastery?" Since the dying man was unable to speak and could only give a sign by nodding, the monk said to the nobleman's son, "See, you notice that your father consents to giving these things." Then the son asked his dying father, "Father, isn't it your will that I hurl this monk down the stairs?" When the father gave the same sign the monk got what he deserved and was thrown down the stairs. Such [deathbed] thefts of the monks were enormous.

All Men Love Leisure, Avoid Work
April 11, 1538 No. 3833

"The greatest temptation in the world [Martin Luther said] is that nobody fulfils his calling faithfully but everybody wishes to indulge in idleness. I am now exhausted and full of cares, yet I am plagued with many duties. Others are idle and unwilling to do anything. I think that if we didn't have to do what we do, if we weren't driven to it, we wouldn't do anything either. I mark well where the pope came from; the lazy, idle lords and princes emptied him from their bowels."

---

[130] The widow of a former mayor of Wittenberg, John Hohndorf.
[131] There had been a Franciscan monastery in Wittenberg.

TABLE TALK

A Scurrilous Attack Evokes a Response
April 16, 1538   *No. 3838*

On April 16 there was talk of the insolence and arrogance of Duke George,[132] who in his temerity wished to curb Luther. To this Luther responded, "I've tolerated his insolence long enough. I offered to have a court decide the matter, but he didn't want this. I've had some letters and arguments of his from the New Testament. I wanted to set the old fellow straight. He ridicules my person in an astonishing fashion; he calls me a changeling, the son of a bathmaid, and he pokes fun at this university[133] as a boys' school. It's not at all becoming for a prince to talk like this. I confess I'm the son of a peasant from Möhra, near Eisenach, but in spite of this I'm a doctor of the Holy Scriptures and an opponent of the pope. One can't blame the pope for holding a grudge against me. He has cause for this, but no right."

Hard Work Can Make a Man Old
April 19, 1538   *No. 3843*

The conversation then turned to Martin Bucer,[134] who as a result of his very great cares and endless labors has grown old, although he is not yet fifty years old. Luther responded, "What one thinks can very well make a person old, and so can work. I used to work too. Often I preached four sermons on one day. During the whole of one Lent I preached two sermons and gave one lecture every day. This was when I first preached on the Ten Commandments[135] to a large congregation, for to preach on the catechism was then a new and uncommon thing."

The Elector's Haste Suggests Danger
April 19, 1538   *No. 3844*

Thereupon he [Martin Luther] spoke of the elector's return

---
[132] Cf. No. 275, n. 118.
[133] The university in Wittenberg.
[134] Cf. No. 184, n. 64.
[135] It was in 1516 and 1517 that Luther preached these sermons.

from Braunschweig,[136] saying that he would come speedily on the next day, the eve of Easter. Luther wondered about the haste and thought it might portend bad news. "Dear God [he prayed], do what needs to be done and govern. It's true that we have princes, cities, people, provisions, and money, but we don't want to rely on these but to put our trust in thee. The cause is thine. Our adversaries have more to lose than we have, and they have just as much at stake."

The Swiss gentleman[137] said, "Our region is prepared for war and for peace. The papists are haughty and very insolent toward us."

Luther responded, "I am glad to see that our meetings are small and are held in small places like Smalcald.[138] Thus the papists have occasion to be proud over against us and will the more quickly be destroyed."

How to Achieve Unity with the Swiss
April 22, 1538   *No. 3848*

On April 22 the Swiss Master Simon[139] set out with a letter from Luther[140] and the following advice: "Go in peace and pray to God for sincere unity! However, this is my counsel to all who thirst after unity, that they make every effort to put an end to the controversies, that they teach the people as plainly as possible without the noise of disputations and raillery, even as we for our part speak gently, and that they do not stir up strife again under any circumstances, for we have been vehement enough. Let us now grow up! So I also advise those who are under the papacy to preach the pure gospel plainly and without commotion. If they do this the pope will fall, for he doesn't stand in the gospel."

---

[136] The elector of Saxony, John Frederick, attended a meeting of German princes in Braunschweig from March 30 to April 16. Cf. No. 3780.

[137] Simon Sulzer, a legate from Bern, in Switzerland, had been in Wittenberg since April 15.

[138] It was in Smalcald that the Smalcald League had been founded in 1531, and the meeting in Braunschweig was a meeting of this Protestant league.

[139] Simon Sulzer. Cf. No. 3844, n. 137.

[140] This letter is not extant.

TABLE TALK

Changing Opinions About the Lord's Supper
April 22, 1538   *No. 3849*

Then he [Martin Luther] sighed: "Alas, Karlstadt[141] and Münzer[142] have done the gospel a great disservice. The sacramentarians[143] have gradually retreated. First they taught that there is nothing but bread and wine [in the Lord's Supper]. Then they taught that the body and blood [of Christ] are present spiritually, that is, speculatively. Finally they taught that they [the body and blood] are received bodily, but [only] in faith. These are nothing but philosophical ideas. Articles of faith are opposed to all philosophy, geometry, and arithmetic, indeed to every creature. It's yes and no, and nobody can make these tally. The landgrave,[144] once the patron of Zwingli,[145] wished to establish unity between us and desired that we call each other brothers, but I was unwilling, although Zwingli declared with tears that he wished to remain in our church and to have no separation between us. I hope he was punished on earth[146] and has come to his right mind. There will always be perils in false brethren. We won't be spared good friends[147] if Christ had to suffer such things."

Luther's Conflict with King Henry VIII
April 23, 1538   *No. 3850*

On April 23 there was mention of the pamphlet with the title, *Luther's Answer to the Lampoon of the King of England*,[148] in which Luther once again attacked the king quite sharply. Luther said, "I was forced by necessity to do this. For when, persuaded

---

[141] Andrew Karlstadt. Cf. No. 356, n. 172.
[142] Thomas Münzer. Cf. No. 291, n. 131.
[143] Cf. No. 314, n. 139.
[144] Landgrave Philip of Hesse. Cf. No. 3514, n. 60.
[145] Huldreich Zwingli. Cf. No. 5005, n. 35.
[146] Latin: *temporaliter*, i.e., not eternally, before his death in 1531.
[147] This remark is intended to be ironical.
[148] This small piece, addressed to King Henry VIII of England in 1527, is reproduced in WA 23, 26-37.

by the king of Denmark,[149] I humbly entreated him[150] to pardon me, doing this in order that I might win him for the gospel (just as I also wrote to Duke George[151] when Master Pack[152] urged me to do so), the king immediately wrote back to 'the most wicked detractor, Martin Luther.' Then I had to defend myself, as may be seen in the same pamphlet, and take back my retraction in exchange for those nits and lice."

Luther Recalls Proceedings in Augsburg
April 27, 1538   *No. 3857*

Then he [Martin Luther] began to tell of the proceedings at Augsburg [in 1518], how he was treated by the cardinal:[153] "When I was cited I went, but with strong legal protection from the elector[154] and with recommendations to the Augsburgers, who with great diligence shielded me from conversation with the Italians, whom I was not to trust, for I didn't know them then. For three full days I was in Augsburg without imperial escort. Meanwhile an Italian came to me now and then, summoned me to the cardinal, and urged me to recant: 'Say only one word, *Revoco*,[155] then the cardinal will commend you to the pope and you will return with glory to your prince.'

"After three days had passed the bishop of Trent, in the name of the emperor, showed the cardinal my safe-conduct. Then I went to the cardinal as a suppliant. First, I fell on my knees; second, I lay down on the ground; and third, I stretched out in a prostrate position. Only after the cardinal had ordered me three times to

---

[149] King Christian II.

[150] For Luther's letter of September 1, 1525, to King Henry VIII, see *WA*, Br 3, 562-565.

[151] For Luther's letter to Duke George of Saxony of December 21, 1525, see *WA*, Br 3, 637-644.

[152] Otto von Pack, a counselor of Duke George.

[153] Cardinal Cajetan (Thomas de Vio of Gaeta) gave Luther a hearing in Augsburg in 1518, shortly after the start of the indulgence controversy. Luther's own account, written immediately after the hearing, is in his *Proceedings at Augsburg*. *LW* 31, 253-292.

[154] Elector Frederick the Wise of Saxony. Cf. No. 131, n. 44.

[155] Latin: "I recant."

arise, did I get up humbly. This greatly pleased the cardinal, and he hoped for a prompt victory. But when, after another day, I was unwilling to recant anything, he said, 'Do you think the pope cares about Germany? Do you imagine that the princes will defend you with arms?'

" 'No.'

" 'Where will you stay?'

" 'Under the sky.'

"Such was the insolence of the pope. This is why his honor and majesty are despised. To him this is more bitter than death, but it can no longer be prevented.

"Then the pope humbled himself in a measure and wrote to the elector, even to Spalatin[156] and Pfeffinger,[157] asking them to hand me over and see to the execution of his command. To the elector he wrote the following declaration: 'Although I do not know you personally, I did see your father Ernest[158] in the city [of Rome]. He was a very obedient son of the church and attended our services with great devotion. I wish that Your Serenity would follow in his footsteps.'

"However, the elector marked well the unaccustomed humility of the pope, his bad conscience, and the fact that he was afraid. The elector also recognized the efficacy of the Scriptures, for my *Explanations*[159] circulated through all Europe in a very few days. So the elector was strengthened in his decision not to carry out the pope's command, and he submitted to the judgment of the Scriptures.

"If the cardinal had acted more modestly in Augsburg and had accepted me as a suppliant, things would never have gone so far, for at that time I still knew little of the errors of the pope. If he had kept quiet, I would probably have kept quiet too. It was the Roman style, in an obscure and inexplicable case, for the pope to say, 'By papal authority we shall reserve this case for ourselves

---

[156] George Spalatin, the elector's secretary. Cf. No. 131, n. 45.
[157] Degenhart Pfeffinger was the elector's collector of revenues.
[158] Ernest, who was elector of Saxony from 1464 to 1486, visited Rome in 1480.
[159] The *Explanations* (1518) were an exhaustive explanation by Luther of his *Ninety-five Theses*. Cf. LW 31, 77-252.

and shall eradicate it altogether.' Then both parties would have been compelled to keep silent. I think the pope would give three cardinals if the matter were back in the condition in which it was then."

There Are Many Things We Do Not Know
May 12, 1538   *No. 3874*

Master Philip[160] examined a student in Anthony Lauterbach's home. He was a schoolmaster in Stargard, and when he answered thoughtlessly Philip said, "Do not answer so abruptly and burst out so heedlessly, for there are more things we do not know than there are things we know."

Luther remarked in connection with this, "Jonas[161] once claimed that he knew everything in the Holy Scriptures and was angry at me because I didn't let this claim pass unnoticed. But I know there are many things I don't know. I have preached for twenty-five years and still don't understand the verse, 'He who through faith is righteous shall live' [Rom. 1:17]."

Difference Between Apostles and Bishops
May 21, 1538   *No. 3880*

"The papists boast that their authority in the church goes beyond the Word, and they use this argument: The apostles changed baptism, and therefore the bishops are permitted to change the sacraments.

"The papists should be given this answer: Supposing the apostles did make some changes, there is nevertheless a great difference between an apostle and a bishop. An apostle is a person who is ordained by God immediately and called with gifts of the Holy Spirit, but a bishop is a person chosen by men for the preaching of the Word and the ordination of ministers in a certain place. Accordingly the apostles had authority, but this is not granted to bishops. So Elijah killed false prophets,[162] but similar power is

---
[160] Philip Melanchthon. Cf. No. 157, n. 59.
[161] Justus Jonas. Cf. No. 347, n. 161.
[162] Cf. I Kings 18:40.

not accorded to any pastor at all. Paul therefore makes a clear distinction: His gifts were that some should be apostles, some doctors, some pastors.[163]

"Among the apostles there was no primacy, but equality. And the apostle is a universal person, above a bishop. However, the definition of the superiority of Peter over the bishops is false because the definition extends beyond what is defined, for the conclusion is drawn that the pope is the supreme authority for ordaining ministers, assembling relics, and transferring kingdoms. We don't concede this definition, for any good definition ought to be framed distinctly, properly, plainly in order that neither more nor less is comprehended in the definition than in that which is defined."

Was Sir Thomas More a Martyr?
May 29, 1538   *No. 3887*

When Luther was asked whether Thomas More[164] was put to death by the king on account of the gospel he replied, "Not at all! For he was a very great tyrant against the gospel and shed much blood of the godly confessors of the gospel. He tortured them with strange instruments like a hangman. First he examined the confessors orally under a green tree. Then he stretched them on the rack in dungeons. Finally, when he had attained a place second to the king, he attacked the king himself in opposition to a decree of the whole realm, and for this he paid the penalty."

Why the Lectures on Genesis Are Poor
May 29, 1538   *No. 3888*

Somebody referred to the lectures on Genesis[165] and said that it would be desirable and useful to have them published. Luther

---

[163] Cf. Eph. 4:11.
[164] Thomas More, lord chancellor of England, was put to death by King Henry VIII on July 6, 1535, for refusing to take the oath of supremacy. He had written a violent book against Luther in 1523 and afterward persecuted adherents of Luther in England.
[165] Luther lectured on Genesis from 1535 to 1545, and these lectures were finally published. Cf. *LW* 1, ix-xii.

replied, "The lectures are hastily thrown together and are imperfect. In them I offer others a stimulus to further reflection. Accordingly it wouldn't be prudent to make them public. They are too poor. A single work like this demands the whole of a man. I'm too busy for it. I can't do justice to such a thing while I'm busy with many tasks. To do much and to do it well don't fit together. A person who is occupied with many tasks can't give his undivided attention to any one thing. Cicero[166] complained that he couldn't easily recover a train of thought once it had been interrupted. It's a wretched business in this life! Those who live in idleness and riches are unwilling to do anything, and the others are kept from accomplishing anything by their poverty and preoccupation with many tasks."

Roman Comedies Made Youth Marry
May 29, 1538   *No. 3891*

"The comedies which the Romans produced please me most. It was their principal purpose to incite young people to marry, for political activity can't exist without marriage. On this account those ingenious people enticed the young people to marry as best they could by means of comedies as well as pictures. For whoring and celibacy are pests to the state."

Disjunction of Faith and Life Criticized
June 20, 1538   *No. 3895*

The wife of Duke Henry, prince of Freiberg,[167] came to Wittenberg on June 20. Luther spoke with her twice about the arrogance and insolence of Dr. Jacob[168] and admonished her to have regard for the offenses he was causing the church, etc. A councilman from Freiberg was also present [in Wittenberg] in order to call another man [as minister], and he reported Jacob's ungodly conduct and departure.[169] He said that Jacob had preached carnal

---

[166] Cf. No. 3528, n. 84.
[167] Duchess Katherine.
[168] Jacob Schenk (1508-1546) adopted antinomian views, and this led to his expulsion from Freiberg. Cf. No. 3554, n. 128.
[169] When he left Freiberg, Schenk moved to Weimar.

license and had taught: "Do what you please. Only believe and you will be saved."

Luther replied, "This is a wicked disjunction. Turn the matter about: 'Dear fellow, believe in God, and then afterward, when you are reborn, are a new man, etc., do whatever comes to hand.' The fools don't know what faith is. They suppose it's just a lifeless idea. It's similar to what the sophists[170] taught about infused faith or unformed faith,[171] which, they said, is a gift of the Holy Spirit even in infants and retains its place in mortal sin. In contrast, they said, there is a formed faith[172] which expresses itself in love and doesn't sin. Thus they taught. However, it's impossible to be reborn of God and yet sin, for these two things contradict each other. Alas, dear God, many offenses will occur because we don't fear God and don't pray and presume, instead, to achieve something with the powers of our own nature."

Danger of Future Schism in the Church
June 27, 1538   *No. 3900*

Luther and Melanchthon had supper together in the former's home after a deposition.[173] They spoke at length and sorrowfully about future times, when there would be many teachers. "There will be great confusion [said Luther]. Nobody will conform with another man's opinions or submit to his authority. Everybody will want to be his own rabbi, as Osiander[174] and Agricola[175] do now, and the greatest offenses and divisions will arise from this. It would have been best, therefore, if the princes had prevented this

---

[170] Scholastic theologians of the late Middle Ages.

[171] Latin: *de fide infusa aut informi*. Grace was thought of as a thing poured (infused) into man, when receptive, through the sacraments. Faith that was not formed (*informis*) by love was regarded as imperfect; faith formed (*formata*) by love was deemed perfect or sinless.

[172] Latin: *formata fides*.

[173] Deposition was the name given to the ceremonial initiation to which older students subjected students who were entering the university. Cf. No. 4714.

[174] Andrew Osiander was charged with being an antinomian. Cf. No. 600, n. 367.

[175] John Agricola. Cf. No. 3179a, n. 62.

by holding some sort of council. But the papists avoid a council, so much do they fear the light."

Thereupon Master Philip[176] responded sadly, "The pope will never be persuaded to have a general council. He proceeds against us only with guile and force."

[Luther observed:] "It's said that Nicholas von Schönberg,[177] bishop of Capua, admonished the pope with the best reasons that he should deal honestly with the issue before the church, make some concessions to the Germans, and not fulminate against them with his authority. The Germans, he said, are men who won't yield in a just and honorable cause, nor can they be overcome with guile or with force. But the pope ridiculed the godly counsel of this man. Would that our princes and estates might call a council and establish some measure of agreement in doctrine and ceremonies in order that everybody who wishes to do so might not burst forth rashly to the scandal of many! This is already beginning to happen. Truly the image of the church is deplorable! The church lies hidden under very great weakness and offense."

What Will Occupy Us in Eternal Life
June 27, 1538 No. 3901

Then they spoke about eternal life and the joy that will exist then. "I often think about it [said Luther] but I can't imagine what it's like, can't understand how we'll spend our time inasmuch as there will be no change, no work, no food and drink, and nothing to occupy us there. But I think we'll have enough to do with God. Accordingly Philip[178] put it well when he said, 'Lord, show us the Father, and we shall be satisfied' [John 14:8]. This will be our very dear preoccupation."

News About Preaching the Gospel in Italy
July 1, 1538 No. 3907

On July 1 news arrived in writing from Italy that recently in

---
[176] Philip Melanchthon. Cf. No. 157, n. 59.
[177] Cardinal Nicholas von Schönberg (1472-1537).
[178] The disciple of Jesus.

Bologna forty-two monks preached the gospel in public with freedom and clarity, that they spoke with as much boldness as it could have been done in Wittenberg, and that their numerous auditors received them with great applause, and yet the bishops and the pope resorted to force against them. When advised to flee, they took care of themselves, but one of them, who had books by Luther and books in translation under the name of Erasmus of Rotterdam,[179] was seized and imprisoned while the books were burned. Master Philip[180] said, "The Word of God doesn't fall into empty space but spreads from here into every land. If it reaches Italy it will be clung to tenaciously, for Italians are persevering, not fickle or inconstant."

One Should Stop Preaching When Finished
July 7, 1538   *No. 3910*

"The Gospel[181] for the Third Sunday after Trinity is an excellent portrait," said Luther, "of how God is disposed toward sinners and of how solicitously he seeks them out. The subject and theme of this gospel is repentance, for it speaks of contrite and penitent sinners, to whom this gospel should be preached."

Thereupon he asked Master Cyriacus,[182] "Did you exhaust this text when you preached yesterday?"

"Yes, indeed," he replied, "I emptied my bag of all that was in it."

To this Luther said, "Then it was time to stop, for I have learned this art: When I have nothing more to say I stop talking." Then he told the story of a certain monk who was a beginner as a preacher. "When he had practiced his sermon and had memorized eight pages of manuscript, he delivered it rapidly word for word. In a quarter of an hour he was finished with the sermon. His bag was empty. Dear God, men like this who knew nothing were supposed to have been rectors of the churches!"

---

[179] Cf. No. 113, n. 25.
[180] Philip Melanchthon. Cf. No. 157, n. 59.
[181] Luke 15:1-10.
[182] Cyriacus Gericke, a former monk who was in Wittenberg at this time, was chaplain in Cöthen.

When his [Luther's] sickness continued[183] Cellarius[184] and the others left. Luther then said, "Pray to the Lord for me that I may become godly. I don't desire to live longer, for I'm of no use. Pray that I may have a blessed and cheerful end."

Difference Between Natural and Positive Law
July 7, 1538   *No. 3911*

"Law is sometimes called knowledge, as in the case of legislation, and is sometimes called ability, as in the case of property.

"Natural law is a practical first principle in the sphere of morality; it forbids evil and commands good. Positive law is a decision that takes circumstances into account and conforms with natural law on credible grounds. The basis of natural law is God, who has created this light, but the basis of positive law is civil authority. When theft is punished by hanging, this occurs according to positive law on acceptable grounds, but not as in the case of the Draconian law[185] which condemned every thief to hang, even if he stole only a chicken; this has no acceptable grounds and is contrary to nature. Consequently it was said that this law was written in blood. Yet the punishment must be applied more severely among more unbridled peoples."

Luther's Illness and Stories About Physicians
July 10, 1538   *No. 3912*

On July 10, when his illness[186] became more serious, he [Martin Luther] took an enema on the recommendation of the physicians. Afterward he said, "Such an act puts an end to modesty, for physicians play with their patients as mothers do with their infants, although they deceive themselves mutually. For example, Dr.

---

[183] Luther had been prevented from preaching the previous day because he was suffering from dysentery, according to No. 3909, here omitted.

[184] About this time John Cellarius moved from a pastorate in Bautzen to a parish in Frankfurt-am-Main.

[185] The code of law said to have been framed by the Athenian Draco about 621 B.C. in which every crime was punishable by death.

[186] Cf. No. 3910, n. 183.

Sturtz[187] was unwilling to give anything to a certain bibulous peasant in Erfurt and told him to take coriander. Since he was quite uninformed the peasant bought four calendars[188] bound in parchment and gulped them down four times after they had been chopped up. He asked that he be permitted to drink too. The physician, recognizing the reason for this request, ordered that the peasant drink as much as he pleased.

"It also happened to a certain physician in Heidelberg that a youth had made a girl pregnant and by mistake took to his physician some of his own healthy urine instead of hers. After scrutinizing it the physician reflected for a long time, looked the youth straight in the face, and said, 'My dear fellow, be careful with whom you associate!' The youth, moved by his conscience, responded, 'Dear Doctor, if the wench is pregnant, tell me and I'll marry her.'

"It's with such things that physicians are occupied."

Luther Faces His Illness with Resignation
July 17, 1538 No. 3916

On July 17 Luther was still suffering greatly. He was aware of the irregularity of his pulse and was consoled by the physician. He [Luther] responded, "I'm subject to the will of God. I've given myself up to him altogether. He'll take care of everything. I'm sure that he won't die because he is himself life and resurrection. Whoever lives and believes in him shall not die; though he die, yet shall he live [John 11:25]. Therefore I submit to his will."

A Marriage Case and Monastic Pollution
July 21, 1538 No. 3921

Dr. Jonas[189] and Master Balthasar[190] presented a marriage case.

---

[187] The physician George Sturtz attended Luther when he was sick in Smalcald the previous year. Cf. No. 3543A.
[188] I.e., the peasant mistook coriander for calendar, an account book.
[189] Justus Jonas. Cf. No. 347, n. 161.
[190] Balthasar Loi was deacon in Wittenberg at this time.

They told how a certain man was desperately in love with a girl and promised to marry her in Leipzig. It was later discovered that she gave him a love potion and made love to him. Afterward he was straightened out again by another woman and his love came to an end. Thereupon Dr. Luther was angry and said, "Why do you bother me with this very open case? This is my opinion, that he take her as his wife or that he demonstrate the circumstances clearly to his magistrate, how he was deceived by a love potion. If we allow this excuse, then everybody who regrets [his promise] will have to be vindicated. One shouldn't joke about these things! When anybody feels that he's a man, he should take a wife and not tempt God. That's why girls have their private parts—to offer him a remedy so that pollutions and adulteries don't result."

Then he lamented the horrible temptations to pollution in the monasteries. "Almost every night the brothers were bothered by them, so that they didn't dare celebrate mass the next day.[191] But when a large number of masses that had been imposed on us and appointed for us had to be omitted on account of our refusal, it became public, and the prior conceded that anybody at all could and should celebrate mass, even if he had had nocturnal pollutions. Phew! All the monasteries and convents ought to be dismantled on account of these shameful pollutions alone. There idle men are fattened in luxury and are incited by drunkenness and sloth to engage in such filth almost the whole day long. Dear God, protect us from such abomination; let us remain in the holy estate of matrimony, where thou dost wink at our infirmity."

Death Comes to All After an Interval
August 1, 1538   *No. 3928*

"Astonishing is the stupidity of a man who fears death.[192] Death is common to all men, and nobody can escape it. Cicero was able to comfort himself very well as a heathen in the first book

---

[191] For an early example of this rule, see Bede, *The Ecclesiastical History of the English Nation*, XXVII, 9th question.

[192] The subject of death was probably introduced in connection with Luther's continuing illness. Cf. No. 3912.

of the Tusculans.[193] How much more ought Christians do this, for they have Christ, the destroyer of death, and have [eternal] life and the resurrection. Even if we'd like to live longer, it's a brief interval at best. It's like many of you traveling to Düben;[194] some of you will arrive there about the fourth hour and others about the seventh or eighth hour, but all of you will have to put up there for the night. So Adam has preceded us by only a few hours; he has hardly had more than one night's rest more than us."

Luther Praises the Hospitals in Italy
August 1, 1538   *No. 3930*

Then Luther spoke about the hospital care of the Italians, how well provided their hospitals are: "They are splendidly built, the best food and drink are at hand, the attendants are very diligent, the physicians are learned, the beds and coverings are very clean, and the bedsteads are painted. As soon as a sick man is brought in, all his clothes are taken off in the presence of a notary and are faithfully kept for him. He is then dressed in a white smock and laid in a handsomely painted bed with clean sheets. Two physicians are fetched at once. Attendants come with food and drink, served in immaculate glass vessels; these are not touched with as much as a finger but are brought on a tray. Honorable matrons, who are completely veiled, come in, minister to the poor for several days without identifying themselves, and then go back to their homes.

"I have myself seen in Florence[195] with what care the hospitals make provision [for the sick]. This is true also of foundling homes in which children are excellently kept, fed, and brought up; they are all dressed alike in the same color and are looked after in a paternal way."

---

[193] *Tusculan Disputations.* Cf. No. 3528, n. 84.
[194] Düben was a village midway between Wittenberg and Leipzig, and travelers usually spent the night there.
[195] In the winter of 1510-1511 Luther journeyed to Rome, and he often spoke of his observations on the way as well as in the city. Cf. Nos. 3478, 3582A.

Luther's Brother Reports About His Prince
August 5, 1538   *No. 3948*

On this day Luther's brother, James Luder,[196] came with Master Coelius.[197] They said many things about Count Albrecht, declaring that he was the plague of his subjects.[198] Luther replied, "I regret that your lot is unfavorable on account of this man's wickedness, which obstructs God's blessing. For when God gives a general blessing, as in the case of the mines, etc., and one man tries to appropriate everything for himself and even to take God captive, then God withdraws with his blessing; he wishes to be free and uncoerced in his gifts."

We Do Not Know About the Future Life
August 7, 1538   *No. 3951*

On August 7 he [Martin Luther] said, "I was so gravely ill with this sickness[199] that I committed my life to God's keeping. Nevertheless, during this time of my illness many things occurred to me. Oh, how I pondered over what eternal life is like and what its joys may be! Although I'm sure that it has been given to us by Christ and that it is ours even now because we have faith, it won't be made known to us until hereafter. It isn't given to us here to know what that creation of the next world is like, for we can't fathom this first creation of the world and its creatures.

"If I'd been with God before the creation of this world, I wouldn't have been able to give him this advice, that he ought to make such a large spherical device out of nothing and attach to it a brooch, the sun, which in its swift course illuminates the whole earth, nor that he ought to fashion man and woman as he did. All this God did for us without our counsel and design. So we must

---

[196] James Luther was in the mining business in Mansfeld, where Martin Luther had spent his childhood. "Luder" was one of several variant spellings of the name.

[197] Michael Coelius. Cf. No. 204, n. 74.

[198] Cf. No. 3783, n. 94.

[199] During the early days of August Luther complained at table about severe pain in his arm at night.

accord him the honor of providing a future life and a new creation and let him remain the Creator."

The Devil, Witches, and Death in Old Age
August 8, 1538   No. 3953

On August 8 there was much talk about epicureans[200] and despisers of God who have given themselves over to Satan, such as the witch, the sorceress, the devil's whores with whom Satan comes together. Then there was talk about the three servants who had bound themselves to Satan and whom the devil led away bodily in Süssen, near Augsburg. Luther responded, "This is the penalty for sin. One is paid according to what one does."

That same evening an aged man, a boatman, died. Born more than ninety years ago, he was a very pious hearer of the Word who, with remarkable constancy and sighs for eternal life, gave up the ghost and fell asleep. Although he had eaten nothing for twenty-two days and had been unable to drink anything for sixteen days, he had great faith and patience and fell asleep in the Lord.

Italian Clothing Is Better Than German
August 8, 1538   No. 3956

He [Martin Luther] spoke at length about the arrogance and carelessness of the craftsmen who take few pains and want high pay. "I have enough cloth but I don't want to have any breeches made. This pair of breeches I have myself mended four times, and I will mend them again before I have new ones made. They [the tailors] are careless, use much material, but don't give it proper shape. They've done the best thing in Italy, where tailors who make nothing but breeches have their own guild. Here [in Germany] breeches, doublets, and coats are all poured into one mold."

---

[200] Luther often used this term for skeptics. In this conversation Luther reflects a belief in demonology and witchcraft which he inherited from the late Middle Ages. See T. K. Oesterreich, *Possession, Demoniacal and Other, Among Primitive Races, in Antiquity, the Middle Ages, and Modern Times* (New York: Richard R. Smith, 1930).

Emperor Charles V Misses an Opportunity
August 14, 1538 *No. 3958*

There was mention of lasting peace and harmony between the emperor and the king of France,[201] and various items of news were reported with reference to this. However, letters from Padua indicated only an armistice for ten years, with this condition, that if one [of the signers] didn't wish to observe the armistice any longer he should give the other six months' notice. To this Luther said with a sigh, "The emperor allows himself to be fleeced like a poltroon. He who was once most fortunate is now unhappy. There is a saying: A favorable opportunity is to be grasped by the forelock, for in the back it's bald. The emperor had in his hand the French king,[202] the pope,[203] and the Turk before Vienna,[204] but he made little of the opportunities. God offered him a blessing but he didn't recognize it. Accordingly Solomon in his Ecclesiastes deplores this "vanity," that God puts decisive power into a man's hands and he doesn't make use of it.[205] This happened to our emperor. He now has to give up Milan and Savoy and let a duke be chosen cardinal. This is a disgraceful catastrophe."

The Plundering of Church Property
August 14, 1538 *No. 3961*

There was mention of the plunder of ecclesiastical property by all bishops and princes. When there was complaint about this, the doctor [Luther] said, "It's a very bad time when the church is neglected, nothing is given to it, and it is robbed of what it has. Kings and princes helped the church formerly; now they rob it, and the church is more ragged than a beggar's coat. Nothing is added to the stipends of the poor and of ministers, but those who

---

[201] On June 18, 1538, Emperor Charles V and King Francis I of France agreed to a ten-year armistice.
[202] At Pavia in 1525.
[203] Through the sack of Rome in 1527.
[204] In the fall of 1532.
[205] Cf. Eccles. 6:2.

distribute [money] for its intended use suffer persecution. Their fate will be like that of St. Laurence, who distributed the goods of the church among the poor contrary to the edict of the emperor."[206]

The Quarreling and Reconciliation of Children
August 17, 1538   No. 3964

On August 17 he [Martin Luther] listened to the quarreling and fighting among his children and afterward watched them as they were again reconciled. Then he said, "Dear God, how pleased you must be with the life and play of such children! Yes, all their sins are nothing else than forgiveness of sins."

Questions Put to Luther to Answer
August 19, 1538   No. 3967

In a letter [which arrived] on August 19 Master Forster[207] set before Luther several questions that troubled him.

First, he asked whether preachers should criticize publicly, although the fraternal rebuke referred to in Matthew 18 [:15] seems to speak only of personal sins. Should not those who have sinned openly by their teaching be rebuked openly, as Moses did to Korah, Dathan, and Abiram,[208] as Elijah did to the Baalites,[209] as Paul did to Peter,[210] and as we publicly opposed the pope? Luther replied, "A brother ought first to be rebuked privately, especially if the fault is new and involves only a few people. But if the error is firmly rooted among many people, so that it's not possible to approach every individual and admonish him separately, the error must be rebuked and refuted publicly."

---

[206] St. Laurence's martyrdom occurred in A.D. 258. According to tradition, when asked to surrender the treasures of the church, St. Laurence gathered some of the sick, old, crippled, and poor and said, "These are our treasures."
[207] John Forster was at the time pastor in Augsburg. It appears that his letter was read at table and that Luther gave oral answers to the questions Forster had raised. See below, n. 220.
[208] Cf. Num. 16:1-40.
[209] Cf. I Kings 18:17-46.
[210] Cf. Gal. 2:11.

The second question: The texts in Numbers 35 [:6] and Deuteronomy 19 [:3] seem to permit private revenge to a person who lays hold of the manslayer of a relative before he betakes himself to a city of refuge. These passages appear to be in conflict with the Scripture that forbids private revenge.[211] He [Luther] replied, "That precept in Moses is judicial and is abrogated, just as the usury of the Jews was permitted among the Gentiles and only ceased when other judicial decisions were made."

The third question: Why did Ruth act according to the law of propinquity when Boaz wasn't the brother of her deceased husband[212] and the law in Deuteronomy 25 [:5] clearly stipulates the brother of the deceased husband? He [Luther] replied, "This passage is an exposition of the law in Deuteronomy 25 [:5], namely, that if the brother of the deceased man is unwilling, then the next to him in blood kinship should marry her. Besides, Ruth didn't demand that Boaz marry her, but he did so because he had had an intimate connection with her when she couldn't be seen by him very well. I have treated this text in the English disputation." [213]

The fourth question: [What may be said] to the Judaizers, who demand testimonies from the Old Testament, namely, that Mary was of the tribe of Judah and belonged to the house of David, when it is plain that the tribes and families were scattered after the Babylonian exile? He [Luther] replied, "Our evangelist expressly states that Mary was of the tribe of Judah.[214] Those who don't want to believe this may remain infidels. Moreover, such Judaizers can't find support for themselves in the last chapter of Judges,[215] where the tribe of Benjamin was disrupted. On account of fornication this tribe was not an honorable people of God, but it was separated and excommunicated from the people of God, and

---

[211] Cf. Rom. 12:19.
[212] Cf. Ruth 3:1–4:17.
[213] In the fall of 1535 and the spring of 1536 a series of discussions was held in Wittenberg between representatives of King Henry VIII of England, headed by Bishop Fox of Hereford, and Luther and his colleagues. While not the main subject under discussion, the question of the king's divorce was introduced in the "English disputation" here alluded to.
[214] Cf. Matt. 2:6.
[215] Cf. Judg. 21:1-24.

accordingly six hundred of them were compelled to take as their wives Gentiles and women who were carried off."

The fifth question concerned the passage of the Scriptures in Joshua 24 [:19], "You cannot serve the Lord; for he is a holy God, he is a jealous God; he will not forgive your transgressions." It seems plain that in these words an ungodly people is rejected, yet immediately after these words we read, "If you forsake the Lord and serve foreign gods" [Josh. 24:20]. These words refer to those who had hitherto been godly and had not yet fallen away. Luther replied, "This was the farewell speech of Joshua. He admonishes the people with extraordinary feeling, as if he would say, 'I fear that you will provoke God's wrath again. If so, God will punish you, for he can't tolerate this. If you provoke him and fall away from him, God will be angry,' etc. Another solution is that the earlier words were said of the ungodly and the later words of the godly, just as we have many psalms in which, here and there, people are praised and are lifted up to heaven and immediately after are put down into hell; by synecdoche, in the former case the godly in the whole people are spoken of, and in the latter case the ungodly. We do the same thing in our churches when we preach; we praise those among the people who are good and then, on the other hand, we reprove the bad and the ungodly. So the church is called holy, although only the smallest part of it is actually holy."

The sixth question: Whether a married man, whose wife was caught in adultery or whose wife left him, can marry another woman while the first is still living? Does not a second wedding seem to be fornication or adultery instead of marriage? He [Luther] replied, "In I Corinthians 7 [:15] Paul expressly declares that second marriage is permitted when he says, 'But if the unbelieving partner desires to separate, let it be so; in such a case the brother or sister is not bound. For God has called us to peace,' etc. It's evident that this passage allows remarriage. See my annotations on this passage." [216] Then Luther told of a case in Eisenach, where a wife was unwilling to cohabit with her husband and repeatedly left him without cause. "At length," he said, "we per-

---

[216] *Das siebente Kapitel S. Pauli zu den Corinthern* (1523). WA 12, 123.

mitted the husband to marry another woman but forbade the guilty party [to marry again]."

The seventh question: When Balaam took counsel so often with a spirit and received different answers,[217] was it the true God whom he consulted, and did he get his answers from the true God? He [Luther] replied, "He should have clung to the Word. But after a time his greed, stirred up by Balak's promises, turned his attention to sorcerers, who spoke otherwise. The third time the true God again resisted him through the angel, but afterward he turned his attention to the sorcerers; and although the text reads that God met Balaam [Num. 23:4], as if the Lord replied, nevertheless the voices were imitated and not the real thing. It's like the papists, who glory in the true God and Christ and yet under his name glory in and do the works of the devil. On this the text is clear."

The eighth question: How is one to understand the passage in Joshua 5 [:9], where it reads, "This day God rolled away from us the reproach of Egypt"? He [Luther] replied, "The answer is easy, for after Moses had circumcised the people according to the law, he said, 'Now you are no longer Egyptians; now that you are circumcised you are no longer heathen.'"

The ninth question: Did David sin when he offered to fight against the people of God in the presence of Achish?[218] He [Luther] replied, "He didn't sin because Saul was then a reprobate and was no longer king of God's people; he was in the place now occupied by the papists. In the second place, David didn't offer his service voluntarily but because he was under the Philistines. He was summoned as a minister by the king, just as our subjects can fight against the church of the papists.

The tenth question: How is the passage in I Samuel 2 [:25][219] to be understood, "If a man sins against a man, God will mediate for him; but if a man sins against the Lord, who can intercede for him"? He [Luther] replied, "It's more tolerable to sin against the

---

[217] Cf. Numbers 22 and 23.
[218] Cf. I Sam. 29:8.
[219] By mistake I Kings 2 was cited here.

second table [of the Decalogue] than against the first. Let him[220] just examine the Decalogue and he'll see that a sin against the first table is greater than a sin against the second."

The eleventh question: Could Saul prophesy by the evil spirit, and if so, what was the prophecy like? He [Luther] replied, "At the time that he prophesied Saul didn't act by the evil spirit. Moreover, his prophecy was an exposition of the law in his home."

Civil Righteousness Versus Monastic Piety
August 22, 1538   No. 3970

On August 22 he [Martin Luther] marveled at the vehemence and malice of Witzel,[221] who undertook to write many things against the Lutherans without cause. "He took the opportunity, wherever he could, to make captious objections to that view of ours according to which we teach that the works of a tax collector are far superior to all the works of the monks. Here the wretched fellow complains about us. He doesn't pay attention to the works of a man's calling but only to works of superstition.

"In his letters Paul wrote about virtues and good works more fully and appropriately than all the philosophers. He extols the civil works of the godly very highly. Were not the battles and wars of David better than all the fasting and praying of the best and most pious monks? Meanwhile I'll remain silent about the superstitious monks—like the one who wanted to conquer his concupiscence by smashing his dear chamber pot. Truly, this was noble mortification!"

Church Fathers Do Not Adhere to Scriptures
August 24, 1538   No. 3975

Then there was talk about the writings of the church fathers on the Bible and how these left the reader in uncertainty. He

---

[220] John Forster. From this reference it appears that Luther was giving oral answers to the questions raised by Forster.

[221] George Witzel wrote much against Luther after first supporting him. Luther may here have reacted against Witzel's work *Detectio Lutheranismi* (1538). Cf. No. 640, n. 371.

[Martin Luther] responded, "I'm not allowed to make judgments about them because they're writers of recognized authority and I'm compelled to be an apostate. But let him who wishes read them, and Chrysostom[222] in particular. He was the supreme orator, but how he digressed from the thing at hand to other matters! While I was lecturing on the letter to the Hebrews[223] and consulted Chrysostom, [I found that] he wrote nothing about the contents of the letter. I believe that as the greatest orator Chrysostom had plenty of hearers but that he taught without fruit. For it ought to be the primary and principal function of a preacher to reflect upon the substance, contents, and sum total of the matter and instruct his hearer accordingly. Once this is done the preacher can use rhetoric and exhort."

A Lie About Bugenhagen and Palladius
August 25, 1538 *No. 3980*

Then somebody reported a lie about Dr. Pomeranus,[224] who was said to have separated a rich wife from her husband in Denmark by divorce and then united her in marriage to Dr. Peter Palladius.[225] Luther responded, "I don't believe it. Such lies are invented against us to crush the gospel, because an insignificant occurrence gives great offense to Christians. So in the *Ecclesiastical History* it was reported that when Christians assembled for the eucharist they were accused of devouring a slain human body.[226] This lie caused a great deal of blood to be shed among Christians at Lyons, in Gaul. In similar fashion we are today imposed upon.

"Would that we could get rid of these marital cases! They keep us from having quiet for study. Such cases arise every day because men are married every day. These matters belong to the civil government."

---

[222] Cf. No. 252, n. 98.
[223] Luther lectured on the Epistle to the Hebrews in 1517.
[224] John Bugenhagen, of Pomerania. Cf. No. 122, n. 36.
[225] Bishop of Zealand (d. 1560), who was a prominent preacher as well as administrator in Denmark.
[226] Eusebius, *Ecclesiastical History*, V, 1, 26.

The Extreme Torment of Sleeplessness
August 27, 1538   *No. 3985*

"Sleep is a beneficial and necessary work of nature. I think it's a most annoying thing for a sleeping person to be disturbed in his rest. Hippolytus[227] wrote from Italy that it's the severest torment not to let robbers sleep when they are being questioned. Such sleeplessness is the worst of all tortures."

There Were Jews in Germany a Long Time
August 29, 1538   *No. 3990*

Then there was talk of the flight of the Jews to Italy and Germany. [Martin Luther said,] "In his oration for Flaccus, Cicero[228] complained about the superstition of the Jews in Italy, and we see traces of them all over Germany, for there's no town or village that doesn't have names, signs, and streets [referring to Jews]. It's said that Jews were living in Regensburg long before the time of Christ. It used to be a populous and mighty people."

Two French Students Visit Wittenberg
August 30, 1538   *No. 3991*

On August 30 two Frenchmen, very honorable men, came here from Italy to see Luther and Wittenberg. They stayed several days, attending lectures and eating breakfast with Dr. Luther and other professors. They said they had lived in Italy for the sake of study, and when they wished to return to France once again they decided to see Germany and Luther beforehand for the sake of piety. Luther said to them, "Here you see our very poor kingdom; you see me, a monk in a monastery; and you see my wonderful companions, namely, my wife and children. You can tell about these things. But be careful not to tell what you've seen but only what you've heard. And God keep you in the constancy of your soul!"

---

[227] Presumably the bishop and theologian of the third century.
[228] Oration at a trial for extortion held in 59 B.C. by Marcus Tullius Cicero, Roman statesman.

Why God Places Christians in the World
August 31, 1538   *No. 3993*

"God placed his church in the midst of the world, among countless external activities and callings, not in order that Christians should become monks but so that they may live in fellowship and that our works and the exercises of our faith may become known among men. For human society, as Aristotle[229] said, is not an end in itself but a means [to an end]; and the ultimate end is to teach one another about God. Accordingly Aristotle said that society isn't made by a physician and a physician, by a farmer and a farmer, etc. There are three kinds of life: labor must be engaged in, warfare must be carried on, governing must be done. The state consists of these three. Consequently Plato[230] said that just as oxen aren't governed by oxen and goats by goats, so men aren't governed by men but by heroic persons."

The Need for a Reform of the Calendar
September 1, 1538   *No. 3996*

He [Martin Luther] said many things about the course of the sun and declared that it is especially necessary that the calendar be corrected by intercalation, which is the function of the princes. "This is necessary," he said, "because the calendar rules the whole world. From the time of Julius Caesar—that is, during the past fifteen hundred years—the calendar has fallen ten days behind.[231]

"In this year 1538 we should have observed Easter on Reminiscere Sunday; the Jews keep their festival promptly, but we observed Easter five weeks late.[232] However, the mathematicians, if they all agreed harmoniously, could easily straighten out the year."

---

[229] Greek philosopher (384-322 B.C.) who had great influence on medieval theology.
[230] Greek philosopher (d. 347 B.C.) who was the teacher of Aristotle.
[231] The Julian calendar, introduced by Julius Caesar in 46 B.C., was finally replaced in 1582 by the Gregorian calendar, so called after Pope Gregory XIII. The correction suppressed, or skipped, ten days.
[232] In 1538 Easter fell on April 21; the year before it fell on April 1. But the date of Easter can vary from year to year as much as five weeks, the span between Reminiscere Sunday and Easter. Cf. *LW* 41, 62.

Contempt for Word and Shortage of Ministers
September 10, 1538   No. 4002

It was said in Lochau[233] that six hundred of the richest parishes in the diocese of Würzburg are vacant. He [Luther] commented, "This will have bad consequences. It will happen among us, too, if contempt for the Word and its ministers continues to be so great. If I wanted to get rich under these circumstances I wouldn't preach but would be a juggler and travel about the country. For the sake of money I'd have plenty of spectators.

"When the visitors[234] reproached the farmers and inquired why they were unwilling to support their parish ministers when they were providing livings for their cattle herders, the farmers replied, 'Because we can't get along without a herder.' For shame, that it has come to this in my lifetime! The antinomians[235] contribute a great deal to this. They increase the presumption among secure people, and I now see so much presumption in the antinomians that under the covering of trust in [God's] mercy they dare to do whatever they please, as if the believer no longer sins and as if believers are so righteous that they don't need any preaching of the law. They dream of a church as righteous as Adam was in paradise, though the wrath of God was revealed from heaven against him[236] when God said, 'Adam, you may eat of every fruit, but if you eat of this tree you shall die.'"[237]

Another Account of the "Tower Experience"
September 12, 1538   No. 4007

"That expression 'righteousness of God' was like a thunderbolt

---

[233] According to an earlier entry, not translated here (No. 3999), Luther had set out for Lochau on September 10 in response to a summons from the elector of Saxony.

[234] Since 1528 clergymen and lawyers had been appointed by the elector of Saxony to make visits of inspection to all parishes. According to a later report of the same incident (No. 5503), the farmers spoke not to the visitors but to Luther himself.

[235] On the antinomians, who claimed that believers were free of the law, see No. 3554.

[236] Cf. Rom. 1:18.

[237] Cf. Gen. 2:16.

in my heart.[238] When under the papacy I read, 'In thy righteousness deliver me' [Ps. 31:1] and 'in thy truth,' I thought at once that this righteousness was an avenging anger, namely, the wrath of God. I hated Paul with all my heart when I read that the righteousness of God is revealed in the gospel [Rom. 1:16, 17]. Only afterward, when I saw the words that follow—namely, that it's written that the righteous shall live through faith [Rom. 1:17]—and in addition consulted Augustine,[239] was I cheered. When I learned that the righteousness of God is his mercy, and that he makes us righteous through it, a remedy was offered to me in my affliction.

"But our antinomian friends[240] wish in their folly to flatter secure men and to make them good by reminding them of righteousness, though such an age as ours is incapable of being terrified by the lightning of the law. On account of the great sense of security it's necessary to thunder and lightning with the law, for farmers and burghers are so ungodly that they don't take care of a single pastor. If the princes and lords didn't provide, we wouldn't last very long. Therefore Isaiah put it well when he said, 'Kings shall be your foster fathers' [Isa. 49:23]. The farmers won't do it, as, alas, we see today from experience with these ungrateful people."

Great Diversity of Nations and Languages
September 19, 1538   No. 4018

On September 19 he [Martin Luther] said various things about the people of Germany and said that they were all simpler and more attached to the truth than Frenchmen, Italians, Spaniards, and Englishmen. "Even the way in which they speak indicates this, for Germans produce sounds ineptly with a lisping and hissing of the tongue. It's said of Frenchmen that they don't speak as they write, or even that they speak differently from what they intend

---

[238] For a parallel account of Luther's so-called "tower experience," see No. 3232c.
[239] Cf. No. 51, n. 4.
[240] Cf. No. 3650a.

in their hearts. The German tongue is the most perfect of all. It bears much resemblance to Greek. On the other hand, the Latin language is quite meager and thin, and it is irregular. It lacks diphthongs like *ps, ch, tz, th*. The Greek language has these in good measure, and German imitates Greek in this respect. There are so many German dialects, however, that the Germans don't understand one another. The Swiss have almost no diphthongs at all. The Swabians and Hessians don't understand each other, and the Bavarians are such barbarians among themselves that at times they can't understand one another.

"All nations are simple in comparison with Saxons. Accordingly if Saxons or Flemings go to Italy, they are worse than the Italians themselves. So it's said that Low Germans are very sly. Beware of an Italo-German! For as soon as a German learns epicureanism in Italy and adopts the hellish art, he becomes more deceitful than Italians.

"Such a man is the bishop of Mainz.[241] He's a real Italo-German. Not enough can be said in praise of him. In his book Schönitz[242] sets forth only the subject; I ought to add the predicate, for his [the bishop's] impudence and wickedness are so great that he laughs at all upright people, and as a result certain margraves in Zerbst regretted that he was of their blood. When, some three years ago, I wrote a very sharp letter to him, he didn't reply, pretended to take no notice of it, and sent back the messenger in a respectful manner. But this one word of mine—my scolding him for his behavior—stirred up all the margraves against me. In this way he tried to provoke all the descendants of the margraves against me, though I had written simply about him personally, for it can happen that a good father can sire a bad son and vice versa. So Hezekiah, a godly king born of an ungodly father, begot an ungodly son."[243]

---

[241] Cardinal Albrecht, archbishop of Mainz. Cf. No. 1362, n. 65.
[242] Anthony von Schönitz. Cf. Luther's *Wider den Bischof zu Magdeburg Albrecht Kardinal* (*Against the Bishop of Magdeburg*) (1539). WA 50, 386-431.
[243] Cf. II Kings 16:1-3; 18:1-3.

Hungarians Not to Have Separate Communion
September 22, 1538 No. 4020

On that day certain Hungarian students asked for the sacrament in both kinds.[244] But since they did not understand the German language they requested that the sacrament be administered to them privately in Latin. Luther replied that the wish to communicate privately would give a bad example in the church. Even if they do not understand the words, nevertheless they know that this is the true ordinance of God and institution of Christ, Christ's testament, and that in our church it is offered publicly and in common through the Word and in the Word. Therefore they ought never separate themselves from the church, for it would be much safer for their consciences and less offensive to the church if they would take the sacrament in the public fellowship. And this is what they did, obediently and thankfully.

Proposal to Publish Luther's Collected Works
September 29, 1538 No. 4025

Men [printers] in Augsburg and Wittenberg urged Luther to allow them to publish his collected works.[245] He replied, "I'll never consent to this proposal of yours. I'd rather that all my books would disappear and the Holy Scriptures alone would be read. Otherwise we'll rely on such writings and let the Bible go. Brenz wrote such a big commentary on twelve chapters of Luke[246] that it disgusts the reader to look into it. The same is true of my commentary on Galatians.[247] I wonder who encourages this mania for writing! Who wants to buy such stout tomes? And if they're bought, who'll read them? And if they're read, who'll be edified by them?"

---

[244] I.e., in evangelical fashion, with distribution of wine as well as bread to the communicants.
[245] For a similar proposal, see No. 3797.
[246] The commentary by John Brenz was published in 1537.
[247] For Luther's commentaries on Galatians, see LW 26 and 27.

TABLE TALK

An Appraisal of the Deceased Erasmus
September 30, 1538 *No. 4028*

"Erasmus of Rotterdam wrote many excellent things because he had talent and leisure, was without worries and official duties, didn't preach or lecture, and was no businessman. In his manner of life he was without God, lived with a sense of great security, and died the same way.[248] When he was in the agony of death he didn't ask for a minister of the Word or for the sacraments. It's a fabrication that in the agony of death he may have spoken these words of confession, 'O Son of God, have mercy on me!' God forbid that in my last hour I shouldn't want to have a godly minister of the Word, that I couldn't summon the nearest one at hand, that I shouldn't want to thank God! That fellow Erasmus learned such things in Rome. But now one ought not talk about this on account of his reputation and his books."

Some Monastic Foundations Might Remain
September 30, 1538 *No. 4031*

On this day some nuns wrote to him [Martin Luther] from Erfurt in the Low Country[249] and commended themselves to his prayers. They were very pious maidens who had always lived in unity from the labors of their hands. Having pity on them, he said, "One should allow such nuns to stay at their pleasure, like the rural monasteries which princes founded for noble persons. But the mendicant orders were nets and harpies that attracted everything, and they deserve to blush with shame. I should especially like to see the rural monasteries and those that have been endowed stay to take care of noble persons and poor ministers. Nor have I proposed anything else from the beginning. From such monasteries suitable men can then be chosen for the church, the state, and economic life."

---

[248] Erasmus died July 12, 1536. Cf. No. 113, n. 25.
[249] Probably should read: "from Herford in Westphalia."

An Experience on a Hunting Trip
October 7, 1538   *No. 4040*

On this day Luther went hunting, and a hare and a fox were seen by all [who were there]. When with a shout Erasmus Spiegel[250] pursued the hare on horseback over the plain, his horse suddenly fell and died. That hare was a specter of Satan.

Then a story was told about many noblemen who were racing on horseback and crying, "The last will be the devil's!" A boy who had two horses galloped off on one horse, leaving the other behind. This horse was snatched up into the air by Satan. Thereupon Luther said, "One shouldn't invite the devil to be a guest. We have enough to do as it is to oppose him with our prayer and watching."

The Word Must Be Rightly Divided
October 7, 1538   *No. 4044*

"The Word of God should be rightly divided,[251] and with care, for people are of two kinds. On the one hand are the contrite, who need consolation. On the other hand are the rigid ones, to whom apply the law, threats, examples of wrath, the fire of Elijah,[252] the waters of the flood, and the destruction of Jerusalem; these must be attacked at once and must be made to feel terror."

The Danger from Antinomian Teaching
October 10, 1538   *No. 4048*

When on this day there was much discussion of Jacob Schenk,[253] he [Martin Luther] said, "I don't want to blame him for his teaching because I still have good hope for him. However,

---

[250] Erasmus (Asmus) Spiegel was captain of the guard in Wittenberg.
[251] Cf. II Tim. 2:15 (KJV).
[252] Cf. I Kings 18:20-40.
[253] Along with John Agricola, Jacob Schenk was charged by Luther with antinomian views; he held that there was no place for the law in the church. Cf. No. 3554.

I can't refrain from suspicion because I've learned from experience. I have to be on my guard, no matter how much one may wish to praise him. Sulla said in jest about Julius Caesar, who was praised by all, 'Have your way, take him, but know that there are many Mariuses in Caesar.'[254] So Peter, the bishop of Alexandria, said of his presbyter Arius[255] that he would be alienated from the glory of Christ. After Peter's death Alexander succeeded to his office, and he also opposed Arius, as did his colleague Athanasius.[256] But Arius held all of them in contempt and fell into the worst heresy."

Antinomian Leaders Are Called Hypocrites
October 11, 1538   No. 4050

"I think well of men who are open, who make a thing clear in word and gesture, and who are not liars and hypocrites like John Agricola and Jacob Schenk,[257] who do everything in a friendly and yet deceitful way. The term 'hypocrite' is a very strong and emphatic designation, and Christ also employed it.[258] One couldn't rebuke a person more sharply than by calling him a hypocrite, that is, the worst possible pest."

A Parable on the Function of the Law
October 13, 1538   No. 4057

On October 13 he [Martin Luther] preached at home on the gospel, Luke 14 [:1-11],[259] since he was unable to go to church. On that day he marveled very much at the impudence of the antinomians,[260] who reject the necessary teaching of the law so

---

[254] Suetonius, *Julius Caesar*, 1.
[255] Cf. No. 3695, n. 24.
[256] Athanasius (d. 373), bishop of Alexandria, is best known as the defender of the orthodox Christology of his time against Arius.
[257] Cf. n. 253, above.
[258] Cf. Luke 6:42.
[259] The Gospel for the Seventeenth Sunday after Trinity. Luther did not feel well enough to go to church.
[260] Cf. No. 3554, n. 128.

strongly and do not see its effect. Augustine[261] depicted the power and function of the law in a beautiful simile: Through the law the sins in us are made transparent and the wrath of God is increased. This is not the fault of the law but of our nature. It is like chalk stone, which is quiescent unless water is poured on it, when it becomes hot, not through the fault of the water but by virtue of its own nature. However, if oil is poured on the chalk, the chalk stays still and does not boil. This parable is excellent.

Opinions on Several Marriage Problems
October 15, 1538   *No. 4068*

Several matrimonial cases were presented on October 15.

Before his marriage a certain engaged man committed murder and fled to an unknown place. Should the engaged woman be regarded as free from him?[262] He [Luther] replied, "This is a civil matter, and the man is dead by civil law. But if the accused man can be cleared before civil law, he ought to take her as his wife in the name of the Lord."

A second case: A certain adulteress of ill repute finally took flight with her adulterer and carried some household utensils off with her. He [Luther] said that she should be summoned to appear, her case should be heard, and then they should be separated. "Cases like this belong to the civil government altogether [said Luther] because marriage is a civil affair. In all its outward circumstances it has nothing to do with the church, except insofar as there may be a case of conscience."

Several Men Are Excluded from the Sacrament
October 15, 1538   *No. 4073b*

Because the prefect[263] in his arrogance had ridiculed God, the ministers of the Word, the university, and the civil authorities, had tried to do many things in opposition to these, and had often been

---

[261] Augustine, *The City of God*, XXI, 4, 3.
[262] An engagement to marry was then regarded as just as binding as a marriage.
[263] Hans Metzsch. On his earlier troubles, see No. 1646.

reprimanded in a fraternal way by Martin Luther, once again on October 15[264] Martin Luther sent two deacons[265] to him with a note, written in his own hand, as follows:

"This is to inform the prefect, first, that the absolution given him the preceding Sunday[266] by the deacon, Master Fröschel, is null and void because he did not examine himself inwardly. Second, that responsibility for receiving the sacrament in his sins, unrepentant, must be borne by him, not by me!" (These are hard words!) "Third, if he wants to be a Christian he must first reconcile himself with us preachers, pastors, the university, and the town" (because he had offended all of these by his tyranny). "So Christ said, 'If you are offering your gift at the altar [and there remember that your brother has something against you, leave your gift there before the altar and go; first be reconciled to your brother, and then come and offer your gift,' Matt. 5:23, 24]. If he will not do this humbly, I shall be content, in place of the pastor,[267] to let him seek salvation elsewhere, for I will not tolerate his wickedness, nor will I be damned on account of his sins. Let this be the second admonition according to Matthew 18 [:15-17], 'If your brother sins,'" etc.

In response to this note the prefect excused himself and said that he was innocent and bore no one hatred of any kind. But as before, so now again, Dr. Martin Luther ordered him not to go to the sacrament or serve as sponsor at a baptism.

The same week Martin Luther rebuked a certain Henry Rieder,[268] a nobleman who was a notorious usurer, to his face and forbade his pastor to admit him to the sacrament because he took thirty gulden a year for one hundred.[269] So great is the godlessness

---

[264] The text mistakenly reads November 15.
[265] Anthony Lauterbach, recorder of this entry, and Sebastian Fröschel were the two deacons.
[266] The text reads: "the next Sunday." The reference is to confession and absolution.
[267] Luther was serving as pastor in Wittenberg during the absence of John Bugenhagen.
[268] The text reads "Ruder" and a variant reads "Ryder," but the reference appears to be to a member of the noble house of Rieder.
[269] I.e., charged 30 per cent interest.

of the nobles that they have no conscience about boasting of their wickedness. One of them claimed he had begotten forty-three children in one year. Another asked why he should not take forty gulden a year for one hundred. Of what use were his eyes, he asked, if not to see with them.

A Farmer who Would Not Sell His Grain
October 23, 1538   No. 4079

In a letter the news was conveyed that a certain rich farmer had recently transported his grain to the city to sell it, but when nobody was willing to buy it at anything like his price, he is reported to have said, "I won't sell it for less. I'd rather take it home again and let the mice eat it."

When the farmer had done this, a very large number of mice suddenly gathered in his house and noisily gnawed at the grain until it was all gone. When the farmer fled from the house to his fields, he found that his standing grain had been eaten away and was ruined by the mice, although the fields of other farmers were unharmed. He [Luther] observed, "If this is true, then it's surely God's punishment and, alas, a sign of his wrath toward the ungrateful world."

Katy Recommended as Teacher of German
November 4, 1538   No. 4081

A certain Englishman,[270] a learned man, sat at the table but could not understand the German language. Luther said, "I recommend my wife[271] to you as a teacher of the German language. She's very fluent. She's such a ready speaker that she's much better at it than I am. However, eloquence in women shouldn't be praised; it's more fitting for them to lisp and stammer. This is more becoming to them.

"In men speech is a great and divine gift. It's with words and

---

[270] Probably a member of the legation sent from England by King Henry VIII. Cf. No. 3967, n. 213.
[271] Cf. No. 49, n. 1.

not with might that wisdom rules men, instructs, edifies, consoles, and soothes in all circumstances of life, especially in affairs of conscience. Therefore God provided his church with audible preaching and visible sacraments. Satan resists this holy ministry in all earnestness, and he would like it to be eliminated altogether because by it alone is Satan overcome. The power of the oral Word is truly remarkable. To think that Satan, that proud spirit, may be put to flight and thrown into confusion by such a frail word on human lips! This is why he attacks it so vigorously in the sacramentarians,[272] who despise it thoroughly, as Karlstadt[273] does when he calls the Word a sibilant sound of the human lips.

"Meanwhile I shall not speak of the Anabaptist scoffers at the oral Word. Paul says, 'You accepted it not as the word of men but as what it really is, the word of God' [I Thess. 2:13]. Likewise in Romans 10 [:14], 'How are they to believe in him of whom they have never heard?' Again in Thessalonians [II Thess. 2:4] Paul speaks of the Antichrist who exalts himself above the God who is preached; otherwise every fanatic would invent a god and special worship apart from this Word. Also Romans 1 [:16], 'It [the gospel] is the power of God for salvation to every one who has faith.' Also, 'It is not you who speak' [Matt. 10:20]. Nevertheless, the sacramentarians impudently dare to reject the oral Word. They argue thus: No external thing is salvatory; the oral Word of God and the sacraments are external things; therefore [they are not salvatory], etc.

"I reply: There is a great difference between the external things of God and of man. God's external things are salvatory and efficacious. The poor people used to think that the external ministry of God was the same as the unfruitful traditions of the papists. The devil worked through such childish inferences: 'The flesh is of no avail' [John 6:63]. If one drew conclusions from this way of reasoning, unspeakable consequences would follow; so one would reject all external means, and ultimately even the humanity of Christ. Satan has considered this, for it is his way to begin with lowly things and eventually to climb up to the heights."

---

[272] Cf. No. 314, n. 139.
[273] Andrew Karlstadt. Cf. No. 356, n. 172.

The Death of a Friend, Nicholas Hausmann
November 6, 1538   No. 4084

On November 6 a letter was brought from Freiberg which reported the sudden death of the very godly and faithful pastor there, Master Hausmann.[274] Although a sick man, he had just undertaken that important position. When he preached for the first time he was so confused and exhausted that he died the same day of apoplexy. We kept this sad news about his very dear friend from the Rev. Father, Dr. Luther. Then we took turns—his wife, Philip,[275] Jonas,[276] and I[277]—in telling him, first, that his friend was not well; second, that he was gravely ill; and finally, that he died quietly. Luther was deeply moved by this death. While sitting among good friends he broke into tears again and again and said, "Thus God takes away those who are good. Afterward he'll burn the chaff. It's in accordance with the saying in the Scriptures, 'The righteous man perishes, . . . devout men are taken away' [Isa. 57:1]. The times are perilous. God will clean out his storehouse. I pray that when I die my wife and children may not live on very long, for dangerous times lie ahead. I wouldn't have expected such wickedness in the world. God help us to remain steadfast in his Word and to better ourselves!

"He was an exceedingly dear friend of mine!"

So he sat in great sorrow the whole day with Justus Jonas, Philip Melanchthon, Master Joachim Camerarius,[278] Caspar von Koeckeritz.[279] Among these he sat, sad and full of tears.

---

[274] Nicholas Hausmann was a native (b. 1478) of Freiberg, in Saxony, where he died on November 3, 1538. Pastor in Zwickau since 1521 and court chaplain in Dessau from 1532 until he moved to Freiberg in 1538, he had been an old and trusted friend of Luther.

[275] Philip Melanchthon. Cf. No. 157, n. 59.

[276] Justus Jonas. Cf. No. 347, n. 161.

[277] Anthony Lauterbach, who wrote this account.

[278] Joachim Camerarius (1500-1574) was, like his friend Philip Melanchthon, a humanist and an educator. He taught in Tübingen and Leipzig, but was in Wittenberg on a visit at this time.

[279] Caspar von Koeckeritz. Cf. No. 3575, n. 146.

Youth Is Characterized by Temerity
November 9, 1538   No. 4091

Then he [Martin Luther] spoke about the brashness of the wiseacres who put too much reliance on speculative knowledge while they have no real experience, although experience is the teacher of reality and ought to regulate everything.

"The philosophers did the right thing," he said, "when they required their students to remain silent for five years, that is, not to express opinions lest they become rash in their judgments. Nor is it for nothing that certain times have been fixed in the universities for the granting of degrees. In Paris nobody is awarded a degree in theology who hasn't worked in that field for ten years. In Erfurt only fifty-year-olds were made doctors of theology. Many took umbrage at my getting the doctorate at the age of twenty-eight, when Staupitz drove me to it.[280]

"In short, youth is impertinent. So we see lawyers who in their first year are masters of all laws, in their second year are Justinians,[281] in their third year are licentiates, in their fourth year give formal opinions, and in their fifth year finally become trembling students. This is the way a boy acts in a bowling alley. First he expects to strike twelve pins, then nine, then six, then three, and at last he's satisfied with one, and probably misses the alley at that. It would be a good thing if young people were wise and old people were strong, but God has arranged things better."

Discussion at Table About Mothers' Milk
November 14, 1538   No. 4105

Afterward there was talk about the excellence of mothers' milk, which is especially good and nourishing. In fact, calves are nourished more by milk than by other food. Infants also become stronger

---

[280] It was at the urging of his monastic superior, John Staupitz, that Luther secured his doctorate in 1512.
[281] Justinian I was the Roman emperor (527-565) under whom a body of civil laws was collected into the so-called Justinian Code, and promulgated under his authority. Hence "a Justinian" was a legal expert.

when they are nursed for a long time. Swiss children are said to go to cows as a rule in order to suckle.

Then there was discussion about breasts, which are an ornament to women if they are well proportioned. Large and flabby breasts cause unhappiness, it was said, because they promise much but produce little. Firm breasts, and even the small ones of tiny women, are fruitful and can provide milk for many children.

Then it was said that it is not good for a pregnant woman to nurse an infant because the fetus in her uterus always draws away the best stuff, takes the cream and leaves only skimmed milk for the guest outside. Accordingly it is the common judgment of all married women that it is better for the child to be weaned early.

Two Kinds of Sinners, Penitent and Secure
November 16, 1538　　　　　　　　　　　　　　　*No. 4114*

"To distinguish between two kinds of sinners, the penitent and the secure, is especially necessary for the preacher, otherwise all Scripture remains closed. Consequently at the beginning of the sermon which he preached before numerous princes in Smalcald,[282] Amsdorf[283] said sharply, 'The gospel belongs to the poor and afflicted and not to you princes and lords who live in luxury, without tribulations.' It was an ill-humored introduction calculated to win favor! Yet it had to be, because this most spiritual teaching of the gospel disturbs even the best and most godly people. We see in the Pauline epistles with what zeal Paul opposes them: 'Put to death therefore what is earthly in you' [Col. 3:5]. 'If, in our endeavor to be justified in Christ, we ourselves were found to be sinners. . .' [Gal. 2:17]. One sees that it's not only the law that makes hypocrites; the disturbing thing is that even the doctrine of grace should make hypocrites. This distinction between two kinds of sinners must therefore be held on to and must be followed by excommunication. My 'No' means as much as your 'Yes.' "

---

[282] At the meeting of the Smalcald League in Smalcald, 1537.
[283] Nicholas Amsdorf. Cf. No. 1421, n. 84.

Dr. Gregory Brück[284] responded, "No, the reason for denying is more plausible than that for affirming, because proof is required of the plaintiff."

The Quibbling of Sophists to Be Avoided
November 17, 1538   No. 4128

"The world must be considered carefully [Martin Luther said]. It's governed by opinions, and therefore it's ruled by sophistical hypocrisy and tyranny. True religion is compelled to serve them as a maidservant. One must therefore be careful and beware of sophistry, which consists not only of equivocation in words but flourishes under all circumstances, so that in religion it possesses a magnificent pretense under the guise of Holy Scripture. There's more harm in sophistry than any man can perceive; our nature, which is prone to lying, can't see the evil in sophistry at all. Plato[285] offers a remarkable description of sophistry: People who can twist everything, repudiate the opinions of others, and draw conclusions on both sides after the manner of Carneades[286] are not to be praised. These are sly tricks. It's the glory of a good character [on the other hand] to seek the truth and to rejoice in guilelessness."

Obedience or Opposition to the Word of God
November 20, 1538   No. 4133

Thereupon he [Martin Luther] spoke of the very great folly of all men which consists of this, that we wretched men wish to make judgments concerning the Word of God, which we ought rather give ear to. "It's as if a vessel tried to teach the potter how to make it," he said, "how many fingers to use in shaping it.[287] Even so we wish to set ourselves up against God, we wretched

---

[284] The old chancellor of the elector of Saxony. Cf. No. 1421, n. 85.
[285] In his *Georgias* Plato attacked the rhetoric of contemporary sophists and declared that it is better to suffer injustice than do it.
[286] Carneades was an Athenian philosopher in the second century B.C. who embraced skeptical views.
[287] Cf. Rom. 9:20, 21.

creatures against our Creator. It is written, 'Listen to him' [Matt. 17:5], and 'Hear, O daughter, consider, and incline your ear; forget your people and your father's house' [Ps. 45:10].

"Yes, even if Adam had not fallen, we would nevertheless have accommodated ourselves to the Word alone. Are we now, in a particular situation and in darkness, to despise that Word? The great folly of the pope's church is that it's based only on the external rule of reason, without the Word of God, and our salvation is supposed to be bound up with outward child's play. If this had only had to do with moral and legal matters!"

The Hatred Between Laymen and Clergymen
November 25, 1538   No. 4143

On November 25 there was discussion of the perpetual hatred between clergymen and laymen. "This is not without reason [Luther said] because untamed people don't want to be corrected, but it is the function of preachers to accuse them. This is an extremely burdensome and dangerous business, and therefore laymen counter by keeping a sharp eye on clergymen. They have to find some fault with them and see some boils, even if they're only on the wives and children of the clergymen. In this way the laymen try to get revenge. If the princes didn't have power over them, the people would pursue them with the same hatred. Only let us abide by the pure Word in order that we may sit on Moses' seat.[288] If life is not so well rounded and perfect, God will have mercy, even if the hatred of the laity should remain according to the old saying, 'When the ocean dries up and Satan is lifted up to the stars, the layman will be the trusted friend of the clergyman.'"

Examples of the Faulty Proofs of the Papists
November 25, 1538   No. 4153

"Since the papists have a bad case they try to defend themselves with very defective arguments which don't prove anything. Their arguments should therefore be repudiated altogether. Here

---

[288] Cf. Matt. 23:2.

is an example: All praise is invocation; the saints should be praised; therefore they should be invoked. I deny the major premise, for all praise is not invocation.

"Another example: Every act of concupiscence is illicit; the marital act is an act of concupiscence; therefore [marriage is illicit]. I reply to the minor premise: The marital act is not an act of concupiscence. Rather, the act which attracts sex to sex is a divine ordinance. Even if by mischance the act is impure on account of original sin, in itself it's still licit and pure.

"Still another example: The teaching of the forgiveness of sins is necessary; an indulgence is a remission of sins; therefore [the teaching of indulgences is necessary]. I reply: Indulgences are not the forgiveness of sins but satisfaction for the remission of penalties, and this is an invention."

The Roman Mass as a Sacrifice to God
December 5, 1538 No. 4173

On December 5 there was much talk about the pestilential error concerning man's own righteousness, which has drawn even the best of men away from the truth of God. "The Jews made their sacrifices *ex opere operato*[289] in order that they might be expiation and satisfaction [for sin], as if they tossed a scrap to angry Cerberus[290] (though the only scrap is Christ), when all their sacrifices ought ultimately to be those of thanks and benevolence. Similar is the error of the papists concerning the sacrifice of the mass *ex opere operato*, when the priest, who is a stupid dolt and knows no Latin, atones for the sins of all men."

Then Luther began to say many things about the profanation of the mass, which has held captive all men, both those who say mass and those who are bystanders. "The severest punishment for

---

[289] A technical term in the late Middle Ages meaning by the mere performance of the act. Aurifaber inserted an explanatory sentence here: "They maintained that if only the external work was performed, sin was thereby appeased and paid for."

[290] A three-headed dog in Greek mythology who guarded the entrance to the lower world.

a mass-priest [he said] was to forbid him to hold masses, for to celebrate mass was to do everything. It's not at all surprising therefore if the mass isn't abrogated very soon in England, for it puts on a great show."

The First Mass of a Priest Was an Occasion
December 5, 1538   *No. 4174*

"The first mass was an occasion for great profit [Martin Luther said]. It was a real time for snaring money by means of fees and presents. The canonical hours were then supplanted for the bridegroom by torches.[291] Amid the weeping of the spectators the young priest had to have the first dance with his mother, if she was living,[292] as Christ danced with his mother. When I celebrated my first mass in Erfurt[293] I almost died because no faith was there. I reflected only on the dignity of my person, that I wasn't a sinner, that I shouldn't leave anything out."

Laws Must Be Interpreted with Equity
December 5, 1538   *No. 4178*

"The strictest right is the greatest wrong,[294] and therefore equity is necessary. This is not a rash relaxation of laws and discipline. It is, rather, an interpretation of laws which in some cases finds mitigating circumstances, especially in cases in which the law doesn't decide on principle. According to the circumstances equity weighs for or against. But the weighing must be of such kind that the law isn't undermined, for no undermining of natural law and divine law must be allowed. The necessary moral duties are to be given preference over ceremonies, except where confession is involved."

---

[291] The newly-ordained priest was married to the church. Hence he was looked upon as a bridegroom and there were wedding torches.
[292] If the mother was dead, Aurifaber added later, the new priest included her among the beneficiaries of the mass and rescued her from purgatory.
[293] May 2, 1507.
[294] Cf. Cicero, *De officiis*, I, 10, 33. Cf. No. 3604A, n. 156.

Some Observations About Life in Heaven
December 6, 1538   *No. 4181*

On the same day[295] Luther spoke admirably about the future eternal life and its unspeakable joy: "Human reason can't grasp it by speculation. With our thoughts we can't get beyond the visible and physical. No man's heart comprehends eternity. One might suppose that according to the saying, 'Even pleasure becomes burdensome,'[296] one would get tired of eternity. What pleasure is like in eternity we can't imagine. Isaiah said, 'Be glad and rejoice for ever in that which I create' [Isa. 65:18]."

Once He Starts, Luther Writes Rapidly
December 12, 1538   *No. 4188*

In these days Luther was excited and anxious while in his mind he was thinking through the plan of his little book, *Against the Bishop of Magdeburg*,[297] but when he began to write his quill moved rapidly. When asked about the swiftness of his pen he replied, "I bring forth what I conceive. I carefully consider all the arguments and every single word from every angle. The outline of a book like this requires a great deal of effort. This was the case with the writing on the abrogation of the mass.[298] On the other hand, the papists and our other opponents simply burst forth and babble; they write whatever comes to mind."

Meditation at Table on Christmas Day
December 25, 1538   *No. 4201*

This evening he [Martin Luther] was very joyful. His conversation, his singing, and his thoughts were about the incarnation of Christ, our Savior. Amid his sighs he said, "Ah, what wretched people we are! To think that we are so cold and slothful in our

---

[295] A previous entry, not translated here, indicates the date.
[296] Marcus Manilius, *Astronomica*, 4, 155. Manilius was a Roman poet about the time of Christ.
[297] Cf. No. 4018, n. 242.
[298] *The Misuse of the Mass* (1521). LW 36, 127-230.

attitude toward this great joy which, after all, happened for us, this great benefaction which is far, far superior to all other works of creation! And yet how hard it is for us to believe, though the good news was preached and sung for us by angels, who are heavenly theologians and have rejoiced in our behalf! Their song is the most glorious. It contains the whole Christian faith. For the *gloria in excelsis*[299] is supreme worship. They wish us such worship and they bring it to us in Christ.

"Ever since the fall of Adam the world knows neither God nor his creation. It lives altogether outside of the glory of God. Oh, what thoughts man might have had about the fact that God is in all creatures, and so might have reflected on the power and the wisdom of God in even the smallest flowers! Of a truth, who can imagine how God creates, out of the parched soil, such a variety of flowers, such pretty colors, such sweet vernal grass, beyond anything that a painter or apothecary[300] could make! Yet God can bring out of the ground such colors as green, yellow, red, blue, brown. Adam and those around him would have been elevated by all this to the praise of God, and they would have made use of all created things with thanksgiving. Now we enjoy all this to overflowing, yet without understanding, like cattle or other beasts trampling the most beautiful blossoms and lilies underfoot.

"For this reason the angels here [in the Christmas story] recall fallen men to faith and love, that is, to glory toward God and peace on earth." [301]

A Fable About the Origin of Monasticism
Between January 12 and 15, 1539   No. 4322

There was mention of the suspicious origin of monasticism and of the monks. It was said that it is manifest that the devil is the author of the monks; when he wished to imitate God, the author of the priests, he made the mold too large, and it turned out to be a monk.

---

[299] Latin: "Glory to God in the highest" (Luke 2:14).
[300] In the sixteenth century paints were prepared and sold by apothecaries.
[301] Cf. Luke 2:14.

"That's an appropriate fable [said Luther], for a monk is useful neither for the church, nor for the state, nor for domestic life. Accordingly the devil has to make monks, who obscure the works of God. In the church they're of no use, civil government they defame, and of marriage they think and teach callously. If the institution of marriage had stood firm, monasticism wouldn't have amounted to anything. Thus Satan obscured the glorious ordinance of God (namely, marriage) with the glittering phantom of the monks. If there had been God-fearing and pure teaching about marriage in the church, the monks and nuns wouldn't have counted for so much."

Are We Rewarded in View of Our Works?

Between January 15 and 21, 1539 *No. 4331*

An Englishman[302] asked Dr. Martin Luther about this question, which is very common in England: Whether godly persons who are already justified should expect some merit on account of the works that follow justification? Dr. Martin Luther replied, "It should be understood at the outset that we who are already justified are still sinners, and so we believe in and pray for forgiveness of sins in this life. 'Therefore let every one who is godly offer prayer to thee' [Ps. 32:6]. 'Enter not into judgment with thy servant [for no man living is righteous before thee,' Ps. 143:2]. This is a certain statement. We're all sinners and live under the grace of the forgiveness of sins.

"In the second place, God promises reward to those who do works, and therefore we earn something, etc. Surely God gives works to individuals, but differently, as one star differs from another. Yet all of these are under the forgiveness of sins. As heaven (that is, justification) is under grace, so much the more are the stars. As the stars don't make heaven but only adorn it, so works don't merit heaven but only adorn justifying faith. This is the only reasoning that solves everything: 'I believe in Jesus Christ,

---

[302] Cf. No. 4081. On the subject at hand, see Philip S. Watson, *Let God Be God: The Theology of Martin Luther* (Philadelphia: Muhlenberg, 1948), pp. 33-48.

who suffered under Pilate for us.' Everything is his; nothing is ours. Afterward, when by grace we are sons of God, we differ in our gifts, just as there are different stars in heaven.

"In short, the article of justification by Christ solves everything. If Christ merits it, we merit nothing. In Christ there are gifts, not merits. Likewise, since capital and substantial righteousness is nothing, how much less will accidental righteousness count in God's sight? Substantial righteousness is the righteousness of faith, but accidental righteousness is gifts, not merits. God crowns nothing but his own gifts, as Augustine said.[303] He expounded the term 'merit' very well against the deceit of the sophists, who said that the Blessed Virgin merited becoming the mother of Christ, the Son of God, because of her virginity; that is, she was suited in her maidenly body to give birth to him. Truly, an excellent merit! It's as if somebody were to say, 'This tree merits the bearing of fruit because God ordained it to do so.' Surely, one should look upon God's gifts and ordinance, not upon our works. Thus Augustine carefully reflected on the term 'merit' and concluded from the words of Mary, 'Behold, I am the handmaid of the Lord' [Luke 1:38] and 'He has regarded the low estate of his handmaiden' [Luke 1:48], that it depends on God's grace and not our merit. The merit of our works is nothing before God. The merit of our justification is grace, or Christ died in vain. Besides, we're all non-doers because there must be a diversity of gifts. This error comes from a confusion of the law and the gospel; when each of these teachings doesn't remain in its place and sphere, we turn heaven into hell and hell into heaven."

How the Pope Tries to Rule the World
February 6, 1539 *No. 4341*

He [Luther] mentioned Sadoletus:[304] "He's an able and learned man, and the papists took him up into the number of the cardinals

---

[303] For this and what follows, see Augustine, *Homilies on the Gospel of John*, Tractate 3, 10; *The Enchiridion*, 106, 107; *Grace and Free Will*, 7, 16.
[304] Jacopo Sadoleto (1477-1547), a brilliant humanist in the service of the Roman curia, was made cardinal in 1536.

in the hope that he might write against us. But he has no understanding, as may be seen clearly in his commentary on Psalm 51.[305] What alien and absurd notions he introduces into the psalm! Dear God, help us! Let thy good Spirit guide us into the right path!

"These arrogant and unlearned papists can't govern the church because they write nothing, they read nothing, but, firmly saddled in the pride of possession, they cry out that the decrees of the fathers are not to be questioned and decisions made are not to be disputed, otherwise one would have to dance to the tune of every little brother. For this reason the pope, possessed by demons, defends his tryranny with the canon 'Si papa.'[306] This canon states clearly: If the pope should lead the whole world into the control of hell, he is nevertheless not to be contradicted. It's a terrible thing that on account of the authority of this man we must lose our souls, which Christ redeemed with his precious blood. Christ says, 'I will not cast out anybody who comes to me' [John 6:37]. On the other hand, the pope says, 'As I will it, so I command it;[307] you must perish rather than resist me.' Therefore the pope, whom our princes adore, is full of devils. He must be exterminated by the Word and by prayer."

A Crucial Political Meeting in Frankfurt Between February 12 and 21, 1539 — No. 4352

"May the merciful God help those who are now in Frankfurt[308] that they may deliberate in an upright and honest fashion and reach conclusions which contribute to the glory of God. It is a small meeting. It seems curious and gives a bad impression to hold a

---

[305] Sadoleto had published *Interpretatio in Psalmum Miserere mei* in 1525.

[306] The first Latin words of the canon which is reported in the next sentence, "If the pope. . . ." *Decreti Magistri Gratiani Prima Pars*, dist. XL, VI. CIC 1, 146.

[307] Juvenal, *Satires*, 6, 223. Luther often applied this quotation to the pope; cf. No. 1346, n. 56.

[308] In February, 1539, the evangelical princes and estates met in Frankfurt-am-Main in a tense atmosphere. Landgrave Philip of Hesse was determined to use force to resist Emperor Charles V, who also seemed ready to take up arms. Conflict was prevented when it was decided in Frankfurt to appoint a commission to negotiate peace.

meeting in an imperial city, but they were challenged or compelled by the adversaries to do so. The foolish papists are trying to take the cities by cunning. They irritate our side with conceit, and then they feign peaceful intent. They wish to tear the body to pieces by inciting controversy among its members. They attack Hamburg, Minden, and Frankfurt. It might be more prudent to attack our forces in an open conflict. In Augsburg they condemned us publicly, and if we hadn't been so patient, things would soon have broken loose there."

On February 16 Dr. Martin Luther ordered that prayers be offered earnestly for the meeting in Frankfurt (which will probably be a small meeting), that peace may be concluded. "Once the landgrave[309] catches on fire [said Luther] there is no stopping him. This is what happened to Philip and me.[310] When we advised him humbly against war he said, 'What if I let you find a way out and I didn't take it?' He's a divine miracle and a heroic man. Although he's a weak prince, he's nevertheless formidable. He forced the bishops,[311] and now he speaks with them in the place of judgment, so that the papists must either take a risk, suffer it, or keep silent and offer peace. The landgrave doesn't provoke conflict, but, being provoked, he seeks peace, though he has a stronger force of horsemen, numbering two thousand. For the Hessians and Saxons are horsemen; when they're sitting in the saddle, they're not easily frightened. The horsemen from the south are easygoing fellows. God preserve the landgrave for us, because much depends on one man. As Augustus[312] used to say, 'I'd rather be in an army of deer under the command of a lion than in an army of lions under the command of a deer."

On February 25 he [Luther] prayed with fiery words and grave countenance for peace and for the meeting in Frankfurt, entreating God that religion, the state, and economic affairs be not disrupted by a destructive and endless civil war. "War is sweet to

---

[309] Philip of Hesse. Cf. No. 3514, n. 60.
[310] In 1534 Luther and Philip Melanchthon had met in Weimar with Philip of Hesse.
[311] The bishops of Würzburg and Bamberg in 1528.
[312] The Roman emperor Augustus (63 B.C.–A.D. 14).

those who don't know it by experience [he said]. God keep us from it! Today soldiers are devils incarnate, and not only the Spaniards but also the Germans. No faith and loyalty are to be found in those who bear arms.[313] The very ones who should be our future defenders will be our misfortune."

Superstition Connected with an English Statue
February 22, 1539　　　　　　　　　　　　　　　*No. 4355*

On February 22 there was talk about the horrible lies of the papists which alienate men from the truth. For in England they had a statue of Christ which was hollow and into which warm water was poured at some stated times, and this water flowed out through the eyes and feet. Such was their superstition that the people flocked to that place to collect the health-bringing water. At length the statue was publicly smashed by Bishop Latimer[314] when he was there on a visitation. There was likewise talk about the appearance of three springs in Rome; when the head of St. Paul had been cut off it leaped up three times at the mention of Jesus' name, and in these three places three springs gushed forth. He [Martin Luther] responded, "Ah, those aren't lies made by human error, but they're satanic. Those who know very well what they're doing give out those lies in ungodly fashion."

The Purpose of a True Council of the Church
Between February 22 and 26, 1539　　　　　　　*No. 4360*

Afterward he [Martin Luther] mentioned the councils and said that through their decisions the pope had arrogated to himself the authority to establish articles of faith and ordain good works and forms of worship. "This is most ungodly," he said, "for the articles of faith and rules about good works and worship had been decided long before the pope's councils. It wasn't necessary to convene councils for such purposes, nor was it appropriate for

---

[313] Cf. Marcus Annaeus Lucan, *Pharsalia*, 10, 405.
[314] Hugh Latimer (d. 1555), English reformer and bishop of Worcester.

them. In my book[315] I am therefore refuting the opinion and the fictitious authority of the pope, who in his councils is constantly increasing articles of faith and works.

"The correct definition of a council is this: A council is a consistory or tribunal of the church in which many bishops assemble to defend the pure doctrine of the faith and to purge the church of new heresies. Accordingly many bishops gather in order to banish and put out a fire. They shouldn't impose burdens on the church but should cleanse it so as to restrain the ungodly. They can introduce ceremonies in councils, but only insofar as the ceremonies remain free.

"So the councils of Nicaea and Ephesus,[316] which were just about the best, decided nothing about faith and works but only cleansed the church of the ungodly heresy of Arius,[317] which was, as it were, a fire threatening the doctrine of the Trinity. The holy bishops didn't there for the first time set up that article concerning the divinity of Christ, but they merely brought to light again what had long before been believed. If some ceremonies are established, however, let it be done not with the purpose and aim that they be binding everywhere and forever but that they be as free as political and economic regulations and that they do not make the conscience captive.

"The papists have taught the twelve articles of the faith in the Creed,[318] but in the meantime they have invented a multitude of others about purgatory, the sacrifice of the mass, the invocation of saints. Thus one error grows out of another. We must therefore restore everything to its right shape—that is, to conformity with the Word of God."

---

[315] Luther's *On the Councils and the Church* was published in March, 1539. Cf. *LW* 41, 3-178.

[316] Councils of the church were held in Nicaea (325) and Ephesus (431).

[317] Cf. No. 3695, n. 24.

[318] It had been customary in the Middle Ages to divide the Apostles' Creed into twelve parts, the authorship of each of which had been attributed to one of the twelve disciples. Although Luther preferred to divide the Creed into three parts, as he did in the *Small Catechism,* he continued at times to employ the other enumeration.

Absolution Is a Form of the Word of God
Between February 22 and 25, 1539   *No. 4362*

Then he [Martin Luther] spoke about the efficacy of the Word of God and about the joy in the church when brethren comfort one another with the Word of God. "There's something great about the employment of the keys and of private absolution when the conscience can be put to rest. Consequently I'm unwilling to discard absolution. For under the papacy I was always a despairing monk, even when I made the greatest efforts. Finally I received comfort from a brother through this one Word. God himself has commanded us to hope. Our salvation is faith in God. Why shouldn't we trust in God, who bids and commands us to hope? Through this Word he gave me life again."

Children Are Ingenuous at Their Play
February 26, 1539   *No. 4364*

On February 26 Master Spalatin[319] and the pastor of Zwickau, Master Leonard,[320] came to supper [in Luther's house]. He [Martin Luther] had some pleasant banter with his little son Martin,[321] who wished to defend his doll with zeal and honor and to dress her and love her. Then he said, "Such was our disposition in paradise —simple, upright, without malice. There must have been real earnestness there, just as this boy speaks about God piously and with supreme trust and just as he is sure of God. Such natural playing is best in children, who are the dearest jesters. The affected play of old fools lacks such grace. Therefore little children are the finest mockingbirds and talk naturally and honestly. Such a man was the jester Claus,[322] who, when he befouled his boots, excused himself to the chamberlain Pfeffinger[323] by saying that a little bird had done it."

---

[319] George Spalatin. Cf. No. 131, n. 45.
[320] Leonard Beyer was made pastor in Zwickau in 1532.
[321] Luther's son Martin was less than eight years old. The word here translated as "doll" is *sponsa* (Latin: "bride") in the text.
[322] Cf. No. 3287a, n. 68.
[323] Degenhart Pfeffinger was chamberlain under Elector Frederick the Wise of Saxony before 1525.

The Simplicity of Faith in Children
February 26, 1539   No. 4367

Afterward, watching his son,[324] he [Martin Luther] praised the boy's ingenuousness and innocence: "Children are better informed in the faith [than adults], for they believe very simply and without any question in a gracious God and eternal life. Oh, how good it is for children to die while they're young. To be sure, it would cause me great grief because part of my body and part of their mother's flesh and blood would die. Such natural feelings don't cease in godly parents, no matter how hardened and calloused they think they are, for feelings like these are a work of divine creation.

"Children live altogether in faith, without reason. It's as Ambrose[325] said, 'There is lack of reason but not of faith.'"

The Consequences of Enforced Celibacy
February 26, 1539   No. 4368

Thereupon the conversation turned to the very harmful superstition of celibacy, which has hindered many good things, like the bringing to life of children, the activity of the state, and economic life. On the other hand, horrible crimes have proceeded from it, like fornication, adultery, incest, fluxes, dreams, fantasies, pollutions. "Ambrose therefore declares in his hymn, 'Let dreams and fantasies of the night withdraw into the distance, lest our bodies should be polluted.' If St. Ambrose, who was burdened with many cares, experienced such temptations, why shouldn't fat and lazy monks feel them? Dear God, this is no way to remedy what God has created."

News of Warlike Activity by Adversaries
March 15, 1539   No. 4396

On March 15 news arrived about the madness of the papists, who conscripted soldiers to attack the evangelicals in Bohemia and

---
[324] The same son Martin is probably meant here.
[325] Ambrose (attributed to), *Hymns*, No. 24.

who have assembled military forces under alien leadership in Braunschweig.[326] He [Martin Luther] said with reference to this, "Give peace, O Lord! Spare us, and don't make us pay for our sins! We are so bad, ungrateful, and secure, but Satan doesn't sleep. Our adversaries could at any time invade our little land here and destroy everything, for we haven't a large citizenry or strong fortress. I rejoice that we don't make the first attack. Even if we should stay in this little land and be massacred, the noise of it will go out beyond the Rhine River, to Bavaria, etc. We Saxons are weak, for here we sit among the thorns and have wicked protectors, the margrave and Duke George.[327] But God is the supreme protector, and he says, 'My will be done.' Although we ought to be more godly, he has patience with us. Only let us not despise his grace! If they attack us, God grant us patience! If they try to win a penny, they must wager a gulden on it, for they have hair and we are bald.[328] The Lord will strike terror into the Amorites and will defend Jacob, as Moses said [Deut. 2:25]. 'If it had not been the Lord who was on our side' [Ps. 124:1], we would long since have collapsed. Even if they slay us, they won't accomplish much."

An Exhortation to Die for Christ's Sake

March 16, 1539   *No. 4400*

On Laetare Sunday, March 16, he delivered a sermon and followed it with a very beautiful exhortation that we suffer death in Christ's name. "Although we are otherwise mortal on account of our sins, if we die in behalf of the Word of God our death will be very costly. We'll all be saints, and our hide will be sold dearly enough. Not for our own sake would we pray for peace, therefore, since our death is gain, but for the sake of our posterity and the church of our descendants."

---

[326] Emperor Charles V was making intensive preparations for war against the Turks, which led to tension and suspicion between evangelicals and Catholics.

[327] Elector Joachim II of Brandenburg and Duke George of Albertine Saxony.

[328] I.e., they have the opportunity. Cf. the proverb in No. 3958.

The Duty of Husband and Wife

March 17, 1539 *No. 4408*

He [Martin Luther] spoke of the estate of marriage, in which each person must do his duty: "The husband should earn and the wife save. Accordingly the wife can make her husband rich but the husband can't make his wife rich, for a penny saved is better than a penny earned. So thrift is the best income. Deservedly I am in the list of the poor, for I keep too many servants."

Some Field Mice Invade Luther's Home

March 18, 1539 *No. 4412*

On March 18 some field mice broke into his [Martin Luther's] house and gnawed to pieces his best ornamental branches of fruit trees and laurels. He was quite annoyed. In a short time he caught a mouse in a mousetrap. It was almost as large as a dormouse, but with a bigger head, a shorter tail, and rather long teeth. When he had looked at it he said, "It looks like a beaver, which can also cut down trees. It has done me harm, but it has paid for it with the highest price."

That same day his wife drowned many mice in some holes in the garden. He [Martin Luther] said, "Mice also serve a useful purpose, for they make diligent housefathers. It's as Augustine said about heretics,[329] that they have the function of inciting and provoking Catholics and theologians not to be so cool toward the Word of God; when the opportunity is met, they begin to boil. It happened so to me. Unless the pope had challenged me with his abominations and false writings I'd never have come to this. Opportunities have taught me."

How Luther Stopped Wearing Habit of Monk

March 18, 1539 *No. 4414*

Then he [Martin Luther] spoke of his life in the monastery. He said that God had not let him become a monk without a great

---

[329] Augustine, *Homilies on the Gospel of John*, Tractate 36, 6.

reason, namely, that instructed by experience he would be able to write against the papacy.

"I was made a monk by my own power against the will of my father and mother, of God and the devil, for in my monastic life I honored the pope with such reverence that I would defy all papists who have lived or still live [to outdo me]. I took the vow not for the sake of my belly but for the sake of my salvation, and I observed all our statutes very strictly."

He also said how painful and difficult it was to lay aside his habit. Again and again his father had asked him to take off his cowl. [Luther continued,] "In return for my book on vows[330] Elector Frederick[331] sent me a piece of the best cloth with the suggestion that I should have a hood or cowl made of it. He is reported to have said, laughing, 'What if he should have a Spanish cloak made for himself?'[332] Dr. Jerome Schurff[333] promised me material for a new cowl because I had worn mine to shreds and had to have it mended.

"Many pious people were offended because I acted one way and taught another. The papists railed against me although I wanted to meet them halfway in external matters, in vestments, celibacy, abstinence from meat, Lenten observance, etc. Many papists shouted, 'If what he teaches were right he'd act accordingly!' And on Palm Sunday the preacher in Bremen, Jacob,[334] set a chicken before me, alongside other dishes, saying, 'If we teach it, why don't we do it?'

"In the year 1523 I finally laid aside my habit to the glory of God and the confusion of Satan, and many approved of my act for the sake of liberty. If I had not myself taken off my cowl,

---

[330] *The Judgment of Martin Luther on Monastic Vows* (1521). LW 44, 243-400.

[331] Frederick the Wise of Saxony (d. 1525).

[332] The Spanish style of dress was introduced into Germany during the reign of Emperor Charles V. So the elector was suggesting that Luther might not only exchange monastic for civilian attire but conventional for ultramodern style.

[333] Cf. No. 1421, n. 86.

[334] Jacob Probst (1486-1562), Reformation leader in Bremen, was in Wittenberg in 1522 and 1523, when the events here recalled took place.

eaten meat [on fast days], and taken a wife, all the papists would have protested that my teaching isn't true because I act otherwise than I teach. I couldn't secure permission anywhere to get rid of the dreadful vestment. It was hard for me to do [but I got rid of it], not because my conscience drove me but for the sake of others to whom I desired to be of service."

A Question About Two Bible Passages
March 19, 1539   *No. 4416*

On March 19 he [Martin Luther] was asked about the passage, '[I the Lord your God am a jealous God] visiting the iniquity of the fathers upon the children to the third and the fourth generation' [Exod. 20:5], and how it agrees with the passage in Ezekiel 18 [:4-20]. He replied, "If a son who is born of sinful parents leads a life of repentance, he doesn't belong to the generation of the ungodly. However, if he perseveres in the iniquity of his parents, as is generally the case, he'll be punished. All history teaches us that the sins of the fathers don't continue in the children beyond the fourth generation because the line of succession goes to ruin, according to the proverb, 'What you get through wrongdoing won't be enjoyed by a third heir.' None of the royal houses of Israel lasted to the fourth generation. Only Jehu was preserved; although he fell into error and idolatry, he had a sure and special promise of God [II Kings 9–10], and this preserved him. Similarly some of the kings of Judah were preserved, but not all. God can wipe them out."

What Fasting Was Like in the Monastery
March 20, 1539   *No. 4422*

On March 20 there was talk about the most sumptuous fasts of the papists—which were nothing less than fasts when the meals of bread and wine were without moderation. "Only truly afflicted consciences fasted in earnest," Martin Luther said. "I almost fasted myself to death, for again and again I went for three days without taking a drop of water or a morsel of food. I was very serious about it. I really crucified the Lord Christ. I wasn't simply an observer but helped to carry him and pierce [his hands and feet]. God forgive me for it, for I have confessed it openly! This is the truth: the most pious monk is the worst scoundrel. He denies that Christ is the mediator and highpriest and turns him into a judge.

"I chose twenty-one saints and prayed to three every day when I celebrated mass; thus I completed the number every week. I prayed especially to the Blessed Virgin, who with her womanly heart would compassionately appease her Son. Ah, if the article on justification hadn't fallen, the brotherhoods, pilgrimages, masses, invocation of saints, etc., would have found no place in the church. If it falls again (which may God prevent!) these idols will return."

The Great Debt of Christians to the Jews
March 20, 1539 No. 4425

Afterward he read in the Psalter and spoke with admiration of David's genius: "Dear God, what people those were! This David was a husband, king, warlord, almost crushed by political affairs and submerged in public business, and yet he wrote such a book!

"In like fashion the New Testament was written by real Jews, for the apostles were Jews. Thus God indicates that we should honor the Word of God in the synagogue. We Gentile Christians have no book that has such authority in the church—except Augustine,[335] who is the only doctor in the church of the Gentiles who stands out above others. Accordingly we Gentiles are in no way equal to the Jews. Paul therefore makes an excellent distinction between Sarai and Hagar and their two sons.[336] Hagar was a woman, too, but far from the equal of Sarai. It was therefore terrible temerity on the part of the pope to dare, as a man without Scripture, to oppose the Holy Scriptures."

Some Questions About Joseph and Mary
March 25, 1539 No. 4435

Then the doctor [Martin Luther] was asked about Joseph's

---

[335] Cf. No. 51, n. 4.
[336] Cf. Gal. 4:24-31.

suspicion of Mary.[337] [He replied,] "He must have had strange thoughts about his bride. With the permission of her fiance she had gone to the mountains, had stayed there a full quarter of a year, and had now returned pregnant. It's as if she had gone on a pilgrimage to Eicha.[338] He took her to be an adulteress. This was a serious suspicion, and the Scriptures can't hold this against him. An angel compelled him to put off any action against her and to postpone judgment. Dear God, with what difficulty these things happen! They're like fables, except that they've been confirmed by great miracles."

Then he was asked whether Mary also had intercourse with Joseph after the birth of Christ, for Matthew says that he 'knew her not until she had borne a son' [Matt. 1:25]. He [Martin Luther] replied, "The church leaves this [to us] and has not decided. Nevertheless, what happened afterward shows quite strongly that Mary remained a virgin. For after she had perceived that she was the mother of the Son of God, she didn't think she should become the mother of a human child and adhered to this vow."

Recollection of the Conflict with Tetzel
March 25, 1539   No. 4446

"At the beginning of the gospel[339] I took steps only very gradually against the impudent Tetzel.[340] Jerome, the bishop of Brandenburg,[341] held me in esteem, and I exhorted him, as the ordinary of the place, to look into the matter and sent him a copy of my

---

[337] Cf. Matt. 1:18-25; Luke 1:39, 56. The festival of the Annunciation on March 25 and the appointed lessons for this day led to the conversation that is here reported. For a brief discussion of Luther's views concerning Mary, see Hans Duefel, "Luthers Stellung zur Marienverehrung," *Luther: Zeitschrift der Luther-Gesellschaft*, XXXV (1964), 122-131, and Bernhard Lohse, *A Short History of Christian Doctrine* (Philadelphia: Fortress Press, 1966), pp. 200-202.
[338] Eicha, near Leipzig, was a popular place of pilgrimage in the late Middle Ages. On the immorality of pilgrims, see No. 5435.
[339] A favorite expression of Luther for the beginning of the Reformation, when the gospel was first recovered.
[340] John Tetzel (*ca.* 1465-1519) was the seller of indulgences with whom Luther came into conflict in 1517.
[341] Jerome Scultetus (d. 1522) had been bishop of Brandenburg since 1507.

341

Explanations[342] before I published them. But nobody was willing to restrain the ranting Tetzel; rather, everybody ventured to defend him. So I proceeded imprudently while others listened and were worn out under the tyranny. Now that I got into the matter I prayed God to help me further. One can never pay the pope as he deserves."

Then somebody said, "He won't stop until the world becomes good." He [Martin Luther] responded, "When the world becomes good the strife will be ended. The seed of the woman will bruise the serpent's head,[343] but the treading on the head and the biting in the heel won't come to an end in this life."

On Receiving the Lord's Supper in One Kind
March 29, 1539   *No. 4451*

Then the question was raised whether people who are living under [papal] tyranny and are unable to have [the sacrament in] both kinds[344] would be excused if in the meantime they receive it in one kind. Dr. Martin Luther replied, "This question is one of general interest and has been put to me very often, but I can answer quite simply. Anybody who still has doubts about the institution of the sacrament may receive it in one kind. But anybody who is certain about the institution of Christ will sin knowingly against his conscience. Many who live under Duke George[345] are scourged thus. This tyrant will die in his impenitence, for he has burdened the consciences of many people. He'd like to go back but can't."

Luther Judges First Writings Critically
March 31, 1539   *No. 4462*

Thereupon he spoke of his earliest books. He was now ashamed of them, he said, because in them he had conceded everything to

---

[342] Luther's explanations of and commentary on his *Ninety-five Theses*. Cf. *LW* 31, 77-252.
[343] Cf. Gen. 3:15.
[344] I.e., are unable to receive the cup as well as the bread.
[345] Cf. No. 275, n. 118.

the pope. "Yes, I'd gladly have defended him because at that time I was like a drowning man, tossed about in the waves. Now I've fought my way through. I see that I tried to bring impossible contradictions into harmony. It was a wretched patchwork. The stitch wouldn't hold. I tried to sew the old on the new, and this caused a very bad rent."

Luther Says that He Is Tired, Worn Out
April 2, 1539   *No. 4465*

Afterward he [Martin Luther] was asked whether he would still like to preach on the passion [of Christ, and he replied]: "It's enough. I've worked with all my might. For one person I've done enough. All that's left is to sink into my grave. I'm done for, except for tweaking the pope's nose a little now and then. I'd still like to attack the canons, the patched mantle of the pope.

"There's no name by which the pope could be called that's as odious as he deserves. Even if he's called greedy, impious, idolatrous, these ascriptions don't come up to his barbarity. Christ put it in a word, 'the desolating sacrilege standing in the holy place' [Matt. 24:15]. In his second epistle Peter [II Pet. 2:1-3] painted the pope in a marvelous way. In his letter to the Thessalonians Paul called him an adversary who exalted himself above all that is called god [II Thess. 2:4]. Daniel also prophesies that he is very exalted and magnifies himself above the God of his fathers [Dan. 11:36].

"Formerly we read and reread these passages and still didn't understand them. Now that the abomination of the pope is made known both in the Word and in experience, I have become so wicked that I have thoughts about it that I'm not pleased to have, namely, that the present knowledge of the Word will fall because the gospel states clearly that Christ will come in the middle of the night, when unfortunately neither daylight nor lamp will be at hand." [346]

---

[346] Cf. Matt. 25:1-13.

Belief in the Gospel Because of the Church?
April 6, 1539 *No. 4470*

"In the passage, 'I would not believe the gospel unless the authority of the church urged me to,' Augustine[347] never wished to embrace the opinion of the papists. He didn't want to write what should be believed but what should be judged, as another passage indicates, 'I do not wish you to believe my writings more than the Holy Scriptures.'[348] But the sophists[349] poked fun at Paul for having written obscurely and confusedly. Ah, dear God, this treasure of the Holy Scriptures belongs only to a contrite heart and a humble and God-fearing spirit. The ungodly must be exposed and their boasting put down. This is what Stephen did in Acts 7 [:2-53], where he spoke against the place of Jerusalem, against the law, against the prosperous people, against a demanding God. Truly it was an excellent and sharp sermon! In the Roman church today the glory of the church is not at all comparable with the glory of Jerusalem and of the people Israel."

Remedy for Shortage of Food in Wittenberg
April 7, 1539 *No. 4472*

In the evening he [Martin Luther] gave Dr. Cruciger[350] an admonition for the town council in which he demanded that the council see to it that the millers provide something for the poor people, lest they starve, for there had been so great a shortage in these days that one could get neither flour nor bread for money. Thus he obliquely reproached the council for its negligence.

That evening one of the burgomasters, Lucas Cranach,[351] came to him [Martin Luther] and excused himself by saying that the town's grain had been impounded in Brandenburg. Dr. Martin

---

[347] Augustine, *Against the Epistle of Manichaeus*, 5, 6.
[348] Augustine, *Epistles*, 82; 148.
[349] Luther's favorite designation for the medieval scholastics.
[350] Caspar Cruciger. Cf. No. 3754, n. 69.
[351] Lucas Cranach the Elder, the artist, was also the mayor of Wittenberg for a time.

Luther replied, "What a pity that our prince isn't at home![352] Great is the treachery of those nobles who buy all the grain from their farmers and keep it off the market, curb the movement of grain, and artificially raise prices, though there was no act of God to produce such a shortage. There's need of a prince to talk to the nobles and point out to them that they don't have the right to keep the country's grain from the common market. It's only human wickedness. What will happen if God's punishment is added? Dear God, if the world is so wicked I'll be glad to die—even of hunger, just so I get away from it."

But afterward he said to the burgomaster, "It's the prefect's[353] fault. Several ships with grain were turned away from our area by him. He once said, 'If the townspeople won't make good beer and sell it cheap, I'll make the price of barley go up before they have time to wipe their mouths!' This statement of his has made me exceedingly suspicious of him. God has in a wonderful way blessed us here on this sandy soil more than he has those who live on richer Thuringian land. Let us pray for our daily bread!

"I tried to get the tax collector to give me several measures of grain for the poor. When in a time of pestilence I once complained to the elector about the shortage in our city and about the three plagues (pestilence, famine, and cold) that resulted from the fact that nothing was imported, I said, 'I'll have to pitch in and help the burghers distribute grain and wood [among the needy].' The elector replied graciously, 'By all means help me to do so.' On the basis of this word of his, I'll venture now to do something for the benefit of the poor."

A Man who Neglected the Sacrament

April 8, 1539 *No. 4473*

There was mention of a citizen of Wittenberg who was an atheist and who confessed publicly before the town council that he had not received communion for fifteen years. To this Dr. Martin Luther said, "We've been sufficiently forbearing with him. After

---

[352] Elector John Frederick of Saxony was in Frankfurt-am-Main at this time.
[353] Hans Metzsch. Cf. No. 342, n. 152.

a couple of admonitions I'll publicly declare that he's excommunicated and is to be treated like a dog. If in view of this anybody associates with him, let him do so at his own risk. If the unbeliever dies in this condition, let him be buried in the carrion pit like a dog. As an excommunicated person we'll turn him over to the civil laws."

Luther Has a Kidney Stone Attack
April 8, 1539   *No. 4479*

On this day he [Martin Luther] was also troubled by kidney stones and said, "This ailment attaches in a peculiar way to Germans, just as the gout is said to be the disease most frequently encountered in England. Various kinds of sickness have been directed at this wretched body of ours, and oh, the pain by which we have been quite broken! Cramps seem to be the least of the ailments, but I think epilepsy is a kind of spasm that occurs in the brain. When it occurs in the legs, a spasm makes motion and travel difficult."

Then he also spoke about bewitching and how the bodies of men are also afflicted by this.

The Pope as Antichrist and the Devil Incarnate
April 11, 1539   *No. 4487*

"I believe the pope is the masked and incarnate devil because he is the Antichrist. As Christ is God incarnate, so the Antichrist is the devil incarnate. The words are really spoken of the pope when it's said that he's a mixed god, an earthly god, that is, a god of the earth. Here god is understood as god of this world. Why does he call himself an earthly god, as if the one, almighty God weren't also on the earth?

"The kingdom of the pope really signifies the terrible wrath of God, namely, the abomination of desolation standing in the holy place.[354] Therefore Christ says that he who reads this should mark it well. To be sure, it's very exasperating that after Christ's

---

[354] Cf. Matt. 24:15; Dan. 12:11.

revelation a man should lift himself up above God in the church. If this had happened among the heathen before the revelation of Christ it wouldn't have been very remarkable. That's why we have been so diligently warned about this deadly pestilence by Daniel, Christ, Paul, Peter, and others. In spite of this, we Christians were so stupid that we asked for all the pope's commands.

"We allowed ourselves to be persuaded that, under the pretext of the patrimony of Peter,[355] he is the lord over the whole world, although neither Christ nor Peter bequeathed any kind of dominion on earth."

A Severe Arraignment of Pope Julius
April 11, 1539　　　　　　　　　　　　　　　　*No. 4488*

"The dialogue of Julius[356] is very true and deserving of immortality. With tragic words it describes the papacy, especially under Julius, who was a monster in power above all others and who was an ungodly, warlike, and fierce man. He presumed to venture everything so that he could be god on earth. With the help of others (namely, of the emperor and the king of France) he put down the Venetians.[357] After this victory he attacked the French before Ravenna with great assurance.[358] If he had overcome the French king, he would have attacked and subdued the Spaniards and the emperor. In short, he was the last flame on the lamp and the final effort of the devil. He fulminated with ban and sword. He waged war with the might of others. As Daniel said,[359] he is powerful, but not in his own strength, as one now discovers. It used to be said that the pope has more strength in one finger than all the princes of Germany. Do you think the pope cares about Germany? However, the shameless harlot, the stain of infamy, and the blemish are assailed by the breath from God's mouth. With

---

[355] The alleged hereditary estates of St. Peter were the lands in Italy which the popes possessed. These were developed and added to especially by Pope Gregory I (590-604).
[356] Cf. No. 1319, n. 32.
[357] The reference is to the defeat of Venice on May 14, 1509.
[358] The Battle of Ravenna occurred on April 11, 1512.
[359] Cf. Dan. 8:24.

iron and sword nothing would be accomplished against him, for the devil doesn't give a hoot about dagger and sword. But if he's struck by the Word of God, the pope will be turned into a dandelion,[360] that is, the flower that rises with the sun and goes down with the sun, like that yellow flower that turns in the evening into a stinking monk."

Terence Not Readily Translated into German
April 11, 1539   *No. 4492*

Then he [Martin Luther] read Terence with the learned annotations of John Rivius[361] in the margins. He said, "It's not strange that Rivius is arrogant. Nor is it any wonder if young fellows think highly of themselves. But if we oldsters have a good opinion of ourselves, then it's quite ridiculous.

"Terence can't be translated into German; our tongue won't permit it. But he can be translated into French because this language is more adaptable."

Jews Seek Salvation in Their Observances
April 12, 1539   *No. 4493*

On April 12 he [Martin Luther] was reading in a Hebrew book in which the prayers and holy days of the Jews, as these are now observed, were described. He wondered at the extraordinary presumption of the Jews. No knowledge of the Scriptures appeared there, but only boasting in special laws that are of mutual benefit. "They understand nothing about grace and justification by faith [he said], but they wish to be holy by nature and by blood, as the heathen try to be by the will of the flesh. However, the papists look for a middle way. They wish to be righteous neither by the will of the flesh nor by blood but by the will of man. But all these ways are rejected, and John says that we must be born of God [John 1:13]."

---

[360] Luther's play on words in Latin, in which *papa* ("the pope") is turned into *papus* ("the dandelion"), cannot be reproduced in English.

[361] An edition of Terence (190-159 B.C.), a Roman playwright, was put out by John Rivius in 1534.

Marriage Laws Must Be Adapted to Times
April 13, 1539　　　　　　　　　　　　　　　　No. 4499

Then Dr. Martin Luther was asked about the causes of divorce, and he spoke about two: "The first is adultery. Here one should make an effort to reconcile the couple again after the guilty party has been sharply rebuked. The second cause: when one deserts the other, thereupon returns again, and finally goes off for the third time. Generally such good-for-nothings are on a seesaw; they have a wife elsewhere, return after a couple of years, make that wife pregnant again, and then go away without consent. Men like this ought to have their heads chopped off.

"It's true that the laws prohibit a woman's marrying another man within five or seven years, but this is civil law that pertains only to citizen soldiers, for at that time[362] military service was hereditary and not voluntary, as it is now. The stupid canon lawyers want to apply laws that were framed in other times and for other reasons. They say, 'Thus it is written in the book,' and they don't see that the times have changed and that former circumstances and laws have passed away.

"They act as if somebody would try to rule Constantinople today with Justinian[363] or if somebody would try to put a burden upon it according to what is written. They act as if the Elbe River were overflowing in one place and somebody wished, according to the prescription of the law, to drive in pilings and erect a dam at another place. This would be to act not according to the need but according to the letter of what's written."

Messages Report the Death of Duke George
April 20, 1539　　　　　　　　　　　　　　　　No. 4509

At the eighth hour in the morning of April 20 a letter came to Dr. Martin Luther concerning the death of Duke George.[364] It was reported that he died at seven o'clock in the evening on

---

[362] I.e., when the law was enacted.
[363] I.e., the Justinian code of laws. See No. 4091, n. 281.
[364] Duke George of Albertine Saxony had been a bitter foe of Martin Luther for two decades and often appears in this light in the Table Talk. Cf. No. 275.

April 17, having received the sacrament before at two o'clock. Soon another letter came which reported that he had died without cross or candle[365] at eight o'clock in the morning on April 17.[366] Here it was reported that he had spent the evening of the previous day, healthy and cheerful, in a brothel, and shortly afterward, in the morning, he had died wretchedly. After a long silence Dr. Martin Luther said, "His death will please some and frighten many other people because he was a terrible tyrant. It is as the landgrave[367] is reported to have said three years ago, 'Our father could do a great deal of good if he'd give up his stubbornness!' But he was obstinate and had to do good after his death. For a well-founded report was circulated a few days before the death of Duke George that the use of the sacrament in both kinds would be permitted, and all the prelates had been summoned to Leipzig on this very day, April 20. This was his intention when he died wretchedly, as if unworthy to accomplish such a change. There's reason to suspect that Duke George died a long time earlier and that this was kept secret on account of his proposals. But let it pass! It's a significant example for all of us. For a short time the father is hidden from our eyes, together with his sons,[368] and proceeds unrepentant to hell. Ah, how I dislike prophesying! But it's his own fault; he ruined the parishes, he exiled the people, he let the university[369] go to pieces, he encouraged exorbitant compound interest and usury. He died as he lived. Like Heinz Probst,[370] a former usurer in Leipzig, in the agony of death he fell into hell."

Good Weather and Promise of Crops
April 25, 1539   *No. 4533*

When fruitful weather set in he [Martin Luther] said with a

---

[365] Monks' Latin: *sine lux sine crux*, i.e., without benefit of a priest's ministrations in the extremity of death.

[366] The second letter reported the time of death correctly.

[367] Landgrave Philip of Hesse had married the daughter of Duke George and accordingly referred to him as his father, i.e., his father-in-law.

[368] Duke John and Duke Frederick had died earlier.

[369] During the rule of Duke George enrolment of students in the university in Leipzig declined to about one-third of what it had been before.

[370] Heinz Wiederkehrer, called Probst, died in 1515.

sigh, "Ah, praise God, this is wonderful weather! God is merciful and grants it to us without our deserving it. Would that we might also become more godly! If this happened we'd have paradise and heaven right here. All pains and troubles would be ended. Caterpillars, ants, and all sorts of worms would no longer harm our fruit, but everything would grow green and ripen in a delightful way. However, the punishment of original sin goes out into the whole world and falls on all creatures. Just now the grain in Thuringia and Meissen must be cut shorter with the sickle because the fertility is excessive. We Saxons don't have to do this, and therefore we have an earlier harvest than they do."

Pleasures of a May Day in Late April
April 28, 1539   *No. 4542*

Afterward he gave thought to the pleasant weather of the month of May, whose blooms are a parable of the resurrection of the dead. "How pleasant the trees are! How delightfully green everything's beginning to be! It's like a charming day in May. I don't recall one like it. If it continues this way it will be a very fruitful year and the world will be crammed full. Ah, would that we could trust God! If God can take such delight in our earthly sojourn, what must it be like in the life to come?"

A Nightingale's Song and Croaking Frogs
April 28, 1539   *No. 4543*

Then he heard a nightingale sing beautifully. On the other hand, he heard the measured noise and the croaking of frogs, which drowned out the sweet sound. He said, "That's the way it is in the world. This nightingale is Christ, who proclaims the gospel. He's drowned out by the clamor of the heretics, of Eck,[371] Cochlaeus,[372] and Faber,[373] who shout with great might."

---

[371] John Eck. Cf. No. 257, n. 107.
[372] John Cochlaeus. Cf. No. 1320, n. 38.
[373] John Faber, archbishop of Vienna. Cf. No. 1320, n. 36.

TABLE TALK

Those who Put Their Trust in Duke George
May 1, 1539   *No. 4556*

The cruelty of Duke George[374] toward his brother was discussed and Dr. Martin Luther said, "God strengthens his own in their suffering and confounds the tyrants, as he exalted David and destroyed Saul in his counsels. This Duke George is a remarkable example of heartlessness. Many say that he had nothing of the Saxon stock in either his physical or his spiritual make-up but was manifestly a supposititious Bohemian or Czech.[375] His fury is now passing by as if it had never been, and all those who put their confidence in him have been deceived and their thoughts have turned to nothing in a single day. Ah, to believe in God is no deception. If only we could stake everything on God!"

The Church Fathers and Biblical Interpretation
May 7, 1539   *No. 4567*

There was talk on May 7 about the clarity of the Scriptures in this age, though in former times much had been written and read but little understood. He [Martin Luther] replied, "Surely a great light has gone up, for we understand both the words and the content [of the Scriptures] according to the testimony of the ancient writers. None of the sophists[376] was able to expound the passage, 'He who through faith is righteous shall live' [Rom. 1:17], for they interpreted 'righteous' and 'righteousness' differently. Except only for Augustine,[377] there was great blindness among the fathers. After the Holy Scriptures, Augustine should especially be read, for he had keen judgment. However, if we turn from the Bible to the commentaries of the fathers, our study will be bottomless.

"Consequently this is the best advice, that one should draw from the source and diligently read the Bible. For a man who

---

[374] Duke George of Albertine Saxony had just died. Cf. No. 4509.
[375] Duke George's mother was a daughter of George Podiebrad, the Hussite king of Bohemia.
[376] The scholastic theologians of the Middle Ages.
[377] Luther generally put Augustine above the other church fathers. Cf. No. 51.

knows the text is also an extraordinary theologian. One passage or one text from the Bible is worth more than the glosses of four writers who aren't reliable and thorough. Suppose I take the text, 'Everything created by God is good' [I Tim. 4:4]; food, marriage, etc., are created by God; therefore [they are good], etc. The glosses contradict this; Bernard,[378] Dominic,[379] and Basil[380] wrote and acted otherwise. But the text itself overcomes the glosses. The dear fathers were held in high esteem; meanwhile what they did to the Bible was wrong. Ambrose[381] and Basil were quite dull, and Gregory Nazianzen[382] was accused of writing nothing honestly about God in his poetry and songs.

"The Holy Spirit doesn't let himself be bound by words but makes the content known. This once happened to me when with the help of certain men I concentrated on a Greek form. Because I insisted on definitions, I said nothing about the matter and couldn't tell about the function, use, or utility of the thing about which I spoke."

A Student Goes Home to See His Sick Father
May 7, 1539   *No. 4568*

Martin Weyer,[383] a student of noble birth from Pomerania, was called back home by his father. Since the father was an old man and was accustomed to papistic usages, the son asked Dr. Martin Luther how he should deal with his father in order to be able to benefit him. He inquired if during the time of his father's illness he ought to attend papistic ceremonies and, in particular, private mass.

Dr. Martin Luther replied that he should in every way accommodate himself to his father, under no circumstances offend him,

---

[378] Bernard of Clairvaux. Cf. No. 494, n. 295.
[379] Dominic (1170-1221) was the founder of the Dominican Order.
[380] Cf. No. 252, n. 99.
[381] Cf. No. 51, n. 6.
[382] Gregory of Nazianzus (329-390), a prominent Eastern theologian, wrote some poems in the artificial, rhetorical style of his day, including many that were autobiographical.
[383] Martin Weyer was matriculated in the University in Wittenberg in 1534 and boarded in Luther's home.

and adapt himself to his fasting, praying, invocation of the saints, and hearing of masses. At the same time, Luther said, through the Word of God the son should instruct his parent in the doctrine of justification and the words of the Creed. Above all, he should diligently impress upon him the preaching of Jesus Christ, and only after all this should he dwell on his upright life and his pure conversation. Then there will be hope for the father. If the father should not be changed by all this, the son must bear his infirmity, pray, and commend him to God. He should take care in every possible way not to offend his father by his liberty but should become the spiritual father of him who is his physical father. If for this purpose he adjusts himself to his father, he will not sin by attending mass and other profane rites.

Another Account of Luther's First Mass
May 8, 1539   *No. 4574*

Afterward he spoke of his monastic life, into which he had been thrust against the will of his parents and all his friends.[384] "When I celebrated my first mass, I was almost desperate at the altar when I read in the canon, 'To thee, eternal and true God.' The next day I asked my father why he was angry at me since everything turned out well. He answered, 'Don't you know the Fourth Commandment, Honor your father and your mother [Exod. 20:12]?' For he wanted to encourage me to study law, and in fact I already possessed a complete *Corpus iuris*.[385] However, God wanted to get a *jube Domine benedicere*[386] out of me, and I first had to learn and know the pope's tricks."

Different Temperaments of Luther and Melanchthon
May 8, 1539   *No. 4577*

Then there was talk about the impudence of the papists against

---

[384] For parallels of this account see Nos. 623, 3556A.
[385] Cf. No. 4091, n. 281.
[386] Latin: "Lord, command me to extol thee." These are the words with which a deacon asked for the priest's blessing in a mass.

our *Confession* in Augsburg.[387] He [Martin Luther] said, "I still have their *Confutation*[388] secretly at home. It deserved to be rejected. I had to attack it more sharply because Philip[389] was too modest. As a result of his modesty, at all events, the papists were puffed up. Out of love Philip wants to be of service to everybody. If the papists came to me this way, I'd send them packing."

Thereupon the conversation turned to the great difference in temperament between Dr. Martin Luther and Philip Melanchthon and to the high measure of agreement between them, which, despite the difference, made them accomplish so much. To this Dr. Martin Luther commented, "In the Acts of the Apostles you have a description of us. James is our Philip, who in his modesty wanted to retain the law voluntarily [Acts 15:13-21]. Peter signifies me, who smashed it: 'Why do you put a yoke on the neck of the disciples' [Acts 15:10]? Philip lets himself be devoured. I devour everything and spare no one. So God accomplishes the same thing in two different persons."

A Rose Suggests a Lesson About God's Gifts
May 14, 1539   *No. 4593*

He [Martin Luther] had a rose in his hand and marveled at it. "A glorious work of art by God," he said. "If a man had the capacity to make just one rose he would be given an empire! But the countless gifts of God are esteemed as nothing because they're always present.

"We see that God gives children to all men, the fruit of their bodies resembling the parents. A peasant is said to have three or

---

[387] The *Augsburg Confession*, drafted and presented at the diet of the empire in Augsburg, 1530.

[388] The so-called *Roman Confutation*, the reply by Roman theologians in 1530 to the *Augsburg Confession*. The original draft of the *Confutation* was rejected by Emperor Charles V as inadequate. The manuscript of this draft was recovered in the Vatican archives about 1890. Cf. *The Lutheran Church Quarterly*, IV (1931), 147-165.

[389] Philip Melanchthon prepared the *Augsburg Confession* in a conciliatory tone. His *Apology of the Augsburg Confession* (1531), which was a reply to the *Roman Confutation*, was more forthright. Even more so was Luther's *Exhortation to All Clergy Assembled at Augsburg* (1530), which has been called Luther's own *Augsburg Confession*. Cf. *LW* 34, 3-61.

four sons who look so much like him that they're easily mistaken for one another. All of these gifts are despised because they're always present. It's not a small thing, even among the heathen, for children to be born who resemble their parents. So Dido said to Aeneas, 'If I had a little Aeneas playing in the palace who resembled you only in the face!'[390] And the Greeks, when they cursed somebody, wished that his children wouldn't look like him."

The Pope Avoids Reformation of the Church
May 15, 1539 *No. 4596*

Then there was talk about the meeting to be held in Nürnberg.[391] It was evident that it displeased Dr. Martin Luther [who said]: "We should submit to the wiles and tricks of the papists, who want nothing less than reformation? We can't recede from that which we confessed in Augsburg[392] and Smalcald[393] without peril to our faith. So we would tear down the teaching of our churches for the sake of external pacification. If Emperor Charles would call together a national council[394] there would still be some hope. The papists don't want to yield; they want to decide with authority."

Philip[395] responded, "It was resolved in Frankfurt after a sharp debate that if the papists or cardinals should come and try to decide with authority, all of us would stand up [to leave], for the pope is to have no authority here."

But Dr. Martin Luther laughed. "This is an invention of the

---

[390] Vergil, *Aeneid*, 4, 328, 329.

[391] At a meeting of princes in Frankfurt from February to April, 1539 (cf. No. 4352), it was decided to continue discussions in Nürnberg in August, 1539. This meeting was not held.

[392] The *Augsburg Confession* had been prepared there in 1530.

[393] The *Smalcald Articles* had been written by Luther for adoption in 1537. Cf. Tappert (ed.), *The Book of Concord*, pp. 287-335.

[394] Long ago Emperor Charles V had threatened to call a German national synod, or council, to defy the pope and introduce reforms. See Jaroslav Pelikan, "Luther's Attitude Toward Church Councils," in Kristen E. Skydsgaard (ed.), *The Papal Council and the Gospel* (Minneapolis: Augsburg, 1961), pp. 37-60.

[395] Philip Melanchthon had been present at the meeting in Frankfurt.

archbishop of Mainz," [396] he said. "We don't need a council for the sake of the Word, but only for the sake of some externals. We can arrange for fasting very well without a council. I shall be glad to help make arrangements for it openly, but without laws that are binding on consciences. Christ didn't institute fasting by means of laws, but he said, 'When the bridegroom is taken away from them, then they will fast in that day' [Mark 2:20]. 'Go, sell all that you possess' [Matt. 19:21]. Then fasting will follow readily."

There Is Danger in Avoiding Marriage
May 29, 1539 *No. 4625*

Thereupon there was conversation about the delightful institution of marriage. [Martin Luther said,] "Through the papists Satan so defiled it that in his little book on the celibacy of priests Cyprian[397] wrote, 'If you hear a woman speak, flee from her as if she were a hissing snake.' That's the way it is. When one is afraid of whores one must fall into Sodomite depravity, as almost happened to St. Jerome.[398]

A Miracle Story and Luther's Estimate of It
June 3, 1539 *No. 4632*

On June 3 a case was related that occurred near Zittau during the famine this year.[399] There an honorable, godly matron of evangelical faith suffered greatly with her two children for want of food. When she had nothing more to live on she dressed herself and her children in festive attire and resolved to go with them to a well and pray there that God might feed her and her children in this time of hunger. On the way a man met her, talked with her, and inquired whether she also intended to eat of the water of the well. She assured him, "To God everything is easy. He who fed the people of Israel with manna for forty years can also sustain me

---

[396] Cardinal Albrecht, archbishop of Mainz. Cf. No. 1362, n. 65.
[397] Cyprian (d. 258), *The Discipline and Advantage of Chastity*.
[398] Cf. No. 51, n. 2.
[399] On the shortage of food in the spring of this year, see No. 4472.

with water." When she adhered with constancy to her claim the man (who was perhaps an angel) said, "Indeed, because you believe firmly, go home. There you will find three measures of meal." And it is said that she really found the meal according to his promise.

In response to this Dr. Martin Luther said, "If this is true, it's a remarkable miracle of faith. But if it's contrived, it was piously and cleverly invented to entice man to believe."

Apart from Its Use a Sacrament Is Nothing
June 3, 1539   *No. 4634*

Then he [Martin Luther] was asked whether the sacraments have a spiritual power in themselves, so that baptism would be consecrated water which by its own strength could wipe out sins, even in case the water were drunk by an ass. He replied, "Because the spiritual power of God doesn't consist of corporeal, inanimate matter, baptism doesn't accomplish anything at all as water existing by itself. But as an action (which would be in its use) baptism has power, so that if anybody sprinkles an infant with water together with a recitation of those words of Christ by which he instituted baptism and promised the forgiveness of sins, that action, and not the water, has divine power. Thus the sacraments are nothing apart from the action and use. Philip Melanchthon [treats] these things." [400]

Luther Rejects the Copernican Cosmology
June 4, 1539   *No. 4638*

There was mention of a certain new astrologer[401] who wanted

---

[400] Compendiously, for example, in Art. 13 of the *Augsburg Confession* and the *Apology of the Augsburg Confession*.

[401] The reference is undoubtedly to Nicholas Copernicus (1473-1543). His revolutionary theory was finally set forth in his *Revolutions of the Celestial Spheres* (1543), but before this it was taught, among other places, in Wittenberg itself. For the historical context, see John Dillenberger, *Protestant Thought and Natural Science* (Garden City, N. Y.: Doubleday, 1960), pp. 28-49; Walter A. Hansen (trans.), Werner Elert, *The Structure of Lutheranism* (St. Louis: Concordia Publishing House), I (1962), 414-431.

to prove that the earth moves and not the sky, the sun, and the moon. This would be as if somebody were riding on a cart or in a ship and imagined that he was standing still while the earth and the trees were moving. [Luther remarked,] "So it goes now. Whoever wants to be clever must agree with nothing that others esteem. He must do something of his own. This is what that fellow does who wishes to turn the whole of astronomy upside down. Even in these things that are thrown into disorder I believe the Holy Scriptures, for Joshua commanded the sun to stand still and not the earth [Josh. 10:12]."

Luther Does Not Wish to Live Much Longer
June 11, 1539 *No. 4647*

On June 11 he [Martin Luther] went to Lichtenberg and had supper with the margrave's wife[402] in the evening. She addressed him in a very friendly way, wished him a long life, and expressed the hope that he could live another forty years. He replied, "God forbid! Even if God were to offer me paradise in order that I might last forty more years in this life, I wouldn't want it. I'd rather hire a hangman to knock my head off. That's how bad the world is now. It's full of nothing but devils, so that one can't wish anything better than a blessed end and to get away. Nor do I bother with physicians. I won't embitter my life, which may last a half year, but in God's name I'll eat whatever tastes good to me."

The Faith that Justifies Is Not Knowledge
June 16, 1539 *No. 4655*

On June 16 there was an examination of candidates for ordination at which the proposition put for debate was: "Faith justifies; faith is a work; therefore works justify." He [Martin Luther] responded, "Faith justifies not as a work, or as a quality, or as knowledge, but as assent of the will and firm confidence in the mercy of

---

[402] Elisabeth, widow of Elector Joachim I of Brandenburg, who had died in 1535. She now lived in the Lichtenberg Castle, in Saxony, and had frequent contacts with Luther. It appears that Anthony Lauterbach, the recorder of this conversation, had accompanied Luther on this as on many other trips.

God. For if faith were only knowledge, then the devil would certainly be saved because he possesses the greatest knowledge of God and of all the works and wonders of God from the creation of the world. Accordingly faith must be understood otherwise than as knowledge. In part, however, it is assent."

The Introduction of Reforms in Leipzig
June 25, 1539   No. 4675

On this day Dr. Caspar Cruciger returned from Leipzig and asked for help in his work of reform.[403] Things are hopeful there, he said, in spite of the hypocrisy of the town council and the rich burghers. Dr. Martin Luther said, "Christ's words are being fulfilled there, 'You cannot serve God and mammon' [Matt. 6:24]. Also, 'How can you believe, who seek glory from one another' [John 5:44]? The Leipzigers take us to be fools because we don't have money as they do. It's as Solomon said in Proverbs 26 [:16], 'The sluggard is wiser in his own eyes than seven men who can answer discreetly.' Nevertheless, their pride and their wisdom are odious to God and men because thereby they drew Duke George (who now stands before God's judgment) altogether to their side."

Continuation of the Preceding Entry
June 25, 1539   No. 4676

Thereupon there was consultation about ceremonies, how communion ought to be observed.[404] He [Martin Luther] said that the Lord's Supper must correspond in every respect with the arrangement in our principality.

Then Philip[405] declared that he had heard it said by many that our ceremonies are so arranged that the people think no change has been made in comparison with former usage. Yet these cere-

---

[403] Caspar Cruciger (cf. No. 3754, n. 69) helped to establish the Reformation in Leipzig, in Albertine Saxony, after the death in 1539 of Duke George (cf. No. 4509), who had opposed Luther bitterly.
[404] This entry is obviously a continuation of the consultation concerning reforms to be introduced in Leipzig.
[405] Philip Melanchthon. Cf. No. 157, n. 59.

monies possess great solemnity, he said, unlike the deformed ceremonies of the Swiss, who communicate while seated at table; soon after the consecration the minister departs, leaving the communicants at the table.

Thereupon Martin Luther said, "It would be good to keep the whole liturgy with its music, omitting only the canon."[406]

The Production of Books Seems Endless
Between July 1 and 10, 1539   No. 4691

He [Martin Luther] deplored the abundance of books and writers: "There will be a boundless flood of books, for any and everybody will be writing a book to feed his pride, while others will increase this evil in quest of gain. So the Bible will be buried under a mass of literature about the Bible, and the text itself will be neglected, though the experts in the text are the best men in every discipline. A good disciple of Bartolus[407] is a good lawyer. But today everybody hastens to consult writers.

"As a young man I made myself familiar with the Bible; by reading it again and again I came to know my way about in it. Only then did I consult writers [of books about the Bible]. But finally I had to put them out of my sight and wrestle with the Bible itself. It's better to see with one's own eyes than with another's. On this account, because of the bad example, I would wish that all my books were buried. Otherwise everybody will imitate me and try to become famous by writing, as if Christ had died for the sake of our fickle glory and not for the hallowing of his name."

Breakdown of Proposed Alliance with England
July 10, 1539   No. 4699

On July 10 he [Martin Luther] began to give thanks to God for having freed our church from that offensive king of England

---

[406] The canon was that part of the Roman mass in which the priest is believed to transubstantiate bread and wine into the body and blood of Christ and to offer these as a sacrifice to God for the sins of men.
[407] Bartolus de Sassoferrato (1314-1357) taught law in Bologna and elsewhere.

who zealously sought an alliance with our princes but was not accepted.[408] "There's no doubt at all [Luther said] that the king was hindered by divine intervention because he had always been very unstable. I'm glad that we're rid of the blasphemer. He wants to be head of the church in England directly after Christ, a title that isn't appropriate for any bishop or prelate, to say nothing of a king. It won't do. There's only one bridegroom and head of the church, Christ. The church is not such an insignificant body as the pope imagines. But the devil rides the king who troubles the church and torments Christ. He put Thomas More[409] to death; however guilty More was before God, he was just toward his king. He's still King Harry, but he'll soon be confounded. I regret that Master Philip wrote his nicest prefaces for the loosest knaves." [410]

Initiation of New Students in Wittenberg
July 23, 1539   *No. 4714*

That evening he [Martin Luther] attended a deposition[411] with many distinguished men and he himself absolved three youths from their fledgling status.[412] Finally he said, "This ceremony is intended to make you humble, so that you may not be haughty and arrogant and given to wickedness. Such vices are horns and other monstrous parts that are not becoming to a student. Therefore humble yourselves. Learn to be patient. You'll be subjected to hazing all your life. When you hold important offices in the future, burghers, peas-

---

[408] Fearing that he might be politically isolated, King Henry VIII of England had sought admission to the Smalcald League, which refused to accept him as a member unless he could embrace the doctrines and practices set forth in the *Augsburg Confession*. Cf. Neelak Tjernagel, *Henry VIII and the Lutherans* (St. Louis: Concordia, 1965).

[409] For Luther's opinion of Sir Thomas More, cf. No. 3887.

[410] Philip Melanchthon's dedication to Archbishop Albrecht of Mainz in 1532 (*C.R.* 2, 611) and to King Henry VIII in 1535 (*C.R.* 2, 920).

[411] A deposition was a ceremony for the initiation of students entering medieval universities. Such students were called "yellow-bills" (*bejani*) and had to be "absolved" from their previous condition of immaturity. Horns and other tokens of folly which had previously been attached to their heads were removed, and wine was poured on their heads to mark their entrance upon a new life. Cf. Belgum (ed.), *The Mature Luther*, pp. 3-5.

[412] Latin: *a beanio absolvebat*.

ants, nobles, and your wives will harass you with various vexations. When this happens, don't go to pieces. Bear your cross with equanimity and your troubles without murmuring. Remember that you have been initiated into annoyances at Wittenberg. Say that you first began to be hazed in Wittenberg when you were a young man, that now that you have become a weightier person you have heavier vexations to bear. So this deposition of yours is only a symbol of human life in its misfortunes and castigations." And so when the wine had been poured on their heads he absolved them from their fledgling status.

Do Marriage Cases Belong to the Church?
July 23, 1539   *No. 4716*

We asked him [Martin Luther] what pastors should do in marriage cases, whether we can with a good conscience stay away from these troublesome things. He replied, "It is my advice that we should by no means take this yoke upon ourselves. First, we have enough work in our proper office. Second, marriage is outside the church, is a civil matter, and therefore should belong to the government. Third, these cases have no limits, extend to the height, the breadth, and the depth, and produce many offenses that bring disgrace to the gospel.

"I know how often we have been put to shame with our advice in these matters, when to prevent future evil we allowed secret acts —just so they were kept secret so as not to be made an example. But people treat us unkindly and draw us into wicked affairs. If things don't turn out well the blame must be ours entirely. Accordingly we prefer to leave this business to civil officials. The responsibility rests on them. If they do well, it's all the better for them. Only in cases of conscience should pastors give counsel to godly people. Controversies and court cases we leave to lawyers and consistories.[413]

---

[413] In February, 1539, a consistory of two clergymen and two lawyers was set up in Electoral Saxony to serve as a court for matrimonial and disciplinary cases.

"Dr. Kilian[414] wished to impose on us ministers the hearing and examination of cases, after which we should await the decisions of the lawyers. I was against this and suggested that the lawyers hear the cases and look to us for decisions. Master Philip[415] persuaded Master Cellarius[416] and me that for the time being we should serve our lacerated churches in such cases."

---

[414] Kilian Goldstein was a lawyer and a member of the consistory.
[415] Philip Melanchthon. Cf. No. 157, n. 59.
[416] John Cellarius was in Wittenberg at this time before going to Dresden as the newly-appointed superintendent there.

TABLE TALK RECORDED BY JOHN MATHESIUS

1540

INTRODUCTION

The pieces numbered 4858 to 5341 in WA, TR 4 and 5 fall in the year 1540 and were recorded by John Mathesius.

A native of Rochlitz, in Saxony, Mathesius was born in 1504, attended the Latin school in Nürnberg, and studied in the university in Ingolstadt. When converted to the evangelical faith he went to Wittenberg for a short period of study and in 1532 became rector of the Latin school in Joachimstal, a prosperous city in northwestern Bohemia that had recently become Lutheran. In 1540 Mathesius returned to Wittenberg to prepare himself for the ministry, and two years later he returned to Joachimstal as an ordained clergyman. He remained there until his death in 1565.[1]

During his second stay in Wittenberg, from 1540 to 1542, Mathesius became intimately acquainted with and warmly attached to Luther. From May until November, 1540, he boarded in Luther's home and afterward visited it from time to time. During his stay in the Reformer's home he took notes of the conversation at table. These notes reflect the active participation of Mathesius himself, who often asked questions or offered comments, which he recorded without apparent self-consciousness. The unusual number of references to Bohemia and Bohemians in 1540 may also be accounted for by his presence.

In addition to reporting what he himself heard at table, Mathesius diligently assembled and copied the notes which others had taken before and after him. Thus he was prepared, after Luther's death, to publish a biography of the Reformer in a series of sermons entitled *Histories of Luther's Life* (1566). Here he recalled: "What I heard and saw there [in Luther's house] I carefully noted. With the help of diligent individuals God also provided me with good *colloquia* and conversations which had been written down before by Master Veit Dietrich, of Nürnberg; Dr. Weller, of Freiberg;

---

[1] *Luthers Tischreden in der Mathesischen Sammlung. Aus einer Handschrift herausgegeben von Ernst Kroker* (Leipzig, 1903), Introduction.

Master Anthony Lauterbach, of Pirna; and afterward by Master Caspar Heydenreich, superintendent in Torgau; Master Jerome Besold, of Nürnberg; Master [George] Plato; and others of the doctor's boarders." [2]

The selection that follows is representative of the conversation that Mathesius himself recorded. What he copied from the notes of others is not included here.

---

[2] *Historien von Martin Luthers Leben* . . . , quoted in WA, TR 4, xxix.

TABLE TALK RECORDED BY JOHN MATHESIUS

Control of Usurious Rates of Interest
Between May 6 and 16, 1540 *No. 4875*

"One must observe a little equity," Martin Luther said. "The value of goods has gone up not a little, and one can now enjoy a greater profit than formerly. Accordingly I'm happy to concede what the law and the emperor allow, namely 5 per cent or 6 per cent. But 20 per cent, 30 per cent, and 40 per cent—this is excessive! Wollensecker[1] is said to be a pious man, and yet he takes 20 per cent[2] and makes forty on every one hundred. This is too much. And Dr. Löffel,[3] I hear, gets four thousand annually on ten thousand, yet he's a doctor of jurisprudence."

Then I[4] spoke about the case of Naevius[5] and added, "In Bohemia it is the general custom, approved by the king and the nobles, to give 10 per cent, and our friend received 6 per cent."

The doctor said, "If the laws permit it, what should I do? Equity should be advised."

God Is More Generous Than We Expect
Between May 6 and 16, 1540 *No. 4885*

"Our Lord God always gives more than we ask for. If we ask properly for a piece of bread he gives us a whole acre. I prayed God to let my Katy live,[6] and he gives her a good year in addition. But I think a really bad time will follow because we're too wicked and are introducing heresies among ourselves."

---

[1] Probably Andreas Wollensecker, book-dealer in Leipzig.
[2] If the following figure is correct, the meaning here must be 20 per cent interest for half a year.
[3] Martin Löffel, a doctor of law, was a town councilman in Leipzig.
[4] John Mathesius, who often introduces himself in the conversation.
[5] John Neefe, physician in Joachimstal and a friend of Mathesius.
[6] At the end of January and beginning of February, 1540, Luther's wife Katherine had been deathly ill.

Bequest of Duke George Before His Death
Between May 6 and 16, 1540 No. 4887

When Hans von Bora[7] said, "Duke George,[8] God be gracious to him!" the doctor [Martin Luther] interrupted by declaring, "Ungracious! If he isn't in hell, Caiaphas[9] isn't in it either, and there's no hell! For that supreme persecutor of the gospel who has died was filled with the greatest hatred, envy, and malice toward his brother.[10] What had his flesh and blood done to him that he wished to disinherit them and make his land a fief?[11] When his counselors resisted what he wanted he would say, 'You are disloyal and betray me!' On the day on which God killed him he made a will and bequeathed all his treasures to the emperor with the stipulation that he use them against his enemies in Germany. But who are the emperor's adversaries but us?

"He [Duke George] was a wicked, envious man. If he knew that Duke Henry's children were now sitting peacefully in his quarters, this would grieve him in hell. But God is our God. He let Duke George and three cardinals die, and the cardinal of Mainz[12] is very sick too. When one knave is removed, however, another comes to take his place. The duke of Braunschweig[13] won't last long either."

The Incarnation of Christ and the Trinity
May 16, 1540 No. 4915

"If anybody takes counsel with reason, he can't agree with our articles of faith.

"The Turk holds his people to their duty more by religion than by arms, for they believe that God is the almighty Creator of

---

[7] Katherine's brother, and thus Luther's brother-in-law.
[8] Duke George of Albertine Saxony, a bitter opponent of Luther, had died the previous year.
[9] Caiaphas, high priest in Jerusalem (Matt. 26:13), is mentioned by Luther below as a similar enemy of Christ and the gospel.
[10] Duke Henry of Saxony succeeded his brother, Duke George.
[11] To Emperor Charles V.
[12] Cardinal Albrecht, archbishop of Mainz.
[13] Duke Henry of Braunschweig/Wolfenbüttel (1489-1568).

heaven and earth, that Christ is a prophet, that by civil uprightness they can merit heaven, etc.

"However, I have learned, not only through the Scriptures but also from severe inner struggles and trials, that Christ is God and has put on flesh, and likewise I have learned the doctrine of the Trinity. Today, therefore, I don't so much *believe* as I *know* through experience that these doctrines are true. In the worst temptations nothing can help us but faith that God's Son has put on flesh, is bone [of our bone], sits at the right hand of the Father, and prays for us. There is no mightier comfort. From the beginning of the world God has defended this doctrine against all heretics, who are innumerable, and defends it today against the Turk and the pope. He always confirms it by miracles, allows us to call his Son the Son of God and true God, and hears us all when we call upon him in Christ's name.

"What will preserve us today in such great perils except prayer to Christ? If anybody should say that Master Philip[14] or I or others will, he would lie to us. God does it for the sake of Christ, about whom the apostles preach today,[15] 'The one whom you hanged seven weeks ago still lives!' If the blindness of the human heart weren't so great they would all have believed on this day. Accordingly we'll abide by these articles, even against reason, for they have stood up and will stand."

Drunkenness a Common Vice of Germans

May 16, 1540   *No. 4917*

The doctor [Martin Luther] said, "Our Lord God must count the drunkenness of us Germans as an everyday sin, for we probably can't stop it, and yet it's such a disgraceful nuisance that it injures body, soul, and goods."

Then Severus[16] said, "Doctor, they said at court that you never inveighed against this vice."

The doctor replied, "I often bore down hard on this subject

---

[14] Philip Melanchthon. Cf. No. 157, n. 59.
[15] This was Whitsunday. Cf. Acts 2:22-24.
[16] Wolfgang Schiefer, an Austrian who had studied in Wittenberg in 1523, was back in Wittenberg in 1539 and 1540.

in the presence of the court.[17] As a matter of fact, I made it rough and tough on the nobles for leading astray and ruining the princes.[18] This pleased the old man[19] very much, for he lived soberly and often kept John Frederick at table until seven o'clock. But it didn't help after that hour. I used to say to the nobles, 'After dinner you ought to practice on the wrestling ground or engage in some other knightly exercise. After that I'd allow you to have a good drinking bout because some tippling's bearable but intoxication's not.'"

John Huss and His Death at the Stake
Between May 16 and 21, 1530   No. 4922

"The blood of Huss[20] still damns the papists today. He was a learned man, as one can see from his book on the church, and I love him very much. He didn't die like the Anabaptists, but like Christ. Although human weakness may be seen in him, the power of God nevertheless manifests itself. It's pleasant to behold the struggle between flesh and spirit in Christ and in Huss. In all classes of men this testimony concerning Huss has endured, that he was a very learned man and that Jerome[21] was a very eloquent one. More than this one can't say. He knew more than the whole world, but he was condemned as an innocent man. From that time the cause of the pope began to go back and collapse."

Severus[22] interjected, "The city of Constance is in a deplorable condition."

[Luther said,] "I believe God has punished it because it was under arms and led Huss to his death."

---

[17] For examples, see Nos. 3468, 3514.

[18] In the margin was inserted here: "Dr. Steiner's wife related that in a sermon [at court] the doctor [Martin Luther] had said, 'You look this morning as if your heads had been soaking in salt water!' And the elector's wife gave the doctor some underclothing as a present."

[19] Elector John of Saxony, the father of John Frederick. Cf. No. 3507, n. 55.

[20] John Huss, Bohemian reformer, was burned at the stake in Constance during sessions of the Council of Constance. One of his most influential writings was the book *De ecclesia*, on the church. See Matthew Spinka, *John Hus's Concept of the Church* (Princeton University Press, 1966).

[21] Jerome of Prague, a follower of Huss, suffered the same fate about a year later.

[22] Wolfgang Schiefer. Cf. No. 4917, n. 16.

The Authorship of Ancient Writings
Between May 21 and June 11, 1540   *No. 4964*

"Genesis is the right book. One should read and learn it. There we see that the ancient patriarchs agree with our faith. In my opinion, however, Genesis was not by Moses, for there were books before his time and books are cited—for example, the Book of the Wars of the Lord and the Book of Jashar.[23] I believe that Adam wrote for several generations, and after him Noah and the rest, to describe what happened to them. For the Jews were writers in very ancient times. The Greeks started late, and the Germans have been writing for barely a thousand years."

Holiness in This and the Future Life
Between May 21 and June 11, 1540   *No. 4991*

Severus[24] said, "Doctor, there is a certain doctor in Linz who is sorely tried because he cannot find perfect righteousness in himself and because, when he prays, blasphemies against Christ always come to his mind.

"This is a good sign," Luther replied. "There are two kinds of blasphemy. First, there is active blasphemy when we consciously and intentionally look for reasons to blaspheme, as Faber,[25] the duke of Braunschweig,[26] and the rest do. God keep us from this! But, second, blasphemy is passive when the devil introduces such perverse thoughts into our heads against our will and in spite of our struggle against them. By means of these thoughts God wishes to occupy us so that we don't get lazy and snore but fight against them and pray. But when the end of life approaches, these temptations cease, for then the Holy Spirit is near to his Christians, keeps the devil at a distance, and gives us a tranquil and quiet mind.

---

[23] Cf. Num. 21:14; Josh. 10:13.
[24] Cf. No. 4917, n. 16.
[25] John Faber, bishop of Vienna. Cf. No. 1320, n. 36.
[26] Duke Henry of Braunschweig. Cf. No. 4887, n. 13.

"This happened to me in Gotha.[27] Being certain that I was about to die I said farewell to everybody, called Pomeranus,[28] commended to him the church, the school, my wife, and the rest, and asked him to absolve me of my sins. I requested my dear Frederick[29] to keep me in his cemetery in Gotha, but he said, 'Doctor, I don't want to have you here; you ought to go back home.' Thus with a peaceful mind and without any struggle at all I would have fallen asleep in Christ. But Christ wished me to live on. So also my Katy,[30] when we had all given up hope for her life, would have died willingly, happily, and with complete peace, and she said nothing at all but, 'In thee, O Lord, do I seek refuge; let me never be put to shame' [Ps. 31:1]. She repeated this more than a thousand times." She was now seated at the table and confirmed this. Then the doctor added, "If we hadn't had children I wouldn't have said one more prayer for her but would have committed her soul to Christ's keeping.

"Wherefore, Dr. Severus, you ought to write that man [in Linz] that he shouldn't torment himself but should have confidence. In his good time the devil will of his own accord stop forcing such blasphemies upon him. As far as perfect righteousness is concerned, I can readily believe that he desires to be perfectly righteous and that he tries to be holy and blameless. But such a life would be a life of angels and it will not be ours except in the future life. I often get angry with myself because I find much impurity in myself. But what should I do? I can't divest myself of my nature. Meanwhile Christ deems us righteous on account of his blood and counts for righteousness the fact that we desire to be righteous, abhor this uncleanness, and love his Word and trust in him.

---

[27] In 1537, after he had been taken ill in Smalcald and was returning to his home in Wittenberg, Luther had stopped in Gotha, where he had suffered a relapse. Cf. above, No. 3543A.

[28] John Bugenhagen, of Pomerania. Cf. No. 122, n. 36.

[29] Frederick Myconius, or Mecum (1490-1546), had since 1524 been pastor in Gotha, where he consolidated reforms previously begun.

[30] Latin: *Catena*, a chain, a frequent play on words; Katy was Luther's "ball and chain." The reference here is to the grave illness of Luther's wife a few months before. Cf. No. 4885, n. 6.

"Surely as far as we and our princes are concerned, we are not pure and holy, and our princes have their faults. But Christ rejoices in a clear and trustful confession. Certainly I esteem it highly. By saying one word and denying the Word our princes[31] could have returned to the favor of king and emperor and lived quietly. But they preferred to lose everything and put themselves, their family, and their land in temporal danger rather than forsake the confession. This is the thing that terrifies the emperor and the pope; it also attracts many of us and encourages more people to confess their faith. I'm a beggar. What can I lose when I have nothing? But they risk the loss of their reputation and their principalities for the name of Christ.

"Consequently, even if we are not perfectly holy, Christ will wash away our sins with his blood and, when we depart from this life, will make us altogether pure in the life to come. In the meantime we are content with that righteousness which exists in hope through faith in Jesus Christ. Amen."

Grammar and Experience in Translating Bible
Between May 21 and June 11, 1540   No. 5002

"It's not enough to know the grammar [of a biblical passage]. One must observe the sense, for a knowledge of the matters treated brings with it an understanding of the words. Lawyers wouldn't understand the law unless it dealt with matters known to them by experience. Nobody could comprehend the words of Vergil's *Eclogues*[32] unless he was first sure about the contents. If he knew whether an eclogue was about Augustus or Julius Caesar[33] it would then be easy to apply the words.

In the case of the Bible I hold fast to the meaning. Often learned grammarians like Forstemius[34] came and I indicated what

---

[31] The allusion here is probably to the steadfastness of the evangelical princes, and especially of the elector of Saxony, at the imperial Diet of Augsburg in 1530, where the *Augsburg Confession* was presented.

[32] The *Eclogues* of Vergil were poems about the life of shepherds.

[33] Roman emperors during and following Vergil's career.

[34] Bernard Ziegler (1496-1556), Hebrew scholar in Leipzig.

something meant to the people as if I understood neither Greek nor Hebrew nor Latin. I said, 'Master Forstemius, can the grammatical construction bear this sense?' Then he replied, 'Most assuredly!' So at last he was convinced that we translated the Bible with great care."

Zwingli Proud of His Knowledge of Greek
Between May 21 and June 11, 1540   No. 5005

"Those people want to be learned even if we don't acknowledge it. When we were in Marburg he [Zwingli][35] always spoke Greek. Once when he was absent I asked, 'Why is it that he's not ashamed of speaking Greek in the presence of such learned Greekists as Oecolampadius,[36] Philip,[37] Osiander,[38] and Brenz?[39] Surely they know and understand it!' These words of mine were reported to him, and so the next morning he justified himself in the presence of the prince[40] by saying, 'Illustrious Prince, I often speak Greek because I have now read the New Testament in Greek for thirteen years.' Ah, no! There's more to it than reading the New Testament; the thirst for glory entirely blinds people. He also speaks German and thinks all people ought to speak in the Swiss dialect."

Severus[41] said about the same man, "When he had been called to the Anabaptists and spoke in Greek, one of them said, 'You have a proud spirit and desire to be famous. Speak German!'"

---

[35] Huldreich Zwingli (1484-1531), the Swiss reformer, is meant here, as parallel entries indicate (Nos. 5006 and 5143, not translated in this selection). Through the mediation of Landgrave Philip of Hesse and Martin Bucer, Luther and Zwingli with a few of their adherents met in Marburg (October, 1529) in an unsuccessful attempt to compose their theological differences. The grammarian Forstemius is not identifiable.
[36] John Oecolampadius (1482-1531), at the Marburg Colloquy as a humanistic supporter of Zwingli, helped introduce the Reformation into Basel.
[37] Philip Melanchthon. Cf. No. 157, n. 59.
[38] Andrew Osiander supported Luther against Zwingli at the Marburg Colloquy. Cf. No. 600, n. 367.
[39] John Brenz, Swabian reformer, was praised by Luther as an exegete.
[40] Landgrave Philip of Hesse. Cf. No. 3514, n. 60.
[41] Wolfgang Schiefer. Cf. No. 4917, n. 16.

What Was God Doing Before the Creation?
Between May 21 and June 11, 1540 No. 5010

Severus said, "The scholastics even disputed about the question of where God was before the creation of the world. I heard Camers[42] reply in Vienna that God was in himself."

The doctor [Martin Luther] said, "Yes, Augustine[43] mentioned this. But once, when he was asked, he said, 'God was making hell for those who are inquisitive.'" Then he added, "Where is God now, after the creation?"

The Place of Reason in the Christian Faith
Between May 21 and June 11, 1540 No. 5015

Severus said, "Doctor, the Jewish physician Ricius[44] writes against our faith and is distressed that Philip[45] wrote that articles of faith cannot be comprehended by reason. He said that if the condition of her body is not perfect a girl cannot conceive in her uterus."

He [Martin Luther] responded, "Ah, what does reason understand? It can't comprehend how man is made from a drop of blood, how a cherry grows from a blossom, how bone and flesh came into existence. The world is full of everyday miracles, but, as Augustine[46] said with reference to John 6 [:9], because they occur so often these things are deemed of little value. Christ once fed several thousand people with five loaves of bread. What does he do every day? But what happens daily is counted of little consequence. God produces wine from stones and makes butter and bread out of sand. So he once formed man out of the ground,[47] and now he creates men every day out of drops of blood. There's no difference. Then he took a clod of earth in his hands and said, 'Be a man!' And today he says to the little drop, 'Be a man!' These

---
[42] John Camers was professor in Vienna until 1528, and Severus (Schiefer) probably was his student there.
[43] Augustine, *Confessions*, XI, 10.
[44] Dr. Paul Ricius wrote *Statera Prudentum* (Regensburg, 1532).
[45] Philip Melanchthon. Cf. No. 157, n. 59.
[46] Augustine, *Homilies on the Gospel of John*, Tractate 24, 1.
[47] Cf. Gen. 2:7.

are great miracles, but because of their frequency they are little esteemed.

"Who can understand anything about these things by means of reason? To be sure, enlightened reason can to some extent understand the Ten Commandments and the religion of the Jews; but articles of faith, like the Trinity and the incarnation of Christ—these don't tally with reason. Let's say that the king of France and a stone are the same thing, or this knife[48] and I are identical—these statements don't tally with reason. It's the same with the statement that God is man. We have to puzzle this out. I can reflect on it but can't understand it. Paul understood a good part of it, though he didn't comprehend all of it by any means. Yet he said with authority, 'In Christ are hid all the treasures of wisdom and knowledge' [Col. 2:3]. For in this Christ all things, every creature, the whole Godhead are known. Here are united the greatest fortitude and the greatest weakness, life and death, righteousness and sin, the grace and the wrath of God. Ah, this is a high doctrine, but few care very much about it."

The Study of the Bible Demands Humility
Between May 21 and June 11, 1540   *No. 5017*

"The Holy Scriptures require a humble reader who shows reverence and fear toward the Word of God and constantly says, 'Teach me, teach me, teach me!' The Spirit resists the proud. Though they study diligently and some preach Christ purely for a time, nevertheless God excludes them from the church if they're proud. Wherefore every proud person is a heretic, if not actually, then potentially. However, it's difficult for a man who has excellent gifts not to be arrogant. Those whom God adorns with great gifts he plunges into the most severe trials in order that they may learn that they're nothing. Paul got a thorn in the flesh to keep him from being haughty.[49] And if Philip[50] were not so afflicted he would have curious notions. When on the other hand Jacob[51] and

---

[48] Luther, seated at table, probably had a knife in his hand.
[49] Cf. II Cor. 12:7.
[50] Philip Melanchthon's physical infirmities may have been in Luther's mind here.
[51] Jacob Schenk, an antinomian. Cf. No. 4048, n. 253.

Agricola[52] are haughty and despise their teachers and learning, I fear it may be done with them. I knew the spirit of Münzer,[53] Zwingli,[54] and Karlstadt.[55] Pride drove the angel out of heaven and spoils many preachers. Accordingly it's humility that's needed in the study of sacred literature."

Christians as Sheep in the Midst of Wolves
Between May 21 and June 11, 1540   *No. 5031*

"Christ fights with the devil in a curious way—the devil with great numbers, cleverness, and steadfastness, and Christ with few people, with weakness, simplicity, and contempt—and yet Christ wins. So he wished us to be sheep and our adversaries to be wolves.[56] But what an unequal contest to fight with ten or a hundred wolves! He sent twelve disciples into the world, twelve among so many wolves. I think it's a remarkable war and a strange fight in which the sheep are killed and the wolves stay alive. But they'll all go to ruin as a result, because God alone performs miracles. He'll preserve his sheep in the midst of the wolves and he'll crush the jaws of the wolves for ever."

Philip of Hesse's Boldness and His Bigamy
Between May 21 and June 11, 1540   *No. 5038*

When news of the bigamy of Hesse[57] spread abroad, the

---

[52] John Agricola was Luther's chief antinomian opponent. Cf. No. 3179a, n. 62.
[53] Thomas Münzer was a radical religious leader in the Peasants' War. Cf. No. 291, n. 131.
[54] Huldreich Zwingli. Cf. No. 5005, n. 35.
[55] Andrew Karlstadt. Cf. No. 356, n. 172.
[56] Cf. Matt. 10:16. Luther expressed similar thoughts in a letter to Philip Melanchthon on June 18, 1540. WA, Br 9, 144-145.
[57] Landgrave Philip of Hesse, a prominent evangelical prince who had been unhappily married to the daughter of Duke George of Saxony (cf. No. 275, n. 118) and had been resorting to a succession of prostitutes, finally decided to end his immoral conduct by marrying Margaret von der Sale. The theologian Martin Bucer (cf. No. 184, n. 64) interceded in his behalf with Luther and Melanchthon, who reluctantly gave their approval to the proposed marriage on condition that the arrangements be kept secret. On March 4, 1540, the marriage took place. When it became widely known soon after, a scandal resulted.

doctor [Martin Luther] said with a serene countenance, "He's a remarkable man. He has his [propitious] star. I think he wishes to obtain it [consent for his bigamy] through the emperor and the pope in order to gratify his desire. It's also possible that he may defect from us as a result of this business."

Then Severus[58] said, "Surely many doubt the constancy of [Philip of] Hesse and suspect him."

The doctor said, "It's remarkable, but up to now he has stood firm. The emperor wanted to concede to him the quiet possession of Katzenelnbogen[59] and Duke George wanted to make him his heir, which the emperor assented to, but Hesse preferred to confess the gospel. He could have become the dear son of the emperor and the pope, but he was unwilling. He has a Hessian head. He can't rest, nor does he give in. If one thing is finished he'll undertake something else shortly after. Perhaps either she or he[60] will die.

"He's always starting something new, and he finishes it too. It was an audacious thing to oppose the bishops,[61] and even more audacious to restore [the duke of] Württemberg and drive out the king.[62] Philip[63] and I used our best rhetoric to dissuade him in Weimar from disgracing the gospel and disturbing the public peace, and he became angry and embarrassed, when otherwise he was straightforward. At the Marburg Colloquy[64] he went about looking like a stable boy and, as great men do, playfully concealed his weighty thoughts. He asked Philip, 'Master Philip, should I tolerate it that the bishop of Mainz drives out my preachers by force?' Philip replied, 'By all means, if the jurisdiction is that of Mainz.'[65] Then Hesse declared, 'I'll let you give me advice, but I won't act

---

[58] Wolfgang Schiefer. Cf. No. 4917, n. 16.
[59] Rival claims for the possession of Katzenelnbogen, a small county, were being advanced by the counts of Nassau as well as by Philip of Hesse.
[60] Either Margaret von der Sale or Philip of Hesse. The death of one or the other might cause the scandal to subside.
[61] The bishops of Würzburg and Bamberg in 1528.
[62] In 1526 Philip of Hesse had supported the duke of Württemberg in his successful attempt to regain his throne in the face of opposition from King Ferdinand of Austria.
[63] Philip Melanchthon. Cf. No. 157, n. 59.
[64] Cf. No. 5005, n. 35.
[65] Cardinal Albrecht, archbishop of Mainz.

according to it.' I said to the old counselor Bemelburg,[66] 'Why don't you oppose the proposals of your prince?' He answered, 'It doesn't help, for once he makes up his mind he can't be turned aside.' When he was on an expedition all his subjects begged him not to ruin the land of Hesse, and he said, 'Don't worry! I won't ruin it for you.'"

The doctor added, "He kept his word. He was honorable. In one hour he shot three hundred and fifty shots into a castle and waited for an answer from Kaaden.[67] In the consultation there [Duke] George said to the king, 'If you can raise an army in two or three days I don't recommend peace, but if you can't do this, then peace must be made.'"

Severus said that only Hans Hofmann[68] opposed the king and his counselors and brought it about that there was peace.

[The doctor then said,] "Because he's such an odd fellow I have to let it go. The emperor doesn't give in to Hesse. Something could have been done about secret concubinage. 'God will act' [Ps. 37:5].

"In Augsburg,[69] when invited together with the rest of the princes by the king,[70] he [Philip of Hesse] said openly to the bishops, 'Make peace! We desire it. If you don't and I must go down to my grave, I'll take at least two of you down with me.' The bishop of Salzburg said to [the bishop of] Mainz, 'How is it that you are so afraid of Hesse? After all, he is only a poor prince!' Mainz replied, 'My dear Sir, if you lived as near to him as I do you would probably speak differently.'"

The doctor continued, "God has hurled this [landgrave of] Hesse into the midst of the Roman Empire. He has four electors and [the duke of] Braunschweig as his neighbors, and yet they're all afraid of him. He enjoys the favor of the common people, and he's a belligerent rooster. Before he restored [the duke of] Würt-

---

[66] Probably Ludwig von Boineburg (1466-1536).
[67] The treaty of Kaaden, in Bohemia (1534), where King Ferdinand returned Württemberg to Duke Ulrich.
[68] In 1534 Severus (Schiefer) had tutored Hofmann's children.
[69] At the Diet of Augsburg in 1530.
[70] King Ferdinand of Austria. Cf. No. 206, n. 77.

temberg, Hesse was in France, and the king lent him two hundred thousand crowns to carry on that war."

Then Severus said, "The Germans often deceive the king of France, and it was not done prudently."

Then the doctor replied, "He was blinded by ambition. Consequently he doesn't remember anything. The king made a gift of fifty thousand crowns to [the duke of] Württemberg."

Scandal Caused by Philip of Hesse's Bigamy
Between May 21 and June 11, 1540 No. 5046

The doctor [Martin Luther] said, "Great is the scandal caused by our Hesse,[71] but the restoration [of Württemberg][72] caused much greater offense. At that time everybody thought Germany would fall to pieces. Bigamy has well-known examples in the Scriptures[73] and could have been kept secret, but to drive out the king, the emperor's brother, from the duchy [of Württemberg] in the face of the raging of the bishops and the pope! That was a great risk. But it was the cause of the man who carried it out. No prudent man would have entered upon that course, but overtaken by a frenzy he [Philip of Hesse] managed the affair cleverly.

"Just be calm! It will blow over. Perhaps she will soon die." [74]

Preaching Should Be Simple, Not Erudite
Between May 21 and June 11, 1540 No. 5047

"Many sects will still arise and Osiander[75] will start one of them, for that fellow can do nothing but criticize others. We translated the Bible, and he took up one and another word with which to attack us. These words and the whole quarrel don't really matter to Christendom, and he doesn't prove anything anyhow. He

---

[71] On Philip of Hesse's bigamy, see No. 5038, n. 57.
[72] Cf. No. 5038, n. 62.
[73] Abraham, Jacob, David, and Solomon are familiar examples in the Old Testament. Cf. Luther's letter to Elector John Frederick, June 10, 1540. Tappert (ed.), *Luther: Letters of Spiritual Counsel*, pp. 288-291.
[74] Philip of Hesse's new bride Margaret was only about nineteen years old and in good health. Cf. No. 5038, n. 60.
[75] Andrew Osiander. Cf. No. 600, n. 367.

offends the church. He could have taken up and debated this matter in private, but he couldn't contain himself and curb his cleverness.

"In Smalcald I preached on a text from the Epistles of John[76] in which it's stated that Christ dwells in us through faith and grace, works in us, and defends and saves us. Just as I fell ill[77] he [Osiander] rebuked me openly, though not by name, in the presence of all the learned men. Christ, he said, dwells in us essentially, etc. Everybody was annoyed by this, especially Brenz.[78] Osiander possesses eloquence, follows an outline, and adheres to rules of rhetoric, but he doesn't instruct the people. On the other hand, Dr. Link[79] and Master Veit[80] instruct them. Today Master Mörlin[81] pleased me very much [when he preached]. He instructed the common people about the duties of wives and maidservants. A wife, he said, should think that she's in a holy estate and that her husband is a gift of God; a maidservant should also think that her estate is holy and that her work is holy. The people can take this home with them, but nobody understands a sermon that is turgid, deep, removed from life.

"I spoke about this to Bucer in Gotha[82] and suggested that he and Osiander should refrain from erudite preaching. Philip[83] doesn't need to be instructed, and I don't teach or lecture for his sake, but we preach publicly for the sake of plain people. Christ could have taught in a profound way but he wished to deliver his message with the utmost simplicity in order that the common people might understand. Good God, there are sixteen-year-old

---

[76] In February, 1537, Luther preached at a meeting of the Smalcald League on I John 4. The sermon is extant and is reproduced in WA 45, 11-24.
[77] Luther had a severe attack of renal calculus. Cf. No. 3543A.
[78] John Brenz. Cf. No. 347, n. 163.
[79] Wenceslaus Link (1483-1547) was a friend of Luther who had succeeded John Staupitz in 1520 as vicar-general of the Augustinians.
[80] Veit Dietrich was the trusted secretary of Luther who recorded some of the Table Talk.
[81] Joachim Mörlin (Mörlein). The "today" suggests that this conversation took place on a Sunday, perhaps June 6. Mörlin (1514-1571) was deacon in the city church in Wittenberg.
[82] In 1537 Martin Bucer (cf. No. 184, n. 64) met with Luther in Gotha.
[83] Philip Melanchthon. Cf. No. 157, n. 59.

girls, women, old men, and farmers in church, and they don't understand lofty matters! If one can present fitting and familiar comparisons, as Link can do in masterful fashion, the people will understand and remember. Accordingly he's the best preacher who can teach in a plain, childlike, popular, and simple way. I prefer to preach in an easy and comprehensible fashion, but when it comes to academic disputations watch me in the university; there I'll make it sharp enough for anybody and will reply, no matter how complicated he wants to be. Some day I'll have to write a book against artful preachers."

Why God Sometimes Winks at Wrong
June 11, 1540   *No. 5059*

The doctor's wife[84] said, "If it were in my hands I would really take vengeance on my adversaries. Why does God spare them so?"

The doctor replied, "If God were to do everything with his might, where would that leave his wisdom and his goodness? Accordingly he overlooks many things so that his wisdom and goodness may become known in our weakness. It will turn out well."

Report of Imprisonment of Robert Barnes
Between June 11 and 19, 1540   *No. 5064*

When it was reported that the king of England had had Dr. Anthony[85] thrown into prison because he had opposed the king's articles,[86] the doctor [Martin Luther] said, "That king wants to be God. He establishes articles of faith and forbids marriage on pain of death, which not even the pope did. I have something of the prophet in me. What I prophesy will usually come true. Therefore I keep it back and don't say much."

---

[84] Katherine Luther. Cf. No. 49, n. 1.

[85] On the continent of Europe Robert Barnes called himself and was called by others, as here, "the English Antonius." Barnes (1495-1540) had spent some time in Wittenberg, was a strong advocate of Protestant views in England, and was burned at the stake as a heretic by King Henry VIII.

[86] Probably the Six Articles, enacted by Parliament on June 28, 1539, which imposed the doctrine of transubstantiation on the English people and dissolved clerical marriages. The Articles were repealed on the death of King Henry VIII in 1547.

Predestination Cannot Be Searched Out
Between June 11 and 19, 1540   No. 5070

"I was troubled," said the doctor [Martin Luther], "by the thought of what God would do with me,[87] but at length I repudiated such a thought and threw myself entirely on his revealed will. We can't do any better than that. The hidden will of God can't be searched out by man. God hides it on account of that very clever spirit, the devil, in order that he may be deceived. For he learned the revealed will from us, but God keeps the hidden will to himself. We have enough to learn about the humanity of Christ, in whom the Father revealed himself. But we are fools who neglect the revealed Word and the will of the Father in Christ and, instead, investigate mysteries which ought only be worshiped. As a result many break their necks."

"He Hardens the Heart of Whomever He Wills"
Between June 11 and 19, 1540   No. 5071

Somebody asked [Martin Luther], "Is the hardening of the heart in the Scriptures[88] to be taken literally or figuratively?"

The doctor replied, "Literally, but not actively, because God doesn't do anything that's bad. Yet his omnipotence does everything, and as he finds man, so he acts on him. Pharaoh was by nature wicked; God acted on him, and Pharaoh continued to be wicked.[89] His heart was hardened because God didn't hinder Pharaoh's ungodly plans by his Spirit and grace. Why God didn't hinder them is not for us to ask. This 'why' destroys many souls when they search after that which is too high for us. God says, 'Why I am doing this you do not know, but ponder my Word, believe in Christ, pray, and I will make everything turn out well.' If God should be asked at the last judgment, 'Why did you permit Adam to fall?' and he answered, 'In order that my goodness toward the human race might be understood when I gave my Son for

---
[87] Luther had just mentioned his book *The Bondage of the Will* (1525) and the circumstances in which he wrote it.
[88] Cf. Rom. 9:18.
[89] Cf. Exod. 7:13.

man's salvation,' we would say, 'Let the whole human race fall again in order that thy glory may become known! Because thou hast accomplished so much through Adam's fall we do not understand thy ways.'

"There is a threefold light: that of reason, that of grace, and that of glory."

What It Means to Be Delivered to Satan
Between June 11 and 19, 1540   No. 5074

Major[90] said, "My dear doctors, I don't understand this passage [where Paul speaks of certain persons who had made a shipwreck of their faith and said he delivered them to Satan that they may learn not to blaspheme, I Tim. 1:19, 20]. Explain it for me."

The doctor [Martin Luther] then said, "At the time of the apostles miracles still occurred often. Accordingly if they wished to punish somebody they delivered his body to the devil to be tormented. The body of such a person was possessed and harassed for a while by the devil. Thereupon the church prayed and the possessed person was set free, as we see in the history of the church. So Nebuchadnezzar was punished for seven years and without doubt was afterward saved." [91]

Pomeranus[92] observed: "One must take the historical context into account."

Then Major asked, "But if they died under this harassment, would they be damned?"

The doctor replied, "This was their penance to be tormented so. Accordingly their soul would be saved."

Characterizations of Some Fellow Germans
Between June 11 and 19, 1540   No. 5081

"The people in Meissen[93] are proud and arrogant in their claim

---

[90] George Major (1502-1574) had since 1537 been court chaplain in Wittenberg.
[91] Cf. Dan. 4:28-37.
[92] John Bugenhagen, of Pomerania. Cf. No. 122, n. 36.
[93] The district of Albertine Saxony in which Dresden was located.

to wisdom which they don't possess. The Thuringians are neglectful of their duty and greedy. The Bohemians outdo all others in haughtiness. The Bavarians are stupid and lacking in talent, which accounts for the fact that they are more upright. The Franconians and Swabians are simple, honorable, and obliging. The Swiss are the most distinguished of the Germans, courageous and candid. The Wends[94] are thieves and a very bad sort of people. The Dutch or Batavians are real buffoons. The Rhinelanders are crafty adventurers who are intent on their own advantage."

Melanchthon's Gentleness, Luther's Roughness
Between June 11 and 19, 1540   *No. 5089*

When there was talk about Philip[95] and it was said that he employed the greatest moderation in negotiations pertaining to the gospel, the doctor [Martin Luther] said, "The little fellow is a godly man, and even if he should do wrong, his intention's not bad, but it's because he's taken captive by others. He hasn't accomplished much by his method, and he used bad judgment in dedicating his books.[96]

"I think, when I reflect on the matter, that my way is still the best. I speak right out and scold my opponents like schoolboys. For a knotty stump requires a tough wedge."

Repercussions from Philip of Hesse's Bigamy
June 18, 1540   *No. 5096*

When a letter arrived from Pontanus,[97] the doctor [Martin Luther] read it and then said, "Philip[98] is almost consumed with grief and has been seized by the tertian fever. Why does the good

---

[94] Slavic people living in various enclaves in Germany.
[95] Philip Melanchthon. Cf. No. 157, n. 59.
[96] It was a humanistic custom to furnish books with dedications to prominent persons. Melanchthon had dedicated books to opponents of the Reformation such as Archbishop Albrecht of Mainz and King Henry VIII of England in the hope of winning them over, but without success. Cf. No. 4699.
[97] Gregory Brück. Cf. No. 1421, n. 85.
[98] Philip Melanchthon was in Weimar, where he was conferring about the bigamy of Philip of Hesse (cf. No. 5038), when he fell ill.

man macerate himself on account of this matter? He can't set it right with his worrying. I wish I were with him! I know how soft he is in his disposition. This scandal grieves him very much. I have developed a thick skin. I'm a peasant and a tough Saxon when it comes to such filthy things.[99] I believe I'll be summoned to go to Philip."

Thereupon somebody said that this might be an impediment to the conference,[100] and the doctor replied, "They'll probably have to wait for us."

Shortly afterward a letter from his prince[101] reached the doctor [Martin Luther], who read it with an earnest countenance and at length said, "The landgrave[102] is altogether out of his mind. Now he's asking the emperor for permission to keep both women!"[103]

With a very earnest countenance he returned to us and said, "It's good to have something to do, for thus we get ideas; otherwise we do nothing but swill and gorge ourselves. How our papists will cry out! Let them cry! Surely it will be to their own ruin. Our cause is good and our life is blameless—at least those who take it seriously. If the landgrave has sinned, it is indeed a sin and an offense. We have often given the best professional opinions. They [our adversaries] have seen our innocence, but they haven't wanted to see it. Hence they're looking for something offensive in [the landgrave of] Hesse. They ought to waste away with offenses because they're unwilling to hear sound doctrine. God won't forsake us and his Word on their account, even if we are guilty of sins, nor will he spare them, for he intends to overthrow the papacy. God has clearly decreed, as it is written in Daniel, that when the pope comes to his end, which is now threatening, nobody will help him [Dan. 11:45]. In the age preceding ours no power could over-

---

[99] The manuscript has an X here, a mark used to indicate that Luther employed some strong expression.
[100] A colloquy was to be held in Hagenau in an effort to reconcile the Catholic and evangelical parties in Germany. Melanchthon was the chief Lutheran spokesman.
[101] John Frederick, elector of Saxony.
[102] Landgrave Philip of Hesse. Cf. No. 3514, n. 60.
[103] I.e., both his first wife, the daughter of Duke George of Saxony, and his second wife, the former Margaret von der Sale.

throw the pope; in this age no power will save the pope because he has been revealed as the Antichrist.

"If there are offenses among us, there were also offenses in the time of Christ. Because of Judas [and his betrayal] the Pharisees must have exulted over the Lord Christ; so very much like Judas is the landgrave! 'Such companions does the new prophet have [the Pharisees must have said]! What good can come from Christ?' But those who didn't want to see miracles had to see Christ hanging on the cross, had to listen to preaching, and afterward had to see and suffer Titus.[104]

"In any case, our sins are forgivable and can easily be removed if the emperor prohibits, or our princes (as they can do by law) intervene, or he [Philip of Hesse] revokes his position. After all, David fell too, and there were probably greater offenses under Moses in the wilderness. He let his own people perish and put many of them to death.[105] How Og and Sihon must have laughed up their sleeves and thought to themselves, 'Now we'll destroy the Jews because they are themselves disunited.'[106] But God had resolved to drive out the heathen, and so the offenses of the Jews couldn't prevent it. So our sins are forgivable, for they despise God, crucify Christ, and defend their blasphemies consciously and intentionally. What do they want to make of it? They kill people while we strive for life—and practice polygamy!" This he said with a pleased look on his face and not without loud laughter.

"God will harass the people. As far as I'm concerned, I'll use the foulest words and tell them, if they're unwilling to look Morolf in the face, to look at his behind.[107] I don't know why I should worry about these things. I'll commit them to our Lord God. If the landgrave defects from us, may Christ stand by us; to him the Lord said, 'Sit at my right hand, till I make your enemies your footstool' [Ps. 110:1]. He has undoubtedly helped us out of greater

---

[104] I.e., some Pharisees lived to see the destruction of Jerusalem under the Roman emperor Titus (A.D. 71-81).

[105] Cf. Num. 16:1-40.

[106] Cf. Num. 21:33, 34.

[107] The allusion is to a gnomic poem of the twelfth century, "Solomon and Morolf," part of which is related in John Aurifaber's later version of this conversation. Cf. WA, TR 4, No. 659.

troubles. The restoration of [the duke of] Württemberg[108] caused more of an uproar than this scandal. The same is true of the sacramentarians[109] and the uprising,[110] but God rescued us from those dangers. In a quarter of a year this tune will be played out too. Would to God that Philip[111] might look at it this way! The papists are Demea now, while I'm Mitio,[112] and a harlot and a mother are in the same house.[113] A son is born.[114] She's without a dowry.[115] So I'm Mitio; may God make it turn out well! This is the way human life is, like a game of dice! I expect worse things than this. If somebody should ask, 'Does that deed[116] please you?' I would reply, 'No!' If I could change it I would. If I can't change it I'll bear it with equanimity. I commit it to the dear Lord. May he preserve his church as it now stands, that it may remain in the unity of faith and doctrine and a sound confession of the Word. Only may it not become worse!"

Then he rose from the table with a very cheerful countenance. "I don't want to do the devil and all the papists the favor of worrying about it," he said. "God will make it turn out well. To his keeping I commit the whole business."

Philip Melanchthon Should Rest from Studies
August 7, 1540   No. 5124

The doctor [Martin Luther] asked Master Philip,[117] "Do you wish to obey God or man?"

"God," he replied, "for it's better to fall into the hands of the Lord than into the hands of men."

---

[108] Cf. No. 5038, n. 62.
[109] Cf. No. 314, n. 139.
[110] The Peasants' War of 1525.
[111] Philip Melanchthon, not Philip of Hesse.
[112] In a play by the Roman playwright Terence, *Adelphoi*, Demea is hard and violent while his brother Mitio is calm and quiet.
[113] Cf. Terence, *op. cit.*, 4, 7, 29.
[114] *Ibid.*, 4, 7, 10. There was a rumor to the effect that Margaret von der Sale had already borne a son. Cf. Luther's letter of June 2, 1540. WA, Br 9, 123-124.
[115] The reference is again to Margaret von der Sale and to Terence, *op. cit.*, 4, 7, 11.
[116] I.e., the bigamy of Philip of Hesse.
[117] Philip Melanchthon. Cf. No. 157, n. 59.

The doctor asked in turn, "Do you wish to hear the Word of God directly from God or through a man?"

"Through a man," replied Philip.

"I therefore command you by divine authority," the doctor said, "that you interrupt your studies and your labor until I command you otherwise, for God wishes us to observe the Sabbath."

The Fame of the University in Wittenberg
Between August 7 and 14, 1540   No. 5126

The doctor [Martin Luther] said, "I said to Dr. Pontanus[118] earlier that whoever speaks disparagingly of this school after my death (that is, if church and school remain at all, for there were also famous schools in Antioch, Constantinople, and Rome but they perished) is a heretic and a perverse man. For it was in this school that God revealed his Word, and today this school and town can compare favorably with all others in doctrine and life, even if we are not yet altogether perfect in life. The most distinguished men today agree with us—such as Amsdorf,[119] Brenz,[120] and Rhegius[121]—and they seek our friendship and write to us. But those who depart from us and secretly insult us have fallen from the faith—men like Agricola and Schenk,[122] and also Zwingli[123]—and can get along by themselves since they haven't learned anything from us. Who knew anything twenty-five years ago? Who stood by me twenty-one years ago when God led me into this business against my will and knowledge? Ah, vainglory is a calamity!"

Scholastics Taught Reliance on Oneself
Between August 7 and 24, 1540   No. 5135

"Scholastic theology agrees on this point, that man can merit

---

[118] Gregory Brück. Cf. No. 1421, n. 85.
[119] Nicholas Amsdorf. Cf. No. 1421, n. 84.
[120] John Brenz. Cf. No. 347, n. 163.
[121] Urbanus Rhegius (1489-1541), an early supporter of Luther, was superintendent of the church in Lüneburg after 1531.
[122] John Agricola and Jacob Schenk were antinomians. Cf. No. 4048, n. 253.
[123] Huldreich Zwingli. Cf. No. 5005, n. 35.

grace *de congruo*[124] by his purely natural powers, and all the schoolmen taught at least this: 'Do what lies in your strength.' But Occam,[125] though he was superior to all the others in mental acumen and refuted all the rest of the positions, expressly said and taught that it isn't to be found in the Scriptures that the Holy Spirit is necessary for good works.

"These men had talent and leisure and grew old as they lectured, but they had no understanding at all of Christ because they despised the Bible and because nobody read the Bible for the sake of meditation but only for the sake of knowledge, as one would read a historical writing."

May Mass Be Said If the Gospel Is Preached? Between August 7 and 24, 1540   No. 5161

The doctor [Martin Luther] was asked by George[126] whether a parish minister could with good conscience say mass, even with the canon[127] omitted, provided that in the meantime he preached the true gospel. For [according to canon law] a priest was permitted to preach but was not permitted to intermit saying masses.

The doctor replied, "Write him as follows: In order to obtain [clothes for] his body—shoes, breeches, doublet—you would sell out everything! How can this be, that a man should destroy himself in order to give others the advantage? How can we compel Ferdinand[128] and the dukes of Bavaria?"[129]

Then George said, "But he who is the worst papist succeeds in office, and this moved the good man [to inquire]."

The doctor replied, "Those who in their dominions forbid [the administration of the sacrament according to the gospel] will be responsible."

---

[124] In scholastic theology merits of congruity may be secured by man in proportion to the good works he performs by his natural powers.

[125] William of Occam (1300-1349) was an English Franciscan theologian who had considerable influence on Luther's early theological development.

[126] George Rörer, who also recorded conversations at Luther's table (cf. p. 117), appears to have asked this question in behalf of a correspondent.

[127] The canon of the mass. Cf. No. 4676, n. 406.

[128] The king of Austria. Cf. No. 206, n. 77.

[129] The dukes of Bavaria were traditional foes of the king of Austria.

Then I[130] interjected, "Doctor, there are similar cases among us. Many abandoned their vocation on account of celibacy, and they were told that this was a mistake."

The doctor responded, "They have had no command to put themselves in danger."

Thereupon I said, "Paul wished that he might be accursed for the sake of his brethren [Rom. 9:3]. Shouldn't a good pastor of the church therefore be useful even at the risk of his soul?"

Philip[131] remarked, "Paul indeed wished to be accursed for the sake of his brethren, but not so as to be damned by God as a guilty person. However, those who act impiously by celebrating mass and committing the sin of adultery defile themselves. God doesn't command it, nor is it a wish of godly men. For evil shouldn't be done in order that good may result."

How to Preach in Three Brief Steps
Between August 7 and 21, 1540   No. 5171b

Conrad Cordatus[132] said to Dr. Martin Luther, "Reverend Father, teach me in a brief way how to preach."

Luther responded briefly, "First, you must learn to go up to the pulpit. Second, you must know that you should stay there for a time. Third, you must learn to get down again."

He added nothing in addition to these words, and as a result Cordatus was quite angry. Yet at length it occurred to him that the doctor had hit the mark very well. Anybody who keeps this order will be a good preacher. First, he must learn to go up to the pulpit, that is, he should have a regular and a divine call. Second, he must learn to stay there for a time, that is, he should have the pure and genuine doctrine. Third, he must also learn to get down again, that is, he should preach not more than an hour (which didn't please Pomeranus).[133]

---

[130] The recorder of this conversation, John Mathesius.
[131] Philip Melanchthon. Cf. No. 157, n. 59.
[132] Cf. No. 165, n. 62.
[133] John Bugenhagen, of Pomerania (cf. No. 122, n. 36), was well known for his excessively long sermons. See Wilhelm Pauck, *The Heritage of the Reformation* (revised ed.; Glencoe: Free Press, 1961), pp. 101-143.

How to Treat Despisers of the Sacrament
Between August 7 and 24, 1540   No. 5174

Somebody asked, "Doctor, what should I do if I should find people in my church who have stayed away from the sacrament for twenty years?"

The doctor [Martin Luther] replied, "Let them go to the devil! And when they die let them be put in the carrion pit!"

The further question was asked, "Ought they be compelled to go to the sacrament?"

The doctor answered, "That would be papistic. By no means! They should be told this." Then he added, "I wonder why they abstain from the sacrament so long. Perhaps they're afraid of private confession."

It Is Christ who Absolves, Not the Minister
Between August 7 and 24, 1540   No. 5176

"This ought especially to be taught, that confession's not made to man but to Christ. Likewise it isn't man who absolves but Christ. But few understand this. Today I replied to the Bohemians,[134] who insist that God alone remits sins and are offended by my little book on the keys. Wherefore one should teach that men make confession to Christ, and Christ absolves through the mouth of the minister, for the minister's mouth is the mouth of Christ and the minister's ear is the ear of Christ. It's to the Word and the command that one should pay attention, not to the person. Christ sits there, Christ listens, Christ answers, not a man."

The Term "Word" Has Various Meanings
Between August 7 and 24, 1540   No. 5177

Somebody asked, "Doctor, is the Word that Christ spoke when he was on earth the same in fact and in effect as the Word preached by a minister?"

---

[134] A Utraquist minister in Jungbunzlau named Gregory was offended by what Luther had written in his work, *The Keys* (1530). *LW* 40, 321-377. Luther's letter is not extant.

The doctor [Martin Luther] replied, "Yes, because he said, 'He who hears you hears me' [Luke 10:16]. And Paul calls the Word 'the power of God' [Rom. 1:16]."

Then the inquirer asked, "Doctor, isn't there a difference between the Word that became flesh [John 1:14] and the Word that is proclaimed by Christ or by a minister?"

"By all means!" he replied. "The former is the incarnate Word, who was true God from the beginning, and the latter is the Word that's proclaimed. The former Word is in substance God; the latter Word is in its effect the power of God, but isn't God in substance, for it has a man's nature, whether it's spoken by Christ or by a minister."

A Case Concerning the Seal of Confession
Between August 7 and 24, 1540   No. 5178

Somebody asked, "Doctor, if a parish minister absolves a woman who has killed her infant child and afterward the matter becomes public through others, should the parish minister, when asked, offer testimony in this case before a judge?"

"By no means," said the doctor [Martin Luther], "for the forum of conscience is to be distinguished from the forum of the civil government. The woman didn't confess anything to me; she confessed to Christ. But if Christ keeps it hidden, I should conceal it and simply deny that I heard anything. But I would say privately to the woman when she came to me for absolution, 'You whore, don't you ever do it again!'"

"Doctor, what if that woman said that she had been absolved by you and wished to be set free for the reason that Christ had discharged her. Therefore, she would say, the judges can't decide anything against her."

The doctor replied, "I repeat that civil matters must be distinguished [from ecclesiastical]. If I were summoned to appear in this case I would deny it again, for I'm not the person who should speak, testify, etc., in the political forum but in the forum of conscience. Therefore I would say, 'I, Martin Luther, don't know anything at all about whether she was absolved. Christ knows, for he's the one with whom she spoke, to whom she confided something or didn't, who (as he certainly knows) absolved her or didn't. I know nothing about it because I don't hear confession; it's Christ who does.'"

Luther Expects No Pay for Teaching

August 24, 1540   *No. 5187*

When somebody asked the doctor [Martin Luther] about a biblical passage, the doctor's wife[135] replied, joking, "Doctor, don't teach them for nothing! They are gathering many things together. Lauterbach[136] in fact has collected the most, and they were useful sayings."

The doctor interjected, "For thirty years I have taught and preached without charging anything. Why should I begin to sell something in my old age?"

Some Preachers Are Much Too Voluble

Between September 2 and 17, 1540   *No. 5199*

"When Mörlin,[137] Medler,[138] or Master Jacob[139] preach it's as if one pulled the bung out of a full barrel. Out it flows as long as there's something in the barrel. Such fluency of speech doesn't benefit the auditors, even if it gives pleasure to some people, nor does it instruct. Accordingly it's better to speak clearly. Thus the hearer can take hold of something."

Disposition of a Boy Possessed by the Devil

Between September 2 and 17, 1540   *No. 5207*

In Dessau there was a twelve-year-old boy like this:[140] he

---

[135] Luther's wife had just intimated (in No. 5181, not translated in this selection) that there was a shortage of money in the household.

[136] Anthony Lauterbach was one of those who took notes of the conversation at Luther's table. Cf. pp. 253-254.

[137] Joachim Mörlin. Cf. No. 5047, n. 81.

[138] Nicholas Medler was at this time pastor in Naumburg. Cf. p. 117.

[139] Possibly Jacob Schenk, although he had a doctor's degree.

[140] In this account Luther is reported to have suggested to friends at his table

devoured as much as four farmers did, and he did nothing else than eat and excrete. Luther suggested that he be suffocated.

Somebody asked, "For what reason?"

He [Luther] replied, "Because I think he's simply a mass of flesh without a soul. Couldn't the devil have done this, inasmuch as he gives such shape to the body and mind even of those who have reason that in their obsession they hear, see, and feel nothing? The devil is himself their soul. The power of the devil is great when in this way he holds the minds of all men captive, but he doesn't dare give full vent to the power on account of the angels."

Then somebody said, "Perhaps Origen did not rightly understand the malice of the devil because he thought that devils would be liberated after the day of judgment." [141]

"Ah," said the doctor, "the sin of the devil is great because he knowingly opposes God, the Creator of all things."

Marriage of a Young Man and an Old Woman
Between September 2 and 17, 1540   No. 5212

[Somebody asked] whether a marriage between a young man and an old woman would be proper when there was no hope of offspring. The doctor [Martin Luther] replied, "Yes, indeed! Of the four reasons I gave in my Genesis[142] the fourth is that such a marriage should be approved for the sake of honoring marriage. However, I'd prefer if at the wedding the words, 'Be fruitful and multiply,' were omitted. Yet I don't like to make ceremonies and regulations, for once one starts there's no end to it any more. One follows another, as in the papacy."

---

that a boy whose condition was such that he lived like a vegetable should be done away with. John Aurifaber's later version (*WA*, TR 5, No. 9) elaborated on the original by stating that Luther had himself seen and touched the boy and that he advised the prince of Anhalt to have the boy drowned. What had at first been the private expression of an opinion here became a formal recommendation to a ruler. It was in this later version that Luther was cited as an advocate of euthanasia in connection with a court case in Germany in 1964. See Erwin Mühlhaupt, "'Spiegel,' 'Stern' und Luther," *Luther: Zeitschrift der Luther-Gesellschaft*, XXXV (1964), 81-88.

[141] Origen taught that the wicked, and even the devil, would ultimately be united with God. Cf. *Against Celsus*, V, 15, 17, 23; VI, 72.

[142] In Luther's *Lectures on Genesis*; e.g., LW 2, 301.

TABLE TALK

A Usurer Should Be Excommunicated
Between September 2 and 17, 1540   No. 5216

The doctor [Martin Luther] said, "Manifest usurers should be excommunicated, that is, they should not be given the sacrament, as I did in the case of the nobleman." [143]

Thereupon somebody asked, "What if he's penitent?"

The doctor replied, "There's a limit to everything. However, he must become a Zacchaeus[144] and return what he stole in excessive interest to those out of whom he sweated it. Otherwise he's not truly repentant. According to civil law, not to speak of divine law, he can't with a good conscience keep this money anyhow. Whoever eats and drinks with him makes himself a participant in his sins. Consequently you, Master Mickell,[145] should never eat with him."

The Story of Joab, David, and Absalom
Between September 2 and 17, 1540   No. 5219

"Joab must have been an untroubled warrior. I like to read these stories[146] because he relied wholly on his fist. He had six hundred soldiers and took to fighting all of Israel. He thought, 'I have good veteran soldiers, and that's a large mob of disorderly people.' And it turned out well for him.

"I don't think David liked to fight against his son, but he was persuaded by the captains to do so. For this reason he commanded that his son be spared.

"But Joab's counsel was best. Down with wicked knaves! They won't improve and will only cause misfortune to others. A young man of eighteen years, whom the judges wished to set free, spoke thus, 'Away with me! I'm in it now. If you set me free I'll start again where I left off. Do away with anybody who has deserved death!' So it is with thieves; they belong on the gallows, as a

---

[143] Probably Henry Rieder. Cf. No. 4073b.
[144] Cf. Luke 19:2-10.
[145] From the form of address this must have been a clergyman. Possibly it was Henry Rieder's pastor.
[146] Cf. II Sam. 18:1-33.

monk belongs in a monastery and a fish in water. I have asked that several persons be set free, but after a few days they were hanged anyhow. Accordingly Joab's counsel was better than David's."

Discussion of Primary and Secondary Causes
Between September 2 and 17, 1540 No. 5221

Somebody said, "Doctor, the fathers[147] seldom mention secondary causes but simply attribute everything, whether great or small, to the first cause."

The doctor [Martin Luther] replied, "Yes, they were aware of secondary causes but they were fully engrossed in the primary cause, which they saw and believed to be operative in secondary causes and, if it should please God, without them."

When some lovely grapes from the doctor's garden were placed before them somebody said, "It's remarkable that such fine fruits are produced in this sandy soil, and I wonder whether this is to be attributed to the seeds, to the vines, to the cultivation, or to the sunshine, or whether it should be said that it's only God who does this."

The doctor said, "Secondary causes are indeed required but they accomplish nothing without the first cause. The Holy Land was once very fertile, but now it's quite unfruitful. I believe the species and the cultivation are not wanting, but if God withdraws the sap down below and takes away his power up above nothing more will grow."

Man Is Not Satisfied with God's Gifts
Between September 2 and 17, 1540 No. 5224

"How rich a God our God is! He gives enough, but we don't notice it. He gave the whole world to Adam, but this was nothing in Adam's eyes; he was concerned about the one tree and had to ask why God had forbidden him to eat of it.[148] That's the way it

---

[147] The fathers of the ancient church. The medieval theologians made fine distinctions among causes, including the first cause, God.
[148] Cf. Gen. 3:1-20.

is today too. God has given us enough to learn in his revealed Word, but we let this go and look for his hidden will[149] without being able to find it. It serves us right if we are crushed as a consequence."

Some Inscrutable Works of Creation
Between September 2 and 17, 1540   No. 5227

"That God is called Creator is an unfathomable thing, and yet God creates every day. As he made Adam out of the dust of the ground,[150] so today he still takes a little semen, in which there's no life, and forms, nourishes, and preserves the fruit in a supernatural way, though physicians have their explanations of a passage from the breast into the womb. Secondary causes obscure the first cause.

"I can't sufficiently marvel at an egg. In this case the matter is outside of the mother's womb. Alien warmth is applied, sometimes even the warmth of another species, as Hans Loeser[151] had his chicks hatched by crows, which he couldn't get rid of otherwise. At times the chicks are hatched with warmth like that of Livia in Suetonius,[152] and God forms a living chick in the shell. These are all miracles. God is in the creature, which he creates and in which he works. But we pay no heed, and meanwhile we look for secondary and philosophical causes. We'll never learn the article about creation rightly in this way."

Plato and the Immortality of the Soul
Between September 2 and 17, 1540   No. 5229

The doctor [Martin Luther] said, "We are indeed poor people. We are poor and despised, as if it will remain so forever."

Then somebody said, "The heathen argued this way: It's bad for good people here; therefore there's another life."

"Yes," said the doctor, "this is the best argument that all the

---
[149] Cf. No. 5070.
[150] Cf. Gen. 2:7.
[151] The marshal of the elector. Cf. No. 2946a, n. 41.
[152] Suetonius, *Tiberius*, 14.

heathen have. Plato's minor premise [to prove the immortality of the soul],[153] that the soul is not made from the elements, and his proof (because our knowledge and such swift motion can't be the effect of elementary nature) don't stand up. Augustine[154] disputed the matter vigorously and produced many facts in support of it, but even a sheep produces swift motion when it sees a wolf! Accordingly their argument isn't adequate. But think of the Creator; this indicates the answer."

Luther Rejects the Pre-existence of the Soul
Between September 2 and 17, 1540   *No. 5230*

Hereupon[155] somebody asked whether Plato's opinion about the soul is true.

"No, indeed!" replied the doctor. "How can Plato speak about this matter? I believe that God made the whole man from the dust of the earth, for the text [Gen. 2:7] says that God made man. 'Man' doesn't mean the body alone but always means the body and the soul, and accordingly the Scriptures call the soul 'the breath of life' [Gen. 2:7]. Since the soul was in that instance made with the body, so when a child is born today the soul is created together with the body, contrary to Plato. Although all others disagree, it's my opinion that the soul isn't added from the outside but is created out of the matter of the semen. This is my reason: If the soul came from somewhere else, it would be made bad by contact with the body, but the soul isn't bad by chance but by nature. Consequently the soul must be born out of corrupt matter and seed and must be created by God out of the matter of a man and a woman."

The Meaning of a Verse in Paul's Romans
Between September 2 and 17, 1540   *No. 5234*

When there was mention of Egranus[156] the doctor [Martin

---

[153] E.g., Plato, *Phaedrus*, 245.
[154] E.g., Augustine, *The City of God*, 12, 23.
[155] This is obviously a continuation of the preceding conversation.
[156] John Sylvius Egranus (i.e., John Wildenauer, of Eger) visited Desiderius Erasmus in 1518 and became a disciple of his.

Luther] said, "He was a proud spirit and maintained that Christ bought it [salvation] and we must earn it. Yes, if Christ were Heinz Scherl,[157] of Leipzig! Ah, no! This is the way it goes when Christ isn't understood properly, for he determines everything."

Then somebody said, "Yet Paul seems to distinguish, Doctor, when he declares, 'Man believes with his heart and so is justified, and he confesses with his lips and so is saved' [Rom. 10:10]."

The doctor replied, "Here confession means perseverance, for St. Paul means to say, 'Faith must express itself and be confessed, and one must abide in it, otherwise faith disappears again. For it isn't as the Priscillianists[158] taught, 'At home and in church confess; before tyrants deny.' Accordingly here confession means perseverance in one's whole life, as Christ said, 'He who endures to the end will be saved' [Matt. 10:22]."

Places in Which the Gospel Is Not Heard
Between September 2 and 17, 1540   No. 5239

The doctor [Martin Luther] said, "I always hope that the day of judgment isn't far away and that we'll live to see it."

Thereupon somebody said, "I believe that at that time the gospel won't be preached openly because Christ said that he would hardly find any faith on the earth [Luke 18:8]."

"Yes, indeed," said the doctor. "What does it amount to that we have the gospel in this little corner? Just reckon that there is no gospel in all of Asia and Africa and that the gospel isn't preached in many parts of Europe, in Greece, Italy, Hungary, Spain, France, England, Poland. This little spot, the house of Saxony, won't prevent the day of judgment."

How Habakkuk Is Quoted by St. Paul
Between September 2 and 17, 1540   No. 5243

Somebody said, "Doctor, Egranus[159] declared that this verse

---
[157] Henry Scherl was the richest burgher in Leipzig.
[158] Followers of Priscillian (d. *ca.* 385), an ascetic and Gnostic sect leader in Spain.
[159] Cf. No. 5234, n. 156.

['The righteous shall live by his faith,' Hab. 2:4] was improperly cited by Paul [in Rom. 1:17] because it deals with the hope for deliverance from Babylon."

The doctor [Martin Luther] replied, "Fools! This is a general statement: 'The righteous shall live by his faith.' Consequently it is rightly applied to Christ. While it's true that in his whole prophecy Habakkuk speaks of deliverance from Babylon, nevertheless he always includes Christ because the ancients couldn't believe that they would be delivered in external ways unless they believed surely in the descendant who was to come. Therefore the verse must be interpreted thus: the Jews were inclined to fall from their hope [and say], 'Now we're done for; we're captives; Christ won't come; the promise is nothing.' Accordingly the prophet combines two things: a) God will deliver you from Babylon and keep his promise; b) the future Christ will really come, and the righteous shall live by his faith."

The Importance of Schools and Schoolmasters Between September 2 and 17, 1540   No. 5247

When Andrew Misenus[160] was mentioned, the doctor [Martin Luther] said, "We must now have stones to fill gaps and many corners. He must be a cornerstone, for schoolmasters have become accustomed in school to speaking, are somewhat bolder, and also learn from their school exercises how to treat and expound verses of the Holy Scriptures. I wish nobody would be chosen preacher unless he had first kept school. Now all the young fellows want to start out as preachers and flee from schoolwork. But if a young man has kept school for about one to ten years, he can leave with a good conscience, for it involves much work and is held in low esteem.

"In a city as much depends on a schoolmaster as on a minister. We can get along without burgomasters, princes, and noblemen, but we can't do without schools, for they must rule the world. One sees that there are no rulers today who aren't compelled to let

---

[160] Andrew Misenus was rector of the Latin school in Altenburg from 1530 to 1553.

themselves be guided by a lawyer or a clergyman. They don't know anything of themselves and are ashamed to study, and so advisers must come from the school. If I weren't a preacher I know no position on earth I'd rather fill [than that of schoolmaster]. But one must not consider how the world esteems and rewards it but how God thinks of it and how he will praise it on the day of judgment."

Should One Preach Law or Gospel More?
Between September 18 and 23, 1540 No. 5269

"Doctor, many men think and say that the law should be emphasized often for the sake of the profane common people, lest they abuse the gospel. Others say that the common man ought not to be cited as a reason but only the command of Christ, who wishes that the goodness of the Father may become known through the gospel. Which of these opinions is the better?"

The doctor [Martin Luther] replied, "This shouldn't and can't be comprehended in a fixed rule. Christ himself preached [the law and the gospel] according to his circumstances. As a passage or text indicates, therefore, one should take up the law and the gospel, for one must have both. It isn't right to draw everything into the gospel alone; nor is it good always to preach the law alone. The Scriptures themselves, if properly adhered to, will give the answer."

Should a Liar Be Given the Sacrament?
Between September 18 and 23, 1540 No. 5270

"Doctor, if there is a scarcity of crops, and I admonish a rich man in confession that he should give something for the use of the poor and he denies that he has anything left over, but I know that he has, should I give the sacrament to such a liar?"

The doctor [Martin Luther] replied, "If he should deny it, what more can you do? If he persists, do what Christ did; he gave the sacrament to the betrayer Judas."[161]

Here somebody else advanced, in opposition, the example of

---
[161] Cf. John 13:25-26.

Ananias and Peter. Peter put the lying Ananias to death at once with a word.[162] The doctor replied, "That was something special. In any case, I believe that Peter did this not of himself but by revelation. God wished to confirm the primitive church by miracles."

Opposition by the Devil a Good Sign
October 3, 1540   *No. 5284*

On the Sunday after St. Michael's Day[163] he [Martin Luther] was cheerful at heart, joked with his friends and with me,[164] and made little of his learning. "I'm a simple man," he said. "You're a scoundrel but more learned than I am in economic and political matters. I'm not interested in such things. I'm concerned about the church and must defend myself against the attacks of the devil. I think that if I became involved in the other matters I would also remember. I believe everybody, and for this reason I can probably be deceived. Once I keep an eye on somebody, however, he won't take anything from me."

Among others he turned to Brother Cellarius[165] and said, "Don't take it ill of me. I'm cheerful and in good spirits because I've heard a great deal of bad news today and I've just read a wicked letter from Mainz,[166] who snatched a citizen from bondage. Because the devil is thus pressing hard upon us, we're in a good way. We have a good, triumphant cause, and God has a hand in it; he'll soon bring it to a glorious conclusion, for they're going too far and are desperate knaves. Ferdinand[167] wishes to pay tribute to the Turk and a bishop tries to set fire to his city.[168] The pope

---

[162] Cf. Acts 5:5.
[163] This was October 3.
[164] John Mathesius, the recorder of this conversation.
[165] John Cellarius, the new superintendent in Dresden, was in Wittenberg on a visit.
[166] Presumably from Cardinal Albrecht, archbishop of Mainz.
[167] The king of Austria. Cf. No. 206, n. 77.
[168] On August 26, 1540, there had been a great fire in Magdeburg. A large number of other fires broke out in central and northern Germany in 1540. Hence the reference to "incendiaries" below.

wants to be a judge and has been found fault with by us. God will judge the earth, and you'll soon know it. Just hold still! They must all go down, even Anthony von Schönberg,[169] unless the Scriptures are mistaken. This is what Staupitz[170] said to me when he was overcome by sadness: God grant patience! After all, nothing remains unpunished. And all history testifies that God's coming. This is the reason some take Luther to be a prophet and apostle, for he has prophesied that there's nothing good in a papist. This is now becoming evident in the incendiaries. Let us wait awhile. They will come running of their own accord, although Braunschweig[171] would like to excuse himself. It doesn't help. The blood of Abel cries out."[172]

From Allegorical to Literal Interpretation
Between October 3 and 19, 1540   No. 5285

The doctor [Martin Luther] said, "I can't work any more, nor can I speak any longer. When I was young I was learned, especially before I came to the study of theology. At that time I dealt with allegories, tropologies, and analogies and did nothing but clever tricks with them.[173] If somebody had them today they'd be looked upon as rare relics. I know they're nothing but rubbish. Now I've let them go, and this is my last and best art, to translate the Scriptures in their plain sense. The literal sense does it—in it there's life, comfort, power, instruction, and skill. The other is tomfoolery, however brilliant the impression it makes."

---

[169] A younger brother of the cardinal Nicholas von Schönberg and at this time counselor of Duke Henry the Pious.

[170] John Staupitz, Luther's superior in the monastery. Cf. No. 94, n. 14.

[171] Duke Henry of Braunschweig was reported to have been responsible for setting some of the fires in 1540. Cf. No. 4887, n. 13.

[172] Cf. Gen. 4:10.

[173] According to the fourfold method of biblical interpretation in the late Middle Ages, scholars sought various meanings in a text. In addition to the literal meaning there were believed to be other meanings: an allegorical (doctrinal), a tropological (moral), and an analogical (pertaining to the future) meaning. Cf. Warren A. Quanbeck, in Gerhard Belgum (ed.), *Luther Today* ("Martin Luther Lectures," Vol. I [Decorah, Iowa: Luther College Press, 1957]), pp. 60-81.

Division of World History into Six Ages
Between October 3 and 19, 1540   No. 5300

"I divide the [history of the] world into six ages:[174] the age of Adam, of Noah, of Abraham, of David, of Christ, and of the pope. Each of the first five has attained about a thousand years together with its posterity. The pope began about five thousand years after the creation of the world, that is, when Hildebrand[175] openly ridiculed the marriage of priests in the time of Henry IV. That was the time when Bernard[176] was born. But the pope won't complete his thousand years."

One Must Not Be Too Rigid About Practice
Between October 19 and November 5, 1540   No. 5314

When the doctor [Martin Luther] was asked whether the sacrament can be carried to the sick,[177] he replied, "We don't think it should be done. To be sure, one must allow it for a while. The practice will probably be dropped, if only because they have no ciborium.[178] What should be done about it? In our churches, too, there's debate about whether the [elements of the] sacrament

---

[174] Cf. John M. Headley, *Luther's View of Church History* (New Haven: Yale University Press, 1963), chap. 3.

[175] Pope Gregory VII (1073-1085), called Hildebrand, came to a showdown with Emperor Henry IV at Canossa. Hildebrand energetically enforced ecclesiastical legislation requiring the celibacy of priests.

[176] Bernard of Clairvaux. Cf. No. 494, n. 295.

[177] The Brandenburg Church Order of 1540, often criticized for making too many concessions to Roman practice, provided for carrying the consecrated bread and wine from the altar to the sick and distributing the elements to them without further ado. At issue was the question whether "consecration" changed the elements. In this conversation Luther informally approved of practices which he seemed to criticize elsewhere. Cf., for example, No. 4634. Luther addressed concrete situations; note here the words "on account of several heretics." On this problem, see Hans Grass, *Die Abendmahlslehre bei Luther und Calvin* (2nd ed.; Gütersloh: C. Bertelsmann, 1954), pp. 118-121.

[178] I.e., because the clergymen in Brandenburg will have no receptacle in which to reserve the bread and wine of the sacrament. Cf. Helmut T. Lehmann (ed.), *Meaning and Practice of the Lord's Supper* (Philadelphia: Muhlenberg Press, 1961), pp. 103-109.

TABLE TALK

should be carried to another altar for consecration. I put up with it on account of several heretics who must be opposed, for there are some who allow that it's a sacrament only while it's in use; what is left over and remains they throw away. That isn't right. We let somebody consume it. One must never be so precise [and say that the sacrament remains a sacrament when carried] four or five steps or when kept so-and-so many hours. What does it matter? How can one bless the bread for each and every one? We also retain the practice of elevating the sacrament on account of several heretics who say it must be done so. It must *not* be done so, for as long as one is engaged in the action even if it extends for an hour or two or even if one carries it to another altar or, as you do" (he said this to Cordatus),[179] "across the street, it is and remains the body of Christ."

Translating the Bible Meant Hard Work
Between October 19 and November 5, 1540   No. 5324

"Nobody believes what labor it cost us—except those who work with us and hear about it, like George.[180] For the rabbis help us very little. I plan to put a new preface in the front of the Bible to warn everybody about the rabbis, for they are blinded and hardened. Even if they already have the book, as Isaiah said [Isa. 29:11-21], they are blind to it.

"This German Bible (this is not praise for myself but the work praises itself) is so good and precious that it's better than all other versions, Greek and Latin, and one can find more in it than in all commentaries, for we are removing impediments and difficulties so that other people may read in it without hindrance. I'm only concerned that there won't be much reading in the Bible, for people are very tired of it and nobody clamors for it any more."

---

[179] Conrad Cordatus, an Austrian by birth, had been called to Brandenburg in 1539 to help introduce the Reformation there. Cf. No. 165, n. 62.

[180] George Rörer, deacon in Wittenberg, helped Luther with the revision of the German Bible, the 1541 edition of which was in preparation at this time. The intended preface to the whole Bible was not published.

RECORDED BY MATHESIUS

The Excellence of the Book of Genesis
Between November 4 and 7, 1540   No. 5332

"This [Genesis] is a charming book and has wonderful stories. I can't altogether understand it, however. I'll have to be dead four years or so before I comprehend fully what creation means and what the omnipotence of God is. Otherwise we can't grasp it and must be content to leave it, like that judge who prayed, 'I believe in God Almigh Ty.' He thought this was God's name, like the nun who called Christ 'Master Scimus' and 'Master Clic.'[181] Nobody can by his study exhaust the meaning of the word 'creation,' though even the heathen have had some thoughts about it. They said there must be a first cause that does and governs all things."

---

[181] Prayers beginning *Magister, scimus* ("Master, we know") and *Magister, dic* ("Master, speak") were not understood by the nuns, who also misread the second as *Magister, clic*.

TABLE TALK RECORDED BY CASPAR HEYDENREICH

1542-1543

INTRODUCTION

The pieces numbered 5379 to 5603 in WA, TR 5 were written by Caspar Heydenreich in 1542 and 1543. Heydenreich was mentioned by John Mathesius as the man who took notes at Luther's table after him. The supposition that these notes were written by Heydenreich is confirmed by the traces of Saxon dialect which appear in them again and again.

Caspar Heydenreich was born in Freiberg, Saxony, in 1516. He matriculated at Wittenberg as early as 1528, when he was only twelve years old. In 1540 he went to Joachimstal, in Bohemia, to succeed John Mathesius as rector of the Latin school there. He remained only a year and returned to Wittenberg to earn his master's degree in 1541. It was probably in the following spring that he began to eat at Luther's table, where he took notes on the conversation. In the fall of the year 1543 he was made chaplain at the court of Duke Henry the Pious in his native Freiberg. On the death of the duke, Heydenreich moved to Torgau as chaplain to the widowed Duchess Katherine and was made superintendent. In his seventieth year, in 1586, he died soon after he suffered a stroke.

One may safely assume that it was through the intervention of Mathesius that Heydenreich found access to Luther's home and through the encouragement of Mathesius that Heydenreich undertook to take notes at Luther's table. A few datable events that are mentioned in the notes, supported by knowledge about the duration of Heydenreich's stay in Wittenberg, make it possible to establish when the reported conversations occurred. About one-fourth of the entries that are known to be Heydenreich's have been selected for this edition.

TABLE TALK RECORDED BY CASPAR HEYDENREICH

Rumor Concerning the Death of John Eck
April, 1542 *No. 5379*

When a report concerning the death of Eck[1] was being circulated [Martin Luther said]: "I can't believe that he's dead, though he was gravely ill. I wonder how he was able to live so long, for he was a man of insatiable lust and inexhaustible addiction to drink. Faber[2] slandered himself to death, Karlstadt[3] slandered himself to death, and now Eck must have slandered himself to death. To sin by mistake can be excused, but to wish consciously and eagerly to sin—this is too much."

Young Men Should Avoid Fornication
April, 1542 *No. 5381*

A certain cobbler here caught his wife in adultery and tore off her nose. [When this was related] the doctor's wife asked what had been decided with respect to the adulterer. After all, he was still a young journeyman. The doctor [Martin Luther] said, "I'm afraid I would have stabbed him."

When the doctor's wife exclaimed, "How can people be so wicked and defile themselves with such sin!" the doctor said, "Ah, dear Katy, people don't pray," and then he added, "I think if God had commanded women to take on every man who happened along and in like manner commanded men to take every woman who came by—in short, if things were the opposite of what they are—people would earnestly have sighed for the institution of marriage.

---

[1] John Eck, a bitter opponent of Luther ever since the indulgence controversy, had been ill for some time, but the rumor of his death was premature; he lived a year longer.

[2] John Faber, bishop of Vienna, died May 21, 1541.

[3] Andrew Karlstadt, Luther's early colleague in Wittenberg and later his left-wing critic, died December 24, 1541.

Accordingly we should pray, 'Lead us not into temptation, but deliver us from evil' [Matt. 6:13]. I'm not so astonished at a young journeyman, for children are children, etc. And it's set right before him! Yet I commend Master Philip Melanchthon's brother;[4] when Philip exhorted him to flee from fornication, the brother said, 'Ah, why do you say that, Brother? I intend to get married. So other women and whores should stay away from me.' A young fellow ought to remember that he hopes some day to take a wife, and therefore he should abstain for the present."

What Heaven Is Like for Moslems
April, 1542   *No. 5386*

"The Turk takes from the New Testament and the Old whatever pleases him. The rest doesn't please him at all. He ridicules the Trinity, the incarnation of Christ, his passion, the sacraments, absolution, marriage. He takes a wife if he likes her, and when he no longer likes her he casts her off again. What kind of marriage is that? The result is that all the children in Turkey are bastards.

"The Turk says that the following will happen after the resurrection: A beautifully set table will stand there with tasteful salvers and excellent drinks. The food will be eels and tender liver. Around the table will stand attractive nude women, whom it will be a delight to look at."

Dr. Pomeranus[5] added, "Thus they'll go 'round and 'round like a rooster among the hens."

Prophetic Words About King Ferdinand
April, 1542   *No. 5389*

When the conversation turned to Ferdinand[6] the doctor [Martin Luther] said, "Ferdinand is Germany's ruin. His [grand]father Maximilian[7] predicted this. He was an astrologer, and when he

---

[4] Philip Melanchthon's brother, George Schwarzerdt, was burgess in Bretten.
[5] John Bugenhagen, of Pomerania. Cf. No. 122, n. 36.
[6] Ferdinand I was king of Austria. Cf. No. 206, n. 77.
[7] Emperor Maximilian I was Ferdinand's grandfather and not his father.

saw his [grand]son's horoscope he is reported to have said, 'If you had drowned at your baptism it would have been best for you.' These were truly prophetic words of the [grand]father. Erasmus[8] also expressed an excellent opinion of the two men;[9] when they were still children he said of them, 'These two young cocks will someday bring great misfortune on Germany.'"

Nothing Strange About Grasping the Chalice
April, 1542 *No. 5390*

Somebody reported that a minister had said to his preacher who was administering the cup to him in communion, "Give me the cup. For it is written, 'Take!' [Matt. 26:26]." This offended those who were standing by and gave them some scruples. The doctor [Martin Luther] said, "What's so strange about that? When I communicate I also take hold of the cup. I do it in order that the minister may not miss my mouth, for I'm always afraid that he won't hit it."

Thereupon somebody said, "The people in Augsburg are exceedingly superstitious about their communion."

The doctor responded, "The Augsburgers are still Zwinglian.[10] Bucer[11] is a scoundrel in every case, part of speech, and rule of grammar. I never trust him because Paul said, 'As for a man who is factious, after admonishing him once or twice, have nothing more to do with him' [Titus 3:10]."

Then another person interjected, "I believe that wealth and glory make people so proud."

The doctor said, "A girl makes a magnificent show in a new dress or with her dark eyes. But this doesn't last, for soon a fever comes and robs her of her beauty. There is reason why Marnholt[12]

---

[8] Desiderius Erasmus. Cf. No. 113, n. 25.
[9] Emperor Charles V and King Ferdinand I.
[10] The reference is probably to the iconoclasm that occurred in Augsburg in 1524 under the leadership of John Schilling and other radicals.
[11] Martin Bucer. Cf. No. 184, n. 64. Reference to Augsburg probably reminded Luther of Bucer.
[12] Ludolf Marnholt was a nobleman in Halberstadt.

and Rantzau[13] are somewhat conceited, but soon some kind of pestilence will come and will undermine their pride. In a war some sort of firearm will pierce the body of a noble who is arrogant, and it's done with him. But glorying about religion—this does special harm and does great evil."

Gifts of God and Our Misuse of Them
Between April 11 and June 14, 1542　　　　*No. 5395*

"Where there's prosperity there are all sorts of sins, for:
> Property produces effrontery,
> Effrontery produces poverty,
> Poverty produces humility.

Accordingly the rich must give a vigorous accounting, for 'to whom much is given, of him will much be required' [Luke 12:48]. Wealth, talent, beautiful form are fine gifts of God, but we misuse them badly. Talent can be an evil thing, too, when we use it to speak in a bad way, for it has been said, 'He who wishes to submit to talent will be nobody.'[14] It's better not to be so handsome to look at. Sickness can come and take beauty from a person, but talent is not so readily changed. It's written, 'you will be like God' [Gen. 3:5]. Yes, indeed! You'll also be as rich as God. This sickness we've inherited from Adam: 'You will be like God.'"

The Ancient Jews Were a Remarkable People
Between April 11 and June 14, 1542　　　　*No. 5396*

"I wonder how the Jews lived in olden days—such a mighty people in a restricted space, for all of Judea was only thirty miles wide and fifty miles long.[15] They must have eaten very sparingly. I think a person spent barely a penny a day for bread. They also had root vegetables which they ate with the bread. Sometimes they ate a fig, of which they had a plenty, and at times a plum or a raisin. They also had to live close to one another, for I believe

---
[13] Paul Rantzau, a knight, was at Luther's table.
[14] Cf. Martial, *Epigrams*, 8, 18.
[15] The figures are of course incorrect.

that about a hundred Jews must have lived in a house like that of Master Ambrosius.[16] Even now four households with wives and children can manage to live in a single room when a table is set up and they also sleep there. It must have been a curious thing!"

Then Dr. Maurice[17] said, "That was a prolific people. In four hundred years seventy persons in Egypt increased to six hundred thousand, not including wives and children—and this while they were in bondage!"

The doctor [Martin Luther] said, "The severe bondage lasted hardly fifty years, and the slaying of children didn't continue long. For Joseph went there in his fortieth year and died when he was one hundred and ten years old, and so he ruled about seventy years, during which things went well. Afterward the nation undoubtedly survived a hundred years under the other patriarchs. It's a remarkable thing! Today such a large population couldn't be governed because it would always have to be fed."

The Fear of Invasion by the Turks
Between April 11 and June 14, 1542   No. 5398

"Pray! For hope no longer lies in arms but in God. If anybody defends us against the Turk,[18] the poor children who pray the Our Father will. Our wall and firearms and all the princes will probably leave the Turk untouched. I told the master builders too, 'Dear Sirs, why are you spending so much time building? Unless prayers build a wall that declares that angels surround you with protection, your wall is worthless.' A wall of angels is fine protection, and it should be called a special wall for Christians, made not of stone, etc. But it doesn't help.

"The theologians don't understand it? Well, then, we nevertheless understand that the Turk and the devil are thumbing their

---

[16] Perhaps the Wittenberg home of Ambrose Berndt, who had married Luther's niece, Magdalene Kaufmann.
[17] It is not clear who is intended here.
[18] There was a new threat of invasion by the Turks at this time. In the spring of 1542 a large imperial army was gathered to defend Germany, and at the same time efforts were made to strengthen the fortified town walls of Wittenberg.

noses at their wall! If there were an iron wall around us, the Turk would occupy the countryside, so that we would have nothing to eat and would starve to death. For our Lord God walks away when people behave so insolently. 'Very well,' he says, 'I'll let you do it alone. You don't want me, so do everything as well as you can.' All the prophets are crying out about it. If you stop doing anything you'll live? Ah, no! We'd have to have firearms in place of farmers! Well, should you flee? One hears no answer. And this is a sign of God's wrath, that nobody hears anything."

Rebuke for Those who Laugh During Singing
Between April 11 and June 14, 1542 No. 5408

"Music doesn't sound right when there is laughter in connection with it, for music is intended to cheer the spirit. The mouth gets no pleasure from it. If one sings diligently, the soul, which is located in the body, plays and derives special pleasure from it." This he [Martin Luther] said when we laughed during the singing [at table].

One Wearies of Most Songs in a Year
Between April 11 and June 14, 1542 No. 5415

"A certain Jew who heard the singing of 'Christ is risen,' said, 'Within a year one gets tired of every song and doesn't sing it any longer. Only this song must be sung year after year and remains unforgettable.'

"A certain wicked priest, when he was chanting the evening prayers on Christmas Eve, said, 'We have to do all this singing although Mary had only one child. What would it be like if she had had more? We'd have to scream ourselves to death!'"

His Most Christian Majesty and His Holiness
Between April 11 and June 14, 1542 No. 5416

"Maximilian[19] once said to the king of England,[20] 'The king

---
[19] Emperor Maximilian I. Cf. No. 3492, n. 31.
[20] King Henry VIII of England.

of France is called His Most Christian Majesty, but this does him an injustice because he never did a Christian thing. I am called His Most Invincible Majesty, but this also does me an injustice because I have often been overcome. The pope is called His Holiness, but this does him an injustice, too, because he is the biggest scoundrel who lives on earth. You are called the wealthiest man, and this is true.'"

When the doctor [Martin Luther] spoke in like fashion and related that the Turkish ambassador in Venice had called the king of France the most beloved brother of his lord and had at that time made him a present of two handsome stallions,[21] the doctor added, "Yes, he may very well be called His Most Turkish Majesty inasmuch as he was before called His Most Christian Majesty! It would not be improper to call him that. Just as Africanus[22] has his name from subjugated Africa and Carthage, so the king is called most Christian because he put many Christians to death."

A Story About a Dog who Was Lutheran
Between April 11 and June 14, 1542 No. 5418

The doctor [Martin Luther] said, "I just received a letter from Jonas.[23] He wrote that a dog had shit into the grave of the bishop of Halle. I believe it's fatal, for it has also happened to others before. Once when there was a procession with banners around a church, the verger put the holy water pot on the ground. A dog came along and pissed into the holy water pot. A priest noticed this because he was sprinkling the water, and he said, 'You impious dog! Have you become a Lutheran too?'"

To Err in Doctrine and to Err in Life
Summer or Fall, 1542 No. 5432

The papists insist: The church cannot err; we are the church; therefore [we do not err]. To the major premise he [Martin Luther]

---

[21] King Francis I of France made a treaty of alliance with the Turks in 1542.
[22] Julius Africanus, Christian historian of the third century.
[23] Justus Jonas had been in Halle since 1541. The letter referred to is not extant.

responded, "The church cannot err, namely, in doctrine, for it can err in deeds. Therefore the church prays, 'Forgive us our debts' [Matt. 6:12], etc. The minor premise I deny altogether. Accordingly when it is argued that whatever the church teaches is true, I concede it. But if it is argued that whatever the church does is right, I do not concede it. Consequently one must always look to the doctrine. The teaching does it! In their books the papists do nothing else than make false accusations about our crimes. They don't attack the chief articles of our faith. False accusations won't do; it's the teaching that matters.

"This is what I do. If I attack somebody I always teach something at the same time in order that he may see what's at stake. The common people approve of this too."

Pilgrimages Provided Occasion for Sin
Summer or Fall, 1542　　　　　　　　　　　　　*No. 5435*

"Every false religion is contaminated by libidinous desires. Just keep an eye on sex.[24] What were pilgrimages [under the papacy] but opportunities to get together? What does the pope do now but besmirch himself unceasingly with lust? In order that they might satisfy lust the more, well-situated places, beautiful fountains, trees, hills, and rivers were sought out for pilgrimages.

"The heathen held marriage in more honor than the pope and the Turk. The pope hates it; the Turk despises it. It is the devil's custom to hate the works of the Lord. He's hostile to whatever God holds dear—the church, marriage, government. He'd like to have whoredom and uncleanness, for if he does, he knows very well that people will no longer trouble themselves about God."

Gross Sinners Excommunicate Themselves
Summer or Fall, 1542　　　　　　　　　　　　　*No. 5438*

"Our usurers, gluttons, drunkards, whoremongers, blasphemers, and scoffers shouldn't be excommunicated by us. They excommuni-

---

[24] In the place of the last word in the sentence the manuscript has a perpendicular line as a symbol to suggest some strong expression by Luther. Cf. No. 5096, n. 99.

cate themselves. They despise the Word of God, enter no church, hear no sermon, receive no sacrament. If they don't want to be Christians, let them be heathen, and forever! Who cares about this anyhow? If they take the goods of ministers and appropriate everything for themselves, the minister shouldn't absolve them or administer the sacrament to them. They shouldn't be allowed to attend any baptism, any honorable wedding, or any funeral. They should behave among us as heathen, which they'll be glad to do! When they are dying, no minister or chaplain should visit them, and when they have died the hangman should drag them outside the town to the carrion pit, and no student or chaplain should escort them. If they want to be heathen we'll treat them as heathen," etc.

Classical Proofs for the Existence of God
Summer or Fall, 1542 No. 5440

"Aristotle is altogether epicurean.[25] He doesn't believe that God cares about human affairs, or if he believes it, he thinks that God governs the world the way a sleepy maidservant rocks a child in a cradle. Cicero,[26] on the other hand, made more progress. I think he collected every good thing that he found in all the Greek writers. The best argument that there is a God—and it often moved me deeply—is this one that he proves from the generation of species: a cow always bears a cow, a horse always bears a horse, etc. No cow gives birth to a horse, no horse gives birth to a cow, no goldfinch produces a siskin. Therefore it is necessary to conclude that there is something that directs everything thus. We may be able to know very well that God exists from the sure and perpetual motion of the heavenly constellations—every year we find the sun rising and setting in its proper place—and likewise from the reliability of the seasons which give us winter and summer with such regularity. These things that happen every day are held to be unimportant and don't astonish us. But if one brought up a child from early childhood in a dark place and after twenty years brought him

---

[25] For Luther, epicurean usually meant skeptic. On Aristotle, cf. No. 3993, n. 229.
[26] Cf. No. 3528, n. 84.

out, he would wonder about the sun, what it is, how it always adheres to a particular course, and how it moves according to a precise schedule of time. To us it is nothing because we pay little attention to what happens every day."

Forcing or Forbidding Children to Marry Is Wrong
Summer or Fall, 1542   No. 5441

"Secret marriages ought not to be considered valid at all, although our lawyers wish to recognize them as such. However, parents ought not urge their children to marry persons for whom they, the children, have no liking. On the other hand, parents ought to give their children permission to marry when they are of marriageable age, and they should not refuse them permission to take the sons or daughters of respectable people in marriage if the young people are attracted to each other.

"We once united a couple here against the will of the parents. The bridegroom was an honorable and well-to-do fellow; the bride was poor and would have been glad to have him but her father did not wish it, for he said he wanted her in the house. I replied, 'There are plenty of maidservants here; hire one for yourself!' And with that I united them in marriage."

Luther Has Low Opinion of Epistle of James
Summer or Fall, 1542   No. 5443

"We should throw the Epistle of James out of this school,[27] for it doesn't amount to much. It contains not a syllable about Christ. Not once does it mention Christ, except at the beginning [Jas. 1:1; 2:1]. I maintain that some Jew wrote it who probably heard about Christian people but never encountered any. Since he heard that Christians place great weight on faith in Christ, he thought, 'Wait a moment! I'll oppose them and urge works alone.' This he did. He wrote not a word about the suffering and resurrection of Christ, although this is what all the apostles preached about.

---

[27] I.e., out of the university in Wittenberg. For a similar judgment of Luther concerning James, see LW 35, 395-397.

Besides, there's no order or method in the epistle. Now he discusses clothing and then he writes about wrath and is constantly shifting from one to the other. He presents a comparison: 'As the body apart from the spirit is dead, so faith apart from works is dead' [Jas. 2:26]. O Mary, mother of God! What a terrible comparison that is! James compares faith with the body when he should rather have compared faith with the soul! The ancients recognized this, too, and therefore they didn't acknowledge this letter as one of the catholic epistles." [28]

Does the Kind of Water Affect Valid Baptism?
Summer or Fall, 1542   No. 5446

The doctor [Martin Luther]: "I wish to ask Dr. Jacob[29] whether children should be baptized in warm water."

Dr. Jacob: "Yes."

Dr. Luther: "This becomes a change of elements,[30] and cold water terrifies like the law."

Dr. Jacob: "The cold is accidental. Besides, the law is often called fire too."

Dr. Luther: "It's true. Water that's too hot can also terrify, if this is to be determinative."

Dr. Jacob: "Should a child be baptized with wine? I hear that such a thing happened," etc.[31]

Dr. Luther: "If it's done, it's done by accident. So in this instance what happened was that in an emergency the poor women laid hold of wine, thinking it was something else. That child shouldn't be baptized again because when I take something to be something—when I think it's water, even if it really is something else

---

[28] Up to the fourth century the Epistle of James was not included in the canon by many Christian leaders, and earlier writers did not quote from it. Cf. Eusebius, *Ecclesiastical History*, II, 23, 25.

[29] Jacob Probst. Cf. No. 4414, n. 334.

[30] It used to be debated whether when heat was added to water the water was changed to another element. Cf. Luther's letter to Melchior Frenzel, July 13, 1542. WA, Br 10, 96-97.

[31] There is a report of such a case when the child of Dr. Melchior Kling was baptized. Cf. No. 5983, which is not included in this edition, where it also appears that an emergency baptism was administered, presumably by midwives.

—there's no danger at all. Under the papacy priests often elevated water instead of wine."[32]

Luther Proposes to Write Against the Jews
Summer or Fall, 1542   No. 5462

"I intend to write against the Jews once again[33] because I hear that some of our lords are befriending them. I'll advise them to chase all the Jews out of their land. What reason do they have to slander and insult the dear Virgin Mary as they do? They call her a stinkpot, a hag, a monstrosity. If I were a lord I'd take them by the throat or they'd have to show cause [why I shouldn't]. They're wretched people. I know of no stronger argument against them than to ask them why they've been in exile so long."

Then somebody said, "In Frankfurt there have hitherto been many Jews, and they aren't harmful, as far as one can judge."

[Luther responded,] "The people in Frankfurt take money from them. Whether this is a good thing to do they must find out for themselves. The Jews put their own flesh and blood to shame when they defame Christ. They bear a grudge against us, who believe in him who was born from their blood."

Adam's Fall Must Have Affected His Body
Summer or Fall, 1542   No. 5475

"Adam grieved incredibly after he lost the innocence in which he had been created by God. As a result of the excessive worry and anxiety of his spirit he failed in his body too. I believe he had been able to see a hundred miles as clearly as we can see a half-mile. The same was true of his other senses. After the fall he must have said, 'O God, what has happened to me? I've become so blind and deaf. Where have I been?' I have no doubt that this is what

---

[32] Priests, especially if nearsighted, easily mistook the cruet of water for the cruet of white wine at the altar. To prevent such confusion the use of red wine was recommended. Cf. Theodore G. Tappert, *The Lord's Supper: Past and Present Practices* (Philadelphia: Muhlenberg Press, 1961), p. 26.

[33] Luther's *The Jews and Their Lies* appeared the next year, 1543. Cf. WA 53, 417-552.

happened. It was a dreadful fall. He used to enjoy the obedience of all creatures and used to play with the serpent."

Rival Claims for Tombs of the Apostles
Summer or Fall, 1542   *No. 5484*

There was discussion of the bodies, or rather the corpses, of the apostles. As many as sixteen apostles have been counted, although there were only twelve, because there has been a great deal of rivalry among the cities for the apostles, every city claiming one. Finally he [Martin Luther] said, "To the present day one doesn't know for sure where any of the apostles is buried. No doubt God didn't wish us to know this in order that we might avoid idolatry. However, this is quite certain, that most of the martyrs were buried in Rome. But now this city has become a harlot.

"I wouldn't take one thousand florins for not having seen Rome[34] because I wouldn't have been able to believe such things if I had been told by somebody without having seen them for myself. We[35] were simply laughed at because we were such pious monks. A Christian was taken to be nothing but a fool. I know priests who said six or seven masses while I said only one. They took money for them and I didn't. In short, there's no disgrace in Italy except to be poor. Murder and theft are still punished a little, for they must do this. Otherwise no sin is too great for them."

Progress of the Gospel Is a Sign of the End
Summer or Fall, 1542   *No. 5488*

"I think the last day is not far away. My reason is that a last great effort is now being made to advance the gospel. It's like a candle. Just before it burns out it makes a last great spurt, as if it would continue to burn for a long time, and then it goes out. So it now appears as if the gospel is going to spread far and wide, but I'm afraid that it will be extinguished in a jiffy and that the

---

[34] Luther made a journey to Rome in the winter of 1510-1511 and he often spoke of it at table. Cf. Nos. 3478, 3479a.
[35] The "we" probably means "we Germans."

day of judgment will follow. That's how it is with a sick person too. When he's about to die he generally seems to be very alert, as if he might recover, and then in a jiffy he's gone."

A Preacher Should Not Say Everything at Once
Summer or Fall, 1542 *No. 5489*

When Katy[36] said that she could understand the preaching of her husband's assistant Polner[37] better than that of Pomeranus[38] because the latter wandered too far from his subject, the doctor [Martin Luther] responded, "Pomeranus preaches the way you women usually talk. He says whatever comes to mind. Dr. Jonas[39] is accustomed to say, 'One shouldn't hail every soldier one meets.' And it's true, Pomeranus often takes everybody he meets along with him. Only a fool thinks he should say everything that occurs to him. A preacher should see to it that he sticks to the subject and performs his task in such a way that people understand what he says. Preachers who try to say everything that occurs to them remind me of the maidservant who is on her way to market. When she meets another maid she stops to chat with her for a while. Then she meets another maid and talks with her. She does the same with a third and a fourth and so gets to market very slowly. This is what preachers do who wander too far from their subject. They try to say everything all at once, but it won't do."

Luther's Wife Comforted When Daughter Is Dying
September, 1542 *No. 5491*

When his wife wept loudly, Martin Luther comforted her: "Think where she's going.[40] She'll get along all right. Flesh is flesh,

---

[36] Luther's wife Katherine. Cf. No. 49, n. 1.

[37] Hans Polner, a son of Luther's sister, began to study in Wittenberg in 1529 and was still living in Luther's home in 1542, where he was serving as the Reformer's *famulus* or assistant.

[38] John Bugenhagen was notoriously long-winded. Cf. No. 5171b, n. 133.

[39] Justus Jonas. Cf. No. 347, n. 161.

[40] Luther's thirteen-year-old daughter Magdalene died September 20, 1542, after a brief illness. Entries No. 5491 to No. 5500 belong together.

spirit is spirit. Children don't argue. They believe what they're told. All things are simple for children. They die without anxiety, complaint, or fear of death, and they have little physical pain, as if they were falling asleep."

We Do Not Believe that God Is Creator

September, 1542   No. 5492

Turning to Master Holstein[41] he [Martin Luther] said, "Master, where were you sixty years ago? Where was I? Where did I come from? Certainly we didn't make ourselves inasmuch as we were nothing. There must be someone who made us. And do we rashly propose to make a bargain with our Lord God to sell him our works, in return for which he is to give us heaven? Isn't it a disgraceful thing for a creature to dare to lift himself up so high and deal with his Creator in such a fashion? It's because we don't believe that God is the Creator. If we believed in him as the Creator we'd surely act differently. But nobody believes in him as the Creator, even if one says so and even if one's conscience convinces one that God is the Creator of all that is ours. If we had been created by another God, it might have made some sense if we approached God and said, 'Lord God, have regard for me on account of my works! I come to thee although thou hast not made me!'"

The Greatest Thing in Death Is Fear

September, 1542   No. 5493

"Fear of death is death itself and nothing else. Anybody who has torn death from deep down in his heart does not have death or taste it."

Somebody inquired about the pains of death, and Martin Luther replied, "Ask my wife if she felt anything when she was really dead."[42]

---

[41] John Sachs (d. 1566), a native of Holstein, was a professor in the philosophical faculty of the university in Wittenberg.
[42] The reference is to the grave illness of Luther's wife Katherine in 1540. Cf. No. 4885.

She herself responded, "Nothing at all, Doctor."

Thereupon Dr. Martin Luther continued, "For this reason I say that the greatest thing in death is the fear of death. It is written in the Epistle to the Hebrews [2:9], 'that by the grace of God he might taste death for every one.' We are blessed if we don't taste death, which is very bitter and sharp. How great the pain of tasting death is we can discern in Christ when he said, 'My soul is very sorrowful, even to death' [Matt. 26:38]. I regard these as the greatest words in all the Scriptures, although it is also a great and inexplicable thing that Christ cried out on the cross, 'Eli, Eli,' etc. [Matt. 27:46]. No angel comprehends how great a thing it was that he sweated blood [Luke 22:44]. This was tasting and fearing death. Creation consoles the Creator[43] and the disciples noticed nothing of these things," etc.

Illness of Luther's Daughter Becomes Graver
September, 1542 No. 5494

When the illness of his daughter[44] became graver he [Martin Luther] said, "I love her very much. But if it is thy will to take her, dear God, I shall be glad to know that she is with thee."

Afterward he said to his daughter, who was lying in bed, "Dear Magdalene, my little daughter, you would be glad to stay here with me, your father. Are you also glad to go to your Father in heaven?"

The sick girl replied, "Yes, dear Father, as God wills."

The father said, "You dear little girl!" [Then he turned away from her and said,][45] "The spirit is willing, but the flesh is weak [Matt. 26:41]. I love her very much. If this flesh is so strong, what must the spirit be?" Among other things he then said, "In the last thousand years God has given to no bishop such great gifts as he has given to me (for one should boast of God's gifts). I'm angry with myself that I'm unable to rejoice from my heart and be thankful to God, though I do at times sing a little song and thank God.

---

[43] Cf. Luke 22:43.
[44] Cf. No. 5491, n. 40.
[45] Text in brackets from the later version of John Aurifaber.

Whether we live or die, we are the Lord's [Rom. 14:8]—in the genitive singular and not in the nominative plural." [46]

Desire to Talk with Christ Before the End
September, 1542   No. 5495

Turning to Rörer[47] he [Martin Luther] said, "Be of good cheer, Master!"

He responded, "I have at some time heard a word from Your Reverence that has often comforted me, namely, 'I have prayed our Lord God that he may grant me a blessed end in order that I may depart from this life, and I'm sure he'll do it. Just before I die I'll speak with Christ, my Lord, even if it should be but a brief word.'"

The doctor said, "I'm afraid I'll go suddenly and silently, without being able to utter a single word."

Philip Melanchthon[48] said, "Whether we live or die we are the Lord's [Rom. 14:8]. Even if you should fall down the stairs or should suddenly expire while you are writing, it wouldn't matter. Let it be! The devil hates us but God protects and keeps us."

Description of the Death of Magdalene Luther
September 20, 1542   No. 5496

When his daughter was in the agony of death, he [Martin Luther] fell on his knees before the bed and, weeping bitterly, prayed that God might will to save her. Thus she gave up the ghost in the arms of her father. Her mother was in the same room, but farther from the bed on account of her grief. It was after the ninth hour on the Wednesday after the Fifteenth Sunday after Trinity in the year 1542.

---

[46] In Latin *Domini sumus* can mean "we are the Lord's" (where *Domini* is taken as genitive singular) or "we are lords" (where *domini* is nominative plural). This was a favorite play on words by Luther. Cf. Tappert (ed.), *Luther: Letters of Spiritual Counsel,* p. 38.

[47] George Rörer. Cf. No. 1421, n. 83.

[48] Cf. No. 157, n. 59.

The Love of Parents for Their Children
September, 1542   No. 5497

Often he [Martin Luther] repeated the words given above: "I'd like to keep my dear daughter because I love her very much, if only our Lord God would let me. However, his will be done! Truly nothing better can happen to her, nothing better."

While she was still living he often said to her, "Dear daughter, you have another Father in heaven. You are going to go to him."

Philip Melanchthon said, "The feelings of parents are a likeness of divinity impressed upon the human character. If the love of God for the human race is as great as the love of parents for their children, then it is truly great and ardent."[49]

Luther's Daughter Magdalene Placed in Coffin
September, 1542   No. 5498

When his dead daughter was placed in a coffin, he [Martin Luther] said, "You dear little Lena! How well it has turned out for you!"

He looked at her and said, "Ah, dear child, to think that you must be raised up and will shine like the stars, yes, like the sun!"

The coffin would not hold her, and he said, "The little bed is too small for her."

[Before this,] when she died, he said, "I am joyful in spirit but I am sad according to the flesh. The flesh doesn't take kindly to this. The separation [caused by death] troubles me above measure. It's strange to know that she is surely at peace and that she is well off there, very well off, and yet to grieve so much!"

The Coffin Is Escorted from the Home
September, 1542   No. 5499

When people came to escort the funeral and friends spoke to him according to custom and expressed to him their sympathy, he [Martin Luther] said, "You should be pleased! I've sent a saint

---

[49] Cf. Isa. 49:15.

to heaven—yes, a living saint. Would that our death might be like this! Such a death I'd take this very hour."

The people said, "Yes, this is quite true. Yet everybody would like to hold on to what is his."

Martin Luther replied, "Flesh is flesh, and blood is blood. I'm happy that she's safely out of it. There is no sorrow except that of the flesh."

Again, turning to others, he said, "Do not be sorrowful. I have sent a saint to heaven. In fact, I have now sent two of them." [50]

Among other things, he said to those who had come to escort the funeral as they were singing the verse in the psalm, "Lord, remember not against us former iniquities" [Ps. 79:8], "O Lord, Lord, Lord, not only former iniquities but also present ones! We are usurers, gougers, etc., and for fifteen years I read mass and conducted the abominations of the mass."

A Girl Is Harder to Raise Than a Boy
September, 1542   *No. 5500*

When she[51] was buried he [Martin Luther] said, "There is a resurrection of the flesh."

When he returned home from the funeral he said, "My daughter is now fitted out in body and soul. We Christians now have nothing to complain about. We know that it should and must be so, for we are altogether certain about eternal life."

Thereupon he consoled himself by saying, "After all, one must make provision for the children, especially for the poor girls. We have no right to expect that somebody else will care for them. I don't worry about the boys because a boy supports himself, no matter what country he's in, as long as he's willing to work. But the poor girls must have a staff to lean on. A boy who is in school can gather alms,[52] and afterward he can become a fine man if he has a will to. A girl can't do this and can easily bring shame on

---

[50] Luther's eight-month-old daughter Elizabeth had died August 3, 1528.
[51] Luther's daughter Magdalene. Cf. No. 5491, n. 40.
[52] It had been customary in Luther's youth for students to beg for alms. Cf. No. 137, n. 48. This practice was forbidden where the Reformation took hold.

herself. I'm very glad to give my daughter to our Lord God. According to the flesh I would gladly have had her, but since God has taken her away I am thankful to him."

Should Ministers Flee in Time of Pestilence?
October, 1542   *No. 5503*

When somebody reported that two preachers in Naumburg had been carried off by the pestilence, somebody else asked whether ministers who were employed only for preaching could deny their service to sick people in time of pestilence. He [Martin Luther] replied, "No! By no means! Preachers must not be all too ready to flee in order not to make the people apprehensive. It is sometimes said that pastors and preachers should be spared and not overburdened in time of pestilence, but the reason for saying this is that wherever the pestilence has carried off some of the chaplains there may be others who would visit the sick; besides, it is also said in order that everybody won't shun the priests at such times, for one sees that nobody wishes to go to them and everybody flees from them. Accordingly it would be a good thing not to burden all with this task [of visiting the sick] but to appoint one or two men and let them risk their lives.

"If the lot fell on me I would not be afraid. I have now lived through three pestilences[53] and have visited several persons who suffered from this sickness. So Schadewald[54] had two sick women, and I touched them, but it didn't do me any harm, thank God! When I came home that time I took hold of my Margaret's face— and she was little at the time[55]—with my unwashed hands. I had in fact forgotten about them, otherwise I wouldn't have done it, for it tempts God.

"It pleases me very much that the Jews apply the psalm, 'He who dwells in the shadow of the Most High' [Psalm 91], to the

---

[53] Wittenberg suffered from the pestilence in the years 1527, 1535, and 1539.
[54] Bartholomew Schadewald, town councilman in Wittenberg, died in 1535, perhaps as a result of the pestilence.
[55] Luther's daughter Margaret was born December 17, 1534. The reference must be to the pestilence in 1535 when she was less than one year old.

pestilence. I would also have pointed the psalm in that direction but I was concerned about the superstition that the psalm would henceforth be prayed against the pestilence in the same manner in which the Gospel of St. John is interpreted as applying to lightning. For when the mass was finished the priest read the Gospel of John with a loud voice, and anybody who had heard it read was said to be safe.[56] In order to confirm their lies the papists introduced a fable into the pulpit. Three men were riding together, it was said, when a storm arose and a voice was heard to say, 'Strike!' Thereupon one of the men was struck down [by lightning]. A second time the voice was heard saying, 'Strike!' and the second man was struck down. When the voice was heard the third time saying, 'Strike!' there was another voice that replied, 'Don't strike because he heard St. John's Gospel today!' So he escaped with his life. Such things the papists preached to confirm their idolatry.

"Likewise there was a story about something that happened not far from here. A man was to marry the wife of Lucas, the painter.[57] He was sitting in a castle with his tailor and having some nice clothes made for his wedding. When he looked out of the window the tailor noticed that a storm was coming and said, 'I'm going to get some [blessed] palm catkins and throw them in the fire because I didn't hear the Gospel of John today. Go out and do the same.' The young man said, 'Ah, what do you mean? Do you think the priest is the only one who can read the Gospel? I can do it just as well as he can.' With that he opened the window and began to read, 'In the beginning,' etc. [John 1:1]. It thundered, and the lightning struck and stripped the breeches clean off the young, handsome, and rich fellow's legs, so that he fell down at once and died. Meanwhile the lightning struck the tailor down below and tore the soles from his feet, but he didn't die. This certainly happened!

"But the story of the peasant was better. When a storm arose

---

[56] The prologue of the Fourth Gospel, John 1:1-14, was read by the priest at the conclusion of the mass, and it was therefore called "the Last Gospel." Sometimes lay people also recited the prologue after mass as an act of private devotion.

[57] Lucas Cranach the Elder, the artist, had been married to Barbara Brengbier, daughter of the mayor in Gotha.

and lightning struck he made the sign of the cross four times and said, 'Matthew, Mark, Pilate, and Herod; may the four evangelists help me!' It was odd under the papacy. Young people today know nothing about it."

Then somebody said that in a certain village not far from Naumburg a parish minister had died of the pestilence, and so also a schoolmaster, etc. Now the people died like beasts without the administration of the sacrament because even before the pestilence had begun to rage they had been unwilling to support a deacon. Thereupon the doctor [Martin Luther] said, "It served them right! Because they thought they didn't need the preacher and chaplain and could get along without them! So the citizens in the village of Zahna once were unwilling to support a pastor. I said to the judge, 'How is it that you don't want to keep a pastor or rector when you keep a cattle herder?[58] You have to pay him what he asks for.' He replied, 'Yes, dear Doctor, we can't very well do without him!' There you see what they're concerned about. Only their bellies! They're attached to anything that produces something for them, otherwise not."

Rites and Ceremonies of Jews and Papists
Winter of 1542-1543   No. 5504

When we were reading at table about the various rites and ceremonies of the Jews in the little book by Anthony Margaritha,[59] a baptized Jew, the doctor [Martin Luther] said, "All religions that depart from the true Christian religion are *ex opere operato*,[60] that is, teach, 'This I will do, and that will please God.' But one must hold fast to the rule that every *opus operatum*[61] is idolatrous. Whatever the papists taught was *opus operatum*. At all events, their

---

[58] For a similar report, see No. 4002.
[59] The principal work of Antonius Margaritha, a contemporary professor of Hebrew in Vienna, was *Der gantz Jüdisch glaub*. For a somewhat similar discussion, see No. 4173.
[60] Latin: by the mere performance of the act. This late medieval formula, which was especially applied to the efficacy of the sacraments, was here extended by Luther to apply to works righteousness.
[61] Latin: the work that is done (in the expectation of receiving a reward for it).

rules and regulations remind me of the Jews, and actually very much was borrowed from the Jews. They also demanded that this and that be done, that a cowl be worn or one's head be shaved. Anybody who didn't do or observe what was prescribed was damned. On the other hand, if it was done by somebody, he couldn't be told for sure whether he was saved thereby or not. Fie on you, Satan! What kind of doctrine is this supposed to be? If one doesn't act according to the rule, one is supposed to be damned, but if one does act accordingly one should be uncertain as to whether it is pleasing to God or not! In such error were we poor people stuck fast."

Then somebody said, "If the world should stand another fifty years, won't many a thing still happen?"

The doctor replied, "God forbid [that it should last that long]! It would become worse than it's ever been, for all sorts of sects would arise that are now still hidden in men's minds. One wouldn't know what to make of them. Come, therefore, dear Lord! Come and strike about thee with thy day of judgment, for no improvement is any longer to be expected!"

Life with Adam and Eve After the Fall
Winter of 1542-1543   *No. 5505*

When asked whether Adam had more children than the three who are mentioned in the Bible,[62] he [Martin Luther] replied, "Yes, indeed! Seth is introduced at once[63] on account of the lineage of Christ, for Christ was born from that line. Adam undoubtedly had many sons and daughters. I think there must have been as many as two hundred, for Adam got to be very old, nine hundred and thirty years. Cain must have been born about thirty years after the fall, when they [Adam and Eve] had been comforted again, for I think they were often comforted by angels; otherwise it wouldn't have been possible for them to sleep together because their fright was so great. After about thirty years they began to beget children.

---
[62] Cain, Abel, and Seth. Cf. Gen. 4:1, 2, 25.
[63] Cf. Gen. 5:1-5.

"At the last judgment Eve's distress will exceed that of all women because no woman has ever come upon the earth who was more sorrowful than she was. Accordingly other women should not speak of their wretchedness in front of Eve. She saw that we must all die on her account. When Cain was born she thought he'd be the [promised] one to do it; she hoped that he'd be the right seed.[64] But he killed Abel and was accursed because of this. That was a disappointment!"

Then somebody said, "Doctor, some hold that Cain was conceived before the promise."

The doctor replied, "By no means! I don't think half a day passed after the fall before the promise was given. They went into the garden about midday. They wanted to eat. She had a great desire for the apple, and there the fall occurred about two o'clock.

"Genesis is a difficult book. One can never stop reading it. The first five chapters aren't understood at all. The whole world was paradise, or at least a very large area 'round about Jerusalem was paradise, for all four rivers[65] belonged to it. But afterward the Flood spoiled it all."

A Substitute for Wine in the Sacrament?

Winter of 1542-1543　　　　　　　　　　　　　　*No. 5509*

When somebody inquired whether, when a sick person wished to have the sacrament but could not tolerate wine on account of nausea, something else should be given in place of the wine, the doctor [Martin Luther] replied, "This question has often been put to me and I have always given this answer: One shouldn't use anything else than wine. If a person can't tolerate wine, omit it [the sacrament] altogether in order that no innovation may be made or introduced. Is it necessary for a person who is dying to have the sacrament again at the last moment?

"Formerly it was said that he who has consumed one kind

---

[64] Cf. Gen. 3:15.
[65] Cf. Gen. 2:10-14.

should think that he has consumed both.[66] Why shouldn't we say, 'If you have taken neither, think that you have taken both'?"

Apparent Conflict Between Two Biblical Texts
Winter of 1542-1543   *No. 5510*

Somebody inquired whether these texts were not in conflict: God said to Abraham that he would spare Sodom if he found ten righteous men in it [Gen. 18:32], and in Ezekiel 14 [:12-23] it is said that even if Noah, etc., prayed, God would not listen. The doctor [Martin Luther] answered, "They are not in conflict. The reason is that in the passage in Ezekiel, Noah and the others were forbidden to pray, and Abraham was not. Accordingly one must observe what the words say. If God says, 'You must not pray,' one may properly stop praying. So I may say, 'Don't pray for my Andrew;[67] if you do, it won't help.' However, if I say, 'If somebody should pray for my Andrew,' that would be different."

Then somebody else asked, "How do we know now when God intends to hear our prayer?"

He replied, "We don't have a command that we shouldn't pray. If we had such a command we ought not pray, but we have a command to pray. Accordingly I would have stopped praying against the Turk long ago if I had such a command, but because I don't, I must pray, although it almost appears as if we never pray."[68]

How One Can Become a Good Theologian
Winter of 1542-1543   *No. 5511*

If anybody wishes to become a theologian, he has a great advantage, first of all, in having the Bible. This is now so clear

---

[66] That is, the medieval church had taught that when laymen received only bread (the body of Christ) in the sacrament of the altar they really received the wine (the blood of Christ) as well, according to the theory of sacramental concomitance. Luther's argument here is ironical.

[67] Andrew Kaufmann, Luther's nephew, was living in the Reformer's home and was probably present.

[68] I.e., from the failure to stem the tide of the Turkish advance into Germany one might suppose that God had not been asked.

that he can read it without any trouble.[69] Afterward he should read Philip's *Loci Communes*.[70] This he should read diligently and well, until he has its contents fixed in his head. If he has these two he is a theologian, and neither the devil nor a heretic can shake him. The whole of theology is open to him, and afterward he can read whatever he wishes for edification. If he wishes, he can read, in addition, Melanchthon's *Romans*[71] and my *Galatians* and *Deuteronomy*.[72] These will give him the art of speaking and a copious vocabulary.

"There's no book under the sun in which the whole of theology is so compactly presented as in the *Loci Communes*. If you read all the fathers and sententiaries[73] you have nothing. No better book has been written after the Holy Scriptures than Philip's. He expresses himself more concisely than I do when he argues and instructs. I'm garrulous and more rhetorical.

"If my advice were taken, only the books of mine that contain doctrine would be printed, such as my *Galatians, Deuteronomy,* and *John*. The rest [of my books] should be read merely for the history, in order to see how it all began,[74] for it was not so easy at first as it is now."

Where the Word Is, There Is Contempt

Winter of 1542-1543   *No. 5512*

"When the Word comes, contempt for it is there too. This is certain. One can see it in the case of the Jews. God sent them the prophets Isaiah, Jeremiah, Amos, etc., sent them Christ himself,

---

[69] Luther seems to be referring here to his German Bible, which was completed in 1534 and continued to be revised thereafter. Cf. M. Reu, *Luther's German Bible* (Columbus: Lutheran Book Concern, 1934), pp. 146-257, and Kooiman, *Luther and the Bible*.

[70] Cf. No. 3695, n. 28.

[71] The text of Melanchthon's *Commentary on the Epistle to the Romans* (1532) is in Robert Stupperich (ed.), *Melanchthons Werke*, V (Gütersloh, 1965), 25-371.

[72] For Luther's lectures on Galatians, see *LW* 26 and 27, and for his lectures on Deuteronomy, see *LW* 9.

[73] Late medieval commentators on Peter Lombard's *Four Books of Sentences*.

[74] I.e., how the Reformation began.

even divided the Holy Spirit among the apostles, who cried out together, 'Be penitent!' But nothing helped. They all had to endure much. Soon Jerusalem lay in ruin, and it remains so to this day. The same thing will happen in Germany. I think a great darkness will follow the present light, and after that the judgment day will come."

The Conscience Bears Witness and Accuses
Winter of 1542-1543 No. 5513

"Caiaphas didn't know that Christ is true God. This is so. But in the meantime he knew this, that harm would be done to that man.[75] So the bishops also think that they are offering service to God[76] by killing Christians; yet they know that they ought not to kill those who are condemned for no cause. But our bishops take it to be nothing but trickery. They oppose what has been demonstrated to be true. William of Bavaria[77] and the bishop of Mainz[78] asked Eck[79] at a meeting whether the things that we taught could be overturned by Holy Scripture, and Eck replied, 'They can't be overthrown by Holy Scripture but only by the teaching of the fathers and the councils.' They confess that we have the Scriptures [on our side], and yet they persecute us.

"At the same meeting the bishop of Mainz said, 'Dear lords, if they had no other article than the one about the marriage of priests, we would be lost, for we don't know how to maintain our position, and we can't.' The scoundrels see this very well, and yet they attack us. Nature teaches them that we are born male and female, and therefore they can't abolish marriage. However, marriage does not consist only of sleeping with a woman—everybody can do that!—but keeping house and bringing up children must also be considered by anybody who intends to take a wife. So the

---

[75] Cf. John 11:47-53.
[76] Cf. John 16:2.
[77] Duke William IV of Bavaria (1493-1550).
[78] Cardinal Albrecht, archbishop of Mainz.
[79] John Eck. Cf. No. 257, n. 107. The meeting was perhaps the imperial Diet in Augsburg, 1530.

bishop of Salzburg[80] also said against Master Philip,[81] 'Why do you argue so much against priests? Priests have never been any good!' Thereupon Philip said, 'This is a matter of conscience.' The bishop then said, 'Are you going to talk a lot about conscience?' These were hard and wicked words. What kind of comfort can a man's poor, terrified conscience have if he doesn't believe anything about conscience? The only thing that concerns a poor sinner is his conscience. Well, then, God will find them out!

"A poor friar once went to Rome to secure a letter concerning a monastery from the pope. A cardinal who gave the letter to the friar demanded three thousand crowns, and the friar asked, 'Do you think I'm God?' Then the cardinal (for he was not so bad) said that the friar should give thirty crowns, one tenth of the amount, and that it was necessary to give this. Thereupon the friar said, 'O Blessed Virgin Mary! Do you at Rome also have a conscience? The conscience is an evil beast who makes a man take a stand against himself.' He correctly defined conscience according to Paul in Romans 2 [:15]."

Distinction Between the Law and the Gospel
Winter of 1542-1543   *No. 5518*

"For a long time I went astray [in the monastery] and didn't know what I was about. To be sure, I knew something, but I didn't know what it was until I came to the text in Romans 1 [:17], 'He who through faith is righteous shall live.' That text helped me. There I saw what righteousness Paul was talking about.[82] Earlier in the text I read 'righteousness.' I related the abstract ['righteousness'] with the concrete ['the righteous One'] and became sure of my cause. I learned to distinguish between the righteousness of the law and the righteousness of the gospel. I lacked nothing before this except that I made no distinction between the law and the gospel. I regarded both as the same thing and held that there was

---

[80] Matthew Lang was bishop of Salzburg. Cf. *WA* 30[III], 294.
[81] Philip Melanchthon. Cf. No. 157, n. 59.
[82] Here Luther once again gives an account of his "tower experience" in a somewhat different context. Cf. above Nos. 3232c, 4007.

no difference between Christ and Moses except the times in which they lived and their degrees of perfection. But when I discovered the proper distinction—namely, that the law is one thing and the gospel is another—I made myself free."

Then Dr. Pomeranus[83] said, "I began to experience a change when I read about the love of God and what it signifies passively, namely, that by which we are loved by God. Before I had always taken love actively [namely, that by which we love God]."

The doctor [Martin Luther] said, "Yes, it is clear—by charity or by love!—that it's often understood [in the Scriptures] of that by which God loves us. However, in Hebrew the genitives of 'love' are difficult."

Then Pomeranus added, "Nevertheless, other passages afterward make these clear."

The Beginning of the Attack on the Papacy
Winter of 1542-1543   No. 5523

"You don't know in what darkness we were under the papacy. Gerson[84] was the best; he began [to attack the papacy], although he was not altogether sure what he was about. Yet he got to the place where he found the distinction in this question, Whether one should in all things submit to the power of the pope? He answered that it's not a mortal sin not to submit, but then he appended the condition, 'if it isn't done out of contempt.' He couldn't make up his mind to make the break [with the pope] complete. Yet what he said was comforting to people; therefore they called him the consolatory doctor. As a consequence he was also condemned. Accordingly the cardinal[85] at Augsburg called me a Gersonist when I appealed from the pope to the Council of Constance. If anybody would blame me for yielding to the pope at first, let him take into

---

[83] John Bugenhagen, of Pomerania. Cf. No. 122, n. 36.
[84] Jean Gerson was a French theologian who became involved in the problem of the relation of councils and the papacy. He was a participant in the Council of Constance (1414-1418).
[85] Cardinal Thomas Cajetan (1469-1534) was sent to Augsburg in 1518 to examine Luther and his teaching. Cf. *LW* 31, 253-292.

account in what darkness I was. Those who didn't live under the papacy suppose that this teaching about the pope isn't necessary, but those who were stuck in it know how necessary it is to inculcate this."

Marriage Requires More Than Fleeting Feeling
Winter of 1542-1543   *No. 5524*

"After Lucas,[86] the artist, had taken a wife and the wedding was over, he always desired to be next to his bride. He had a good friend who said to him, 'Friend, don't do that. Before a half-year is gone you will have had enough of that. There won't be a maid in your house whom you won't prefer to your wife.' And so it is. We hate the things that are present and we love those that are absent. As Ovid wrote, 'What we may have [does not please us]; it's what we may not have that excites our passion.'[87] This is the weakness of our nature. Then the devil comes and introduces hatred, suspicion, and concupiscence on both sides, and these cause desertion. It's easy enough to get a wife, but to love her with constancy is difficult. A man who can do this has reason to thank our Lord God for it.

"Accordingly if a man intends to take a wife, let him be serious about it and pray to God, 'Dear Lord God, if it be thy divine will that I continue to live without a wife, help me to do so. If not, bestow upon me a good, pious girl with whom I may spend all my life, whom I hold dear, and who loves me.' There's more to it than a union of the flesh. There must be harmony with respect to patterns of life and ways of thinking. The bonds of matrimony alone won't do it."

Heretics Perform Unwitting but Useful Service
Winter of 1542-1543   *No. 5525*

"Heretics are useful. We don't realize how good it is for us

---

[86] Lucas Cranach the Younger was married in February, 1541, to the daughter of Chancellor Gregory Brück. Cf. No. 1421, n. 85.
[87] Ovid, *Amores*, 2, 19, 3.

to have opponents. If Cerinthus[88] hadn't lived, John would never have written what we have of his. Cerinthus attacked the person of Christ, and this compelled John to write and declare, 'In the beginning was the Word' [John 1:1]. John made the distinction of the three persons [of the Trinity] so clear that it couldn't be made clearer. So, too, Eck[89] provoked me. He made me wide awake. I wished from the bottom of my heart that he would return to the way [of salvation], and therefore I wanted to strike out against him with my fist in the hope that he might be converted. But if he was always to remain as he had been, I wished him the papacy. He would have deserved it. He took all kinds of work upon himself, although he was in part paid for this, for he received income of seven hundred gulden from the parish in Ingolstadt alone. He would have been an inexpensive pope. They had nobody else who might have done it. He gave me my first ideas, and without him I would never have got this far. Accordingly our opponents are very useful to us, although they think they do us harm."

Three Rules Used for Translating the Bible
Winter of 1542-1543   *No. 5533*

"Münster's Bible[90] pleases me, but I wish he had been here and had conferred with us here.[91] He still makes too many concessions to the rabbis, although he is also hostile to the Jews, but

---

[88] Cerinthus was a gnostic in Asia Minor during the second century. He taught that Jesus was the natural son of Joseph and Mary who was united at his baptism with a higher Christ and that he did not suffer and die. Irenaeus later suggested that John wrote his gospel against Cerinthus.

[89] John Eck was an early opponent of Luther who died on February 10, 1543. Cf. No. 257, n. 107.

[90] Sebastian Münster (1489-1552), a student of the eminent scholar John Reuchlin, translated the Old Testament from the Hebrew into Latin in two volumes published in 1534-1535. On the subject in general, see W. Schwarz, *Principles and Problems of Biblical Translation: Some Reformation Controversies* (Cambridge: University Press, 1955).

[91] Luther had assembled a commission (he called it the Sanhedrin) in Wittenberg to assist him in revising his translation of the Old Testament. Reu, *Luther's German Bible*, pp. 233-240.

he doesn't take it so much to heart as I do. It helped Dr. Forster and Ziegler[92] very much that they talked with us here, for when we translated the Bible I gave them three rules: First, the Bible speaks and teaches about the works of God. About this there is no doubt. These works are divided in three hierarchies: the household, the government, the church. If a verse does not fit the church, we should let it stay in the government or the household, whichever it is best suited to. Second, whenever equivocal words or constructions occur, that one would have to be taken which (without, however, doing injustice to the grammar) agrees with the New Testament. Third, sometimes a sentence seems to be in conflict with the whole [message of the] Bible. So the rabbis have greatly corrupted all the Scriptures with their glosses and relate everything only to the coming of the Messiah, to his supplying us with food and drink, and to his dying afterward. This is rubbish! Accordingly we simply throw it out, and we have taken many sentences like this from Forster. When he said, 'Ah, the rabbis interpret it this way,' I said, 'Could your grammar and points[93] allow you to render the sentence so that it rhymes with the New Testament?'

"Answer: 'Yes.'

"'Then take it!'

"The result was that they themselves marveled and said they never in their lives would have believed it."

Man Is a Whole and Not Merely Body or Soul
Winter of 1542-1543   *No. 5534*

Some said that after the soul has escaped from the mortal body, it immediately migrates to heaven, as Christ said, "Today you will be with me in Paradise" [Luke 23:43].

To this he [Martin Luther] responded, "Yes, what does this word 'today' mean? It's true that souls hear, feel, and see after

---

[92] John Forster and Bernard Ziegler were members of the Bible commission in Wittenberg.
[93] The vowel points in the Masoretic text of the Hebrew Bible.

death, but how this occurs we don't understand. Where do those stay who hang on the gallows? If we try to figure this out according to [our conception of time in] this life, we're fools. Christ has given his answer, for his disciples were undoubtedly just as curious. [He said,] 'He who believes in me, though he die, yet shall he live' [John 11:25]. Similarly [Paul wrote], 'Whether we live or whether we die, we are the Lord's' [Rom. 14:8]."

Before this he had said to his wife,[94] "Yes, you, too, are already in heaven. Christians, both those who are dead and those who are living, await a resurrection of the dead. Abraham lives too. God is God of the living [Matt. 22:32]. Now, if one should say that Abraham's soul lives with God but his body is dead, this distinction is rubbish. I will attack it. One must say, 'The whole Abraham, the whole man, shall live.' The other way you tear off a part of Abraham and say, 'It lives.' This is the way the philosophers speak: 'Afterward the soul departed from its domicile,' etc.[95] That would be a silly soul if it were in heaven and desired its body!"

Somebody observed that the dispute about the location of hell is similar, inasmuch as no certain place was assigned to the demons. Luther added, "The Scriptures say so. Peter declares in II Peter 2 [:4] that God cast them [the angels who sinned] into hell. There they don't suffer punishment as yet, although they are condemned. For if they were already punished, the devils wouldn't engage in so much knavery."

Then somebody said, "It is nevertheless asserted in the Creed, 'he descended into hell.'" Luther responded, "This must be believed. We can't understand it. That's the way it is. There will be debate about how the Trinity is in the unity (when there's no relation between the infinite and the finite), how nature can produce such a strange marvel as a God-man, etc. [While occupied thus with disputation] men will let the article concerning justifica-

---

[94] This earlier conversation between Luther and his wife Katherine shifts the question from "When does the soul go to heaven?" to "Is the soul separated from the body at death?"

[95] Luther seems not to have had any particular philosopher in mind here but to have referred to the interest which philosophers in general showed in the question of the immortality of the soul.

tion go. If only we would study in the meantime how to believe and pray and become godly! We're not content with that which we can understand and insist on disputing about something higher, which we can't possibly understand and which our Lord God doesn't want us to understand. That's the way human nature is. It wishes to do what is forbidden; the rest it ignores and then starts asking, Why? Why? Why? This is what happens when philosophy is introduced into theology. When the devil went to Eve with the question Why? the game was up. One should be on one's guard against this. It's better to fall on one's knees and pray an Our Father. This will help more.

"Dear Lord God, protect us from the devil, and also from ourselves!"

Luther Suffers Pain and Expects His End
Winter of 1542-1543 No. 5537

When he had for some days felt a severe pain in his head, he [Martin Luther] said at table one evening, "Katy, if I don't feel better tomorrow I'll have our Hans brought back from Torgau,[96] for I'd like to have him here at my end."

Thereupon Katy said, "See to it, Sir, that you don't imagine things."

"No, Katy," the doctor replied, "this is not imagination. I won't die so suddenly. I'll first lie down and be sick, but I won't lie there very long. I'm fed up with the world, and it is fed up with me. I'm quite content with that. The world thinks that if it is only rid of me everything will be fine, and it will accomplish this. After all, it's as I've often said: I'm like a ripe stool and the world's like a gigantic anus, and so we're about to let go of each other. I thank thee, dear God, that thou dost allow me to stay in thy little flock that suffers persecution for the sake of thy Word. It's certainly not on account of harlotry or usury that I'm persecuted; of this I'm sure."

---

[96] Luther's oldest son John, who was almost seventeen years old at this time, was living in the home of Marcus Crodel in Torgau, where he was going to school.

It Is Fortunate that God Governs Everything

Winter of 1542-1543   No. 5538

"In a house there is only one servant, and this is the master. Princes don't like to be princes. If they did, all the difficult business would be heaped on them. This is why they have chancellors and lawyers who bear the burden, for everybody prefers to cut boards where they are thinnest. So our Lord God comes and hurls a man into the office of prince as he tosses a young fellow into marriage; the latter sees the girl only from the outside and doesn't know the consequences. In the case of rulers the appearance is similar; the office appears to be something precious, but when one looks at it more closely one sees what it is. I would not like to rule; it's not in my nature."

Thereupon Master Philip[97] said, "You have the sun in your horoscope."

The doctor [Martin Luther] replied, "I don't care a fig about your astrology. I know and experience my nature. Staupitz[98] used to quote this sentence from the Song of Solomon [8:12], 'My vineyard, my very own, is for myself,' and used to interpret it to mean that God has taken the dominion upon himself so that everybody wouldn't strut about haughtily. God says, 'I'll take care of everything by myself. I'll be the pastor, the rector, the man in the house, the wife who brings up the children. In short, I'll do everything alone.' It is good, and it pleases me, that he has taken the rule over all things into his hands. For the pastor, the bishop, the man, and the wife make mistakes, but God doesn't make mistakes. If something worked out well for us we would be proud. Hence it is written,[99] 'Fortune makes a fool out of the man whom it favors too much.' It's impossible for a man not to be proud when things turn out well. Accordingly God must make us pastors, rectors, housefathers, etc. If he doesn't it will be worse for us when we

---

[97] On Philip Melanchthon's interest in astrology, see No. 3520.
[98] John Staupitz, Luther's superior in the monastery in Erfurt. Cf. No. 94, n. 14.
[99] Publilius Syrus, *Sententiae*, 173; these were versified maxims of the first century B.C.

assume these offices. [If we say,] 'Ah, I didn't want to be a bishop, a preacher, a housefather,' then when our hair curls behind our ears it will be well with us. Otherwise, unless he makes us rule, our wisdom can't hold us in check. As it is in the fable,[100] God commanded Peter to rule over the goats, etc. We must have rule over us or else we wouldn't know who we are. It is as Moses said, 'Who am I, O Lord, that I should bring forth these children as a nurse?' [Num. 11:12]. He, too, was afraid enough about his duties. This is our Lord God's way of eliminating our pride.

"Thus the Italians made an arch to please the emperor. On one side was written, 'Utrecht planted,' because it was the birthplace of Adrian.[101] On the other side was inscribed, 'Louvain watered,' because Adrian had studied there. At the top was written, 'The emperor gave the growth,' because he had made him pope. Then a bad boy came along and scribbled on the bottom of the arch, 'Here God did nothing!'"

The Book of Proverbs Is Good for Rulers
Winter of 1542-1543　　　　　　　　　　　　　　　　*No. 5541*

"Proverbs is an excellent book. Rulers ought to read it. There one can see how things happen in the world. There's nothing in the book but 'Fear God' and 'Pray.' On the other hand, we proceed with mathematics and counting and say that something amounts to so and so much. In this way we propose to force our Lord God. Then he says, 'Ah, dear fellow, don't force me. No! No!' And after three years he turns his back on you.[102] It's nothing. 'The blessing of the Lord makes rich' [Prov. 10:22]. It's so, too, with mining. That's the blessing of the Lord. They try to force our Lord God and his grace, but he won't let himself be forced. And then we lose everything. When we undertake something, no matter how

---

[100] A common fable which was used, among others, by Hans Sachs in his "St. Peter and the She-Goat," in E. Goetze (ed.), *Sämtliche Fabeln und Schwänke von Hans Sachs* (3 vols.; Stuttgart, 1893), I, 441.

[101] Pope Adrian VI (1522-1523) had been born in Utrecht and had been professor in Louvain. The alleged inscription is an allusion to I Cor. 3:6.

[102] There is an allusion here to "Solomon and Morolf." Cf. No. 5096, n. 107.

small it may be, we should call upon our Lord God and pray and pray, even if he gives us only a piece of bread and a healthy body. Yet, we wish to blindfold him; we don't want him to see anything because we want to do it ourselves. This is what we do and experience to our great loss. This is what happens to princes and lords. They can't say with David, 'Thou who givest victory to kings and subduest my people under me' [Ps. 144:10, 2]."

Promise for the Jews, Mercy for the Gentiles
Winter of 1542-1543   No. 5544

When the gospel was read at table by his son Martin,[103] "I was sent only to the lost sheep of the house of Israel" [Matt. 15:24], the doctor [Martin Luther] said, "Christ seems to contradict himself because in this gospel he said, 'I was sent only to the lost sheep,' etc., and yet he saved the daughter of the [Canaanite] woman."

Master Holstein[104] asked how this contradiction might be resolved. Thereupon he [Martin Luther] replied, "He wasn't sent to the heathen, but if they came to him he didn't reject them."

Then somebody else said, "Then he did not come for our sake?"

The doctor responded, "Christ was a servant to the circumcised to show God's truthfulness, as Paul wrote [Rom. 15:8]. But when he came he found many Samaritans and Sadducees, as there are many epicureans[105] today, but he was supposed to preach in that land, and afterward he preached to the whole world through the apostles. Paul said that the Word of God should be spoken 'first to you, but if you reject it, then we turn to the Gentiles' [Acts 13:46]. Christ was therefore sent to the Jews in person because they had the promise of his person. The Gentiles didn't have the promise but they had mercy [Rom. 15:9]. He didn't speak to us but about us. He wished to test the woman's faith, and when she said, 'Lord, it's true, I don't deserve it, and I know that I didn't have the promise,' he heard her prayer."

---

[103] Martin was eleven years old at this time.
[104] John Sachs, of Holstein. Cf. No. 5492, n. 41.
[105] I.e., skeptics.

Schools Are the Preservers of the Church

Winter of 1542-1543 No. 5557

"When schools flourish, things go well and the church is secure. Let us make more doctors and masters. The youth is the church's nursery and fountainhead. When we are dead, where are others [to take our place] if there are no schools? God has preserved the church through schools. They are the preservers of the church. Schools don't have a beautiful appearance, and yet they are very useful. Little boys have learned at least the Lord's Prayer and the Creed in the schools, and the church has been remarkably preserved through such small schools."

Wealth the Most Insignificant Gift of God

Winter of 1542-1543 No. 5559

"Riches are the most insignificant things on earth, the smallest gift that God can give a man. What are they in comparison with the Word of God? In fact, what are they in comparison even with physical endowments and beauty? What are they in comparison with gifts of the mind? And yet we act as if this were not so! The matter, form, effect, and goal of riches are worthless. That's why our Lord God generally gives riches to crude asses to whom he doesn't give anything else."

The Meaning of Large Numbers in the Bible

Winter of 1542-1543 No. 5560

"When one often reads [in the Bible] that great numbers of people were slain—for example, eighty thousand—I believe that hardly one thousand were actually killed. What is meant is the whole people. Whoever strikes the king strikes everything he possesses. So if the king of France should be defeated with ten thousand of his men, it is said that eighty thousand were defeated because he has that many in his power, etc. Otherwise I can't reconcile the numbers."

RECORDED BY HEYDENREICH

To Believe and to Comprehend Are Not the Same
Spring, 1543   *No. 5562*

When Dr. Jonas[106] said that the mind of man cannot comprehend articles of faith and that it is enough that we begin only to assent, the doctor [Martin Luther] said, "Yes, dear Dr. Jonas, if one could believe them the way they're written, our hearts would leap for joy. That's certain. Accordingly we won't arrive at the place where we comprehend them. In Torgau a wretched little woman once came to me and said, 'Ah, dear Doctor, I have the idea that I'm lost and can't be saved because I can't believe.' Then I replied, 'Do you believe, dear lady, that what you pray in the Creed is true?' She answered with clasped hands, 'Oh yes, I believe it; it's most certainly true!' I replied, 'Then go in God's name, dear lady. You believe more and better than I do.'

"It's the devil who puts such ideas into people's heads and says, 'Ah, you must believe better. You must believe more. Your faith is not very strong and is insufficient.' In this way he drives them to despair. We are so constructed by nature that we desire to have a conscious faith. We'd like to grasp it with our hands and shove it into our bosom, but this doesn't happen in this life. We can't comprehend it, but we ought to apprehend it. We should hold to the Word and let ourselves drag along in this way."

Everybody Must Believe for Himself
Spring, 1543   *No. 5565*

When he was asked whether somebody else's faith will secure salvation for a person, he [Martin Luther] replied, "By all means! In fact, the faith of one person may obtain another's whole conversion. Accordingly it's said that Paul was converted and saved by Stephen's prayer.[107] However, Paul wasn't accepted on account of Stephen's faith, but Stephen's faith obtained faith for Paul from God and by this faith he was saved in God's sight. Many people

---

[106] Justus Jonas, who had been in Halle since 1541, visited Wittenberg in April, 1543.
[107] Cf. Acts 7:59, 60.

have been preserved by prayer, as we prayed Philip back to life.[108] Ah, prayer accomplishes much."

Somebody else asked, "But, Doctor, wasn't Paul converted long after the death of Stephen?"

The doctor responded, "Not at all! He was converted that same year. He was still a fine, young man and was learned. He adhered to the righteousness of the law: 'By doing these things a man shall live' [Lev. 18:5; Rom. 10:5]. He thought he was pleasing God in this way. It's impossible that God shouldn't hear a prayer of faith. Whether he always does is another matter. God doesn't give according to the prescribed measure, but he presses it down and shakes it together, as he said [Luke 6:38].

"This is what Augustine's mother did.[109] She prayed to God that her son might be converted. But nothing seemed to help. She approached all sorts of learned men and asked them to persuade her son. At length she proposed to him that he marry a Christian girl in order that she might bring him back, but it didn't work. But when our Lord God came along he acted effectively and made such an Augustine out of him that he's now called an ornament of the church. So James said well, 'Pray for one another,' etc., for 'the prayer of a righteous man has great power in its effects' [Jas. 5:16]. This is one of the best verses in that epistle.[110] Prayer is a powerful thing, if only one believes in it, for God has attached and bound himself to it [by his promises]."

Fanatics Are Surer Than Good Christians

Spring, 1543　　　　　　　　　　　　　　　　　　*No. 5568*

"The Turk has just one argument, and this is: Cursed be all those who worship more than one God; the Christians do this; therefore [cursed be the Christians]. I concede the minor premise because Christians believe in God the Father, the Son, and the

---

[108] When Philip Melanchthon was in Weimar in 1540 he was overtaken by a grave illness. Luther was convinced that his prayers brought his friend back from the edge of the grave. Cf. *WA*, Br 9, 170-171.

[109] Augustine reported his mother Monica's efforts in his behalf in his *Confessions*, 3, 11; 6, 1; 8, 12.

[110] For Luther's opinion of the Epistle of St. James, see No. 5443.

Holy Spirit. No matter how one tells the Turks, they can't believe that three are one. But I'll keep my faith without effort and work, even while I sleep. I know that, and I'll cling to what I've taught even if I stumble. A Christian never holds so steadfastly to his Christ as a Jew or a fanatic[111] holds to his teaching, for although a Christian also continues to believe until he dies, yet he often stumbles and begins to doubt. This isn't so in the case of the fanatics, for they stand firm.

"Mark[112] was like this. When I told him that he should be careful that he didn't make a mistake, he said, 'Not even God himself will change my mind!' Drechsel[113] also came to me and said that he had a message to proclaim. I asked him what it was, and he replied, 'The wrath of God toward the world has increased.' I believed this and knew it quite well before, but since he had been sent by God, as he claimed, he should have told me what I hadn't known before. However, he repeated the same words again and again. Finally, I interrupted him and told him to be off if he couldn't add anything else. He departed angrily and said that in six weeks Wittenberg would be destroyed."

Then somebody asked whether Jews or fanatics should be allowed [to serve as sponsors] at baptisms. The doctor [Martin Luther] replied, "By no means! You shouldn't allow usurers, adulterers, or drunkards to stand as sponsors, much less a fanatic, for he's supposed to be there to help your child get true faith but he doesn't himself believe what is right."

Procedure When a Husband or Wife Deserts
Spring, 1543   *No. 5569*

"Here we proceed in this way. When a man or a woman deserts a spouse, we wait not longer than a year if he or she has a good reputation. However, the circumstances must also be taken into account, which is quite possible among us. No sepa-

---

[111] German: *Schwermer* (*Schwärmer*). Cf. No. 342, n. 155.
[112] Thomas Stübner, one of the radicals who caused trouble in Wittenberg during Luther's absence at the Wartburg in 1521-1522.
[113] Drechsel was an adherent of Stübner (above).

rated man or woman returns to this land, for my gracious lord[114] pays strict attention to this, and it should be so. If the individual is in the neighborhood, especially if his precise location is known and he is unwilling to appear, we take legal action. We have removed many offenses by such legal action and by forbidding clandestine marriages."

It Is Faith that Justifies, Not Works

Spring, 1543   No. 5570a

"That works don't merit life, grace, and salvation is clear from this, that works are not spiritual birth but are fruits of this birth. We are not made sons, heirs, righteous, saints, Christians by means of works, but we do good works once we have been made, born, created such. So it's necessary to have life, salvation, and grace before works, just as a tree doesn't deserve to become a tree on account of its fruit but a tree is by nature fitted to bear fruit. Because we're born, created, generated righteous by the Word of grace, we're not fashioned, prepared, or put together as such by means of the law or works. Works merit something else than life, grace, or salvation—namely, praise, glory, favor, and certain extraordinary things—just as a tree deserves to be loved, cultivated, praised, and honored by others on account of its fruit. Urge the birth and substance of the Christian and you will at the same time extinguish the merits of works insofar as grace and salvation from sin, death, and the devil are concerned.

"Infants who have no works are saved by faith alone, and therefore faith alone justifies. If the power of God can do this in one person it can do it in all, because it's not the power of the infant but the power of faith. Nor is it the weakness of the infant that does it, otherwise that weakness would in itself be a merit or be equivalent to one. We'd like to defy our Lord God with our works. We'd like to become righteous through them. But he won't allow it. My conscience tells me that I'm not justified by works, but nobody believes it. 'Thou art justified in thy sentence; against thee only have I sinned and done that which is evil in thy sight'

---

[114] Elector John Frederick of Saxony. Cf. No. 3468, n. 6.

[Ps. 51:4]. What is meant by 'forgive us our debts' [Matt. 6:12]? I don't want to be good. What would be easier than for a man to say, 'I am a sinful man' [Luke 5:8]? But thou art a righteous God. That would be bad enough, but we are our own tormentors. The Spirit says, 'Righteous art thou' [Ps. 119:137]. The flesh can't say this: 'Thou art justified in thy sentence' [Ps. 51:4]."

A Proper Mixture of Praise and Punishment
Spring, 1543　　　　　　　　　　　　　　　　　　*No. 5571*

When somebody asked how this sentence ['Do not provoke your children to anger,' Eph. 6:4] should be understood, he [Martin Luther] replied, "Have you read your Terence? 'After the customary fashion of fathers I found fault with him every day,' etc.[115] This sentence therefore suggests that children should be brought up in such a way that they don't become timid. A father who is a Demea[116] makes his children either dispirited or hopeless; accordingly they do what they would otherwise probably avoid doing. A child should be disciplined, but he should be given food and drink in order that he may see that one would like him to be good. So Solomon said, 'Discipline your son while there is hope; do not set your heart on his destruction' [Prov. 19:18]. As long as there is hope, one should push a child forward. But if one sees that there's no hope, that the child can't learn, one shouldn't flog him to death on that account but should accustom him to something else.

"Some teachers are as cruel as hangmen. I was once beaten fifteen times before noon, without any fault of mine, because I was expected to decline and conjugate although I had not yet been taught this. Anthony Tucher,[117] of Nürnberg, was accustomed to say, 'Praise and punishment belong together; one should be very friendly to people and yet at the same time be ready to whip them.'"

---

[115] The Roman playwright Terence in *Heautontimerumenos*, 1, 1, 49.
[116] In Terence, *Adelphoi*, the character Demea was stern and severe. Cf. No. 5096, n. 112.
[117] Antonius Tucher (1457-1524) was tax collector in Nürnberg.

A Sharp Criticism of Contemporary Astrology

Spring, 1543   *No. 5573*

"There are many reasons I can't believe astrologers, and of these the principal reasons are the following: First, the calendars never agree. One astrologer prophesies that it will be warm, another that it will be cold. I think it should be understood that this is so: it's cold outside and warm behind the stove. Second, when a child is born, the rays of all the signs above the horizon or of all the planets or stars are said to reach that child. For the child is, as it were, a poppy seed in comparison with the smallest star. Now, I ask, why is it that all stars don't affect that child equally if all reach him equally? Third, why does the effect occur outside of the uterus, at the very hour and minute when the infant comes out of the uterus, and not in the uterus? Shouldn't the stars have influence in the uterus as well as outside of it? Do you mean to suggest that the stars care about a little skin on the woman's belly when otherwise the sun gives life to every member? Fourth, Esau and Jacob were born under one sign and in rapid succession.[118] Where did the diversity of their natures come from? The astrologers rack their brains about this but they can't offer a solid explanation."

Thereupon somebody said, "Doctor, many astrologers agree that in the case of your horoscope the constellations that presided over your birth showed that you would bring about a great change."

The doctor [Martin Luther] replied, "There's nothing sure about the time of my birth. Philip[119] and I disagree by a year on this. In the second place, do you think that our cause and my activity have been placed under the direction of your uncertain art? Ah, no! It's something else. It's God's work alone. You'll never persuade me otherwise."

Then the same person said, "However, manifest experience teaches that those born to distinguished parents have accomplished something great." The doctor replied, "The contrary is true. I am the son of a peasant, and peasants have become kings and emperors.

---

[118] Esau and Jacob were twins. Cf. Gen. 25:21-28.
[119] Philip Melanchthon held at one time that Luther had been born in 1484, but later agreed with the best family tradition that the year was 1483.

In short, I set no store on this. You draw a conclusion from one, two, three, or four examples. What about the other hundred who were born the same hour under the same sign and don't have any correspondence at all with such advancement?"

A Choice Between a Wife and the Ministry
Spring, 1543   *No. 5578*

This case was put to the doctor [Martin Luther]: There is a certain schoolmaster in Frankfurt on the Oder, a learned and godly man.[120] He set his heart on theology and preached several times to the great admiration of his auditors. At length he was called to the office of deacon. But his wife, since she had a haughty spirit, was altogether unwilling to consent to that kind of life. She simply did not want to have a parson for a husband. The question was asked, "What should the good man do? Should he abandon his wife or the ministry of the Word?"

The doctor replied at first with a jest, "If he married a widow, as you say, he must do what she wishes." A little later he said, "If there were a real government there, it could compel the old hag. For a wife is bound to follow her husband, not a husband his wife. She must be a wicked woman—indeed, a devil—to be ashamed of the ministry in which the Lord Christ himself and the dear angels were. The devil tries to slander and defame the ministry. If she were my wife I'd say to her, 'Will you go with me? Say quickly, No or Yes.' If she said No, I would at once take another wife and leave her. The trouble is that the government isn't there with its performance and doesn't watch over the ministry."

On Administering the Sacrament to Oneself
Spring, 1543   *No. 5579*

The doctor [Martin Luther] was asked whether a man who was about to die and couldn't have the whole sacrament[121] from the papists did the right thing when he administered the sacrament

---
[120] This appears to have been Jerome Schwolle.
[121] I.e., the wine as well as the bread in the Lord's Supper.

to himself. He replied, "No! At least two persons must always be there, the one who gives and the one who receives. So in an emergency a woman can baptize, but the child doesn't baptize himself. If a person can't have access to the sacrament, faith is enough, according to that word, 'Your faith has made you well' [Matt. 9:22]. On the other hand, if he can have it, he should not despise it.

"Ambrose said something similar in a certain passage.[122] He had a catechumen whom he converted to the faith. When he was on a journey to go to Ambrose in order to be baptized by him, the catechumen died on the way. This gave Ambrose troubled thoughts and he said, 'I have a pain in my stomach.' He misused the words in the prophet [Jer. 4:19]. By these words he meant to signify that he deplored that the catechumen should be lost to the people. At length, after long disputation, he also concluded that the catechumen was saved by his faith without baptism inasmuch as he thought properly of baptism and didn't despise it and would have had himself baptized in this faith if he had been able to. I have had many questions like this, especially from Meissen during the tyranny of Duke George.[123] But it isn't right for a person to administer the sacrament to himself."

The Baptism of Children in a Special Case
Spring, 1543   *No. 5588*

A question was put to the doctor [Martin Luther]. "There is a chaplain[124] who can't baptize because his left hand is shaky or because he can't use it for other reasons." He [Luther] was asked whether the chaplain could have the verger hold the child and pour water with the other hand, which he could use. Luther replied, "If the chaplain preaches well and the congregation hears him gladly, this may be done, especially if the common people are not offended by it. If they approve of it, it's permissible."

---

[122] Cf. Ambrose, *Epistles*, 33.
[123] Until the death of Duke George, evangelicals were persecuted in Albertine Saxony, whose capital was in the county of Meissen.
[124] The administration of the sacraments was often left to the deacons or chaplains, who were assistants of pastors or rectors.

Then somebody else suggested, "How would it be if he took hold of the child with both hands and dipped only his feet into the water?" The doctor replied, "Ah, no! Innovation isn't good. If the chaplain can't baptize, the pastor ought to do it himself."

Thereupon somebody said, "Yes, Doctor, but he might be annoyed by this and feel that it is beneath his dignity, for he might be taken to be the chaplain while the chaplain would be taken to be the pastor." The doctor responded, "Ah, it isn't good for ministers to look for dignity and honor in the works of God. What should one say about dignity? No minister and no angel in heaven is worthy in his person to baptize a child. The ministry is a high office, so why should a pastor be ashamed to baptize? I regret to hear that men wish to mingle their dignity and honor in things of God."

Elevation of the Host Abolished in Wittenberg

Spring, 1543   *No. 5589*

The doctor [Martin Luther] was asked what the origin of the elevation[125] was in the papistic mass. He replied, "It was taken from the Old Testament. Two words are used there. One is *thruma* and the other is *thumpha*. *Thruma* meant the taking of a sacrificial offering in a basket or something else and lifting it up over one's head, as we used to lift up the host, in order to show it to our Lord God, that he might see it. Afterward it was taken and eaten or burned. *Thumpha* referred to the sacrificial offering that was not lifted up but pointed to the four ends of the earth, as we [the

---

[125] In the Roman mass the priest, after consecrating the bread (and later, the wine), lifted it up so that the people could see it and adore it. In 1521 Luther wrote that "it would make no difference if there were no elevation, for that is something men have invented" (*LW* 36, 183). Two years later he suggested that elevation could be continued "for the benefit of the weak in faith who might be offended if such an obvious change in this rite of the mass were suddenly made" (*LW* 53, 28). The argument against elevation was that it presupposed transubstantiation and implied the sacrifice of the mass. The argument for it was that it defied Zwingli and other radicals (*LW* 40, 127-132). John Bugenhagen omitted elevation in the church orders he prepared, and in 1542 Luther approved of its abolition in the parish church in Wittenberg.

papists][126] used to make the sign of the cross or make fencing thrusts in the mass, and that's where we got the practice from."

He then made signs of the cross with extraordinary movements of his fingers but could not fully recover the old usage, and he said, "Mary, mother of God! How we were bothered by the mass, and especially by the crossings! Mecum[127] often told me that he was never in his life able to make those signs. Ah, we were poor people! It was nothing but idolatry, pure and simple. We were real idolaters! Some, and especially those who were good men who took things seriously, were so terrified by the words of consecration that they trembled all over when they repeated the words, 'This is my body,' etc. [I Cor. 11:24]. They were required to pronounce these words without any hesitation. Anybody who stammered or omitted a word was said to have committed a great sin. He had to read the words without having any alien thoughts and in such a way that only he heard them and not those who were nearby. I, too, was a pious monk like this for about fifteen years. God forgive me for it!"

Thereupon somebody asked, "Are there other reasons than adoration [of the host] for abolishing elevation?" He answered, "I know no other."

The former suggested, "Doctor, in places where the gospel has not been preached so long one might tolerate this patiently and not abolish elevation, especially where the people are not yet established in their faith." The doctor replied, "Yes, it's of little consequence to us. We don't care if it's abolished or not, provided the abuse—that is, the adoration—is not there. Some churches have seen that we have dropped the elevation [in Wittenberg] and have imitated us. We are pleased with that."

---

[126] Text in brackets from a later variant. For a description of *tenūphā* (wave offering) and *terūmāh* (heave offering), see James Hastings (ed.), *A Dictionary of the Bible* (4 vols.; Edinburgh, 1898-1902), II, 588.

[127] Frederick Myconius (1490-1546), a former Franciscan, was one of the earliest followers of Luther and helped to introduce the Reformation into Albertine Saxony after the death there of Duke George.

The Necessity of the Sacrament Not Absolute
Spring, 1543   *No. 5596*

When he was asked whether it was enough for a person to confess his sins and believe in absolution and not use the sacrament [of the altar], he [Martin Luther] replied, "No! It is stated in the words of institution, 'Do this in remembrance of me' [I Cor. 11:25]. Everything that is required of a Christian must be in the sacrament: acknowledgment of sin (which we call contrition), faith, giving of thanks, confession. These things must not be separated from one another."

Then somebody said, "Doctor, if it's always necessary to use the sacrament, then those under the papacy did wrong, and still do wrong in our time, who are content with private absolution and don't make use of the sacrament, although they could have it in their neighborhood." [128]

To this he responded, "That's different! There necessity excuses them."

Love in Relation to Men, Faith to God
Spring, 1543   *No. 5601*

"In their books and writings the sacramentarians[129] have pestered us with 'love.' They say to us, 'You Wittenbergers have no love.' But if one asks, 'What is love?' we are told that it means to be united in doctrine and to stop religious controversies. Yes, do you hear? There are two tables [of the Decalogue], the first and the second. Love belongs in the second table. It's superior to all other works there. On the other hand, [in the first table] it is commanded: 'Fear God. Listen to his Word.' The sacramentarians don't bother with this. 'He who loves father and mother more than me is not worthy of me' [Matt. 10:37], said Christ. You should have love for your parents, for your children. Love, love! Be good

---

[128] The reference here is to evangelicals living in Catholic territories where only "the abomination of the mass" was available. Luther repeatedly advised such people to avoid the sacrament altogether. Cf. No. 4451.
[129] Cf. No. 314, n. 139.

to your father and mother! However, 'he who loves them more than me.' When this 'me' comes, love stops. Accordingly I'm glad to be called obstinate, proud, headstrong, uncharitable, and whatever else they call me. Just so I'm not a participant [in their doctrine]. God keep me from that!"

TABLE TALK RECORDED BY JEROME BESOLD

1544

INTRODUCTION

The pieces numbered 5659 to 5675 in WA, TR 5 are believed to have come from the pen of Jerome Besold in the year 1544, and about half of these have been selected for inclusion in this edition. Besold undoubtedly took more notes of the conversation at Luther's table than are here attributed to him, but only these few can be credited to him with any assurance.

Jerome Besold, born in Nürnberg in 1520, was matriculated at Wittenberg in 1537. Armed with recommendations from Veit Dietrich, he was welcomed into Luther's house and lived there from 1542 until the Reformer's death in 1546. In this year he returned to his native city, first as a teacher and then as a preacher and pastor. Together with his father-in-law Andrew Osiander, he gave up his position in protest against the Interim, a temporary political agreement in 1548 according to which Catholic rites and ceremonies were reintroduced in evangelical churches, but he was soon restored to his office. Besold completed the preparation for the press of Luther's lectures on Genesis after death interrupted Veit Dietrich's work on this project. In 1562, when he was only forty-two years old, death also claimed Besold during the pestilence which raged in Nürnberg.

Although there is good reason to believe that Besold took notes on Luther's conversation, as his correspondence with Veit Dietrich indicates, there is no compelling evidence that the particular pieces that follow originated with him. They are attributed to him partly because his name was mentioned by John Mathesius as the man who, after Caspar Heydenreich, was among the last to take notes at Luther's table.[1]

---

[1] See pp. 367-368.

TABLE TALK RECORDED BY JEROME BESOLD

Criticism of Schwenckfeld's Christology

1544   *No. 5659*

Schwenckfeld[1] had sent the doctor [Martin Luther] his booklet about the creatureliness of Christ, the title of which is *Of the Glory*.[2] The doctor said, "That's a poor wretch who doesn't have talent or spirit. Like all the fanatics, he's ecstatic. He doesn't know what he's talking about. However, this is his opinion and his principle: One shouldn't worship the creature because it is written, 'You shall worship the Lord your God and him only shall you serve' [Matt. 4:10]. Then he thinks, 'Christ is a creature and therefore I shouldn't worship Christ as a human being.' He invents two Christs. He maintains that after the ascension and glorification Christ was transformed into the Godhead. Hence he should be worshiped, but Schwenckfeld befouls the people who bear the glorious name of Christ, and does so, as he writes, to the glory of Christ! Children recite without being offended, 'I believe in Jesus Christ, his only Son, our Lord, who was conceived by the Holy Spirit,' etc.[3] So the fool makes two Christs: one who hangs on the cross, and another who ascends to his Father. He says I'm not to worship the Christ who hangs on the cross, who walks on the earth.

---

[1] Caspar Schwenckfeld (1498-1561), a nobleman in Silesia, left his native land in 1529, after he had been influenced by the Reformation. He came into conflict with Luther, especially concerning the Lord's Supper and Christology. He found some support for his views among the Swabian aristocracy, but his free-church spiritualism was not conducive to the organization of churches. In the eighteenth century some of his adherents found their way to America and formed a few congregations in eastern Pennsylvania.

[2] Cf. E. E. S. Johnson *et al.* (eds.), *Corpus Schwenckfeldianorum* (19 vols.; Leipzig: Breitkopf & Härtel, 1907-1961), VIII, 685-723. Cf. also Paul L. Maier, *Caspar Schwenckfeld on the Person and Work of Christ* (Assen: Van Gorcum, 1959).

[3] Words from the Apostles' Creed with which children were familiar.

Yet Christ allowed himself to be worshiped when that man[4] fell down before him, and Christ himself said, 'He who believes in me believes in him who sent me' [John 12:44]. The fantastic fellow stole some phrases from my book, *The Last Words of David*.[5] With these—for example, 'exchange of attributes' and 'oneness of the person'—the simpleton tries to make himself look nice. He mixes these phrases among others and afterward he says, 'That's what I meant too!'

"When he came from Silesia he tried to persuade Dr. Pomeranus[6] and me that his view of the sacrament is right. Since he couldn't hear well he asked us to pray for him. Yes, I wanted to pray that he become dumb as well! At all events, he now proposes to teach me what Christ is and how I should worship him. Thank God, I know this better than he does. I know my Christ well. So he'd better let me alone."

Katy[7] interrupted, "Ah, dear Sir, that's much too coarse!" And he [Martin Luther] replied, "They are the ones who teach me to be so coarse. This is the way one must talk to the devil. Let him renounce his fanaticism about the sacrament in a public writing and let him bring me testimonials from Dr. Hess[8] and Moibanus.[9] Otherwise I won't believe him, even if he swears an oath and puts his finger in the wound." [10]

He [Martin Luther] gave the following answer to the messenger: "My dear messenger, give your master, Caspar Schwenckfeld, the answer that I have received the little book and the letter.[11] Would to God that he'd stop! For in former times he started a fire against the sacraments in Silesia, and it hasn't been extinguished yet, but it will burn against him forever. He goes even further with

---

[4] Probably the doubting Thomas. Cf. John 20:24-29.
[5] *Von den letzten Worten Davids* (1543). WA 54, 28-100.
[6] John Bugenhagen, of Pomerania. Cf. No. 122, n. 36.
[7] Luther's wife Katherine. Cf. No. 49, n. 1.
[8] John Hess (1490-1547), pastor in Breslau.
[9] Ambrose Moibanus (1494-1554), also pastor in Breslau.
[10] Cf. John 20:27.
[11] On October 12, 1543, Schwenckfeld had sent Luther a long letter in which he expounded his Christology (cf. WA, Br 10, 420-429) and also sent along some of his booklets. See also above, n. 1.

his Eutychianism[12] and creatureliness and confuses the church, although God hasn't commanded him or sent him. The stupid fool, who is possessed by the devil, has no understanding, and doesn't know what he's mumbling about. If he won't stop, at least let him not bother me with his books, which the devil is spitting up and spewing out of him. Let him have this as my final judgment and answer:[13] The Lord rebuke you, Satan! And the spirit who called you, the course which you take, and all the sacramentarians[14] and Eutychians who side with you in your blasphemies—to hell with you! As it is written, 'I did not send the prophets, yet they ran; I did not speak to them, yet they prophesied' [Jer. 23:21]."

Can the Minister Affect the Sacrament?
1544 *No. 5661*

[The question was asked] whether it would be permissible to receive the sacrament from a minister who himself thinks and teaches that the body and blood [of Christ] are not in the sacrament, but Christ is present spiritually, as he is present everywhere in his grace. Some say Yes on the ground that there should be no respect of persons or of the worthiness of those who administer the sacrament. Dr. Martin [Luther] said No on the ground that in this instance it is not the worthiness of the person but the thing itself that would cease.

"There's no sacrament there," he said. "Likewise if the minister doesn't observe the sacrament in the right way, the people dare not act contrary to the Christ who shed his blood for them. O Lord God, anybody who can't believe that Christ is in the bread, in the grain of wheat, will believe the creation even less! That all of creation was made from nothing is a higher article of faith. Much less will he believe that God became man, and least of all that there are three persons in one substance. Reason lets this

---

[12] The teaching of Eutyches, who was excommunicated in 448 for maintaining that in the incarnation the human nature of Christ was absorbed into the divine and that therefore Christ only seemed to be a man.

[13] A later variant suggests that what follows was written by Luther in his own hand.

[14] Cf. No. 314, n. 139.

alone. It's an easy thing for me to believe that the body of Christ is in the bread, but it's hard to believe that so many excellent bodies in heaven and on earth should have come from nothing. I can't comprehend this. It's impossible for me. Much less can I comprehend that the Son was born of the Virgin Mary and that the other two persons [of the Trinity] did not become incarnate. If people are offended by this article, if they don't learn the ABC's, how will they learn their Donatus?[15] The article of creation is a lofty thing which no man can comprehend. So the Holy Scriptures remain hidden to the clever and the wise, as St. Paul said [I Cor. 1:18–2:13]. If they don't believe this, the consequence will quickly follow. The Word of God—no, God himself—is seated at the right hand of the Father, and yet I am here in the living Word of God. 'In him we live and move and have our being' [Acts 17:28]. Where, then, will my life remain?"

The Church, the Lawyers, and Dismantled Monasteries
1544   *No. 5663*

Somebody objected that our princes embraced the gospel in order that they might seize church property. He [Martin Luther] responded, "The contrary is true. It's Ferdinand[16] and the emperor[17] and the bishop of Mainz[18] who do that. Ferdinand has imposed a tax on all monasteries,[19] and the diocese of Würzburg recently had to pay ten thousand florins for that tax. The emperor has taken possession of the bishopric of Utrecht.[20] The Bavarians are the greatest plunderers; they have rich monasteries there too. My lord[21] and the landgrave[22] have poor mendicant houses, to

---

[15] The Latin grammar by Aelius Donatus, who lived in the fourth century, was so widely used at the close of the Middle Ages that his name had become synonymous with grammar.
[16] Ferdinand was king of Austria. Cf. No. 206, n. 77.
[17] Emperor Charles V.
[18] Cardinal Albrecht, archbishop of Mainz. Cf. No. 1362, n. 65.
[19] Probably the special tax to support the war against the Turks.
[20] Emperor Charles V had taken possession of the government of the diocese of Utrecht in 1528.
[21] Elector John Frederick of Saxony. Cf. No. 3468, n. 6.
[22] Landgrave Philip of Hesse. Cf. No. 3514, n. 60.

which they even have to contribute. Maurice[23] has three monasteries that amount to something.

"This is the general opinion: that the papists would like to have a foothold in the land through the monasteries. When it was proposed at the diet[24] to deliver up the monasteries to the emperor so that he could place his captains in them, I proposed, and would still propose, that it would be better to tear the monasteries down. Who would tolerate an imperial officer in his land? It's the bishop of Mainz's doing. The same fellows would like to have got the upper hand over the monasteries. So they would have done the same thing that the pope did, who has devoured all the monasteries in Italy and all the abbies. Since they can't have it [a similar arrangement here], they cry out, 'One should leave the property to the emperor; do him the honor!' No, I tell you! We owe the property to godly and learned men, to schoolmasters, to schools. The lawyers are also crying: 'The property belongs to the church! Return the monasteries to the church so that there may be monks and nuns and that mass may be held; they'll also let you preach.'

"Yes, where will we get our support?

"'We'll let you worry about that,' they say.

"Yes, the devil thank them for it.

"We theologians have no worse enemies than the lawyers. If one asks, 'What is the church?' they answer, 'It's an assembly of bishops, abbots, etc., and those are properties of the church; therefore they belong to the bishops.' This is their logic. No, we have a different logic at the right hand of the Father, and this says that they are tyrants, wolves, and robbers. Consequently we condemn all the lawyers on this score, even the godly ones, because they don't know what the church is. Even if they pore over all their books, they won't discover what the church is. Accordingly they shouldn't try to reform us here. Every lawyer is either a good-for-nothing or a know-nothing. If a lawyer wants to dispute this, tell him, 'You hear? A lawyer shouldn't talk until a sow breaks wind!' Then he should say, 'Thank you, dear grandmother, I haven't

---

[23] Duke Maurice (Moritz) of Albertine Saxony (1521-1553) succeeded Duke George; cf. No. 4509.

[24] The imperial Diet of Spires in 1544.

heard a sermon for a long time!' They shouldn't teach us what 'church' means. There's an old proverb: 'A lawyer's a bad Christian.' And it's true."

No Need for One External Head in the Church
1544   *No. 5666*

Against Amerbach[25] and like men who wish to establish the Roman pontiff as the external head in the church [Martin Luther] said, "Greece has never been under the pope, nor have India or Scythia, as Jerome[26] wrote, although there were many godly Christians there. Where do they get the rotten argument that the church ought to have an external head in Rome? All of history is against it. All of the West has not been under the pope, nor has all of the East. It's nothing but pride on Amerbach's part. O Lord God, a man who falls away in this way suffers a fall above all falls! I'm sorry for him because he will happen upon other misfortunes. Men like this are poor people who don't think of the last hour which will befall them."

Man Should Be Different from an Animal
1544   *No. 5671*

"Human nature must be far, far superior to brute nature, for there's no animal, no matter how strong and wild it may be, that isn't afraid of man and thinks, 'It is written, Have dominion over every living thing' [Gen. 1:28]. That a man should live like a pig doesn't agree at all with his nature as one who has dominion. It's characteristic of the pig to obtain things not by work but by accident. This isn't what is written about man, but 'Do something! Be a part of the government in political and economic matters! Have dominion! Have dominion! Don't be a lazy man! Don't devour what other people gather!'

"Cicero's argument from the conversation of species is a beau-

---

[25] Veit Amerbach (1503–1557), an evangelical who relapsed into the Roman church, was at this time professor in Ingolstadt.
[26] Cf. No. 51, n. 2.

tiful one: An apple tree doesn't become a pear tree, a cow doesn't become an ass, etc.; therefore it's necessary to conclude that the world is ruled by divine providence.[27] Against the alchemists Aristotle said, 'Let them enjoy the genera and species.'[28] No, nobody will make it otherwise: an ox remains an ox, a man a man, etc.

"If I had lived at the time of Epicurus[29] and had been a wicked scoundrel, I would like to have played a trick on him. I would have taken his wife and child and put them to shame. Then I would have said, 'Oh, there's no divine providence! God doesn't care about this. Look out for it yourself!' Cicero was an excellent philosopher because he worked very hard, even if he didn't reach his goal. He will sit much higher [in the world to come] than Duke George[30] or the margrave,[31] who died between two whores. Oh, if they sat where Cicero does they would be saved!"

Legends of Saints Are Full of Lies
1544 No. 5674

"It's a singular calamity from the devil that we have no legend of a saint that's untainted. The legends of the saints are so full of shameful lies that it's astonishing. It takes hard work to correct them."

He [Martin Luther] was at that time reading the legend of St. Catherine,[32] and he said, "This is in conflict with all of Roman history. Maxentius[33] drowned in the Tiber at Rome and never got to Alexandria. Maximinus[34] was there, and one can read about him in Eusebius.[35] Since the time of Julius Caesar,[36] and long before,[37]

---

[27] Cicero, *De natura deorum*, 2, 29-30. Cf. No. 5440.
[28] Aristotle, *Posterior Analytics*, 1, 83.
[29] Cf. No. 466, n. 267.
[30] On the death of Duke George of Albertine Saxony, see No. 4509.
[31] Margrave Joachim I of Brandenburg.
[32] The feast of Catherine of Alexandria was November 25.
[33] Marcus Aurelius Valerius Maxentius was Roman emperor from A.D. 306 to 312.
[34] Galerius Valerius Maximinus was Roman emperor from A.D. 308 to 314.
[35] Eusebius, *Ecclesiastical History*, 8, 14.
[36] Caius Julius Caesar (100-44 B.C.).
[37] I.e., before the time of Catherine, who was a daughter of a king of Egypt, according to the legend.

there was no king in Egypt. It must have been a desperate scoundrel who so troubled Christendom with such lies. Surely he must be sitting at the bottom of hell.

"We used to believe such monstrous things and didn't dare utter a sound against them, even if we recognized them as such; but we didn't. Therefore give thanks to our Lord God, you young fellows, and be godly, so that you don't some day believe such things or even more outrageous ones!"

Luther's Last Observation Left in a Note[38]
February 16, 1546 No. 5677

"Nobody can understand Vergil in his *Bucolics* and *Georgics*[39] unless he has first been a shepherd or a farmer for five years.

"Nobody understands Cicero[40] in his letters unless he has been engaged in public affairs of some consequence for twenty years.

"Let nobody suppose that he has tasted the Holy Scriptures sufficiently unless he has ruled over the churches with the prophets for a hundred years. Therefore there is something wonderful, first, about John the Baptist; second, about Christ; third, about the apostles. 'Lay not your hand on this divine Aeneid, but bow before it, adore its every trace.' [41]

"We are beggars. That is true."

These were the last thoughts of Dr. Martin Luther on the day before he died.

---

[38] Two versions, each a little different from the other, of this note left behind by Luther at his death, are extant. Who recorded No. 5677, translated here, is not certain. The other version, No. 5468, begins: When he was in Eisleben in 1546 and had only two days to live, Dr. Martin Luther wrote these words in Latin on a slip of paper and left it lying on his table. I, John Aurifaber, made a copy of it, and Dr. Justus Jonas, the superintendent in Halle who was also present in Eisleben [when Luther died], kept the paper.

[39] Vergil was the greatest of the Latin poets (70-19 B.C.); his *Bucolics* are poems about the life of shepherds and his *Georgics* are poems about agriculture and farmers.

[40] Cf. No. 3528, n. 84.

[41] Cf. Publius Papinius Statius, *Thebais*, XII, 816-817.

INDEXES

INDEX OF NAMES AND SUBJECTS

Aachen, 240
Absolution, 104, 334, 394-395, 463
Adoration, 102
Adrian VI, 450
Adultery, 24, 66, 154, 160, 218, 244, 302, 315, 335, 349, 415
Aegidius of Viterbo, 208
Aesop, 72, 210-213
Africanus, Julius, 421
Agricola, John, 23, 191, 220, 233, 248, 290, 313-314, 379, 391
Aland, Kurt, xv
Albrecht of Brandenburg, margrave, 191
Albrecht of Mainz, archbishop, 60, 86, 144, 171, 230, 256, 265, 310, 357, 370, 380, 387, 405, 441, 472
Albrecht of Mansfeld, count, 233, 272-273
Alexander V, 81
Alexander VI, 230
Alexander the Great, 64
Allegory, 46-47, 406
Altenstaig, John, 8
Ambrose, 8, 26, 34, 259, 335, 353, 460
Amerbach, Veit, 474
Amsdorf, Nicholas, xxiii, 150, 214, 219, 226, 264, 321, 391
Anabaptists, 48, 113, 140, 152, 163, 174, 318, 376
Angels, 172
Anselm of Canterbury, 84
Antichrist, 101, 346, 347
Antinomianism, 233, 248, 289-290, 308-309, 313-314, 391
Apology of the Augsburg Confession, 187, 358
Apostles' Creed, 9, 17, 333
Aquinas, Thomas, 12, 38, 39, 264
Arians, 41
Aristotle, 61, 184, 243, 307, 423, 475
Arius, 36, 60, 259, 314, 333
Arnoldi of Usingen, Bartholomew, 127
Articles, Six, 384
Astrology, 33, 172-173, 219-220, 416-417, 449, 458
Athanasius, 314
Augsburg, 39, 182, 231, 285, 331, 375, 381, 417
Augsburg Confession, 34, 39, 137, 139, 186-187, 355-356, 358, 362
Augustine, 10, 18, 26, 34, 49, 50, 61, 111, 177, 242, 259-260, 270, 309, 315, 329, 337, 340, 344, 352, 377, 401, 454
Augustinians, 18, 30, 44
Augustus, 331, 375
Aurifaber, Andrew, 269, 324
Aurifaber, John, xi-xix, xxiii-xxv, 8, 20-22, 30, 61, 84, 88, 133, 135, 143, 389, 397
Authority, civil (*see* Government, civil)
Authority, parental, 67
Authorship of Genesis, 373

Bainton, Roland H., 43
Baptism, 20, 287, 358, 425, 460-461
 infant, 55-57, 98, 113, 242
 prenatal, 61
Barge, Hermann, 107
Barnes, Robert, 384
Bartolus de Sassoferrato, 361
Basil the Great, 34, 353
Bavaria, 336, 392

Bavarians, 310, 387, 472
Beer, 132, 172, 178
Begging, 20
Belgum, Gerhard, xxii, 54, 362, 406
Bell, Henry, xv
Bembo, Pietro, 208
Benedict of Nursia, 270
Bernard of Clairvaux, 84, 105, 353, 407
Berndt, Ambrose, 419
Besold, Jerome, xii, 368, 467
Beyer, Leonard, 194, 334
Biel, Gabriel, 264
Bigamy, 379, 382, 387, 390 (*see also* Digamy)
Bindseil, Heinrich Ernst, xiii
Birds, 192
Bishops, 287, 288, 299, 333, 380, 441, 473
Black Cloister, ix, 46, 132, 181, 193, 267
Blank, Christopher, 214
Blasphemy, 373
Boccaccio, Giovanni, xxii, 208
Boehmer, Heinrich, xxii
Bohemia, 40, 367
Bohemians, 48, 220, 352, 367, 387, 394
Boineburg, Ludwig von, 381
Bonaventure, 112, 264
Boniface VIII, 239
Books, 141, 163, 213, 274, 292, 311, 326, 342, 361, 387, 440
Bora, Hans von, 370
Bora, Katherine von (*see* Luther, Katherine)
Bowling, 320
Brandenburg, 407
Brenz, John, 50, 311, 376, 383, 391
Brück, Gregory, 139, 150, 228, 274, 322, 387, 391, 444
Brunet, Gustave, xv
Brutus, 247
Bucer, Martin, 25, 196, 205, 262, 282, 376, 379, 383, 417
Buchwald, Georg, 37
Buchwald, Reinhard, xxvi
Bünau, Günther von, 135
Bugenhagen, John, ix, xxi, 15, 23, 49, 52, 75, 89, 142, 156, 158, 180, 214-217, 231, 257, 271, 305, 316, 374, 386, 393, 416, 428, 443, 461, 470
Bullinger, Henry, 89
Butcher, 188

Caesar, Julius, 79, 247, 307, 314, 375, 475
Cajetan (Thomas de Vio of Gaeta), 285, 443
Calendar, 307, 458
Caligula, 278
Callistus, St., 209
Camerarius, Joachim, 319
Camers, John, 377
Campeggio, Lorenzo, 215
Cannons, 232
Carneades, 322
Castration, 177
Catechism, 163, 235, 258
Catherine of Alexandria, 475
Cato, Dionysius, 211
Causes, 399-400
Celibacy, 141-142, 218, 270, 335, 338, 357, 393
Cellarius, John, 196, 293, 364, 405
Ceremonies, 49, 68, 195, 333, 360-361, 397, 436
Cerinthus, 445

478

INDEX

Certainty, 18, 182, 455
Chalice, 417
Charles V, 28, 143, 182, 229, 299, 330, 336, 338, 356, 370, 417, 472
Children, 157-158, 163, 177, 234-235, 245, 267, 296, 300, 334-335, 339, 355-356, 424, 429, 433
Christ, 35-36, 42, 45, 79, 84, 92, 111, 143, 146, 154, 371, 378-379, 469-471
Christian II of Denmark, 285
Christian III of Denmark, 271
Christmas, 248-249, 326-327, 420
Chrysostom, John, 33, 305
Church, 78-79, 119, 130, 185, 195, 261-262, 265, 268, 291, 299, 307, 344, 421-422, 473
Cicero, 136, 171, 190, 223, 241, 243, 246-247, 289, 295, 306, 325, 423, 474-476
Cilli, Barbara of, 220
Circumcision, 55-57
Clemen, Otto, xxvi
Clement VII, 140, 143
Coburg, 11, 196
Cochlaeus, John, 71, 94, 137, 262, 351
Coelius, Michael, 27, 297
Cologne, 271-272, 275
Comestor, Peter, 26
Compostella (Santiago), 148, 238, 247
Concubines, 135, 230, 243
Confession, 394, 402, 404
  seal of, 395
Confutation, Roman, 137, 187, 355
Conscience, 25, 64, 66, 395, 442
Consecration, 119, 244
Constance, 215, 263, 372, 443
Copernicus, Nicholas, 358-359
Cordatus, Conrad, x, xi, xiii, xvi, 5, 24, 121, 133, 140, 145, 169, 207, 393, 408
Corpus Christi, 19
Council, 215-216, 230-231, 261-263, 273, 291, 332-333, 356-357, 441
Cranach, Lucas, the Elder, 153, 217, 222, 267, 344, 435
  the Younger, 444
Cranz, F. Edward, 180
Creation, 44, 200, 245, 297, 327, 377, 400
Crodel, Marcus, 448
Cross, sign of the, 462
Cruciger, Caspar, xiii, 268, 344, 360
Cyprian, 357

Dancing, 76, 207, 222
Day, last, 27, 128, 134, 402, 427-428, 437
Death, 33, 65, 145, 165, 190, 227, 238, 295-296, 298, 312, 319, 336, 349-350, 415, 429-433, 448
Defense, 279
Degree, academic, 54, 320
Demonology, 298
Demons, 172
Demosthenes, 223
Denmark, 257, 271, 305
Deposition, 290, 362-363
Devil, 16, 24, 29, 34, 51, 78, 82, 83, 86, 93-94, 96, 105, 128-129, 151, 241, 275-276, 279-280, 298, 313, 318, 379, 397, 453
Didymus, Gabriel (Zwilling), 244
Diet, 277
Dietrich, Veit, xii, xvi, xix, xxiii, 5, 23, 26, 30, 31, 59, 75, 79, 82, 95, 97, 102, 111, 125, 147, 156, 169, 225, 367, 383, 467
Digamy, 243
Dillenberger, John, 358
Dionysius the Areopagite, 112
Discipline, 157, 235, 457
Divorce, 349
Doberstein, John W., 72
Doctrine, 110, 422, 463
Dölen, Bernard von, 235
Dog, 37, 175, 188, 421
Dolzig, Hans von, 26

Dominic, 353
Dominicans, 261
Donatus, Aelius, 211, 235, 472
Doubt, 59, 61
Dreams, 18, 89-90
Drechsel, 455
Drinking, 18, 20, 76, 205-206, 210, 219
Drought, 192
Drunkenness, 205-207, 219, 278, 295, 371
Duefel, Hans, 341
Durant, Will, 278
Dutch, 387

Easter, 307
Eck, John, 35, 54, 137, 197, 259, 351, 415, 441, 445
Eells, Hastings, 25
Egranus, John Silvius, 401-402
Eisleben, 19
Elert, Werner, 358
Elevation, 408, 426, 461-462
England, 332, 346, 384, 402
English, 151, 309, 317, 328
Ephesus, 333
Epicurus, 78, 475
Epitaph, 227, 238
Equity, 44, 325, 369
Erasmus, Desiderius, xxii, 13, 19, 50, 68-69, 71, 73, 77, 81, 84, 136, 147, 189, 245, 247, 292, 311, 401, 417
Erfurt, 15, 24, 29
Erikson, Erik H., 193, 234
Ernest of Saxony, 286
Eusebius of Caesarea, 274, 305
Euthanasia, 397
Eutyches, 471
Excommunication, 159, 185, 346, 398, 404, 422, 423
Experience, 7, 274, 320, 338, 371, 375

Faber, John, 27, 137, 351, 373, 415
Faith, 39, 74, 104, 157, 290, 453, 456, 460
Fall, 224, 426
Famine, 344-345
Fasting, 178, 338-339, 357
Fausel, Heinrich, xxvi
Faustus, Johannes, 241
Fear, 149
Fellowship, 268, 276, 307
Fend, Melchior, 154
Ferdinand I, 28, 46, 139, 143, 152, 159, 269, 380-381, 405, 416-417, 472
Firearms, 232, 419
Fish, 199-200, 267
Flemings, 310
Florence, 296
Förstemann, Karl Eduard, xiii
Forgiveness, 16, 34, 43, 51, 69-70
Forstemius, 176
Forster, John, xiii, 300, 304, 446
France, 306, 382, 402, 421
Francis I, 143, 299
Francis of Assisi, 270
Franciscans, 261
Franconians, 387
Frankfurt-am-Main, 330-331
Frederick the Wise of Saxony, 19, 54, 164, 180, 194-195, 338
Freiberg, 134
Freitag, Albert, 117
French, 151, 306, 309, 348
Fröschel, Sebastian, 316
Fugger, Anton, 28

Gambling, 206
Games, 221-222
George of Brandenburg, margrave, 60
George of Saxony, duke, xvii, 38, 60, 71, 82, 86, 93-94, 104, 111, 159, 181, 185, 239, 265, 273, 282, 285, 336, 349-350, 352, 360, 370, 379-382, 460
Gericke, Cyriacus, 292

479

German, 311, 348, 376
Germans, 151, 262, 265, 278, 291, 309, 332, 371, 373
Germany, 229, 278, 306, 347
Gerrish, B. A., 183
Gerson, Jean, 42, 133, 142, 443
Ghost, 258
God, 69, 72, 73, 75, 78, 127-128, 155, 269, 423, 429
  knowledge of, 34, 35
  omnipresence of, 32
  service of, 84
  speech of, 88
  wrath of, 15, 34, 190, 270, 308, 420
Göde, Henning, 140, 246, 269
Goetze, E., 450
Goldstein, Kilian, 364
Gospel, 42, 106, 111, 127, 147, 157, 275-276, 344, 402, 404, 427
Gospel, Last, 435
Gotha, 374, 383
Government, civil, 179, 199, 307, 315, 363, 395 (*see also* Magistrate)
Grass, Hans, 407
Gratian, 26
Greece, 402, 474
Greek, 310, 373, 376
Gregory VII, 407
Gregory XIII, 307
Gregory of Nazianzus, 353
Gregory the Great, 8, 26, 85, 104, 259, 347
Greifenklau, Richard von, 139
Grisar, Hartmann, xxii
Grünenberg, Hans, 141
Gypsies, 234

Hausmann, Nicholas, 24, 145, 319
Hazlitt, William, xv, xviii, xx
Headley, John M., 407
Heaven, 416
Hebrew, 43, 348, 376
Henry IV, emperor, 407
Henry VIII of England, 284-285, 317, 362, 384, 387, 420
Henry of Braunschweig/Wolfenbüttel, 217, 279, 370, 373, 406
Heresy, 41
Herodotus, 155
Herte, Adolf, 137
Hess, John, 470
Hessians, 310, 331
Heydenreich, Caspar, xiii, 368, 413
Hilary, 26, 34, 271
Hill, Charles L., 260
Hippolytus, 306
History, 407
Hofmann, Hans, 381
Hohndorf, John, 54, 188, 281
Holmio, Armas K. E., 239
Holy year, 239, 240
Hoppe, A. F., xiv, xv
Horace, 249
Hospitals, 296
Hoyer of Mansfeld, count, 272
Hudson, Hoyt H., 136
Hungarians, 311
Hungary, 402
Hunting, 279, 313
Huss, John, 40, 81, 83, 94, 110, 220, 372

Icarus, 65
Idleness, 281, 295
Immortality, 401, 447
India, 474
Indulgences, 160, 174, 264, 324, 341, 342
Interest, 316, 369, 398
Italians, 140, 151, 207, 256, 262, 266, 296, 309-310
Italy, 229, 238, 265 291-292, 306, 402

Jagow, Matthias, 219
James, Epistle of, 424-425

Jerome, 8, 33, 44, 47, 49, 72, 104, 177, 259, 270, 274, 357, 474
Jerome of Prague, 372
Jerusalem, 238
Jester, court, 194, 334
Jews, 43, 208, 209, 238, 241, 306, 340, 348, 373, 420, 426, 434, 436-437, 455
Joachim I of Brandenburg, 359, 475
Joachim II of Brandenburg, 62, 86, 219, 336
Job, 79
John of Anhalt, 279
John of Küstrin, 263
John of Saxony, elector, 54, 180, 182, 194, 217, 228, 372
John Frederick of Saxony, elector, 164, 218, 226, 233, 239, 255, 257, 263, 270, 272, 283, 345, 388, 456, 472
Jonas, Justus, ix, xiii, 49, 136, 138, 155, 184, 222, 287, 294, 319, 421, 428, 451
Josquin de Prez, 130
Jubilee year, 239-240
Judgment, last (*see* Day, last)
Julius II, 136, 347
Justification, 10, 68, 176, 240, 328, 329, 348, 359, 456, 457
Justinian I, 320
Juvenal, 330

Kaaden, 381
Karg, George, 255
Karlstadt, Andrew, xxii, 51, 54, 60, 64-65, 81, 91, 107, 147, 174, 232, 245, 284, 318, 379, 415
Katzenelnbogen, 380
Kaufmann, Andrew, 439
Kaufmann, George, 205
Kepler, Thomas S., xv
Kingdoms, two, 199
Kling, Melchior, 214, 425
Koeckeritz, Caspar von, 236, 319
Köhler, Franz, 38
Kooiman, Willem J., 13, 440
Kraft, John, xiii
Krapp, Katharine, 224
Krause, John, 106
Kroker, Ernst, xvi, 117, 136, 253, 367

Laity, 120, 323
Lang, Matthew, 442
Latimer, Hugh, 332
Latin, ix-xxii, 235, 376
Latomus (*see* Masson, Jacobus)
Laurence, St., 300
Lauterbach, Anthony, xii, xiv, xvi, xvii, xxvi, 157, 203, 253, 257, 277, 287, 316, 319, 359, 368, 396
Law, 10, 42, 43, 106, 111, 127, 222, 232, 241-242, 246, 248, 275-276, 293, 313-315, 325, 349, 404
  canon, 14, 144
  natural, 67, 103, 293
Lawyer, 21, 66, 69, 103, 128, 131, 144, 150-151, 214, 236, 243, 246, 274, 320, 375, 449, 473-474
Lazareth, William H., 192
Left-wing, 43
Legends of saints, 475
Lehmann, Helmut T., 407
Lehmann, Martin, 49
Leipzig, 197, 256, 350, 360
Life, future, 41, 291, 297-298, 326, 400-401
Link, Wenceslaus, 383
Lochau, 308
Löffel, Martin, 369
Loeser, Hans, 184, 225, 400
Lohse, Bernhard, 341
Loi, Balthasar, 294
Lord's Supper, 12, 25, 45, 58, 89, 91-92, 100, 113, 196, 199, 231, 284, 311, 342, 345-346, 350, 394, 407, 417, 438, 459-460, 463, 471

INDEX

Lotther, Melchior, Jr., 141
Love, 28, 70, 74, 223, 463, 464
Lucan, Marcus Annaeus, 332
Lucullus, Lucius Licinius, 163
Ludovicus of Bologna, 208
Lufft, Hans, 269
Lunn, Arnold, 154
Luther, Elizabeth, 33, 433
Luther, Hans, 27, 109
Luther, James, 297
Luther, John, 9, 29, 157, 163, 190, 448
Luther, Katherine, née von Bora, 22, 25, 62, 89, 90, 127, 145, 153, 162, 165, 174, 191, 199, 216, 222, 226, 228, 258, 270, 317, 319, 369, 374, 384, 396, 415, 428-431, 447, 448, 470
Luther, Magdalene, 9, 428-433
Luther, Margaret, 434
Luther, Martin
  birth of, 458
  childhood of, 235
  collected works of, 274, 311
  correspondence of, 206
  entrance into monastery, 14, 109, 234
  excommunication of, 30
  expectation of death, 133, 134, 152-153
  false report of death, 238
  first mass of, 156, 234, 325, 354
  illnesses of, 23, 154-155, 189, 225-228, 232, 237, 266, 293-295, 297, 314, 346, 374, 383, 448
  income of, 181
  journey to Rome, 208-209, 237, 296, 427
  lectures of, 207, 288
  as monk, 15, 85, 87, 95, 129, 182, 337-340
  parents of, 178, 188
  self-analysis of, 26, 50, 355, 387-388, 405
  as student, 14, 39, 127
  "tower experience" of, 193-194, 308-309, 442
  work of, 23, 382
  as writer, 83, 326, 342, 343
Luther, Martin, Jr., 150, 158-159, 162, 177, 334-335, 451
Lyra, Nicholas, 14

Macaronic, XIX-XX
McDonough, Thomas M., 107
Magdeburg, Liborius, 262
Magic, 58, 241
Magistrate, 28, 180 (*see also* Government, civil)
Maier, Paul L., 469
Major, George, 386
Manicheans, 36
Manilius, Marcus, 326
Manna, 146-147
Manschreck, Clyde L., 23, 260
Mansfeld, 287
Mantua, 215, 216, 222, 230
Mantuanus, 208
Marburg, 376
Margaret of Navarre, XXII
Margaritha, Antonius, 436
Marlowe, Christopher, 244
Marnholt, Ludolf, 417
Marriage, 24-25, 31, 64-67, 80, 138, 141-142, 151, 161, 171, 176-177, 181, 191, 194, 218, 222-224, 244, 271, 289, 294-295, 301-302, 305, 315, 324, 328, 337, 349, 363, 397, 415, 416, 422, 424, 441, 444, 449, 455-456, 459
Mary, 15, 32, 84-85, 247, 301, 329, 341, 420, 426
Mass, 13, 20, 161, 182, 215, 234, 264-266, 295, 324-325, 340, 354, 392-393, 461
Masson, Jacobus (Latomus), 77
Mathesius, John, X, XII, XVI-XVIII, XXII, 367, 369, 393, 405, 413
Maugis, Ferdinand von, XIII
Maurice of Saxony, duke, 473

Maxentius, Marcus Aurelius Valerius, 475
Maximilian I, 416, 420
Maximilian II, x, 213
Maximinus, Galerius Valerius, 475
Medicine, 53-54, 102-103, 237, 266, 277
Medler, Nicholas, XIII, 117, 147, 396
Meissen, 351, 386
Melancholy, 15-18, 74-75, 95-96, 203, 275-276
Melanchthon, Anna, 268
Melanchthon, Philip, IX, XI, 23, 24, 33-34, 44, 50, 54, 64, 79, 89, 132-133, 153, 155-156, 158, 162, 173, 184, 187, 191, 209, 214, 217, 219-220, 222, 224-225, 231, 233, 245-246, 257-258, 260, 268, 277, 287, 290-291, 319, 331, 355-356, 358, 360, 364, 371, 376-378, 380, 383, 387, 390, 393, 416, 431-432, 440, 442, 449, 454
Menius, Justus, 50
Metzsch, Hans, 47, 159, 220, 315, 345
Michalec, Martin, 45
Mickell, 398
Milich, Jacob, 268
Milk, 320-321
Miltitz, Karl von, 195
Minister, 37, 47-48, 395, 471
Ministry, 12, 80, 90, 100-101, 107, 318, 459
Minkwitz, George von, 205
Minkwitz, Wolfgang von, 172-173
Miracles, 111, 357, 358, 386
Misenus, Andrew, 403
Möller, Wilhelm, 107
Mörlin, Joachim, 383, 396
Moibanus, Ambrose, 470
Monastery, 234-235, 295, 312, 473
Monasticism, 134, 178
Monks, 68, 188, 268, 281, 304, 307, 327-328
Monica, 260, 454
Monner, Basilius, 245
Monstrosity, 44, 58
Moravia, 239
More, Thomas, 288, 362
Morolf, 389, 450
Moslem, 416
Mulert, Hermann, XXVI
Münster, Sebastian, 445
Münzer, Thomas, XXII, 41, 60, 86, 144, 233, 284, 379
Music, 130, 205-206, 246, 420
Muth, Conrad, 69
Myconius, Frederick, 374, 462

Nature, 24, 474
Naumburg, 190, 436
Neefe, John, 369
Nettl, Paul, 130
Neuheler, Jodocus, 233
Nicaea, 333
Ninety-five Theses, 286, 342
Norway, 271
Nürnberg, 82, 356
Nuns, 134, 188, 312

Obedience, 67
Oecolampadius, John, 12, 23, 75, 86, 95, 147, 173, 262, 376
Oertel, Veit, 257
Oesterreich, T. K., 298
Offense, 62, 73
Opponents, 445
Ordination, 100-101, 119, 359
Origen, 22, 47, 397
Oschatz, 38, 181
Osiander, Andrew, 107, 249, 290, 376, 382-383
Osterlandt, James, 279
Ovid, 150, 444

Pack, Otto von, 285
Palladius, Peter, 305
Parents, 355-356, 424, 432

481

Partridge, Eric, xxii
Pastor, Ludwig, 229
Patrimony of Peter, 347
Patripassians, 36
Pauck, Wilhelm, 393
Paul III, 219, 229
Pavia, 299
Peasants, 72, 132, 142, 152, 163, 180, 241, 282, 294, 435, 458
Peasants' War, 180, 390
Pederasty, 278
Pegis, Anton C., 39
Pelikan, Jaroslav, 81, 356
Perknowsky, Ignatius, 48-49, 59, 82, 92, 160, 173, 183
Pestilence, 15, 152, 345, 434-436
Peter Lombard, 26, 260, 440
Pfeffinger, Degenhart, 286, 334
Phaeton, 65
Philip of Hesse, landgrave, 218, 263, 284, 330, 350, 376, 379-382, 387-389, 472
Physician, 24, 51, 53-54, 102-103, 237, 266, 277, 293-294, 296
Pilgrimage, 238, 340-341, 422
Plato, 35, 112, 307, 322, 401
Plato, George, xiii, 368
Plautus, 14
Pluralism, 144
Podiebrad, George, 352
Poland, 402
Polner, Hans, 428
Poltergeist, 279, 280
Polygamy, 109 (see also Bigamy)
Ponikau, John von, 227-228
Pope, 13, 19, 41, 46, 48, 66, 130, 158, 185, 228-229, 263, 265, 286, 288, 291, 323, 330, 333, 343, 346-347, 421, 443, 474
Poverty, 132, 137
Prayer, 18, 38, 52-53, 85, 259, 340, 439, 454
Preacher, 31, 137-138, 180, 213, 214, 300, 384, 403-404, 428
Preaching, 90, 100, 157-158, 160, 179, 182, 192, 206, 235-236, 271, 282, 292, 383-384, 393, 396, 428
Predestination, 87, 90-91, 249, 385
Preger, Wilhelm, xvi, 125
Prenter, Regin, 91
Prices, high, 209-210
Prierias, Sylvester, 83, 263, 265
Printer, 141
Priscillian, 402
Prisoners, 269
Probst, Jacob, 338, 425 (see also Wiederkehrer, Heinz)
Proles, Andrew, 72
Property, 279, 299, 472-473
Providence, 475
Prudentius, Aurelius Clemens, 147
Purgatory, 259

Quanbeck, Warren A., 406

Rantzau, Paul, 418
Ravenna, 347
Reason, 60, 71, 105, 183-184, 323, 326, 377-378
Rebenstock, Henry Peter, xiv
Reformation, 231, 273, 356
Reissenbusch, Wolfgang, 83
Relics, 131, 247, 273, 288
Reu, M., 39, 440, 445
Reuchlin, John, 261, 445
Revenge, 301
Rhegius, Urbanus, 391
Rhinelanders, 387
Richenthal, Ulrich von, 215
Riches, 452
Ricius, Paul, 377
Rieder, Henry, 316, 398
Righteousness, 121, 193, 308-309, 324, 329, 348, 373-374, 403, 442
Rivius, John, 348

Rörer, George, xii, 117, 120, 150, 163, 392, 408, 431
Rome, 208-209, 237-238, 272, 286, 299, 332, 427
Rose, golden, 195
Rosheim, Josel, 239
Rossig, Gregory, 256
Rubeanus, Crotus, 108, 171
Ruccius, Walter M., 257
Rupp, Gordon, xv

Sabbatarians, 239
Sabbath, 51-52
Sabellius, 35
Sabinus, George, 268
Sachs, John, 429, 450-451
Sacramentarians, 43, 89, 91, 97, 100, 138, 162-163, 274, 284, 318, 390, 463, 471
Sacraments, 47, 119-120, 358, 394, 470 (see also Baptism, Lord's Supper)
Sacrifice, 139
Sadoleto, Jacopo, 329
Saints, 70, 92, 259, 260, 324, 340, 353, 475
Sale, Margaret von der, 379, 388, 390
Sasse, Hermann, 91
Satan (see Devil)
Saxons, 310, 331, 336, 351
Saxony, 402
Schadewald, Bartholomew, 434
Scheel, Otto, 193
Schenk, Jacob, 289, 313-314, 378, 391, 396
Scherl, Henry, 402
Schiefer, Wolfgang, x, 371-374, 376-377, 381-382
Schilling, John, 417
Schlaginhaufen, John, xii, xvi, xxiii, 5, 125, 129, 132, 149, 154-156, 164, 169
Schneidewein, Henry, 75, 265
Schönberg, Anthony von, 406
Schönberg, Nicholas von, 291, 406
Schönitz, Anthony von, 310
Scholastics, 9, 63, 249, 260, 264, 275, 290, 344, 352, 391-392
Schoolmasters 403-404, 459
Schools, 403-404, 452, 473
Schreiber, Clara S., 7
Schurff, Jerome, 150, 180, 236, 246, 262, 264, 275, 338
Schwärmer, 48, 50
Schwarz, W., 445
Schwarzerdt, George, 416
Schwenckfeld, Caspar, 186-187, 469
Schwolle, Jerome, 459
Scotus, John Duns, 38-39, 264
Scriptures, 13, 42-43, 50-51, 111, 121, 127, 165, 185, 198, 260, 344, 352-353, 361, 378, 392, 406, 408, 440-441, 446, 476
Scultetus, Jerome, 341
Scythia, 474
Seberger, Wolfgang, 22
Seidemann, Johann Karl, xvi, 253
Servants, 270, 337
Servetus, Michael, 32
Sex, 324, 422
Shakespeare, William, xxii
Sick, communion of the, 407
Sickingen, Francis von, 217
Sigismund, emperor, 220
Sin, 60-61, 321
 original, 20, 34, 37
Skeptic, 69
Skydsgaard, Kristen E., 356
Sleeplessness, 306
Smalcald, 225, 228, 231-232, 238, 266, 283, 321, 374, 383
Smalcald Articles, 215, 356
Smalcald League, 271, 362
Smith, Preserved, x, xxvi, 13
Socrates, 218
Solitude, 140, 203, 268, 277
Sophistry, 332
Sorcery, 241

482

INDEX

Soul, 297, 446-448
Spain, 402
Spalatin, George, 19, 195, 286, 334
Spaniards, 229, 269, 309, 332, 347
Spanish, 338
Speculation, 35, 44, 112
Speech, 317
Spiegel, Erasmus, 313
Spinka, Matthew, 142, 372
Spires (Speyer), 473
Spyridion, 271
Statius, Publius Papinius, 476
Staupitz, John, 11, 19, 30, 72, 94, 97, 133, 230, 320, 383, 406, 449
Stolt, Birgit, xxi
Stolz, John, xii
Stokes, F. G., 261
Strabo, Walafried, 14
Student, 179, 221, 287, 311, 320, 353, 362, 433
Stübner, Thomas, 455
Stupperich, Robert, 440
Sturtz, George, 294
Suetonius, 400
Suicide, 29
Sulzer, Simon, 283
Superstition, 332
Swabians, 310, 387
Swiss, 361, 387
Syphilis, 65
Syrus, Publilius, 449

Tacitus, Cornelius, 277-278
Tailors, 298
Taubenheim, Hans von, 205
Temptation, 75, 133, 158
Ten Commandments, 9-10, 25, 282
Terence, 80, 246, 348, 390, 457
Tetzel, John, 341-342
Teutleben, Caspar von, 156
Theodosius, 260
Theologian, 22, 31, 39, 69, 111, 144, 150, 214, 439-440
Theology, 22, 50, 51, 71, 112, 157, 448
Theophylactos, 34
Thompson, Craig R., 19
Thuringia, 351
Thuringians, 387
Tjernagel, Neelak, 362
Torgau, 37, 219, 277, 448
Translation, 42-43, 135, 210, 375-376, 408, 445-446
Trent, 215
Trinity, 31, 371, 378, 416
Tucker, Anthony, 457
Turks, 27, 40, 46, 55, 58, 131, 143, 148-149, 269, 299, 336, 416, 419-422, 454-455

Ubiquity, 92
Ulm, 272
Unity, 283, 284
Usury, 369, 398
Utrecht, 472

Vajta, Vilmos, 69
Venice, 347
Verbosity, 136
Vergil, 14, 80, 356, 375, 476
Visions, 259
Visitation, 308
Vorstius, Peter, 228, 232
Vows, 13

Wahl, Adalbert, xxiii
Waldensians, 114, 176, 177
War, 279, 283, 335, 336
Watson, Philip S., 328
Weber, James, xii
Wedding, 269, 435
Weller, Jerome, xiii, 275
Weller, Peter, 75, 150, 152, 203, 367
Wends, 387
Werdenberg, Felix von, 139
Weyer, Martin, 353
Widow, 242
Wiederkehrer, Heinz (Probst), 350
Wilbur, Earl M., 32
Wild, Mrs. Stephen, 156
Wildenauer, John, 401
Will, free, 260
  last, 178, 281
William IV of Bavaria, 441
William of Occam, 392
Wine, 71, 163, 172, 178, 424-425, 438
Wisloff, C. J. F., 91
Witchcraft, 188, 298, 346
Wittenberg, 15, 134, 169, 282, 391, 419
Wittenberg Concord, 205
Witzel, George, 108, 304
Wollensecker, Andreas, 369
Women, 8, 15, 59, 135, 160-161, 171, 175, 183, 205, 221, 223, 317, 320-321, 428, 438
Word of God, 13, 18, 55, 57, 63, 192, 193, 197-198, 244, 313, 318, 322-323, 334, 394-395
Worms, Diet of, 30, 160
Worship, 84, 195 (*see also* Ceremonies)
Wrampelmeyer, H., xvi, 169
Württemberg, 380, 382, 390
Würzburg, 308, 472
Wycliffe, John, 110

Youth, 64-65

Zahna, 436
Zerbst, 310
Zieger, Balthasar, 155
Ziegler, Bernard, 375-376, 446
Zoch, Lorenz, 138, 268
Zwickau, 145
Zwilling, Gabriel (*see* Didymus, Gabriel)
Zwingli, Huldreich, 11, 22-23, 41, 51, 60, 65, 73, 75, 86, 88, 91-92, 147, 152, 173, 232, 262, 284, 376, 379, 391, 417

INDEX TO SCRIPTURE PASSAGES

Genesis
1:1 — 159
1:1-31 — 89
1:9 — 200
1:22 — 200
1:28 — 59, 175
1:31 — 198
2:7 — 377, 400, 401
2:10-14 — 438
2:16 — 308
3:1-7 — 175
3:1-20 — 399
3:5 — 418
3:15 — 41, 342, 438
3:17 — 105
3:18 — 198
3:19 — 267
3:20 — 223
4:1-2 — 437
4:4 — 56
4:6 — 121
4:7 — 121
4:8-15 — 41
4:10 — 406
4:19 — 244
4:23 — 41
4:25 — 437
5:1-5 — 437
7:20 — 256
9:13 — 56
13:15-16 — 41
16:1-4 — 109
17:10 — 68
17:23 — 56
18:32 — 439
22:1-13 — 68
24:1–35:29 — 91
25:21-28 — 458
25:22 — 88
29:21–30:13 — 244
33:5 — 59

Exodus
1:11-14 — 270
3, 4 — 12
5:7-19 — 270
7:13 — 385
14:15 — 129
16:14, 21 — 147
19:17–20:17 — 114
20:2 — 9, 75
20:5 — 339
20:7 — 12
20:12 — 67, 109, 161, 267, 354
20:13 — 66, 128
21:15, 17 — 68
21:17 — 180
22:18 — 173

Leviticus
18:5 — 454

Numbers
6:2 — 40
11:11-15 — 64
11:12 — 30, 450
16:1-40 — 300, 389
21:4-9 — 97
21:14 — 373
21:33-34 — 389
22, 23 — 303
23:3 — 88

23:4 — 303
24:1 — 88
35:6 — 301

Deuteronomy
2:25 — 336
19:3 — 301
24:6 — 276
25:5 — 301
25:5-10 — 109
32:51-52 — 145

Joshua
5:9 — 303
6 — 187
10:12 — 359
10:13 — 373
17:14-18 — 175
24:19 — 302
24:20 — 302

Judges
7:1-23 — 47
11:30-39 — 59
11:38 — 59
14–16 — 79
16:1 — 31
21:1-24 — 301

Ruth
3:1–4:17 — 301

I Samuel
1:1-11 — 13
1:2-18 — 59
2:25 — 303
14:6 — 149
15:22 — 84
29:8 — 303

II Samuel
1:1-16 — 21
11:2-12:25 — 145
18:1-33 — 398

I Kings
1:1-4 — 75
11:3 — 109
18:17-46 — 300
18:20-40 — 313
18:40 — 287

II Kings
9–10 — 339
16:1-3 — 310
18:1-3 — 310
19:35-37 — 148

II Chronicles
7:14 — 244
14:9-12 — 148

Job
1:21 — 225
2:6 — 129
2:10 — 183, 225

Psalms
2:10 — 128
2:11 — 21
6:1 — 275
8:6 — 280

18:20 — 62
18:24 — 62
31:1 — 309, 374
32:6 — 328
37:5 — 381
40:6-8 — 84
41:6-9 — 107
44:6 — 183
44:22 — 276
45:3 — 186
45:10 — 323
50:7 — 75
51:4 — 457
58:11 — 28
60:6 — 21
82:6-7 — 36
86:2 — 70
110:1 — 389
112:1 — 136
113:5-6 — xviii
119:29 — 59
119:137 — 457
144:2 — 451
144:10 — 451
145:18-19 — 192
147:5 — 9

Proverbs
10:22 — 450
26:16 — 360
27:23 — 76

Ecclesiastes
1:1-2 — 98
1:2 — 98
2:26 — 98
4:10 — 16, 276
6:2 — 299

Isaiah
7:14 — xviii
9:6 — xviii
29:11-21 — 408
37:36-37 — 130
49:15 — 432
49:23 — 309
53:2-3 — 262
54:1 — 19
57:1 — 310
65:18 — 326
66:2 — xviii

Jeremiah
4:19 — 460
7:23 — 84
10:2 — 173
20:7-12 — 64
20:14 — 30
23:21 — 471
26:15 — 65
29:26-27 — 261

Ezekiel
14:12-23 — 439
18:4-20 — 339
33:11 — 14, 16

Daniel
4:28-37 — 386
8:24 — 347
11:36 — 110, 343
11:36–12:13 — 46
11:38 — 110

484

INDEX

11:45 – 46, 388
12:11 – 346

Habakkuk
2:4 – 403

Matthew
1:18-25 – 341
1:25 – 341
2:6 – 301
3:1 – 276
4:1-11 – 79, 276
4:10 – 469
5:12 – 96
5:23-24 – 316
5:27-28 – 218
6:9 – 9
6:12 – 422, 457
6:13 – 416
6:24 – 360
9:22 – 460
10:16 – 379
10:20 – 318
10:22 – 402
10:30 – 24
10:37 – 463
13:8 – 19
13:31-32 – 88
14:25-32 – 197
15:9 – 97
15:24 – 451
17:5 – 89, 323
18:3 – 105, 120, 159
18:15 – 300
18:15-17 – 316
18:16-20 – 66
18:21-22 – 107
19:5 – 67
19:6 – 66
19:21 – 357
20:28 – 112
22:14 – 86
22:32 – 447
23:2 – 323
23:10 – 54
24:15 – 343, 346
24:21 – 76
24:22 – 76
24:37-38 – 77
25:1-13 – 343
25:21 – 74
26:26 – 417
26:26-27 – 196
26:36-46 – 107
26:38 – 430
26:39 – 65
26:41 – 430
26:47-50 – 37, 106, 107
26:52 – 152
27:4 – 276
27:46 – 430
28:19 – 113
28:19-20 – 55

Mark
1:30 – 271
1:44 – 111
2:20 – 357
3:4-12 – 53
8:22-25 – 53
9:19 – 30
10:14 – 55
16:16 – 114

Luke
1:26 – 85
1:38 – 329
1:39 – 329
1:48 – 329
1:56 – 329

2:8-14 – 249
2:14 – 327
6:38 – 91, 454
6:42 – 314
10:16 – 395
12:48 – 418
14:1-11 – 314
16:15 – xviii
16:24-25 – 162
16:29 – 48, 259
18:8 – 402
19:2-10 – 398
19:12-27 – 80
19:22 – 78
22:43 – 430
22:44 – 65, 430
23:39-43 – 17, 198
23:43 – 446
24:21 – 149
24:49 – 149

John
1:1-14 – 435
1:1-67 – 435, 445
1:13 – 348
1:14 – 197, 395
3:18 – 152
4:27 – 154
4:38 – 85
5:21 – 65
5:24 – 65
5:43 – 198
5:44 – 360
6:9 – 377
6:37 – 330
6:63 – 318
6:71 – 108
8:2-11 – 154
8:3-11 – 218
8:24 – 148
8:44 – 41, 128
11:25 – 294, 447
11:47-53 – 441
12:6 – 108
12:27-29 – 127
12:39 – 63
12:44 – 470
13:21-30 – 107
13:25-26 – 404
13:29 – 108
14:1 – 112
14:8 – 291
14:12 – 88
14:27 – 96
16:2 – 441
16:13-14 – 70
16:15 – 112
16:23 – 192
18:2-5 – 107
18:15-18 – 108
18:25-27 – 108
20:17 – 208
20:19 – 149
20:19-31 – 149
20:22 – 470
21:15 – 31
21:15-17 – 86

Acts
2:22-24 – 371
5:5 – 405
7:2-53 – 344
7:59-60 – 453
10:1-48 – 63
10:38 – 53
10:44-47 – 113
13:46 – 451
15:10 – 355
15:13-21 – 355
17:28 – 472
27:23-24 – 146

27:33 – 277
28:14-15 – 146
28:15 – 277

Romans
1:16 – 12, 318, 395
1:16-17 – 309
1:17 – 193, 287, 309, 403, 442
1:18 – 308
2:15 – 442
4:17 – 146
5:12 – 36
9:3 – 393
9:15 – 87, 90
9:16 – 87
9:18 – 385
9:20-21 – 322
9:21 – 260
10:5 – 454
10:10 – 402
10:14 – 318
10:19 – 62
11:33 – 91
12:19 – 301
13:10 – 233
14:8 – 431, 447
15:8 – 451
15:9 – 451

I Corinthians
1:1 – 119
1:18-2:13 – 472
1:23-26 – 119
2:9 – 51
6:9 – 160
7:8 – 271
7:15 – 302
10:3 – 107
11:23 – 113, 196
11:24 – 91, 92, 462
11:25 – 463
11:28 – 58
15:31 – 37

II Corinthians
2:11 – 41
6:4 – 58
7:10 – 75
12:1-4 – 36
12:7 – 95, 378
12:9 – 95

Galatians
1:13 – 17
2:11 – 300
2:17 – 321
4:24-31 – 340
5:6 – 74

Ephesians
2:2 – 93
4:11 – 288
6:4 – 457

Philippians
4:4 – 16

Colossians
2:3 – 378

I Thessalonians
2:4 – 318
2:13 – 318

II Thessalonians
1:9 – 33
2:4 – 46, 77, 101, 343

485

TABLE TALK

I Timothy
1:19-20 — 386
3:1 — 95
4:4 — 353
4:5 — 244

II Timothy
2:15 — 313
3:1 — 101

Titus
1:1 — 73, 146
1:6 — 107
3:10 — 417

Hebrews
1:14 — 9
2:9 — 430
13:8 — 113

James
1:1 — 424
2:1 — 424
2:20 — 176
2:26 — 425
5:16 — 52, 454

I Peter
5:9 — 275

II Peter
2:1-3 — 343
2:4 — 447
3:18 — 143

I John
1:1 — 198
5:14 — 58

Revelation
18 — 76
21:4 — 134

APOCRYPHA
Ecclesiasticus
1:13 — 22
35:15 — 181

Type used in this book
Body, 10 on 13 Caledonia
Display, Bulmer and Caledonia
Paper: Standard White Antique